TensorFlow 1.x Deep Learning Cookbook

Over 90 unique recipes to solve artificial-intelligence driven problems with Python

Antonio Gulli

Amita Kapoor

BIRMINGHAM - MUMBAI

TensorFlow 1.x Deep Learning Cookbook

Copyright © 2017 Packt Publishing

First published: December 2017

Production reference: 1081217

Published by Packt Publishing Ltd.
Livery Place
35 Livery Street
Birmingham
B3 2PB, UK.
ISBN 978-1-78829-359-4

www.packtpub.com

Credits

Authors
Antonio Gulli
Amita Kapoor

Reviewers
Nick McClure
Narotam Singh
Corrado Zoccolo

Commissioning Editor
Sunith Shetty

Acquisition Editor
Tushar Gupta

Content Development Editor
Tejas Limkar

Technical Editor
Danish Shaikh

Copy Editors
Safis Editing
Vikrant Phadkay

Project Coordinator
Manthan Patel

Proofreader
Safis Editing

Indexer
Rekha Nair

Graphics
Tania Dutta

Production Coordinator
Deepika Naik

About the Authors

Antonio Gulli is a transformational software executive and business leader with a passion for establishing and managing global technological talent for innovation and execution. He is an expert in search engines, online services, machine learning, information retrieval, analytics, and cloud computing. So far, he has been lucky enough to gain professional experience in four different countries in Europe and manage teams in six different countries in Europe and America. Currently, he works as site lead and director of cloud in Google Warsaw, driving European efforts for Serverless, Kubernetes, and Google Cloud UX. Previously, Antonio helped to innovate academic search as the vice president for Elsevier, a worldwide leading publisher. Before that, he drove query suggestions and news search as a principal engineer for Microsoft. Earlier, he served as the CTO for Ask.com, driving multimedia and news search. Antonio has filed for 20+ patents, published multiple academic papers, and served as a senior PC member in multiple international conferences. He truly believes that to be successful, you must have a great combination of management, research skills, just-get-it-done, and selling attitude.

I thank every reader of this book for your attention and for the trust. I am humbled by the number of comments received on LinkedIn and Facebook: You, the reader, provided immense help in making this book better. I would also like to thank various people for providing support during the process of writing the book. In no order: Susana, Ewa, Ignacy, Dawid, Max, Jarek, Jerzy, Nina, Laura, Antonella, Eric, Ettore, Francesco, Liubov, Marco, Fabio, Giacomo, Saskia, Christina, Wieland, and Yossi. I am very grateful to my coauthor, Amita, for her valuable comments and suggestions. I am extremely thankful to the reviewers of this book, Eric Brewer, Corrado Zoccolo, and Sujit Pal, for going through the entire book content. Special thanks to my manager, Eyal, for supporting me during the writing process and for the trust constantly offered. Part of this book has been written in Charlotte Menora (http://bistrocharlotte.pl/), a pub in Warsaw, where I found myself writing pages after work. This is an inspirational place, which I definitively recommend if you are visiting Poland. Modern and cool as the city of Warsaw is these days. Last and not the least, I am grateful to the entire editorial team of Packt, especially Tushar Gupta and Tejas Limkar for all the support, constant reminders regarding the schedule, and continuous motivation. Thanks for your patience.

Amita Kapoor is an associate professor in the Department of Electronics, SRCASW, University of Delhi. She has been actively teaching neural networks for the last 20 years. She did her master's in electronics in 1996 and PhD in 2011. During her PhD, she was awarded the prestigious DAAD fellowship to pursue a part of her research work in Karlsruhe Institute of Technology, Karlsruhe, Germany. She had been awarded the best presentation award at International Conference Photonics 2008 for her paper. She is a member of professional bodies such as OSA (Optical Society of America), IEEE (Institute of Electrical and Electronics Engineers), INNS (International Neural Network Society), and ISBS (Indian Society for Buddhist Studies). Amita has more than 40 publications in international journals and conferences to her credit. Her present research areas include machine learning, artificial intelligence, neural networks, robotics, Buddhism (philosophy and psychology) and ethics in AI.

This book is an attempt to summarize what all I had learned in the field of deep neural networks. I have presented it in a manner that readers find easy to understand and apply, and so the prime motivation of this book comes from you, the readers. I thank every reader of this book for being consistently present at the back of my mind, especially when I felt lazy. I would also like to thank professor Parongama Sen, University of Calcutta, for introducing me to the subject in 1994, and my friends Nirjara Jain and Shubha Swaminathan for the hours spent in college library discussing Asimov, his stories, and the future that neural networks behold for our society. I am very grateful to my coauthor, Antonio Guili, for his valuable comments and suggestions and the reviewers of this book, Narotam Singh and Nick McClure, for painstakingly going through the entire content and rechecking the codes. Last and not the least, I am grateful to the entire editorial team of Packt, especially Tushar Gupta and Tejas Limkar for all the support, constant reminders regarding schedule, and continuous motivation.

About the Reviewers

Narotam Singh has been with India Meteorological Department, Ministry of Earth Sciences, India, since 1996. He has been actively involved with various technical programs and training of officers of GoI in the field of information technology and communication. He did his post-graduation in the field of electronics in 1996 and both diploma and post-graduate diploma in the field of computer engineering in 1994 and 1997 respectively. He is currently working in the enigmatic field of neural networks, machine learning, and deep learning.

Nick McClure is currently a senior data scientist at PayScale Inc in Seattle, Washington, USA. Previously, he worked at Zillow and Caesar's Entertainment. He has degrees in applied mathematics from the University of Montana and the College of Saint Benedict and Saint John's University. Nick has also authored *TensorFlow Machine Learning Cookbook* by Packt Publishing.

He has a passion for learning and advocating for analytics, machine learning, and artificial intelligence. Nick occasionally puts his thoughts and musings on his blog, fromdata.org, or through his Twitter account at @nfmcclure.

Corrado Zoccolo is a Senior Staff Software Engineer at Google, with 10+ years of experience in distributed indexing and information retrieval systems.

I would like to show my gratitude to the many people who helped me succeed in my studies and my carreer, in particular: my wife Ermelinda, that supported me over the many years I dedicated to computer science; Prof. Marco Vanneschi who introduced me to the beautiful world of Distributed Systems; my first manager at Google, Peter Dickman, who set me on the right track for my career, and all my colleagues from which I keep learning every day.

www.PacktPub.com

For support files and downloads related to your book, please visit `www.PacktPub.com`. Did you know that Packt offers eBook versions of every book published, with PDF and ePub files available? You can upgrade to the eBook version at `www.PacktPub.com`and as a print book customer, you are entitled to a discount on the eBook copy. Get in touch with us at `service@packtpub.com` for more details. At `www.PacktPub.com`, you can also read a collection of free technical articles, sign up for a range of free newsletters and receive exclusive discounts and offers on Packt books and eBooks.

`https://www.packtpub.com/mapt`

Get the most in-demand software skills with Mapt. Mapt gives you full access to all Packt books and video courses, as well as industry-leading tools to help you plan your personal development and advance your career.

Why subscribe?

- Fully searchable across every book published by Packt
- Copy and paste, print, and bookmark content
- On demand and accessible via a web browser

Customer Feedback

Thanks for purchasing this Packt book. At Packt, quality is at the heart of our editorial process. To help us improve, please leave us an honest review on this book's Amazon page at www.amazon.com/dp/1788293592.

If you'd like to join our team of regular reviewers, you can email us at customerreviews@packtpub.com. We award our regular reviewers with free eBooks and videos in exchange for their valuable feedback. Help us be relentless in improving our products!

This book is dedicated to my son Lorenzo - for your growing passion for algorithms - to my son Leonardo - for your curiosity to explore the world -, and to my daughter Aurora - for your love. A special thought to Elio and Maria, my father and my mother.

All my royalties will go to theschoolfund.org *a non-profit organization devoted to helping fund scholarships for high potential students who cannot afford to attend school.*

- Antonio Gulli

This book is dedicated to the loving memory of my mother Late Smt Swarnlata Kapoor, who instilled in me the value of education, and motivated me to continue learning despite odds, and my father Mr Anil Mohan Kapoor for all his love and support.

A part of my royalties will go to smilefoundation.org *a non-profit organization based in India working in the welfare projects on education, healthcare, livelihood, and women empowerment in remote villages and slums across different states of India.*

- Amita Kapoor

Table of Contents

Preface   1

Chapter 1: TensorFlow - An Introduction   9

  Introduction   10
  Installing TensorFlow   12
    Getting ready   12
    How to do it...   13
    How it works...   15
    There's more...   16
  Hello world in TensorFlow   17
    How to do it...   17
    How it works...   19
  Understanding the TensorFlow program structure   20
    How to do it...   20
    How it works...   21
    There's more...   22
  Working with constants, variables, and placeholders   23
    How to do it...   24
    How it works...   28
    There's more...   29
  Performing matrix manipulations using TensorFlow   30
    How to do it...   30
    How it works...   32
    There's more...   32
  Using a data flow graph   32
    How to do it...   32
  Migrating from 0.x to 1.x   34
    How to do it...   34
    There's more...   35
  Using XLA to enhance computational performance   35
    Getting ready   36
    How to do it...   37
  Invoking CPU/GPU devices   38
    How to do it...   38
    How it works...   41

TensorFlow for Deep Learning	41
How to do it...	43
There's more	47
Different Python packages required for DNN-based problems	47
How to do it...	48
See also	49
Chapter 2: Regression	51
Introduction	51
Choosing loss functions	54
Getting ready	54
How to do it...	55
How it works...	56
There's more...	57
Optimizers in TensorFlow	57
Getting ready	57
How to do it...	58
There's more...	60
See also	60
Reading from CSV files and preprocessing data	61
Getting ready	61
How to do it...	62
There's more...	64
House price estimation-simple linear regression	64
Getting ready	64
How to do it...	64
How it works...	67
There's more...	69
House price estimation-multiple linear regression	70
How to do it...	70
How it works...	74
There's more...	74
Logistic regression on the MNIST dataset	75
How to do it...	75
How it works...	78
See also	81
Chapter 3: Neural Networks - Perceptron	83
Introduction	83
Activation functions	87

Getting ready   87
How to do it...   88
How it works...   93
There's more...   94
See also   94
Single layer perceptron   94
Getting ready   95
How to do it...   95
There's more...   97
Calculating gradients of backpropagation algorithm   97
Getting ready   98
How to do it...   99
How it works...   102
There's more...   102
See also   102
MNIST classifier using MLP   102
Getting ready   102
How to do it...   103
How it works...   105
Function approximation using MLP-predicting Boston house prices   106
Getting ready   106
How to do it...   106
How it works...   110
There's more...   111
Tuning hyperparameters   112
How to do it...   112
There's more...   114
See also   114
Higher-level APIs-Keras   114
How to do it...   115
There's more...   116
See also   116
Chapter 4: Convolutional Neural Networks   117
Introduction   117
Local receptive fields   118
Shared weights and bias   118
A mathematical example   118
ConvNets in TensorFlow   119

Pooling layers	120
Max pooling	120
Average pooling	121
ConvNets summary	122
Creating a ConvNet to classify handwritten MNIST numbers	122
Getting ready	122
How to do it...	123
How it works...	129
Creating a ConvNet to classify CIFAR-10	129
Getting ready	129
How to do it...	130
How it works...	132
There's more...	133
Transferring style with VGG19 for image repainting	133
Getting ready	133
How to do it...	134
How it works...	144
There's more...	144
Using a pretrained VGG16 net for transfer learning	145
Getting ready	145
How to do it...	146
How it works...	149
There's more...	149
Creating a DeepDream network	150
Getting ready	150
How to do it...	151
How it works...	154
There's more...	155
See also	155
Chapter 5: Advanced Convolutional Neural Networks	157
Introduction	157
Creating a ConvNet for Sentiment Analysis	158
Getting ready	158
How to do it...	159
How it works...	161
There is more...	162
Inspecting what filters a VGG pre-built network has learned	163
Getting ready	163

How to do it... | 164
How it works... | 167
There is more... | 168
Classifying images with VGGNet, ResNet, Inception, and Xception | 168
VGG16 and VGG19 | 169
ResNet | 170
Inception | 171
Xception | 172
Getting ready | 172
How to do it... | 172
How it works... | 182
There is more... | 182
Recycling pre-built Deep Learning models for extracting features | 183
Getting ready | 183
How to do it... | 183
How it works... | 184
Very deep InceptionV3 Net used for Transfer Learning | 184
Getting ready | 185
How to do it... | 185
How it works... | 187
There is more... | 188
Generating music with dilated ConvNets, WaveNet, and NSynth | 188
Getting ready | 191
How to do it... | 191
How it works... | 194
There is more... | 194
Answering questions about images (Visual Q&A) | 195
How to do it... | 196
How it works... | 203
There is more... | 203
Classifying videos with pre-trained nets in six different ways | 203
How to do it... | 206
How it works... | 206
There is more... | 207
Chapter 6: Recurrent Neural Networks | 209
Introduction | 209
Vanishing and exploding gradients | 212
Long Short Term Memory (LSTM) | 213

Gated Recurrent Units (GRUs) and Peephole LSTM   215
Operating on sequences of vectors   217
Neural machine translation - training a seq2seq RNN   218
Getting ready   221
How to do it...   221
How it works...   224
Neural machine translation - inference on a seq2seq RNN   226
How to do it...   227
How it works...   227
All you need is attention - another example of a seq2seq RNN 228
How to do it...   229
How it works...   230
There's more...   232
Learning to write as Shakespeare with RNNs   232
How to do it...   233
How it works...   235
  First iteration   235
  After a few iterations   236
There's more...   237
Learning to predict future Bitcoin value with RNNs   238
How to do it...   238
How it works...   248
There's more...   249
Many-to-one and many-to-many RNN examples   249
How to do it...   250
How it works...   250
Chapter 7: Unsupervised Learning   251
Introduction   251
Principal component analysis   252
Getting ready   252
How to do it...   253
How it works...   256
There's more...   256
See also   257
k-means clustering   258
Getting ready   258
How to do it...   260
How it works...   263
There's more...   263

See also   264
Self-organizing maps   264
Getting ready   265
How to do it...   267
How it works...   271
See also   272
Restricted Boltzmann Machine   272
Getting ready   273
How to do it...   274
How it works...   277
See also   277
Recommender system using RBM   278
Getting ready   278
How to do it...   278
There's more...   280
DBN for Emotion Detection   280
Getting ready   281
How to do it...   282
How it works...   288
There's more...   289

Chapter 8: Autoencoders   291
Introduction   291
See Also   293
Vanilla autoencoders   294
Getting ready   295
How to do it...   295
How it works...   299
There's more...   300
Sparse autoencoder   301
Getting Ready...   301
How to do it...   302
How it works...   307
There's More...   308
See Also   308
Denoising autoencoder   309
Getting Ready   309
How to do it...   309
See Also   314

Convolutional autoencoders   314
Getting Ready...   315
How to do it...   315
How it Works...   319
There's More...   319
See Also   319
Stacked autoencoder   320
Getting Ready   320
How to do it...   320
How it works...   325
There's More...   326
See Also   326

Chapter 9: Reinforcement Learning   327
Introduction   327
Learning OpenAI Gym   329
Getting ready   329
How to do it...   330
How it works...   331
There's more...   332
See also   333
Implementing neural network agent to play Pac-Man   333
Getting ready   333
How to do it...   334
Q learning to balance Cart-Pole   337
Getting ready   338
How to do it...   340
There's more...   345
See also   346
Game of Atari using Deep Q Networks   346
Getting ready   346
How to do it...   348
There's more...   356
See also   357
Policy gradients to play the game of Pong   357
Getting ready   357
How to do it...   358
How it works...   363
There's more...   364

AlphaGo Zero | 364
See also | 365

Chapter 10: Mobile Computation | 367

Introduction | 367
TensorFlow, mobile, and the cloud | 369
Installing TensorFlow mobile for macOS and Android | 369
Getting ready | 369
How to do it... | 369
How it works... | 376
There's more... | 377
Playing with TensorFlow and Android examples | 377
Getting ready | 377
How to do it... | 378
How it works... | 381
Installing TensorFlow mobile for macOS and iPhone | 381
Getting ready | 382
How to do it... | 382
How it works... | 385
There's more... | 386
Optimizing a TensorFlow graph for mobile devices | 386
Getting ready | 386
How to do it... | 386
How it works... | 389
Profiling a TensorFlow graph for mobile devices | 389
Getting ready | 389
How to do it... | 389
How it works... | 391
Transforming a TensorFlow graph for mobile devices | 392
Getting ready | 392
How to do it... | 392
How it works... | 395

Chapter 11: Generative Models and CapsNet | 397

Introduction | 397
So what is a GAN? | 398
Some cool GAN applications | 400
Learning to forge MNIST images with simple GANs | 405
Getting ready | 405
How to do it... | 405

How it works... 410
Learning to forge MNIST images with DCGANs 412
Getting ready 412
How to do it... 412
How it works... 418
Learning to forge Celebrity Faces and other datasets with DCGAN 420
Getting ready 421
How to do it... 421
How it works... 422
There's more... 423
Implementing Variational Autoencoders 424
Getting ready... 425
How to do it... 425
How it works... 433
There's More... 434
See also... 435
**Learning to beat the previous MNIST state-of-the-art results with
Capsule Networks** 435
Getting ready 438
How to do it... 438
How it works... 449
There's more... 454

Chapter 12: Distributed TensorFlow and Cloud Deep Learning 455
Introduction 455
Working with TensorFlow and GPUs 459
Getting ready 460
How to do it... 460
How it works... 461
Playing with Distributed TensorFlow: multiple GPUs and one CPU 461
Getting ready 461
How to do it... 461
How it works... 463
Playing with Distributed TensorFlow: multiple servers 463
Getting ready 463
How to do it... 463
How it works... 465
There is more... 465
Training a Distributed TensorFlow MNIST classifier 465

Getting ready	465
How to do it...	466
How it works...	469
Working with TensorFlow Serving and Docker	**469**
Getting ready	469
How to do it...	470
How it works...	471
There is more...	471
Running Distributed TensorFlow on Google Cloud (GCP) with Compute Engine	**471**
Getting ready	471
How to do it...	472
How it works...	475
There is more...	475
Running Distributed TensorFlow on Google CloudML	**475**
Getting ready	475
How to do it...	476
How it works...	477
There is more...	477
Running Distributed TensorFlow on Microsoft Azure	**477**
Getting ready	478
How to do it...	478
How it works...	481
There's more...	481
Running Distributed TensorFlow on Amazon AWS	**482**
Getting ready	483
How to do it...	484
How it works...	486
There is more...	487
Appendix A: Learning to Learn with AutoML (Meta-Learning)	**489**
Meta-learning with recurrent networks and with reinforcement learning	**490**
Meta-learning blocks	**492**
Meta-learning novel tasks	**493**
Siamese Network	**496**
Applications of Siamese Networks	498
A working example - MNIST	499
Appendix B: TensorFlow Processing Units	**501**
Components of TPUs	**501**

Advantages of TPUs — 503
Accessing TPUs — 503
Resources on TPUs — 504

Index — 505

Preface

In this book, you will learn how to efficiently use TensorFlow, Google's open source framework for deep learning. You will implement different deep learning networks such as **Convolutional Neural Networks (CNNs)**, **Recurrent Neural Networks (RNNs)**, **Deep Q-learning Networks (DQNs)**, and **Generative Adversarial Networks (GANs)** with easy to follow independent recipes. You will learn how to make Keras as backend with TensorFlow.

You will understand how to implement different deep neural architectures to carry out complex tasks at work. You will learn the performance of different DNNs on some popularly used data sets such as MNIST, CIFAR-10, Youtube8m, and more. You will not only learn about the different mobile and embedded platforms supported by TensorFlow but also how to set up cloud platforms for deep learning applications. Get a sneak peek of TPU architecture and how they will affect DNN future.

By the end of this book, you will be an expert in implementing deep learning techniques in growing real-world applications and research areas such as reinforcement learning, GANs, autoencoders and more.

What this book covers

Chapter 1, *TensorFlow - An Introduction*, discusses TensorFlow the Google's open source framework, and why it is useful for deep learning. We will discuss how to install TensorFlow on MAC, Windows and Ubuntu for both CPU and GPU. We will also discuss other python packages that we will use throughout the book. We will explain the two components of TensorFlow codes, the definition of graph and its execution. We will learn about using the TensorBoard to see the graph structure. We will understand the difference between TensorFlow constants, variables and placeholders. And we will also get a taste of TensorFlow estimators.

Chapter 2 , *Regression*, talks about regression and its applications. We will discuss the concepts involved in regression, understand how it is different from clustering and classification. We will learn about different types of loss functions possible and how to implement them in Tensorflow. We learn how to implement L1 and L2 regularizations. We will discuss the gradient descent algorithm, learn how to optimize it and implement it in Tensorflow. We will briefly learn about cross-entropy function and its implementation.

Chapter 3 , *Neural Networks - Perceptron*, covers artificial neural networks and explains why it can do the wonderful tasks as claimed recently by DNN. We will learn about different choices of activation functions. We will use all this to build a simple perceptron and use it for function modeling. We will learn about regularization of data before training. We will also learn to build a multilayer perceptron (MLP) layer by layer. We will see how the auto-differentiator of TensorFlow makes our work easier.

Chapter 4 , *TensorFlow - Convolutional Neural Networks*, discusses the process of convolution and how it is able to extract features. We will learn about three important layers of CNN: convolutional layers, pooling layer and fully connected layer. We will also learn about dropout, how it can increase performance and different CNN architectures such as LeNET and GoogleNET.

Chapter 5, *CNN in Action*, covers some wow success stories of CNN like face recognition. We will write a recipe for using CNNs for sentiment analysis. We will discuss pre-tuning CNN and learn how to implement transfer learning. We will learn how to use VGG16 for transfer learning. We will learn classification of images with VGGNet, ResNet, Inception and Xception. We will Generate music using dilated ConvNets, Wavenet and Nsynth. We will also learn how to do Visual Q & A. We will learn how to classify videos.

Chapter 6, *Recurrent Neural Networks*, discusses Recurrent Neural networks. We will learn the basic unit of RNNs the RNN cell. We will learn about word embeddings and time sequencing. We will briefly discuss LSTM networks. We will learn about seq2seq RNNs. We will learn how RNNs can be employed for machine translation, generating text, and predicting future values

Chapter 7, *Unsupervised Learning*, teaches the unsupervised learning paradigm. We will learn about clustering and dimensionality reduction. We will learn about techniques like Principal Component Analysis (PCA) and see how they can be used for dimensionality reduction. We will learn about k-means clustering. We will understand the concept of Topographic maps and learn how to train self-organizing maps. We will learn about Restricted Boltzmann Machines (RBM). We will discuss the architecture and training of RBMs. We learn how to stack RBMs to make Deep Belief Networks, and we will learn how to train them. We will train DBN using the concept of pre-training and fine tuning for emotion detection.

Chapter 8, *Autoencoders*, demystifies autoencoders. We will learn about autoencoders and their applications. We will discuss various real-life examples where auto-encoders can be used. We will discuss the process of encoding and subsequent reconstruction. We will learn about reconstruction error. We will learn about sparse autoencoders, the concept of KL divergence. We will learn Denoising Autoencoders and use them to reconstruct clean images given noisy images. We will learn how to build Convolutional Autoencoders and Stacked Autoencoders.

Chapter 9, *Reinforcement Learning*, covers different reinforcement learning algorithms. We will learn the Q-learning algorithm. We will discuss Bellman-Ford equation and how to choose learning rate, discount factor. We will learn how to use OpenAI gym framework. We will learn about the concepts of Experience Replay and buffering to implement value-iteration Q network. We will use Q learning and policy gradients to build game playing agents. And finally, we will learn how to make our own Deep Q-learning Network (DQN). A brief description of AlphaGo Zero and its grand win.

Chapter 10, *TensorFlow Mobile Computation*, covers TensorFlow mobile. We will learn about different applications of mobile deep learning. We will learn how to use Tensorflow with Android studio on Windows platform. We will learn how to use Tensorflow along with XCode to make IOS based apps. We will learn how to optimize the Tensorflow graphs for mobile devices. We will also learn how to transform Tensorflow graphs for mobile devices.

Chapter 11, *TensorFlow – Generative Adversarial Networks (GANs), Variational Autoencoders, and Capsule networks*, starts with generative adversarial networks and their strength over other DNNs. We explore different predictive models. We understand the motivation behind GANs and their working intuitively. We learn about the basic GAN architecture. We will explore some very cool applications of GANs. We will learn about another generative network the Variational Autoencoder. Lastly, we will learn about the recently proposed Capsule Networks

Chapter 12, *Distributed TensorFlow and Cloud Deep Learning*, explains the cloud environment, dockers, containers, and how to use them. *We learn how to work with distributed Tensorflow with multiple GPUs, and multiple servers. We learn how to setup AWS for deep learning.* We learn how to setup Google cloud for deep learning applications. We learn how to setup Microsoft Azure cloud for deep learning applications. We learn about other available cloud services

Appendix A, *Learning to Learn with AutoML (Meta-Learning)*, briefly talks about AutoML and Siamese Networks.

Appendix B, *TensorFlow Processing Unit*, covers Tensor Processing Unit, its basic architecture, and how it will affect DNN's future.

What you need for this book

For this book, you will need Python version 3.5 (`https://www.continuum.io/downloads`) along with TensorFlow (`www.tensorflow.org`). The following hardware specifications are recommended:

- CPU architecture: x86_64
- System memory: 8-32 GB
- CPUs: 4-8 cores
- GPUs: (Optional, minimum NVDIA ® GTX 650)

Who this book is for

This book is intended for data scientists, machine learning practitioners, and deep learning enthusiasts who want to perform machine learning tasks on a regular basis. People who are slightly familiar with deep neural networks and now want to gain expertise working with CNN and RNN will find this book useful.

Sections

In this book, you will find several headings that appear frequently (Getting ready, How to do it..., How it works..., There's more..., and See also). To give clear instructions on how to complete a recipe, we use these sections as follows.

Getting ready

This section tells you what to expect in the recipe, and describes how to set up any software or any preliminary settings required for the recipe.

How to do it...

This section contains the steps required to follow the recipe.

How it works...

This section usually consists of a detailed explanation of what happened in the previous section.

There's more...

This section consists of additional information about the recipe in order to make the reader more knowledgeable about the recipe.

See also

This section provides helpful links to other useful information for the recipe.

Conventions

In this book, you will find a number of text styles that distinguish between different kinds of information. Here are some examples of these styles and an explanation of their meaning. Code words in text, database table names, folder names, filenames, file extensions, pathnames, dummy URLs, user input, and Twitter handles are shown as follows: "Create a new user for JIRA in the database and grant the user access to the `jiradb` database we just created using the following command:"

A block of code is set as follows:

```
<Contextpath="/jira"docBase="${catalina.home}
/atlassian- jira" reloadable="false" useHttpOnly="true">
```

Any command-line input or output is written as follows:

```
mysql -u root -p
```

New terms and **important words** are shown in bold. Words that you see on the screen, for example, in menus or dialog boxes, appear in the text like this: "Select **System info** from the **Administration** panel."

Warnings or important notes appear like this.

 Tips and tricks appear like this.

Reader feedback

Feedback from our readers is always welcome. Let us know what you think about this book-what you liked or disliked. Reader feedback is important for us as it helps us develop titles that you will really get the most out of. To send us general feedback, simply e-mail feedback@packtpub.com, and mention the book's title in the subject of your message. If there is a topic that you have expertise in and you are interested in either writing or contributing to a book, see our author guide at www.packtpub.com/authors .

Customer support

Now that you are the proud owner of a Packt book, we have a number of things to help you to get the most from your purchase.

Downloading the example code

You can download the example code files for this book from your account at http://www.packtpub.com. If you purchased this book elsewhere, you can visit http://www.packtpub.com/support and register to have the files e-mailed directly to you. You can download the code files by following these steps:

1. Log in or register to our website using your e-mail address and password.
2. Hover the mouse pointer on the **SUPPORT** tab at the top.
3. Click on **Code Downloads & Errata**.
4. Enter the name of the book in the **Search** box.
5. Select the book for which you're looking to download the code files.
6. Choose from the drop-down menu where you purchased this book from.
7. Click on **Code Download**.

You can also download the code files by clicking on the **Code Files** button on the book's webpage at the Packt Publishing website. This page can be accessed by entering the book's name in the **Search** box. Please note that you need to be logged in to your Packt account. Once the file is downloaded, please make sure that you unzip or extract the folder using the latest version of:

- WinRAR / 7-Zip for Windows
- Zipeg / iZip / UnRarX for Mac
- 7-Zip / PeaZip for Linux

The code bundle for the book is also hosted on GitHub at `https://github.com/PacktPublishing/TensorFlow-1x-Deep-Learning-Cookbook`. We also have other code bundles from our rich catalog of books and videos available at `https://github.com/PacktPublishing/`. Check them out!

Errata

Although we have taken every care to ensure the accuracy of our content, mistakes do happen. If you find a mistake in one of our books-maybe a mistake in the text or the code- we would be grateful if you could report this to us. By doing so, you can save other readers from frustration and help us improve subsequent versions of this book. If you find any errata, please report them by visiting `http://www.packtpub.com/submit-errata`, selecting your book, clicking on the **Errata Submission Form** link, and entering the details of your errata. Once your errata are verified, your submission will be accepted and the errata will be uploaded to our website or added to any list of existing errata under the Errata section of that title. To view the previously submitted errata, go to `https://www.packtpub.com/books/content/support` and enter the name of the book in the search field. The required information will appear under the **Errata** section.

Piracy

Piracy of copyrighted material on the Internet is an ongoing problem across all media. At Packt, we take the protection of our copyright and licenses very seriously. If you come across any illegal copies of our works in any form on the Internet, please provide us with the location address or website name immediately so that we can pursue a remedy. Please contact us at `copyright@packtpub.com` with a link to the suspected pirated material. We appreciate your help in protecting our authors and our ability to bring you valuable content.

Questions

If you have a problem with any aspect of this book, you can contact us at
questions@packtpub.com, and we will do our best to address the problem.

1
TensorFlow - An Introduction

Anyone who has ever tried to write code for neural networks in Python using only NumPy, knows how cumbersome it is. Writing code for a simple one-layer feedforward network requires more than 40 lines, made more difficult as you add the number of layers both in terms of writing code and execution time.

TensorFlow makes it all easier and faster reducing the time between the implementation of an idea and deployment. In this book, you will learn how to unravel the power of TensorFlow to implement deep neural networks.

In this chapter, we will cover the following topics:

- Installing TensorFlow
- Hello world in TensorFlow
- Understanding the TensorFlow program structure
- Working with constants, variables, and placeholders
- Performing matrix manipulations using TensorFlow
- Using a data flow graph
- Migrating from 0.x to 1.x
- Using XLA to enhance computational performance
- Invoking CPU/GPU devices
- TensorFlow for deep learning
- Different Python packages required for DNN-based problems

Introduction

TensorFlow is a powerful open source software library developed by the Google Brain team for **deep neural networks (DNNs)**. It was first made available under the Apache 2.x License in November 2015; as of today, its GitHub repository (`https://github.com/tensorflow/tensorflow`) has more than 17,000 commits, with roughly 845 contributors in just two years. This by itself is a measure of both the popularity and performance of TensorFlow. The following graph shows a comparison of the popular deep learning frameworks where it is clearly visible that TensorFlow is the leader among them:

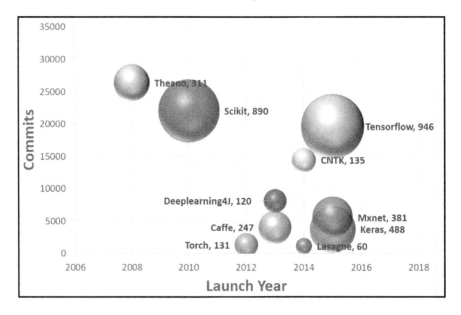

The Figure is based on data taken from the Github repositories of each as on 12 July 2017. Each Bubble has a legend: (Framework, contributors).

Let's first learn what exactly TensorFlow is and why is it so popular among DNN researchers and engineers. TensorFlow, the open source deep learning library allows one to deploy deep neural networks computation on one or more CPU, GPUs in a server, desktop or mobile using the single TensorFlow API. You might ask, there are so many other deep learning libraries such as Torch, Theano, Caffe, and MxNet; what makes TensorFlow special? Most of other deep learning libraries like TensorFlow have auto-differentiation, many are open source, most support CPU/GPU options, have pretrained models, and support commonly used NN architectures like **recurrent neural networks (RNNs)**, **convolutional neural networks (CNNs)**, and **deep belief networks (DBNs)**. So, what more is there in TensorFlow? Let's list them for you:

- It works with all the cool languages. TensorFlow works with Python, C++, Java, R, and Go.
- TensorFlow works on multiple platforms, even mobile and distributed.
- It is supported by all cloud providers--AWS, Google, and Azure.
- Keras, a high-level neural network API, has been integrated with TensorFlow.
- It has better computational graph visualizations because it is native while the equivalent in Torch/Theano is not nearly as cool to look at.
- TensorFlow allows model deployment and ease of use in production.
- TensorFlow has very good community support.
- TensorFlow is more than a software library; it is a suite of software that includes TensorFlow, TensorBoard, and TensorServing.

The Google research blog (`https://research.googleblog.com/2016/11/celebrating-tensorflows-first-year.html`) lists some of the fascinating projects done by people around the world using TensorFlow:

- Google Translate is using TensorFlow and **tensor processing units** (TPUs)
- Project Magenta, which can produce melodies using reinforcement learning-based models, employs TensorFlow
- Australian marine biologists are using TensorFlow to find and understand sea-cows, which are on the verge of extinction
- A Japanese farmer used TensorFlow to develop an application to sort cucumbers using physical parameters like size and shape

The list is long, and the possibilities in which one can use TensorFlow are even greater. This book aims to provide you with an understanding of TensorFlow as applied to deep learning models such that you can adapt them to your dataset with ease and develop useful applications. Each chapter contains a set of recipes which deal with the technical issues, the dependencies, the actual code, and its understanding. We have built the recipes one on another such that, by the end of each chapter, you have a fully functional deep learning model.

Installing TensorFlow

In this recipe, you will learn how to do a fresh installation of TensorFlow 1.3 on different OSes (Linux, Mac, and Windows). We will find out about the necessary requirements to install TensorFlow. TensorFlow can be installed using native pip, Anaconda, virtualenv, and Docker on Ubuntu and macOS. For Windows OS, one can use native pip or Anaconda.

As Anaconda works on all the three OSes and provides an easy way to not only install but also to maintain different project environments on the same system, we will concentrate on installing TensorFlow using Anaconda in this book. More details about Anaconda and managing its environment can be read from `https://conda.io/docs/user-guide/index.html`.

The code in this book has been tested on the following platforms:

- Windows 10, Anaconda 3, Python 3.5, TensorFlow GPU, CUDA toolkit 8.0, cuDNN v5.1, NVDIA® GTX 1070
- Windows 10/ Ubuntu 14.04/ Ubuntu 16.04/macOS Sierra, Anaconda3, Python 3.5, TensorFlow (CPU)

Getting ready

The prerequisite for TensorFlow installation is that the system has Python 2.5 or higher installed. The recipes in this book have been designed for Python 3.5 (the Anaconda 3 distribution). To get ready for the installation of TensorFlow, first ensure that you have Anaconda installed. You can download and install Anaconda for Windows/macOS or Linux from `https://www.continuum.io/downloads`.

After installation, you can verify the installation using the following command in your terminal window:

```
conda --version
```

Once Anaconda is installed, we move to the next step, deciding whether to install TensorFlow CPU or GPU. While almost all computer machines support TensorFlow CPU, TensorFlow GPU can be installed only if the machine has an NVDIA® GPU card with CUDA compute capability 3.0 or higher (minimum NVDIA® GTX 650 for desktop PCs).

CPU versus GPU: Central Processing Unit (CPU) consists of a few cores (4-8) optimized for sequential serial processing. A **Graphical Processing Unit (GPU)** on the other hand has a massively parallel architecture consisting of thousands of smaller, more efficient cores (roughly in 1,000s) designed to handle multiple tasks simultaneously.

For TensorFlow GPU, it is imperative that CUDA toolkit 7.0 or greater is installed, proper NVDIA® drivers are installed, and cuDNN v3 or greater is installed. On Windows, additionally, certain DLL files are needed; one can either download the required DLL files or install Visual Studio C++. One more thing to remember is that cuDNN files are installed in a different directory. One needs to ensure that directory is in the system path. One can also alternatively copy the relevant files in CUDA library in the respective folders.

How to do it...

We proceed with the recipe as follows:

1. Create a conda environment using the following at command line (If you are using Windows it will be better to do it as Administrator in the command line):

```
conda create -n tensorflow python=3.5
```

2. Activate the conda environment:

```
# Windows
activate tensorflow
#Mac OS/ Ubuntu:
source activate tensorflow
```

3. The command should change the prompt:

```
# Windows
(tensorflow)C:>
# Mac OS/Ubuntu
(tensorflow)$
```

4. Next, depending on the TensorFlow version you want to install inside your conda environment, enter the following command:

```
## Windows
# CPU Version only
(tensorflow)C:>pip install --ignore-installed --upgrade
https://storage.googleapis.com/tensorflow/windows/cpu/tensorflow-1.
```

```
3.0cr2-cp35-cp35m-win_amd64.whl

# GPU Version
(tensorflow)C:>pip install --ignore-installed --upgrade
https://storage.googleapis.com/tensorflow/windows/gpu/tensorflow_gp
u-1.3.0cr2-cp35-cp35m-win_amd64.whl

## Mac OS
# CPU only Version
(tensorflow)$ pip install --ignore-installed --upgrade
https://storage.googleapis.com/tensorflow/mac/cpu/tensorflow-1.3.0c
r2-py3-none-any.whl

# GPU version
(tensorflow)$ pip install --ignore-installed --upgrade
https://storage.googleapis.com/tensorflow/mac/gpu/tensorflow_gpu-1.
3.0cr2-py3-none-any.whl

## Ubuntu
# CPU only Version
(tensorflow)$ pip install --ignore-installed --upgrade
https://storage.googleapis.com/tensorflow/linux/cpu/tensorflow-1.3.
0cr2-cp35-cp35m-linux_x86_64.whl

# GPU Version
(tensorflow)$ pip install --ignore-installed --upgrade
https://storage.googleapis.com/tensorflow/linux/gpu/tensorflow_gpu-
1.3.0cr2-cp35-cp35m-linux_x86_64.whl
```

5. On the command line, type `python`.

6. Write the following code:

```
import tensorflow as tf
message = tf.constant('Welcome to the exciting world of Deep Neural
Networks!')
with tf.Session() as sess:
    print(sess.run(message).decode())
```

7. You will receive the following output:

```
🖥 Command Prompt - python

C:\Users\am>activate tensorflow

(tensorflow) C:\Users\am>python
Python 3.5.3 |Continuum Analytics, Inc.| (default, Feb 22 2017, 21:28:42) [MSC v.1900 64 bit (AMD64)] on win32
Type "help", "copyright", "credits" or "license" for more information.
>>> import tensorflow as tf
>>> message = tf.constant('Welcome to the exciting world of Deep Neural Networks!')
>>>
>>> with tf.Session() as sess:
...     print(sess.run(message).decode())
...
2017-06-04 15:23:17.129659: W c:\tf_jenkins\home\workspace\release-win\device\gpu\os\windows\tensorflow\core\platfc
2017-06-04 15:23:17.129809: W c:\tf_jenkins\home\workspace\release-win\device\gpu\os\windows\tensorflow\core\platfc
2017-06-04 15:23:17.129961: W c:\tf_jenkins\home\workspace\release-win\device\gpu\os\windows\tensorflow\core\platfc
2017-06-04 15:23:17.130111: W c:\tf_jenkins\home\workspace\release-win\device\gpu\os\windows\tensorflow\core\platfc
2017-06-04 15:23:17.130264: W c:\tf_jenkins\home\workspace\release-win\device\gpu\os\windows\tensorflow\core\platfc
2017-06-04 15:23:17.130392: W c:\tf_jenkins\home\workspace\release-win\device\gpu\os\windows\tensorflow\core\platfc
2017-06-04 15:23:17.130504: W c:\tf_jenkins\home\workspace\release-win\device\gpu\os\windows\tensorflow\core\platfc
2017-06-04 15:23:17.130991: W c:\tf_jenkins\home\workspace\release-win\device\gpu\os\windows\tensorflow\core\platfc
2017-06-04 15:23:17.466909: I c:\tf_jenkins\home\workspace\release-win\device\gpu\os\windows\tensorflow\core\commor
name: GeForce GTX 1070
major: 6 minor: 1 memoryClockRate (GHz) 1.683
pciBusID 0000:01:00.0
Total memory: 8.00GiB
Free memory: 6.66GiB
2017-06-04 15:23:17.467072: I c:\tf_jenkins\home\workspace\release-win\device\gpu\os\windows\tensorflow\core\commor
2017-06-04 15:23:17.468448: I c:\tf_jenkins\home\workspace\release-win\device\gpu\os\windows\tensorflow\core\commor
2017-06-04 15:23:17.468824: I c:\tf_jenkins\home\workspace\release-win\device\gpu\os\windows\tensorflow\core\commor
Welcome to the exciting world of Deep Neural Networks!
>>>
```

8. Deactivate the conda environment at the command line using the command `deactivate` on Windows and `source deactivate` on MAC/Ubuntu.

How it works...

TensorFlow is distributed by Google using the wheels standard. It is a ZIP format archive with the `.whl` extension. Python 3.6, the default Python interpreter in Anaconda 3, does not have wheels installed. At the time of writing the book, wheel support for Python 3.6 exists only for Linux/Ubuntu. Therefore, while creating the TensorFlow environment, we specify Python 3.5. This installs pip, python, and wheel along with a few other packages in the conda environment named `tensorflow`.

Once the conda environment is created, the environment is activated using the `source activate/activate` command. In the activated environment, use the `pip install` command with appropriate TensorFlow-API URL to install the required TensorFlow. Although there exists an Anaconda command to install TensorFlow CPU using conda forge TensorFlow documentation recommends using `pip install`. After installing TensorFlow in the conda environment, we can deactivate it. Now you are ready to execute your first TensorFlow program.

When the program runs, you may see a few warning (W) messages, some information (I) messages, and lastly the output of your code:

```
Welcome to the exciting world of Deep Neural Networks!
```

Congratulations for successfully installing and executing your first TensorFlow code! We will go through the code in more depth in the next recipe.

There's more...

Additionally, you can also install Jupyter notebook:

1. Install `ipython` as follows:

```
conda install -c anaconda ipython
```

2. Install `nb_conda_kernels`:

```
conda install -channel=conda-forge nb_conda_kernels
```

3. Launch the `Jupyter notebook`:

```
jupyter notebook
```

This will result in the opening of a new browser window.

If you already have TensorFlow installed on your system, you can use `pip install --upgrade tensorflow` to upgrade it.

Hello world in TensorFlow

The first program that you learn to write in any computer language is Hello world. We maintain the convention in this book and start with the Hello world program. The code that we used in the preceding section to validate our TensorFlow installation is as follows:

```
import tensorflow as tf
message = tf.constant('Welcome to the exciting world of Deep Neural
Networks!')
 with tf.Session() as sess:
     print(sess.run(message).decode())
```

Let's go in depth into this simple code.

How to do it...

1. Import `tensorflow` this imports the TensorFlow library and allows you to use its wonderful features.

   ```
   import tensorflow as tf
   ```

2. Since the message we want to print is a constant string, we use `tf.constant`:

   ```
   message = tf.constant('Welcome to the exciting world of Deep Neural
   Networks!')
   ```

3. To execute the graph element, we need to define the Session using `with` and run the session using `run`:

   ```
   with tf.Session() as sess:
        print(sess.run(message).decode())
   ```

4. The output contains a series of warning messages (W), depending on your computer system and OS, claiming that code could run faster if compiled for your specific machine:

   ```
   The TensorFlow library wasn't compiled to use SSE instructions, but
   these are available on your machine and could speed up CPU
   computations.
   The TensorFlow library wasn't compiled to use SSE2 instructions,
   but these are available on your machine and could speed up CPU
   computations.
   The TensorFlow library wasn't compiled to use SSE3 instructions,
   ```

```
but these are available on your machine and could speed up CPU
computations.
The TensorFlow library wasn't compiled to use SSE4.1 instructions,
but these are available on your machine and could speed up CPU
computations.
The TensorFlow library wasn't compiled to use SSE4.2 instructions,
but these are available on your machine and could speed up CPU
computations.
The TensorFlow library wasn't compiled to use AVX instructions, but
these are available on your machine and could speed up CPU
computations.
The TensorFlow library wasn't compiled to use AVX2 instructions,
but these are available on your machine and could speed up CPU
computations.
The TensorFlow library wasn't compiled to use FMA instructions, but
these are available on your machine and could speed up CPU
computations.
```

5. If you are working with TensorFlow GPU, you also get a list of informative messages (I) giving details of the devices used:

```
Found device 0 with properties:
name: GeForce GTX 1070
major: 6 minor: 1 memoryClockRate (GHz) 1.683
pciBusID 0000:01:00.0
Total memory: 8.00GiB
Free memory: 6.66GiB
DMA: 0
0:   Y
Creating TensorFlow device (/gpu:0) -> (device: 0, name: GeForce
GTX 1070, pci bus id: 0000:01:00.0)
```

6. At the end is the message we asked to print in the session:

```
Welcome to the exciting world of Deep Neural Networks
```

How it works...

The preceding code is divided into three main parts. There is the **import block** that contains all the libraries our code will use; in the present code, we use only TensorFlow. The import tensorflow as tf statement gives Python access to all TensorFlow's classes, methods, and symbols. The second block contains the graph definition part; here, we build our desired computational graph. In the present case, our graph consists of only one node, the tensor constant message consisting of byte string, "Welcome to the exciting world of Deep Neural Networks". The third component of our code is **running the computational graph** as Session; we created a Session using the with keyword. Finally , in the Session, we run the graph created above.

Let's now understand the output. The warning messages that are received tell you that TensorFlow code could run at an even higher speed, which can be achieved by installing TensorFlow from source (we will do this in a later recipe in this chapter). The information messages received inform you about the devices used for computation. On their part, both messages are quite harmless, but if you don't like seeing them, adding this two-line code will do the trick:

```
import os
os.environ['TF_CPP_MIN_LOG_LEVEL']='2'
```

The code is to ignore all messages till level 2. Level 1 is for information, 2 for warnings, and 3 for error messages.

The program prints the result of running the graph created the graph is run using the sess.run() statement. The result of running the graph is fed to the print function, which is further modified using the decode method. The sess.run evaluates the tensor defined in the message. The print function prints on stdout the result of the evaluation:

```
b'Welcome to the exciting world of Deep Neural Networks'
```

This says that the result is a byte string. To remove string quotes and **b** (for **byte**), we use the method decode().

Understanding the TensorFlow program structure

TensorFlow is very unlike other programming languages. We first need to build a blueprint of whatever neural network we want to create. This is accomplished by dividing the program into two separate parts, namely, definition of the computational graph and its execution. At first, this might appear cumbersome to the conventional programmer, but it is this separation of the execution graph from the graph definition that gives TensorFlow its strength, that is, the ability to work on multiple platforms and parallel execution.

Computational graph: A computational graph is a network of nodes and edges. In this section, all the data to be used, in other words, tensor Objects (constants, variables, and placeholders) and all the computations to be performed, namely, Operation Objects (in short referred as ops), are defined. Each node can have zero or more inputs but only one output. Nodes in the network represent Objects (tensors and Operations), and edges represent the Tensors that flow between operations. The computation graph defines the blueprint of the neural network but Tensors in it have no value associated with them yet.

To build a computation graph we define all the constants, variables, and operations that we need to perform. Constants, variables, and placeholders will be dealt with in the next recipe. Mathematical operations will be dealt in detail in the recipe for matrix manipulations. Here, we describe the structure using a simple example of defining and executing a graph to add two vectors.

Execution of the graph: The execution of the graph is performed using Session Object. *The Session Object encapsulates the environment in which tensor and Operation Objects are evaluated.* This is the place where actual calculations and transfer of information from one layer to another takes place. The values of different tensor Objects are initialized, accessed, and saved in Session Object only. Up to now the tensor Objects were just abstract definitions, here they come to life.

How to do it...

We proceed with the recipe as follows:

1. We consider a simple example of adding two vectors, we have two inputs vectors v_1 and v_2 they are to be fed as input to the Add operation. The graph we want to build is as follows:

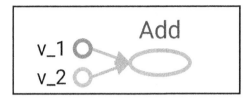

2. The corresponding code to define the computation graph is as follows:

```
v_1 = tf.constant([1,2,3,4])
v_2 = tf.constant([2,1,5,3])
v_add = tf.add(v_1,v_2)   # You can also write v_1 + v_2 instead
```

3. Next, we execute the graph in the session:

```
with tf.Session() as sess:
    prin(sess.run(v_add))
```

The above two commands are equivalent to the following code. The advantage of using `with` block is that one need not close the session explicitly.

```
sess = tf.Session()
print(ses.run(tv_add))
sess.close()
```

4. This results in printing the sum of two vectors:

```
[3 3 8 7]
```

Remember that each Session needs to be explicitly closed using the `close()` method, `with` block implicitly closes the session when it ends.

How it works...

The building of a computational graph is very simple; you go on adding the variables and operations and passing them through (flow the tensors) in the sequence you build your neural network layer by layer. TensorFlow also allows you to use specific devices (CPU/GPU) with different objects of the computation graph using `with tf.device()`. In our example, the computational graph consists of three nodes, v_1 and v_2 representing the two vectors, and Add is the operation to be performed on them.

Now, to bring this graph to life, we first need to define a session object using `tf.Session()`; we gave the name `sess` to our session object. Next, we run it using the `run` method defined in Session class as follows:

```
run (fetches, feed_dict=None, options=None, run_metadata)
```

This evaluates the tensor in `fetches`; our example has tensor `v_add` in fetches. The `run` method will execute every tensor and every operation in the graph leading to `v_add`. If instead of `v_add`, you have `v_1` in fetches, the result will be the value of vector `v_1`:

```
[1,2,3,4]
```

Fetches can be a single tensor/operation object or more, for example, if the fetches is `[v_1, v_2, v_add]`, the output will be the following:

```
[array([1, 2, 3, 4]), array([2, 1, 5, 3]), array([3, 3, 8, 7])]
```

In the same program code, we can have many session objects.

There's more...

You must be wondering why we have to write so many lines of code for a simple vector addition or to print a small message. Well, you could have very conveniently done this work in a one-liner:

```
print(tf.Session().run(tf.add(tf.constant([1,2,3,4]),tf.constant([2,1,5,3]))))
```

Writing this type of code not only affects the computational graph but can be memory expensive when the same operation (OP) is performed repeatedly in a for loop. Making a habit of explicitly defining all tensor and operation objects not only makes the code more readable but also helps you visualize the computational graph in a cleaner manner.

 Visualizing the graph using TensorBoard is one of the most useful capabilities of TensorFlow, especially when building complicated neural networks. The computational graph that we built can be viewed with the help of Graph Object.

If you are working on Jupyter Notebook or Python shell, it is more convenient to use `tf.InteractiveSession` instead of `tf.Session`. `InteractiveSession` makes itself the default session so that you can directly call run the tensor Object using `eval()` without explicitly calling the session, as described in the following example code:

```
sess = tf.InteractiveSession()

v_1 = tf.constant([1,2,3,4])
v_2 = tf.constant([2,1,5,3])

v_add = tf.add(v_1,v_2)

print(v_add.eval())

sess.close()
```

Working with constants, variables, and placeholders

TensorFlow in the simplest terms provides a library to define and perform different mathematical operations with tensors. A tensor is basically an n-dimensional matrix. All types of data, that is, scalar, vectors, and matrices are special types of tensors:

Types of data	Tensor	Shape
Scalar	0-D Tensor	[]
Vector	1-D Tensor	$[D_0]$
Matrix	2-D Tensor	$[D_0, D_1]$
Tensors	N-D Tensor	$[D_0, D_1, ...D_{n-1}]$

TensorFlow supports three types of tensors:

- Constants
- Variables
- Placeholders

Constants: Constants are the tensors whose values cannot be changed.

Variables: We use variable tensors when the values require updating within a session. For example, in the case of neural networks, the weights need to be updated during the training session, which is achieved by declaring weights as variables. The variables need to be explicitly initialized before use. Another important thing to note is that constants are stored in the computation graph definition; they are loaded every time the graph is loaded. In other words, they are memory expensive. Variables, on the other hand, are stored separately; they can exist on the parameter server.

Placeholders: These are used to feed values into a TensorFlow graph. They are used along with feed_dict to feed the data. They are normally used to feed new training examples while training a neural network. We assign a value to a placeholder while running the graph in the session. They allow us to create our operations and build the computation graph without requiring the data. An important point to note is that placeholders do not contain any data and thus there is no need to initialize them as well.

How to do it...

Let's start with constants:

1. We can declare a scalar constant:

```
t_1 = tf.constant(4)
```

2. A constant vector of shape [1,3] can be declared as follows:

```
t_2 = tf.constant([4, 3, 2])
```

3. To create a tensor with all elements zero, we use tf.zeros(). This statement creates a zero matrix of shape [M,N] with dtype (int32, float32, and so on):

```
tf.zeros([M,N],tf.dtype)
```

   Let's take an example:

```
zero_t = tf.zeros([2,3],tf.int32)
# Results in an 2×3 array of zeros: [[0 0 0], [0 0 0]]
```

4. We can also create tensor constants of the same shape as an existing Numpy array or tensor constant as follows:

```
tf.zeros_like(t_2)
# Create a zero matrix of same shape as t_2
tf.ones_like(t_2)
```

```
# Creates a ones matrix of same shape as t_2
```

5. We can create a tensor with all elements set to one; here, we create a ones matrix of shape [M,N]:

```
tf.ones([M,N],tf.dtype)
```

Let's take an example:

```
ones_t = tf.ones([2,3],tf.int32)
# Results in an 2×3 array of ones:[[1 1 1], [1 1 1]]
```

Let's proceed to sequences:

1. We can generate a sequence of evenly spaced vectors, starting from start to stop, within total num values:

```
tf.linspace(start, stop, num)
```

2. The corresponding values differ by (stop-start)/(num-1).

3. Let's take an example:

```
range_t = tf.linspace(2.0,5.0,5)
# We get: [ 2.    2.75  3.5   4.25  5.  ]
```

4. Generate a sequence of numbers starting from the start (default=0), incremented by delta (default =1), until, but not including, the limit:

```
tf.range(start,limit,delta)
```

Here is an example:

```
range_t = tf.range(10)
# Result: [0 1 2 3 4 5 6 7 8 9]
```

TensorFlow allows **random tensors** with different distributions to be created:

1. To create random values from a normal distribution of shape [M, N] with the mean (default =0.0) and standard deviation (default=1.0) with seed, we can use the following:

```
t_random = tf.random_normal([2,3], mean=2.0, stddev=4, seed=12)

# Result: [[ 0.25347459  5.37990952  1.95276058], [-1.53760314
1.2588985   2.84780669]]
```

2. To create random values from a truncated normal distribution of shape [M, N] with the mean (default =0.0) and standard deviation (default=1.0) with seed, we can use the following:

```
t_random = tf.truncated_normal([1,5], stddev=2, seed=12)
# Result: [[-0.8732627 1.68995488 -0.02361972 -1.76880157
-3.87749004]]
```

3. To create random values from a given gamma distribution of shape [M, N] in the range [minval (default=0), maxval] with seed, perform as follows:

```
t_random = tf.random_uniform([2,3], maxval=4, seed=12)

# Result: [[ 2.54461002  3.69636583  2.70510912], [ 2.00850058
3.84459829  3.54268885]]
```

4. To randomly crop a given tensor to a specified size, do as follows:

```
tf.random_crop(t_random, [2,5],seed=12)
```

Here, t_random is an already defined tensor. This will result in a [2,5] tensor randomly cropped from tensor t_random.

Many times we need to present the training sample in random order; we can use tf.random_shuffle() to randomly shuffle a tensor along its first dimension. If t_random is the tensor we want to shuffle, then we use the following:

```
tf.random_shuffle(t_random)
```

5. Randomly generated tensors are affected by the value of the initial seed. To obtain the same random numbers in multiple runs or sessions, the seed should be set to a constant value. When there are large numbers of random tensors in use, we can set the seed for all randomly generated tensors using tf.set_random_seed(); the following command sets the seed for random tensors for all sessions as 54:

```
tf.set_random_seed(54)
```

Seed can have only integer value.

Let's now turn to the variables:

1. They are created using the variable class. The definition of variables also includes the constant/random values from which they should be initialized. In the following code, we create two different tensor variables, `t_a` and `t_b`. Both will be initialized to random uniform distributions of shape `[50, 50]`, `minval=0`, and `maxval=10`:

```
rand_t = tf.random_uniform([50,50], 0, 10, seed=0)
t_a = tf.Variable(rand_t)
t_b = tf.Variable(rand_t)
```

Variables are often used to represent weights and biases in a neural network.

2. In the following code, we define two variables weights and bias. The weights variable is randomly initialized using normal distribution, with mean zeros and standard deviation of two, the size of weights is 100×100. The bias consists of 100 elements each initialized to zero. Here we have also used the optional argument name to give a name to the variable defined in the computational graph.

```
weights = tf.Variable(tf.random_normal([100,100],stddev=2))
bias = tf.Variable(tf.zeros[100], name = 'biases')
```

3. In all the preceding examples, the source of initialization of variables is some constant. We can also specify a variable to be initialized from another variable; the following statement will initialize `weight2` from the weights defined earlier:

```
weight2=tf.Variable(weights.initialized_value(), name='w2')
```

4. The definition of variables specify how the variable is to be initialized, but we must explicitly initialize all declared variables. In the definition of the computational graph, we do it by declaring an initialization Operation Object:

```
intial_op = tf.global_variables_initializer().
```

5. Each variable can also be initialized separately using `tf.Variable.initializer` during the running graph:

```
bias = tf.Variable(tf.zeros([100,100]))
 with tf.Session() as sess:
     sess.run(bias.initializer)
```

6. **Saving variables**: We can save the variables using the `Saver` class. To do this, we define a `saver` Operation Object:

```
saver = tf.train.Saver()
```

7. After constants and variables, we come to the most important element placeholders, they are used to feed data to the graph. We can define a placeholder using the following:

```
tf.placeholder(dtype, shape=None, name=None)
```

8. `dtype` specifies the data type of the placeholder and must be specified while declaring the placeholder. Here, we define a placeholder for x and calculate `y = 2 * x` using `feed_dict` for a random 4×5 matrix:

```
x = tf.placeholder("float")
y = 2 * x
data = tf.random_uniform([4,5],10)
with tf.Session() as sess:
    x_data = sess.run(data)
    print(sess.run(y, feed_dict = {x:x_data}))
```

How it works...

All constants, variables, and placeholders will be defined in the computation graph section of the code. If we use the print statement in the definition section, we will only get information about the type of tensor, and not its value.

To find out the value, we need to create the session graph and explicitly use the `run` command with the desired tensor values as `fetches`:

```
print(sess.run(t_1))
# Will print the value of t_1 defined in step 1
```

There's more...

Very often, we will need constant tensor objects with a large size; in this case, to optimize memory, it is better to declare them as variables with a trainable flag set to `False`:

```
t_large = tf.Variable(large_array, trainable = False)
```

TensorFlow was designed to work impeccably with Numpy, hence all the TensorFlow data types are based on those of Numpy. Using `tf.convert_to_tensor()`, we can convert the given value to tensor type and use it with TensorFlow functions and operators. This function accepts Numpy arrays, Python Lists, and Python scalars and allows interoperability with tensor Objects.

The following table lists some of the common TensorFlow supported data types (taken from `TensorFlow.org`):

Data type	TensorFlow type
DT_FLOAT	tf.float32
DT_DOUBLE	tf.float64
DT_INT8	tf.int8
DT_UINT8	tf.uint8
DT_STRING	tf.string
DT_BOOL	tf.bool
DT_COMPLEX64	tf.complex64
DT_QINT32	tf.qint32

Note that unlike Python/Numpy sequences, TensorFlow sequences are not iterable. Try the following code:

```
for i in tf.range(10)
```

You will get an error:

```
#TypeError("'Tensor' object is not iterable.")
```

Performing matrix manipulations using TensorFlow

Matrix operations, such as performing multiplication, addition, and subtraction, are important operations in the propagation of signals in any neural network. Often in the computation, we require random, zero, ones, or identity matrices.

This recipe will show you how to get different types of matrices and how to perform different matrix manipulation operations on them.

How to do it...

We proceed with the recipe as follows:

1. We start an interactive session so that the results can be evaluated easily:

```
import tensorflow as tf

#Start an Interactive Session
sess = tf.InteractiveSession()

#Define a 5x5 Identity matrix
I_matrix = tf.eye(5)
print(I_matrix.eval())
# This will print a 5x5 Identity matrix

#Define a Variable initialized to a 10x10 identity matrix
X = tf.Variable(tf.eye(10))
X.initializer.run()  # Initialize the Variable
print(X.eval())
# Evaluate the Variable and print the result

#Create a random 5x10 matrix
A = tf.Variable(tf.random_normal([5,10]))
A.initializer.run()

#Multiply two matrices
product = tf.matmul(A, X)
print(product.eval())

#create a random matrix of 1s and 0s, size 5x10
b = tf.Variable(tf.random_uniform([5,10], 0, 2, dtype= tf.int32))
b.initializer.run()
```

```
print(b.eval())
b_new = tf.cast(b, dtype=tf.float32)
#Cast to float32 data type

# Add the two matrices
t_sum = tf.add(product, b_new)
t_sub = product - b_new
print("A*X _b\n", t_sum.eval())
print("A*X - b\n", t_sub.eval())
```

2. Some other useful matrix manipulations, like element-wise multiplication, multiplication with a scalar, elementwise division, elementwise remainder of a division, can be performed as follows:

```
import tensorflow as tf

# Create two random matrices
a = tf.Variable(tf.random_normal([4,5], stddev=2))
b = tf.Variable(tf.random_normal([4,5], stddev=2))

#Element Wise Multiplication
A = a * b

#Multiplication with a scalar 2
B = tf.scalar_mul(2, A)

# Elementwise division, its result is
C = tf.div(a,b)

#Element Wise remainder of division
D = tf.mod(a,b)

init_op = tf.global_variables_initializer()
with tf.Session() as sess:
    sess.run(init_op)
    writer = tf.summary.FileWriter('graphs', sess.graph)
    a,b,A_R, B_R, C_R, D_R = sess.run([a , b, A, B, C, D])
    print("a\n",a,"\nb\n",b, "a*b\n", A_R, "\n2*a*b\n", B_R,
"\na/b\n", C_R, "\na%b\n", D_R)

writer.close()
```

 tf.div returns a tensor of the same type as the first argument.

How it works...

All arithmetic operations of matrices like add, sub, div, multiply (elementwise multiplication), mod, and cross require that the two tensor matrices should be of the same data type. In case this is not so they will produce an error. We can use `tf.cast()` to convert Tensors from one data type to another.

There's more...

If we are doing division between integer tensors, it is better to use `tf.truediv(a,b)` as it first casts the integer tensors to floating points and then performs element-wise division.

Using a data flow graph

TensorFlow has TensorBoard to provide a graphical image of the computation graph. This makes it convenient to understand, debug, and optimize complex neural network programs. TensorBoard can also provide quantitative metrics about the execution of the network. It reads TensorFlow event files, which contain the summary data that you generate while running the TensorFlow Session.

How to do it...

1. The first step in using TensorBoard is to identify which OPs summaries you would like to have. In the case of DNNs, it is customary to know how the loss term (objective function) varies with time. In the case of Adaptive learning rate, the learning rate itself varies with time. We can get the summary of the term we require with the help of `tf.summary.scalar` OPs. Suppose, the variable loss defines the error term and we want to know how it varies with time, then we can do this as follows:

   ```
   loss = tf...
   tf.summary.scalar('loss', loss)
   ```

2. You can also visualize the distribution of gradients, weights, or even output of a particular layer using `tf.summary.histogram`:

   ```
   output_tensor  = tf.matmul(input_tensor, weights) + biases
   tf.summary.histogram('output', output_tensor)
   ```

3. The summaries will be generated during the session. Instead of executing every summary operation individually, you can define `tf.merge_all_summaries` OPs in the computation graph to get all summaries in a single run.

4. The generated summary then needs to be written in an event file using `tf.summary.Filewriter`:

   ```
   writer = tf.summary.Filewriter('summary_dir', sess.graph)
   ```

5. This writes all the summaries and the graph in the `'summary_dir'` directory.

6. Now, to visualize the summaries, you need to invoke TensorBoard from the command line:

   ```
   tensorboard --logdir=summary_dir
   ```

7. Next, open your browser and type the address `http://localhost:6006/` (or the link you received after running the TensorBoard command).

8. You will see something like the following, with many tabs on the top. The **Graphs** tab will display the graph:

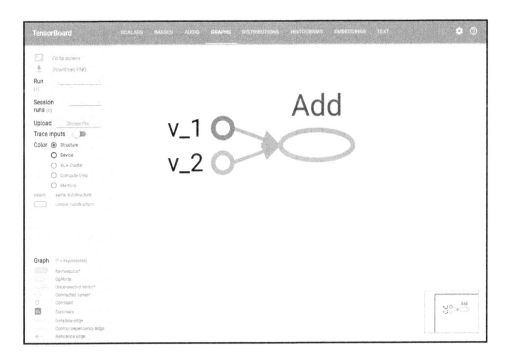

Migrating from 0.x to 1.x

TensorFlow 1.x does not offer backward compatibility. This means that the codes that worked on TensorFlow 0.x may not work on TensorFlow 1.0. So, if you have codes that worked on TensorFlow 0.x, you need to upgrade them (old GitHub repositories or your own codes). This recipe will point out major differences between TensorFlow 0.x and TensorFlow 1.0 and will show you how to use the script tf_upgrade.py to automatically upgrade the code for TensorFlow 1.0.

How to do it...

Here is how we proceed with the recipe:

1. First, download tf_upgrade.py from https://github.com/tensorflow/tensorflow/tree/master/tensorflow/tools/compatibility.

2. If you want to convert one file from TensorFlow 0.x to TensorFlow 1.0, use the following command at the command line:

   ```
   python tf_upgrade.py --infile old_file.py --outfile
   upgraded_file.py
   ```

3. For example, if you have a TensorFlow program file named test.py, you will use the preceding command as follows:

   ```
   python tf_upgrade.py --infile test.py --outfile test_1.0.py
   ```

4. This will result in the creation of a new file named test_1.0.py.

5. If you want to migrate all the files of a directory, then use the following at the command line:

   ```
   python tf_upgrade.py --intree InputDIr --outtree OutputDir
    # For example, if you have a directory located at
   /home/user/my_dir you can migrate all the python files in the
   directory located at /home/user/my-dir_1p0 using the above command
   as:
   python tf_upgrade.py --intree /home/user/my_dir --outtree
   /home/user/my_dir_1p0
   ```

6. In most cases, the directory also contains dataset files; you can ensure that non-Python files are copied as well in the new directory (`my-dir_1p0` in the preceding example) using the following:

```
python tf_upgrade.py --intree /home/user/my_dir --outtree
/home/user/my_dir_1p0 -copyotherfiles True
```

7. In all these cases, a `report.txt` file is generated. This file contains the details of conversion and any errors in the process.

8. Read the `report.txt` file and manually upgrade the part of the code that the script is unable to update.

There's more...

`tf_upgrade.py` has certain limitations:

- It cannot change the arguments of `tf.reverse()`: you will have to manually fix it
- For methods with argument list reordered, like `tf.split()` and `tf.reverse_split()`, it will try to introduce keyword arguments, but it cannot actually reorder the arguments
- You will have to manually replace constructions like `tf.get.variable_scope().reuse_variables()` with the following:

```
with tf.variable_scope(tf.get_variable_scope(), resuse=True):
```

Using XLA to enhance computational performance

Accelerated linear algebra (XLA) is a domain-specific compiler for linear algebra. According to `https://www.tensorflow.org/performance/xla/`, it is still in the experimental stage and is used to optimize TensorFlow computations. It can provide improvements in execution speed, memory usage, and portability on the server and mobile platforms. It provides two-way **JIT (Just In Time)** compilation or **AoT (Ahead of Time)** compilation. Using XLA, you can produce platform-dependent binary files (for a large number of platforms like x64, ARM, and so on), which can be optimized for both memory and speed.

Getting ready

At present, XLA is not included in the binary distributions of TensorFlow. One needs to build it from source. To build TensorFlow from source, knowledge of LLVM and Bazel along with TensorFlow is required. `TensorFlow.org` supports building from source in only MacOS and Ubuntu. The steps needed to build TensorFlow from the source are as follows (`https://www.tensorflow.org/install/install_sources`):

1. Determine which TensorFlow you want to install--TensorFlow with CPU support only or TensorFlow with GPU support.

2. Clone the TensorFlow repository:

   ```
   git clone https://github.com/tensorflow/tensorflow
   cd tensorflow
   git checkout Branch #where Branch is the desired branch
   ```

3. Install the following dependencies:

   - Bazel
   - TensorFlow Python dependencies
   - For the GPU version, NVIDIA packages to support TensorFlow

4. Configure the installation. In this step, you need to choose different options such as XLA, Cuda support, Verbs, and so on:

   ```
   ./configure
   ```

5. Next, use bazel-build:

6. For CPU only version you use:

   ```
   bazel build --config=opt
   //tensorflow/tools/pip_package:build_pip_package
   ```

7. If you have a compatible GPU device and you want the GPU Support, then use:

   ```
   bazel build --config=opt --config=cuda
   //tensorflow/tools/pip_package:build_pip_package
   ```

8. On a successful run, you will get a script, `build_pip_package`.

9. Run this script as follows to build the `whl` file:

   ```
   bazel-bin/tensorflow/tools/pip_package/build_pip_package
   /tmp/tensorflow_pkg
   ```

10. Install the `pip` package:

```
sudo pip install /tmp/tensorflow_pkg/tensorflow-1.1.0-py2-none-
any.whl
```

Now you are ready to go.

How to do it...

TensorFlow generates TensorFlow graphs. With the help of XLA, it is possible to run the TensorFlow graphs on any new kind of device.

1. **JIT Compilation:** This is to turn on JIT compilation at session level:

```
# Config to turn on JIT compilation
 config = tf.ConfigProto()
 config.graph_options.optimizer_options.global_jit_level =
tf.OptimizerOptions.ON_1

 sess = tf.Session(config=config)
```

2. This is to turn on JIT compilation manually:

```
jit_scope = tf.contrib.compiler.jit.experimental_jit_scope

x = tf.placeholder(np.float32)
with jit_scope():
    y = tf.add(x, x)   # The "add" will be compiled with XLA.
```

3. We can also run computations via XLA by placing the operator on a specific XLA device `XLA_CPU` or `XLA_GPU`:

```
with tf.device \
("/job:localhost/replica:0/task:0/device:XLA_GPU:0"):
    output = tf.add(input1, input2)
```

AoT Compilation: Here, we use tfcompile as standalone to convert TensorFlow graphs into executable code for different devices (mobile).

TensorFlow.org tells about tfcompile:

> *tfcompile takes a subgraph, identified by the TensorFlow concepts of feeds and fetches, and generates a function that implements that subgraph. The feeds are the input arguments for the function, and the fetches are the output arguments for the function. All inputs must be fully specified by the feeds; the resulting pruned subgraph cannot contain placeholder or variable nodes. It is common to specify all placeholders and variables as feeds, which ensures the resulting subgraph no longer contains these nodes. The generated function is packaged as a cc_library, with a header file exporting the function signature, and an object file containing the implementation. The user writes code to invoke the generated function as appropriate.*

For advanced steps to do the same, you can refer to `https://www.tensorflow.org/performance/xla/tfcompile`.

Invoking CPU/GPU devices

TensorFlow supports both CPUs and GPUs. It also supports distributed computation. We can use TensorFlow on multiple devices in one or more computer system. TensorFlow names the supported devices as `"/device:CPU:0"` (or `"/cpu:0"`) for the CPU devices and `"/device:GPU:I"` (or `"/gpu:I"`) for the ith GPU device.

As mentioned earlier, GPUs are much faster than CPUs because they have many small cores. However, it is not always an advantage in terms of computational speed to use GPUs for all types of computations. The overhead associated with GPUs can sometimes be more computationally expensive than the advantage of parallel computation offered by GPUs. To deal with this issue, TensorFlow has provisions to place computations on a particular device. By default, if both CPU and GPU are present, TensorFlow gives priority to GPU.

How to do it...

TensorFlow represents devices as strings. Here, we will show you how one can manually assign a device for matrix multiplication in TensorFlow. To verify that TensorFlow is indeed using the device (CPU or GPU) specified, we create the session with the `log_device_placement` flag set to `True`, namely, `config=tf.ConfigProto(log_device_placement=True)`:

1. If you are not sure about the device and want TensorFlow to choose the existing and supported device, you can set the `allow_soft_placement` flag to `True`:

```
config=tf.ConfigProto(allow_soft_placement=True,
log_device_placement=True)
```

2. Manually select CPU for operation:

```
with tf.device('/cpu:0'):
    rand_t = tf.random_uniform([50,50], 0, 10, dtype=tf.float32,
seed=0)
    a = tf.Variable(rand_t)
    b = tf.Variable(rand_t)
    c = tf.matmul(a,b)
    init = tf.global_variables_initializer()

sess = tf.Session(config)
sess.run(init)
print(sess.run(c))
```

3. We get the following output:

```
electing_devices
C:\Users\am\Anaconda3\envs\tensorflow\python.exe D:/PyCharmProjects/Book_TF/Selecting_devices.py
Device mapping:
/job:localhost/replica:0/task:0/gpu:0 -> device: 0, name: GeForce GTX 1070, pci bus id: 0000:01:00.0
Variable_1: (VariableV2): /job:localhost/replica:0/task:0/gpu:0
Variable_1/read: (Identity): /job:localhost/replica:0/task:0/gpu:0
Variable: (VariableV2): /job:localhost/replica:0/task:0/gpu:0
Variable/read: (Identity): /job:localhost/replica:0/task:0/gpu:0
MatMul: (MatMul): /job:localhost/replica:0/task:0/gpu:0
random_uniform/sub: (Sub): /job:localhost/replica:0/task:0/gpu:0
random_uniform/RandomUniform: (RandomUniform): /job:localhost/replica:0/task:0/gpu:0
random_uniform/mul: (Mul): /job:localhost/replica:0/task:0/gpu:0
random_uniform: (Add): /job:localhost/replica:0/task:0/gpu:0
Variable_1/Assign: (Assign): /job:localhost/replica:0/task:0/gpu:0
Variable/Assign: (Assign): /job:localhost/replica:0/task:0/gpu:0
init: (NoOp): /job:localhost/replica:0/task:0/gpu:0
random_uniform/max: (Const): /job:localhost/replica:0/task:0/gpu:0
random_uniform/min: (Const): /job:localhost/replica:0/task:0/gpu:0
random_uniform/shape: (Const): /job:localhost/replica:0/task:0/gpu:0
[[ 1405.24316406  1441.74121094  1364.38000488 ...,   1480.22509766
   1279.00634766  1620.09387207]
 [ 1232.65893555  1344.44580078  1169.70922852 ...,   1205.12854004
   1040.5567627   1421.96716309]
 [ 1209.31665039  1180.32080078  1158.13964844 ...,   1200.03430176
   1014.03210449  1222.51074219]
 ...,
```
```
    TODO    Python Console    Terminal
and Plugin Updates: PyCharm Community Edition is ready to update. (today 18:29)
```

We can see that all the devices, in this case, are `'/cpu:0'`.

4. Manually select a single GPU for operation:

```
with tf.device('/gpu:0'):
    rand_t = tf.random_uniform([50,50], 0, 10, dtype=tf.float32,
seed=0)
    a = tf.Variable(rand_t)
    b = tf.Variable(rand_t)
    c = tf.matmul(a,b)
    init = tf.global_variables_initializer()

sess = tf.Session(config=tf.ConfigProto(log_device_placement=True))
sess.run(init)
print(sess.run(c))
```

5. The output now changes to the following:

```
Selecting_devices
C:\Users\am\Anaconda3\envs\tensorflow\python.exe D:/PyCharmProjects/Book_TF/Selecting_devices.py
Device mapping:
/job:localhost/replica:0/task:0/gpu:0 -> device: 0, name: GeForce GTX 1070, pci bus id: 0000:01:00.0
Variable_1: (VariableV2): /job:localhost/replica:0/task:0/gpu:0
Variable_1/read: (Identity): /job:localhost/replica:0/task:0/gpu:0
Variable: (VariableV2): /job:localhost/replica:0/task:0/gpu:0
Variable/read: (Identity): /job:localhost/replica:0/task:0/gpu:0
MatMul: (MatMul): /job:localhost/replica:0/task:0/gpu:0
random_uniform/sub: (Sub): /job:localhost/replica:0/task:0/gpu:0
random_uniform/RandomUniform: (RandomUniform): /job:localhost/replica:0/task:0/gpu:0
random_uniform/mul: (Mul): /job:localhost/replica:0/task:0/gpu:0
random_uniform: (Add): /job:localhost/replica:0/task:0/gpu:0
Variable_1/Assign: (Assign): /job:localhost/replica:0/task:0/gpu:0
Variable/Assign: (Assign): /job:localhost/replica:0/task:0/gpu:0
init: (NoOp): /job:localhost/replica:0/task:0/gpu:0
random_uniform/max: (Const): /job:localhost/replica:0/task:0/gpu:0
random_uniform/min: (Const): /job:localhost/replica:0/task:0/gpu:0
random_uniform/shape: (Const): /job:localhost/replica:0/task:0/gpu:0
[[ 1405.24316406  1441.74121094  1364.38000488 ...,  1480.22509766
   1279.00634766  1620.09387207]
 [ 1232.65893555  1344.44580078  1169.70922852 ...,  1205.12854004
   1040.5567627   1421.96716309]
 [ 1209.31665039  1180.32080078  1158.13964844 ...,  1200.03430176
   1014.03210449  1222.51074219]
 ...,
```

TODO   Python Console   Terminal

and Plugin Updates: PyCharm Community Edition is ready to update. (today 18:29)

6. The '/cpu:0' after each operation is now replaced by '/gpu:0'.

7. Manually select multiple GPUs:

```
c=[]
for d in ['/gpu:1','/gpu:2']:
    with tf.device(d):
        rand_t = tf.random_uniform([50, 50], 0, 10,
dtype=tf.float32, seed=0)
        a = tf.Variable(rand_t)
```

```
            b = tf.Variable(rand_t)
            c.append(tf.matmul(a,b))
            init = tf.global_variables_initializer()

    sess =
    tf.Session(config=tf.ConfigProto(allow_soft_placement=True,log_devi
    ce_placement=True))
    sess.run(init)
    print(sess.run(c))
    sess.close()
```

8. In this case, if the system has three GPU devices, then the first set of multiplication will be carried on by `'/gpu:1'` and the second set by `'/gpu:2'`.

How it works...

The `tf.device()` argument selects the device (CPU or GPU). The `with` block ensures the operations for which the device is selected. All the variables, constants, and operations defined within the `with` block will use the device selected in `tf.device()`. Session configuration is controlled using `tf.ConfigProto`. By setting the `allow_soft_placement` and `log_device_placement` flags, we tell TensorFlow to automatically choose the available devices in case the specified device is not available, and to give log messages as output describing the allocation of devices while the session is executed.

TensorFlow for Deep Learning

DNNs today is the buzzword in the AI community. Many data science/Kaggle competitions have been recently won by candidates using DNNs. While the concept of DNNs had been around since the proposal of Perceptrons by Rosenblat in 1962 and they were made feasible by the discovery of the Gradient Descent Algorithm in 1986 by Rumelhart, Hinton, and Williams. It is only recently that DNNs became the favourite of AI/ML enthusiasts and engineers world over.

The main reason for this is the availability of modern computing power such as GPUs and tools like TensorFlow that make it easier to access GPUs and construct complex neural networks in just a few lines of code.

As a machine learning enthusiast, you must already be familiar with the concepts of neural networks and deep learning, but for the sake of completeness, we will introduce the basics here and explore what features of TensorFlow make it a popular choice for deep learning.

Neural networks are a biologically inspired model for computation and learning. Like a biological neuron, they take weighted input from other cells (neurons or environment); this weighted input undergoes a processing element and results in an output which can be binary (fire or not fire) or continuous (probability, prediction). **Artificial Neural Networks (ANNs)** are networks of these neurons, which can be randomly distributed or arranged in a layered structure. These neurons learn through the set of weights and biases associated with them.

The following figure gives a good idea about the similarity of the neural network in biology and an artificial neural network:

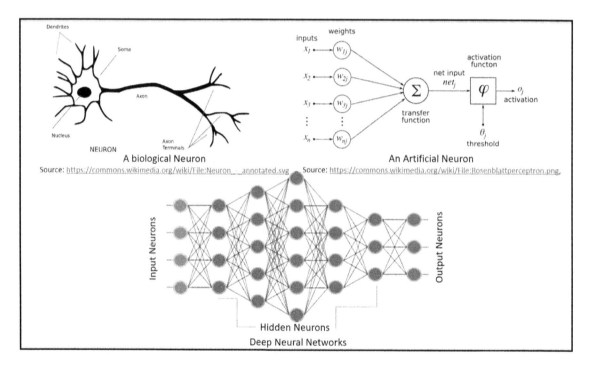

Deep learning, as defined by Hinton et al. (`https://www.cs.toronto.edu/~hinton/absps/NatureDeepReview.pdf`), consists of computational models composed of multiple processing layers (hidden layers). An increase in the number of layers results in an increase in learning time. The learning time further increases due to a large dataset, as is the norm of present-day CNN or **Generative Adversarial Networks (GANs)**. Thus, to practically implement DNNs, we require high computation power. The advent of GPUs by NVDIA® made it feasible and then TensorFlow by Google made it possible to implement complex DNN structures without going into the complex mathematical details, and availability of large datasets provided the necessary food for DNNs. TensorFlow is the most popular library for deep learning for the following reasons:

- TensorFlow is a powerful library for performing large-scale numerical computations like matrix multiplication or auto-differentiation. These two computations are necessary to implement and train DNNs.
- TensorFlow uses C/C++ at the backend, which makes it computationally fast.
- TensorFlow has a high-level machine learning API (`tf.contrib.learn`) that makes it easier to configure, train, and evaluate a large number of machine learning models.
- One can use Keras, a high-level deep learning library, on top of TensorFlow. Keras is very user-friendly and allows easy and fast prototyping. It supports various DNNs like RNNs, CNNs, and even a combination of the two.

How to do it...

Any deep learning network consists of four important components: Dataset, defining the model (network structure), Training/Learning, and Prediction/Evaluation. We can do all these in TensorFlow; let's see how:

- **Dataset**: DNNs depend on large amounts of data. The data can be collected or generated or one can also use standard datasets available. TensorFlow supports three main methods to read the data. There are different datasets available; some of the datasets we will be using to train the models built in this book are as follows:
- **MNIST**: It is the largest database of handwritten digits (0 - 9). It consists of a training set of 60,000 examples and a test set of 10,000 examples. The dataset is maintained at Yann LeCun's home page (`http://yann.lecun.com/exdb/mnist/`). The dataset is included in the TensorFlow library in `tensorflow.examples.tutorials.mnist`.

- **CIFAR10**: This dataset contains 60,000 32 x 32 color images in 10 classes, with 6,000 images per class. The training set contains 50,000 images and test dataset--10,000 images. The ten classes of the dataset are: airplane, automobile, bird, cat, deer, dog, frog, horse, ship, and truck. The data is maintained by the Computer Science Department, University of Toronto (`https://www.cs.toronto.edu/~kriz/cifar.html`).

- **WORDNET**: This is a lexical database of English. It contains nouns, verbs, adverbs, and adjectives, grouped into sets of cognitive synonyms (Synsets), that is, words that represent the same concept, for example, shut and close or car and automobile are grouped into unordered sets. It contains 155,287 words organised in 117,659 synsets for a total of 206,941 word-sense pairs. The data is maintained by Princeton University (`https://wordnet.princeton.edu/`).

- **ImageNET**: This is an image dataset organized according to the WORDNET hierarchy (only nouns at present). Each meaningful concept (synset) is described by multiple words or word phrases. Each synset is represented on average by 1,000 images. At present, it has 21,841 synsets and a total of 14,197,122 images. Since 2010, an annual **ImageNet Large Scale Visual Recognition Challenge (ILSVRC)** has been organized to classify images in one of the 1,000 object categories. The work is sponsored by Princeton University, Stanford University, A9, and Google (`http://www.image-net.org/`).

- **YouTube-8M**: This is a large-scale labelled video dataset consisting of millions of YouTube videos. It has about 7 million YouTube video URLs classified into 4,716 classes, organized into 24 top-level categories. It also provides preprocessing support and frame-level features. The dataset is maintained by Google Research (`https://research.google.com/youtube8m/`).

Reading the data: The data can be read in three ways in TensorFlow--feeding through `feed_dict`, reading from files, and using preloaded data. We will be using the components described in this recipe throughout the book for reading, and feeding the data. In the next steps, you will learn each one of them.

1. **Feeding:** In this case, data is provided while running each step, using the `feed_dict` argument in the `run()` or `eval()` function call. This is done with the help of placeholders and this method allows us to pass Numpy arrays of data. Consider the following part of code using TensorFlow:

   ```
   ...
   y = tf.placeholder(tf.float32)
   x = tf.placeholder(tf.float32).
   ...
   ```

```
with tf.Session as sess:
    X_Array = some Numpy Array
    Y_Array = other Numpy Array
    loss= ...
sess.run(loss,feed_dict = {x: X_Array, y: Y_Array}).
...
```

Here, x and y are the placeholders; using them, we pass on the array containing X values and the array containing Y values with the help of `feed_dict`.

2. **Reading from files**: This method is used when the dataset is very large to ensure that not all data occupies the memory at once (imagine the 60 GB YouTube-8m dataset). The process of reading from files can be done in the following steps:

   - A list of filenames is created using either string Tensor `["file0", "file1"]` or `[("file%d"i) for in in range(2)]` or using the `files = tf.train.match_filenames_once('*.JPG')` function.

   - **Filename queue**: A queue is created to keep the filenames until the reader needs them using the `tf.train.string_input_producer` function:

     ```
     filename_queue = tf.train.string_input_producer(files)
     # where files is the list of filenames created above
     ```

     This function also provides an option to shuffle and set a maximum number of epochs. The whole list of filenames is added to the queue for each epoch. If the shuffling option is selected (`shuffle=True`), then filenames are shuffled in each epoch.

   - **Reader** is defined and used to read from files from the filename queue. The reader is selected based on the input file format. The read method a key identifying the file and record (useful while debugging) and a scalar string value. For example, in the case of `.csv` file formats:

     ```
     reader = tf.TextLineReader()
     key, value = reader.read(filename_queue)
     ```

- **Decoder**: One or more decoder and conversion ops are then used to decode the `value` string into Tensors that make up the training example:

```
record_defaults = [[1], [1], [1]]
col1, col2, col3 = tf.decode_csv(value,
record_defaults=record_defaults)
```

3. **Preloaded data**: This is used when the dataset is small and can be loaded fully in the memory. For this, we can store data either in a constant or variable. While using a variable, we need to set the trainable flag to False so that the data does not change while training. As TensorFlow constants:

```
# Preloaded data as constant
training_data = ...
training_labels = ...
with tf.Session as sess:
    x_data = tf.Constant(training_data)
    y_data = tf.Constant(training_labels)
...

# Preloaded data as Variables
training_data = ...
training_labels = ...
with tf.Session as sess:
    data_x = tf.placeholder(dtype=training_data.dtype,
shape=training_data.shape)
    data_y = tf.placeholder(dtype=training_label.dtype,
shape=training_label.shape)
    x_data = tf.Variable(data_x, trainable=False, collections[])
    y_data = tf.Variable(data_y, trainable=False, collections[])
...
```

Conventionally, the data is divided into three parts--training data, validation data, and test data.

4. **Defining the model**: A computational graph is built describing the network structure. It involves specifying the hyperparameters, variables, and placeholders sequence in which information flows from one set of neurons to another and a loss/error function. You will learn more about the computational graphs in a later section of this chapter.

5. **Training/Learning**: The learning in DNNs is normally based on the gradient descent algorithm, (it will be dealt in detail in `Chapter 2`, *Regression*) where the aim is to find the training variables (weights/biases) such that the error or loss (as defined by the user in step 2) is minimized. This is achieved by initializing the variables and using `run()`:

```
with tf.Session as sess:
    ....
    sess.run(...)
    ...
```

6. **Evaluating the model**: Once the network is trained, we evaluate the network using `predict()` on validation data and test data. The evaluations give us an estimate of how well our model fits the dataset. We can thus avoid the common mistakes of overfitting or underfitting. Once we are satisfied with our model, we can deploy it in production.

There's more

In TensorFlow 1.3, a new feature called TensorFlow Estimators has been added. TensorFlow Estimators make the task of creating the neural network models even easier, it is a higher level API that encapsulates the process of training, evaluation, prediction and serving. It provides the option of either using pre-made Estimators or one can write their own custom Estimators. With pre-made Estimators, one no longer have to worry about building the computational or creating a session, it handles it all.

At present TensorFlow Estimator has six pre-made Estimators. Another advantage of using TensorFlow pre-made Estimators is that it also by itself creates summaries that can be visualised on TensorBoard. More details about Estimators are available at `https://www.tensorflow.org/programmers_guide/estimators`.

Different Python packages required for DNN-based problems

TensorFlow takes care of most of the neural network implementation. However, this is not sufficient; for preprocessing tasks, serialization, and even plotting, we need some more Python packages.

How to do it...

Here are listed some of the common Python packages used:

1. **Numpy:** This is the fundamental package for scientific computing with Python. It supports n-dimensional arrays and matrices. It also has a large collection of high-level mathematical functions. It is a necessary package required by TensorFlow and therefore, with `pip install tensorflow`, it is installed if not already present.

2. **Matplolib**: This is the Python 2D plotting library. You can use it to create plots, histograms, bar charts, error charts, scatterplots, and power spectra with just a few lines of code. It can be installed using `pip`:

```
pip install matplotlib
# or using Anaconda
conda install -c conda-forge matplotlib
```

3. **OS**: This is included in the basic Python installation. It provides an easy and portable way of using operating system-dependent functionality like reading, writing, and changing files and directories.

4. **Pandas**: This provides various data structures and data analysis tools. Using Pandas, you can read and write data between in-memory data structures and different formats. We can read from `.csv` and text files. It can be installed using either `pip install` or `conda install`.

5. **Seaborn**: This is a specialized statistical data visualization tool built on Matplotlib.

6. **H5fs**: H5fs is a filesystem for Linux (also other operating systems with FUSE implementation like macOS X) capable of operations on an **HDFS (Hierarchical Data Format Filesystem)**.

7. **PythonMagick**: It is the Python binding of the `ImageMagick` library. It is a library to display, convert, and edit raster image and vector image files. It supports more than 200 image file formats. It can be installed using source build available from `ImageMagick`. Certain `.whl` formats are also available for a convenient `pip install` (http://www.lfd.uci.edu/%7Egohlke/pythonlibs/#pythonmagick).

8. **TFlearn**: TFlearn is a modular and transparent deep learning library built on top of TensorFlow. It provides a higher-level API to TensorFlow in order to facilitate and speed up experimentation. It currently supports most of the recent deep learning models, such as Convolutions, LSTM, BatchNorm, BiRNN, PReLU, Residual networks, and Generative networks. It works only for TensorFlow 1.0 or higher. To install, use `pip install tflearn`.

9. **Keras**: Keras too is a high-level API for neural networks, which uses TensorFlow as its backend. It can run on top of Theano and CNTK as well. It is extremely user-friendly, adding layers to it is just a one-line job. It can be installed using `pip install keras`.

See also

Below you can find some weblinks for more information on installation of TensorFlow

- `https://www.tensorflow.org/install/`
- `https://www.tensorflow.org/install/install_sources`
- `http://llvm.org/`
- `https://bazel.build/`

2
Regression

This chapter shows how regression can be done using TensorFlow. In this chapter, we will cover the following topics:

- Choosing loss functions
- Optimizers in TensorFlow
- Reading from CSV files and preprocessing data
- House price estimation-simple linear regression
- House price estimation-multiple linear regression
- Logistic regression on the MNIST dataset

Introduction

Regression is one of the oldest and yet quite powerful tools for mathematical modelling, classification, and prediction. Regression finds application in varied fields ranging from engineering, physical science, biology, and the financial market to social sciences. It is the basic tool in the hand of a data scientist.

Regression is normally the first algorithm that people in machine learning work with. It allows us to make predictions from data by learning the relationship between the dependent and independent variables. For example, in the case of house price estimation, we determine the relationship between the area of the house (**independent variable**) and its price (**dependent variable**); this relationship can be then used to predict the price of any house given its area. We can have multiple independent variables impacting the dependent variable. Thus, there are two important components of regression: the **relationship** between independent and dependent variables, and the **strength of impact** of the different independent variable on the dependent variable.

There are various types of regression methods available:

- **Linear regression**: This is one of the most widely used modelling technique. Existing for more than 200 years, it has been explored from almost all possible angles. Linear regression assumes a linear relationship between the input variables (X) and the single output variable (Y). It involves finding a linear equation for predicted value Y of the form:

$$Y_{hat} = W^T X + b$$

  Here, $X = (x_1, x_2, ..., x_n)$ are the n input variables and $W = (w_1, w_2, ...w_n)$ are the linear coefficients, with b as the bias term. The goal is to find the best estimates for the coefficients W, such that the error in the predicted Y is minimized. The linear coefficients Ws are estimated using the method of least squares, that is, minimizing the sum of squared differences between predicted values (Y_{hat}) and observed values (Y). Thus, we try to minimize the *loss* function:

$$loss = \sum_{i=1}^{p} Y_i - Y_{hat_i}$$

  Here, the sum is over all the training samples. Depending on the number and type of input variable X, there are different types of linear regression: simple linear regression (one input variable, one output variable), multiple linear regression (many independent input variables, one output variable), or multivariate linear regression (many independent input variables and multiple output variables). For more on linear regression, you can refer to `https://en.wikipedia.org/wiki/Linear_regression`.

- **Logistic regression**: This is used to determine the probability of an event. Conventionally, the event is represented as a categorical dependent variable. The probability of the event is expressed using the `logit` function (`sigmoid` function):

$$P(Y_{hat} = 1 | X = x) = \frac{1}{1 + e^{-(b + W^T X)}}$$

The goal now is to estimate weights $W = (w1, w2, ...wn)$ and bias term b. In logistic regression, the coefficients are estimated using either maximum likelihood estimator or stochastic gradient descent. The loss is conventionally defined as a cross-entropy term given as follows:

$$loss = \sum_{i=1}^{p} Y_i \log(Y_{hat_i}) + (1 - Y_i)\log(1 - Y_{hat_i})$$

Logistic regression is used in classification problems, for example, given medical data, we can use logistic regression to classify whether a person has cancer or not. In case the output categorical variable has two or more levels, we can use multinomial logistic regression. Another common technique used for two or more output variables is one versus all. For multiclass logistic regression, the cross-entropy *loss* function is modified as follows:

$$loss = \sum_{i=1}^{p} \sum_{j=1}^{K} Y_{ij} \log\left(Y_{hat_{ij}}\right)$$

Here, K is the total number of classes. More about logistic regression can be read at https://en.wikipedia.org/wiki/Logistic_regression.

These are the two popularly used regression techniques.

- **Regularization**: When there are a large number of input features, then regularization is needed to ensure that the predicted model is not complex. Regularization can help in preventing overfitting of data. It can also be used to obtain a convex *loss* function. There are two types of regularization, L1 and L2 regularization, which are described in the following points:

  - **L1 regularization** can also work when the data is highly collinear. In L1 regularization, an additional penalty term dependent on the absolute sum of all the coefficients is added to the *loss* function. The regularization penalty term for L1 regularization is as follows:

$$L1\_penalty = \lambda \sum_{i=1}^{n} |W_i|$$

- **L2 Regularization** provides sparse solutions. It is very useful when the number of input features is extremely large. In this case, the penalty term is the sum of the square of all the coefficients:

$$L2\_penalty = \lambda \sum_{i=1}^{n} W_i^2$$

Above the Greek letter, lambda (λ) is the regularization parameter.

Choosing loss functions

As discussed earlier, in regression we define the `loss` function or objective function and the aim is to find the coefficients such that the loss is minimized. In this recipe, you will learn how to define `loss` functions in TensorFlow and choose a proper `loss` function depending on the problem at hand.

Getting ready

Declaring a `loss` function requires defining the coefficients as variables and the dataset as placeholders. One can have a constant learning rate or changing learning rate and regularization constant. In the following code, let m be the number of samples, n the number of features, and P the number of classes. We should define these global parameters before the code:

```
m = 1000
n = 15
P = 2
```

How to do it...

Let us now see how to proceed with the recipe:

1. In the case of standard linear regression, we have only one input variable and one output variable:

    ```
    # Placeholder for the Training Data
    X = tf.placeholder(tf.float32, name='X')
    Y = tf.placeholder(tf.float32, name='Y')

    # Variables for coefficients initialized to 0
    w0 = tf.Variable(0.0)
    w1 = tf.Variable(0.0)

    # The Linear Regression Model
    Y_hat = X*w1 + w0

    # Loss function
    loss = tf.square(Y - Y_hat, name='loss')
    ```

2. In the case of multiple linear regression, the input variables are more than one, while the output variable remains one. Now you can define X placeholder of shape [m, n], where m is the number of samples and n is the number of features, then the code is as follows:

    ```
    # Placeholder for the Training Data
    X = tf.placeholder(tf.float32, name='X', shape=[m,n])
    Y = tf.placeholder(tf.float32, name='Y')

    # Variables for coefficients initialized to 0
    w0 = tf.Variable(0.0)
    w1 = tf.Variable(tf.random_normal([n,1]))

    # The Linear Regression Model
    Y_hat = tf.matmul(X, w1) + w0

    # Multiple linear regression loss function
    loss = tf.reduce_mean(tf.square(Y - Y_hat, name='loss')
    ```

3. In the case of logistic regression, the `loss` function is defined by cross-entropy. Now output `Y` will have dimensions equal to the number of classes in the training dataset. With `P` number of classes, we will have the following:

```
# Placeholder for the Training Data
X = tf.placeholder(tf.float32, name='X', shape=[m,n])
Y = tf.placeholder(tf.float32, name='Y', shape=[m,P])

# Variables for coefficients initialized to 0
w0 = tf.Variable(tf.zeros([1,P]), name='bias')
w1 = tf.Variable(tf.random_normal([n,1]), name='weights')

# The Linear Regression Model
Y_hat = tf.matmul(X, w1) + w0

# Loss function
entropy = tf.nn.softmax_cross_entropy_with_logits(Y_hat,Y)
loss = tf.reduce_mean(entropy)
```

4. If we want to add L1 regularization to loss, then the code is as follows:

```
lamda = tf.constant(0.8)   # regularization parameter
regularization_param = lamda*tf.reduce_sum(tf.abs(W1))

# New loss
loss += regularization_param
```

5. For L2 regularization, we can use the following:

```
lamda = tf.constant(0.8)   # regularization parameter
regularization_param = lamda*tf.nn.l2_loss(W1)

# New loss
loss += regularization_param
```

How it works...

You learned how to implement different types of `loss` functions. Depending on the regression task at hand, you can choose the corresponding `loss` function or design your own. It is also possible to combine L1 and L2 regularization in the loss term.

There's more...

The `loss` function should be convex in shape to ensure convergence. A smooth, differentiable, convex `loss` function provides better convergence. As the learning proceeds, the value of the `loss` function should decrease and eventually become stable.

Optimizers in TensorFlow

From your high school math, you must know that a function's first derivative is zero at its maxima and minima. The gradient descent algorithm is based on the same principle--the coefficients (weights and biases) are adjusted such that the gradient of the `loss` function decreases. In regression, we use gradient descent to optimize the `loss` function and obtain coefficients. In this recipe, you will learn how to use the gradient descent optimizer of TensorFlow and some of its variants.

Getting ready

The update of coefficients (*W* and *b*) is done proportionally to the negative of the gradient of the `loss` function. There are three variations of gradient descent depending on the size of the training sample:

- **Vanilla gradient descent**: In vanilla gradient descent (also sometimes called **batch gradient descent**), the gradient of the `loss` function is calculated for the entire training set at each epoch. This process can be slow and intractable for very large datasets. It is guaranteed to converge to the global minimum for convex `loss` function, but for non-convex `loss` function, it might settle at the local minimum.
- **Stochastic gradient descent**: In stochastic gradient descent, one training sample is presented at a time, the weights and biases are updated such that the gradient of `loss` function decreases, and then we move to the next training sample. The whole process is repeated for a number of epochs. As it performs one update at a time, it is faster than vanilla, but at the same time, due to frequent updates, there can be a high variance in the `loss` function.
- **Mini-batch gradient descent**: This combines the best qualities of both the previous ones; here, the parameters are updated for a batch of the training sample.

How to do it...

We proceed with the recipe as follows:

1. The first thing we decide is the optimizer that we want. TensorFlow provides you with a wide variety of optimizers. We start with the most popular and simple one, the gradient descent optimizer:

   ```
   tf.train.GradientDescentOptimizer(learning_rate)
   ```

2. The `learning_rate` argument to `GradientDescentOptimizer` can be a constant or tensor. Its value can lie between 0 and 1.

3. The optimizer must be told about the function to be optimized. This is done using its method, minimize. This method computes the gradients and applies the gradients to learning coefficients. The function as defined in TensorFlow docs is the following:

   ```
   minimize(
        loss,
        global_step=None,
        var_list=None,
        gate_gradients=GATE_OP,
        aggregation_method=None,
        colocate_gradients_with_ops=False,
        name=None,
        grad_loss=None
    )
   ```

4. Combining it all, we define the computational graph:

   ```
   ...
   optimizer = tf.train.GradientDescentOptimizer(learning_rate=0.01)
   train_step = optimizer.minimize(loss)
   ...

   #Execution Graph
   with tf.Session() as sess:
        ...
        sess.run(train_step, feed_dict = {X:X_data, Y:Y_data})
        ...
   ```

5. The X and Y data fed to `feed_dict` can be single X and Y points (stochastic gradient), the entire training set (vanilla), or batch.

6. Another variation in gradient descent is adding the momentum term (we will find out more about this in Chapter 3, *Neural Networks - Perceptrons*). For this, we use the optimizer `tf.train.MomentumOptimizer()`. It takes both `learning_rate` and `momentum` as init arguments:

```
optimizer = tf.train.MomentumOtimizer(learning_rate=0.01,
momentum=0.5).minimize(loss)
```

7. We can have an adaptive, monotonically decreasing learning rate if we use `tf.train.AdadeltaOptimizer()`, which uses two init arguments, `learning_rate` and decay factor `rho`:

```
optimizer = tf.train.AdadeltaOptimizer(learning_rate=0.8,
rho=0.95).minimize(loss)
```

8. TensorFlow also supports Hinton's RMSprop, which works similarly to Adadelta--`tf.train.RMSpropOptimizer()`:

```
optimizer = tf.train.RMSpropOptimizer(learning_rate=0.01,
decay=0.8, momentum=0.1).minimize(loss)
```

 There are some fine differences between Adadelta and RMSprop. To find out more about them, you can refer to http://www.cs.toronto.edu/~tijmen/csc321/slides/lecture_slides_lec6.pdf and https://arxiv.org/pdf/1212.5701.pdf.

9. Another popular optimizer supported by TensorFlow is the Adam optimizer. The method computes individual adaptive learning rates for the different coefficients using the estimates of the first and second moments of gradients:

```
optimizer = tf.train.AdamOptimizer().minimize(loss)
```

10. Besides these, TensorFlow also provides the following optimizers:

```
tf.train.AdagradOptimizer   #Adagrad Optimizer
tf.train.AdagradDAOptimizer #Adagrad Dual Averaging optimizer
tf.train.FtrlOptimizer #Follow the regularized leader optimizer
tf.train.ProximalGradientDescentOptimizer #Proximal GD optimizer
tf.train.ProximalAdagradOptimizer # Proximal Adagrad optimizer
```

There's more...

It is often recommended that you start with a high value of learning rate and reduce it as the learning progresses. This helps in fine-tuning the training. We can use the TensorFlow `tf.train.exponential_decay` method to achieve this. According to the TensorFlow docs:

> *When training a model, it is often recommended to lower the learning rate as the training progresses. This function applies an exponential decay function to a provided initial learning rate. It requires a global_step value to compute the decayed learning rate. You can just pass a TensorFlow variable that you increment at each training step. The function returns the decayed learning rate.*
> *Args:*
> *learning_rate: A scalar float32 or float64 Tensor or a Python number. The initial learning rate.*
> *global_step: A scalar int32 or int64 Tensor or a Python number. Global step to use for the decay computation. Must not be negative.*
> *decay_steps: A scalar int32 or int64 Tensor or a Python number. Must be positive. See the decay computation described earlier.*
> *decay_rate: A scalar float32 or float64 Tensor or a Python number. The decay rate.*
> *staircase: Boolean. If True decay the learning rate at discrete intervals*
> *name: String. Optional name of the operation. Defaults to 'ExponentialDecay'.*
> *Returns:*
> *A scalar Tensor of the same type as learning_rate. The decayed learning rate.*

To implement an exponentially decaying learning rate, consider the following code example:

```
global_step = tf.Variable(0, trainable = false)
initial_learning_rate = 0.2
learning_rate = tf.train.exponential_decay(initial_learning_rate,
global_step, decay_steps=100000, decay_rate=0.95, staircase=True)
# Pass this learning rate to optimizer as before.
```

See also

Below are some good links for different optimizers:

- `https://arxiv.org/pdf/1609.04747.pdf`: The paper provides a good overview of different optimization algorithms.

- `https://www.tensorflow.org/api_guides/python/train#Optimizers`: This is the TensorFlow.org link, which details how to use different optimizers included in TensorFlow.
- `https://arxiv.org/pdf/1412.6980.pdf`: The paper on Adam optimizer.

Reading from CSV files and preprocessing data

Most of you will already be familiar with Pandas and its usefulness in handling large dataset files. TensorFlow also offers methods to read from the files. In the first chapter, we went through the recipe for reading from files in TensorFlow; in this recipe, we will focus on how to read from CSV files and preprocess the data before training.

Getting ready

We will consider the Boston housing price dataset (`http://lib.stat.cmu.edu/datasets/boston`) collected by Harrison and Rubinfield in 1978. The dataset contains 506 sample cases. Each house is assigned 14 attributes:

- **CRIM**: per capita crime rate by town
- **ZN**: Proportion of residential land zoned for lots over 25,000 sq.ft
- **INDUS**: Proportion of non-retail business acres per town
- **CHAS**: Charles River dummy variable (1 if tract bounds river; 0 otherwise)
- **NOX**: Nitric oxide concentration (parts per 10 million)
- **RM**: Average number of rooms per dwelling
- **AGE**: Proportion of owner-occupied units built prior to 1940
- **DIS**: Weighted distances to five Boston employment centres
- **RAD**: Index of accessibility to radial highways
- **TAX**: Full-value property-tax rate per $10,000
- **PTRATIO**: Pupil-teacher ratio by town
- **B**: $1000(Bk - 0.63)^2$ where Bk is the proportion of blacks by town
- **LSTAT**: percent lower status of the population
- **MEDV**: Median value of owner-occupied homes in $1,000's

How to do it...

We proceed with the recipe as follows:

1. Import the modules required and declare global variables:

```
import tensorflow as tf

# Global parameters
DATA_FILE = 'boston_housing.csv'
BATCH_SIZE = 10
NUM_FEATURES = 14
```

2. Next, we define a function that will take as argument the filename and return tensors in batches of size equal to BATCH_SIZE:

```
def data_generator(filename):
    """
    Generates Tensors in batches of size Batch_SIZE.
    Args: String Tensor
    Filename from which data is to be read
    Returns: Tensors
    feature_batch and label_batch
    """
```

3. Define the filename that is f_queue and reader:

```
f_queue = tf.train.string_input_producer(filename)
reader = tf.TextLineReader(skip_header_lines=1) # Skips the first
line
 _, value = reader.read(f_queue)
```

4. We specify the data to use in case data is missing. Decode the .csv and select the features we need. For the example, we choose RM, PTRATIO, and LSTAT:

```
record_defaults = [ [0.0] for _ in range(NUM_FEATURES)]
data = tf.decode_csv(value, record_defaults=record_defaults)
features = tf.stack(tf.gather_nd(data,[[5],[10],[12]]))
label = data[-1]
```

5. Define parameters to generate batch and use `tf.train.shuffle_batch()` for randomly shuffling the tensors. The function returns the tensors-- `feature_batch` and `label_batch`:

```
# minimum number elements in the queue after a
dequeuemin_after_dequeue = 10 * BATCH_SIZE

# the maximum number of elements in the queue
capacity = 20 * BATCH_SIZE

# shuffle the data to generate BATCH_SIZE sample pairs
feature_batch, label_batch = tf.train.shuffle_batch([features,
label], batch_size=BATCH_SIZE,
                                        capacity=capacity,
min_after_dequeue=min_after_dequeue)

return feature_batch, label_batch
```

6. We define another function to generate the batches in the session:

```
def generate_data(feature_batch, label_batch):
    with tf.Session() as sess:
        # intialize the queue threads
        coord = tf.train.Coordinator()
        threads = tf.train.start_queue_runners(coord=coord)
        for _ in range(5): # Generate 5 batches
            features, labels = sess.run([feature_batch,
label_batch])
            print (features, "HI")
        coord.request_stop()
        coord.join(threads)
```

7. Now, we can use these two functions to get the data in batches. Here, we are just printing the data; when learning, we will perform the optimization step at this point:

```
if __name__ =='__main__':
    feature_batch, label_batch = data_generator([DATA_FILE])
    generate_data(feature_batch, label_batch)
```

There's more...

We can use the TensorFlow control ops and tensor manipulations that we covered in the first chapter to preprocess the data. For example, in the case of Boston house price, there are about 16 data rows where the MEDV is 50.0. In most probability, these data points contain missing or censored values and it would be advisable not to consider them for the training. We can remove them from the training dataset with the following code:

```
condition = tf.equal(data[13], tf.constant(50.0))
data = tf.where(condition, tf.zeros(NUM_FEATURES), data[:])
```

Here, we first define a tensor boolean condition, which will be true if MEDV is equal to 50.0. Then we use TensorFlow tf.where() Op to assign all zeros if the condition is true.

House price estimation-simple linear regression

In this recipe, we will perform simple linear regression based on the number of rooms (RM) on the Boston house price dataset.

Getting ready

Our goal is to predict the house price given in the last column (MEDV). In this recipe, we load the dataset from the TensorFlow Contrib dataset directly. We optimize the coefficients for an individual training sample using the stochastic gradient descent optimizer.

How to do it...

We proceed with the recipe as follows:

1. The first step is to import all the packages that we will need:

```
import tensorflow as tf
import numpy as np
import matplotlib.pyplot as plt
```

2. In neural networks, all the inputs are added linearly to generate activity; for effective training, the inputs should be normalized, so we define a function to normalize the input data:

```python
def normalize(X):
    """ Normalizes the array X"""
    mean = np.mean(X)
    std = np.std(X)
    X = (X - mean)/std
    return X
```

3. Now we load the Boston house price dataset using TensorFlow `contrib` datasets and separate it into `X_train` and `Y_train`. We can choose to normalize the data here:

```python
# Data
boston = tf.contrib.learn.datasets.load_dataset('boston')
X_train, Y_train = boston.data[:,5], boston.target
#X_train = normalize(X_train)  # This step is optional here
n_samples = len(X_train)
```

4. We declare the TensorFlow placeholders for the training data:

```python
# Placeholder for the Training Data
X = tf.placeholder(tf.float32, name='X')
Y = tf.placeholder(tf.float32, name='Y')
```

5. We create TensorFlow variables for weight and bias with initial value zero:

```python
# Variables for coefficients initialized to 0
b = tf.Variable(0.0)
w = tf.Variable(0.0)
```

6. We define the linear regression model to be used for prediction:

```python
# The Linear Regression Model
Y_hat = X * w + b
```

7. Define the `loss` function:

```python
# Loss function
loss = tf.square(Y - Y_hat, name='loss')
```

8. We choose the gradient descent optimizer:

```
# Gradient Descent with learning rate of 0.01 to minimize loss
optimizer =
tf.train.GradientDescentOptimizer(learning_rate=0.01).minimize(loss
)
```

9. Declare the initializing operator:

```
# Initializing Variables
init_op = tf.global_variables_initializer()
total = []
```

10. Now, we start the computation graph. We run the training for 100 epochs:

```
# Computation Graph
with tf.Session() as sess:
    # Initialize variables
    sess.run(init_op)
    writer = tf.summary.FileWriter('graphs', sess.graph)
    # train the model for 100 epochs
    for i in range(100):
        total_loss = 0
        for x,y in zip(X_train,Y_train):
            _, l = sess.run ([optimizer, loss],
feed_dict={X:x, Y:y})
            total_loss += l
        total.append(total_loss / n_samples)
        print('Epoch {0}: Loss {1}'.format(i,
total_loss/n_samples))
    writer.close()
    b_value, w_value = sess.run([b,w])
```

11. View the result:

```
Y_pred = X_train * w_value + b_value
print('Done')
# Plot the result
plt.plot(X_train, Y_train, 'bo', label='Real Data')
plt.plot(X_train,Y_pred,  'r', label='Predicted Data')
plt.legend()
plt.show()
plt.plot(total)
plt.show()
```

How it works...

From the plot, we can see that our simple linear regressor tries to fit a linear line to the given dataset:

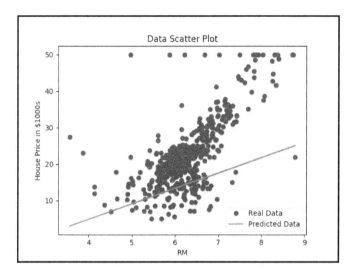

In the following graph, we can see that as our model learned the data, the `loss` function decreased, as was expected:

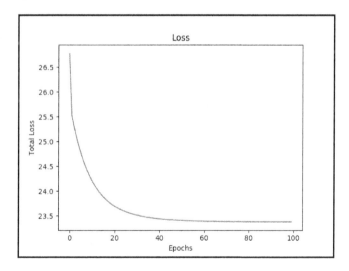

The following is the TensorBoard graph of our simple linear regressor:

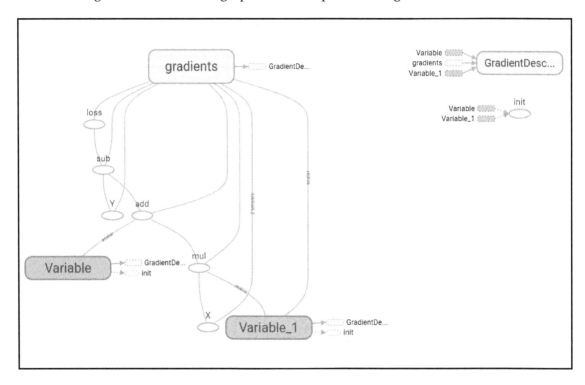

The graph has two name scope nodes, **Variable** and **Variable_1**, they are the high-level nodes representing bias and weights respectively. The node named gradient is also a high-level node; expanding the node, we can see that it takes seven inputs and computes the **gradients** that are then used by `GradientDescentOptimizer` to compute and apply updates to weights and bias:

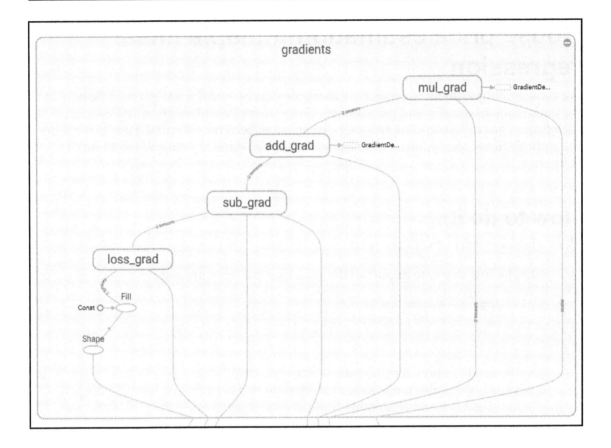

There's more...

Well, we performed simple linear regression, but how do we find out the performance of our model? There are various ways to do this; statistically, we can compute R^2 or divide our data into train and cross-validation sets and check the accuracy (the loss term) for the validation set.

House price estimation-multiple linear regression

We can do multiple linear regression on the same data by making a slight modification in the declaration of weights and placeholders. In the case of multiple linear regression, as each feature has different value ranges, normalization becomes essential. Here is the code for multiple linear regression on the Boston house price dataset, using all the 13 input features.

How to do it...

Here is how we proceed with the recipe:

1. The first step is to import all the packages that we will need:

```
import tensorflow as tf
import numpy as np
import matplotlib.pyplot as plt
```

2. We need to normalize the feature data since the data ranges of all the features are varied. We define a normalize function for it. Also, here we combine the bias to weights by adding another input always fixed to one value; to do this we define the function append_bias_reshape(). This technique is sometimes used to simplify programming:

```
def normalize(X)
    """ Normalizes the array X """
    mean = np.mean(X)
    std = np.std(X)
    X = (X - mean)/std
    return X

def append_bias_reshape(features,labels):
    m = features.shape[0]
    n = features.shape[1]
    x = np.reshape(np.c_[np.ones(m),features],[m,n + 1])
    y = np.reshape(labels,[m,1])
    return x, y
```

3. Now we load the Boston house price dataset using TensorFlow contrib datasets and separate it into X_train and Y_train. Observe that this time, X_train contains all features. We can choose to normalize the data here, we also use append the bias and reshape the data for the network:

```
# Data
boston = tf.contrib.learn.datasets.load_dataset('boston')
X_train, Y_train = boston.data, boston.target
X_train = normalize(X_train)
X_train, Y_train = append_bias_reshape(X_train, Y_train)
m = len(X_train)   #Number of training examples
n = 13 + 1   # Number of features + bias
```

4. Declare the TensorFlow placeholders for the training data. Observe the change in the shape of the X placeholder.

```
# Placeholder for the Training Data
X = tf.placeholder(tf.float32, name='X', shape=[m,n])
Y = tf.placeholder(tf.float32, name='Y')
```

5. We create TensorFlow variables for weight and bias. This time, weights are initialized with random numbers:

```
# Variables for coefficients
w = tf.Variable(tf.random_normal([n,1]))
```

6. Define the linear regression model to be used for prediction. Now we need matrix multiplication to do the task:

```
# The Linear Regression Model
Y_hat = tf.matmul(X, w)
```

7. For better differentiation, we define the loss function:

```
# Loss function
loss = tf.reduce_mean(tf.square(Y - Y_hat, name='loss'))
```

8. Choose the right optimizer:

```
# Gradient Descent with learning rate of 0.01 to minimize loss
optimizer =
tf.train.GradientDescentOptimizer(learning_rate=0.01).minimize(loss
)
```

9. Define the initialization operator:

```
# Initializing Variables
init_op = tf.global_variables_initializer()
total = []
```

10. Start the computational graph:

```
with tf.Session() as sess:
    # Initialize variables
    sess.run(init_op)
    writer = tf.summary.FileWriter('graphs', sess.graph)
    # train the model for 100 epcohs
    for i in range(100):
        _, l = sess.run([optimizer, loss], feed_dict={X: X_train, Y:
Y_train})
        total.append(l)
        print('Epoch {0}: Loss {1}'.format(i, l))
    writer.close()
    w_value, b_value = sess.run([w, b])
```

11. Plot the loss function:

```
plt.plot(total)
plt.show()
```

Here too, we find that loss decreases as the training progresses:

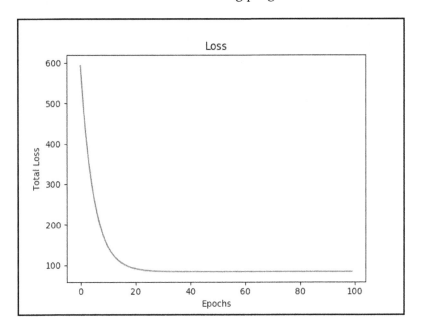

How it works...

In this recipe, we used all the 13 features to train the model. The important differences between simple and multiple linear regression are in weights and the number of coefficients is always equal to the number of input features. The following is the TensorBoard graph for the multiple linear regression model that we built:

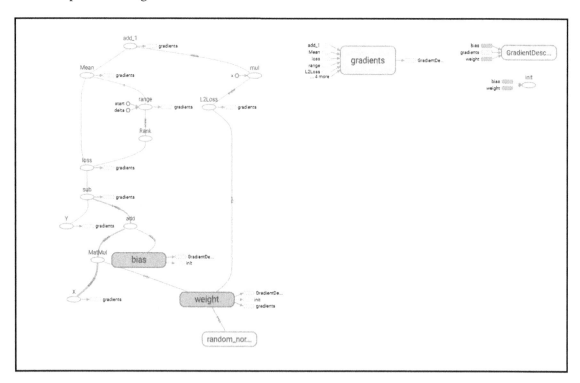

There's more...

We can predict the house price now using the coefficients learned from the model:

```
N= 500
X_new = X_train [N,:]
Y_pred =  (np.matmul(X_new, w_value) + b_value).round(1)
print('Predicted value: ${0}  Actual value: / ${1}'.format(Y_pred[0]*1000,
Y_train[N]*1000) , '\nDone')
```

Logistic regression on the MNIST dataset

This recipe is based on the logistic regressor for MNIST provided at `https://www.tensorflow.org/get_started/mnist/beginners`, but we will add some TensorBoard summaries to understand it better. Most of you must already be familiar with the MNIST dataset--it is like the ABC of machine learning. It contains images of handwritten digits and a label for each image, saying which digit it is.

For logistic regression, we use one-hot encoding for the output Y. Thus, we have 10 bits representing the output; each bit can have a value either 0 or 1, and being one-hot means that for each image in label Y, only one bit out of the 10 will have value 1, the rest will be zeros. Here, you can see the image of the handwritten numeral 8, along with its hot encoded value [0 0 0 0 0 0 0 0 1 0]:

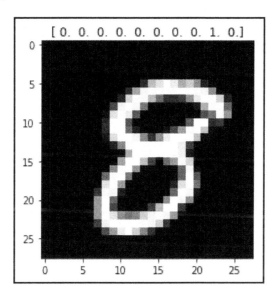

How to do it...

Here is how we proceed with the recipe:

1. The first step is, as always, importing the modules needed:

```
import tensorflow as tf
import matplotlib.pyplot as plt,  matplotlib.image as mpimg
```

2. We take the input data of MNIST from the TensorFlow examples given in the module `input_data`. The `one_hot` flag is set to `True` to enable `one_hot` encoding of labels. This results in generating two tensors, `mnist.train.images` of shape [55000,784] and `mnist.train.labels` of shape [55000,10]. Each entry of `mnist.train.images` is a pixel intensity with the value ranging between 0 and 1:

```
from tensorflow.examples.tutorials.mnist import input_data
mnist = input_data.read_data_sets("MNIST_data/", one_hot=True)
```

3. Create placeholders for the training dataset inputs x and label y to the TensorFlow graph:

```
x = tf.placeholder(tf.float32, [None, 784], name='X')
y = tf.placeholder(tf.float32, [None, 10],name='Y')
```

4. Create the learning variables, weights, and bias:

```
W = tf.Variable(tf.zeros([784, 10]), name='W')
b = tf.Variable(tf.zeros([10]), name='b')
```

5. Create the logistic regression model. The TensorFlow OP is given the `name_scope("wx_b")`:

```
with tf.name_scope("wx_b") as scope:
    y_hat = tf.nn.softmax(tf.matmul(x,W) + b)
```

6. Add summary OPs to collect data while training. We use the histogram summary so that we can see how weights and bias change relative to each other's value with time. We will be able to see this in the TensorBoard Histogram tab:

```
w_h = tf.summary.histogram("weights", W)
b_h = tf.summary.histogram("biases", b)
```

7. Define the `cross-entropy` and `loss` function, and also add name scope and summary for better visualization. Here, we use the scalar summary to obtain the variation in the `loss` function over time. The scalar summary is visible under the Events tab:

```
with tf.name_scope('cross-entropy') as scope:
    loss =
tf.reduce_mean(tf.nn.softmax_cross_entropy_with_logits(labels=y,
logits=y_hat)
    tf.summary.scalar('cross-entropy', loss)
```

8. Employ the TensorFlow `GradientDescentOptimizer` with learning rate `0.01`. Again, for better visualization, we define a `name_scope`:

```
with tf.name_scope('Train') as scope:
    optimizer =
tf.train.GradientDescentOptimizer(0.01).minimize(loss)
```

9. Declare the initializing op for the variables:

```
# Initializing the variables
init = tf.global_variables_initializer()
```

10. We combine all the summary operations:

```
merged_summary_op = tf.summary.merge_all()
```

11. Now, we define the session and store the summaries in a defined folder:

```
with tf.Session() as sess:
    sess.run(init)  # initialize all variables
    summary_writer = tf.summary.FileWriter('graphs', sess.graph)   #
Create an event file
    # Training
    for epoch in range(max_epochs):
        loss_avg = 0
        num_of_batch = int(mnist.train.num_examples/batch_size)
        for i in range(num_of_batch):
            batch_xs, batch_ys = mnist.train.next_batch(100)   # get
the next batch of data
            _, l, summary_str = sess.run([optimizer,loss,
merged_summary_op], feed_dict={x: batch_xs, y: batch_ys})   # Run
the optimizer
            loss_avg += l
```

```
            summary_writer.add_summary(summary_str,
        epoch*num_of_batch + i)   # Add all summaries per batch
              loss_avg = loss_avg/num_of_batch
              print('Epoch {0}: Loss {1}'.format(epoch, loss_avg))
          print('Done')
          print(sess.run(accuracy, feed_dict={x: mnist.test.images,y:
        mnist.test.labels}))
```

12. We get an accuracy of 86.5 percent after 30 epochs, 89.36 percent after 50 epochs, and, after 100 epochs, the accuracy increases to 90.91 percent.

How it works...

We launch the TensorBoard using the tensor `tensorboard --logdir=garphs`. In the browser, navigate to the web address `localhost:6006`, to view the TensorBoard. The graph of the preceding model is as follows:

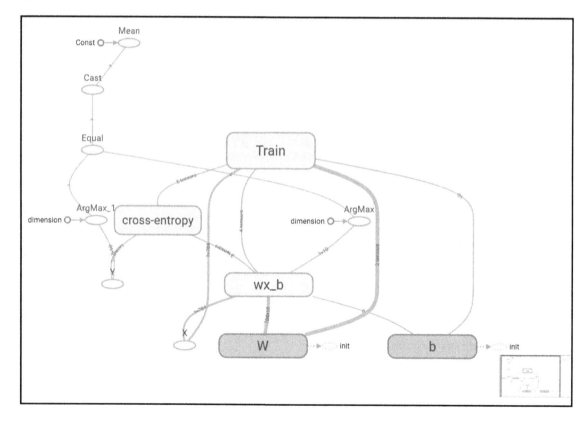

Under the Histogram tab, we can see the histograms for **weights** and **biases**:

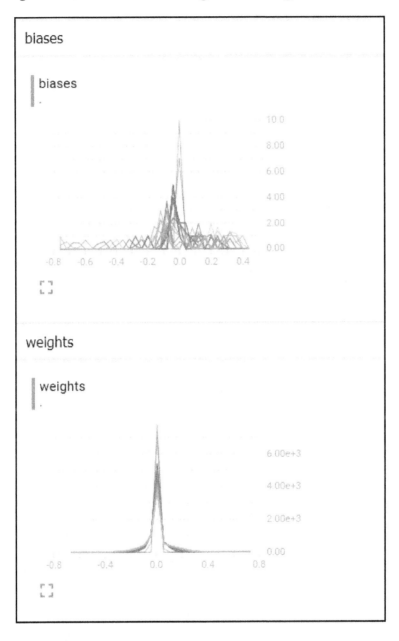

The distribution of **weights** and **biases** is as follows:

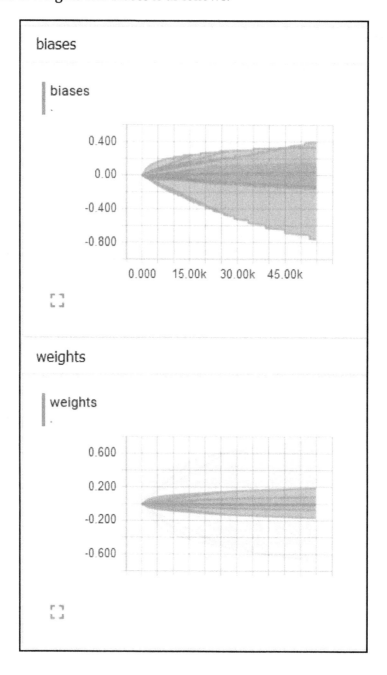

We can see that, with each time step, bias and weight both changed. The bias in our case had a greater spread, which we can see from distributions in TensorBoard.

Under the Events tab, we can see the scalar summary, in this case, cross entropy. The following graph shows that cross entropy loss decreases with time:

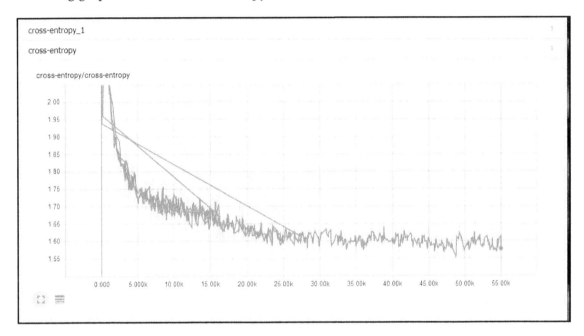

See also

These are some of the good resources if you are interested in finding out more:

- About TensorBoard and visualizing: `https://www.tensorflow.org/get_started/summaries_and_tensorboard`
- This is a good course on statistics and probability: `https://www.khanacademy.org/math/statistics-probability/describing-relationships-quantitative-data`
- More details about regression: `https://onlinecourses.science.psu.edu/stat501/node/250`

3
Neural Networks - Perceptron

Since the last decade, neural networks have been at the forefront of machine learning research and applications. **Deep neural networks** (**DNNs**), transfer learning, and availability of computationally efficient GPUs have helped achieve significant progress in the field of image recognition, speech recognition, and even text generation. In this chapter, we will concentrate on the basic neural network perceptron, a fully connected layered architecture of artificial neurons. The chapter will include the following recipes:

- Activation functions
- Single layer perceptron
- Calculating Gradients of Backpropagation algorithm
- MNIST classifier using MLP
- Function approximation using MLP--predicting Boston house prices
- Tuning hyperparameters
- Higher level APIs-Keras

Introduction

Neural networks, also conventionally known as **connectionist models**, are inspired by the human brain. Like the human brain, neural networks are a collection of a large number of artificial neurons connected to each other via synaptic strengths called **weights**. Just as we learn through examples provided to us by our elders, artificial neural networks learn by examples presented to them as training datasets. With a sufficient number of training datasets, artificial neural networks can generalize the information and can then be employed for unseen data as well. Awesome, they sound like magic!

Neural networks are not new; the first neural network model, McCulloch Pitts (MCP) (`http://vordenker.de/ggphilosophy/mcculloch_a-logical-calculus.pdf`) Model, was proposed as early as 1943. (Yes, even before the first computer was built!) The model could perform logical operations like AND/OR/NOT. The MCP model had fixed weights and biases; there was no learning possible. This problem was resolved a few years later by Frank Rosenblatt in 1958 (`https://blogs.umass.edu/brain-wars/files/2016/03/rosenblatt-1957.pdf`). He proposed the first learning neural network called **Perceptron**.

From that time, it was known that adding multiple layers of neurons and building a deep and dense network will help neural networks solve complex tasks. Just as a mother is proud of her child's achievements, scientists and engineers made tall claims about what they can achieve using **Neural Networks (NN)** (`https://www.youtube.com/watch?v=jPHUlQiwD9Y`). The claims were not false, but it was simply not possible to accomplish them at that time because of the hardware computation limitation and complex network structure. This resulted in what is known as the **AI Winters** in the 1970s and 1980s; during these chills, the progress in this field slowed down due to very little or almost no funding to AI-based projects.

With the advent of DNNs and GPUs, the situation changed; today we have networks that can perform better with less tuning parameters, techniques like dropout and transfer learning the further reduce the training time, and lastly, the hardware companies that are coming up with specialized hardware chips to perform fast NN-based computations.

The artificial neuron is at the heart of all neural networks. It consists of two major components--an adder that (weighted) sums all the inputs to this neuron, and a processing unit that takes the weighted sum and generates an output based on a predefined function, called **activation function**. Each artificial neuron has its own set of weights and thresholds (biases); it learns these weights and thresholds through different learning algorithms:

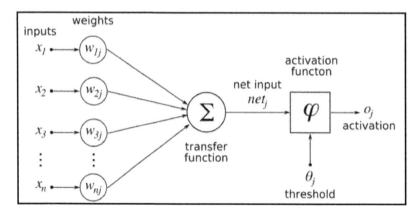

Source: https://commons.wikimedia.org/wiki/File:Rosenblattperceptron.png

When only one layer of such neurons is present, it is called Perceptron. The input layer is called the **zeroth layer** as it simply buffers the input. The only layer of neurons present form the output layer. Each neuron of the output layer has its own weights and thresholds. When many such layers are present, the network is termed **multi-layered perceptron (MLP)**. An MLP has one or more hidden layers. These hidden layers have a different number of hidden neurons. The neurons of each hidden layer have the same activation function:

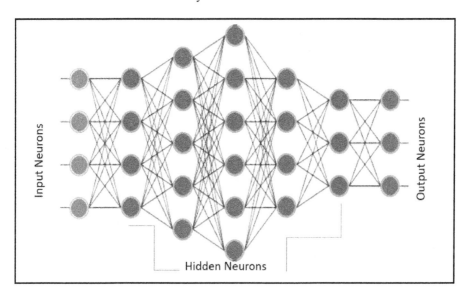

The preceding figure shows an MLP with four inputs, five hidden layers, each with 4, 5, 6, 4, and 3 neurons respectively, and three neurons in the output layer. In MLP, all neurons of the lower layer are connected to all the neurons of the layer just above it. Therefore, MLPs are also called **fully connected layers**. The flow of information in MLPs is always from input to output; there are no feedback or jumps present, therefore these networks are also known as **feedforward networks**.

Perceptrons are trained using **gradient descent algorithms**. In Chapter 2, *Regression*, you learned about gradient descent; here we look at it a little deeper. Perceptrons learn through supervised learning algorithms, that is, the network is provided by the desired output for all the inputs present in the training dataset. At the output, we define an error function or objective function *J(W)*, such that when the network has completely learned all the training data, the objective function will be minimum.

The weights of the output layer and the hidden layers are updated such that the gradient of the objective function decreases:

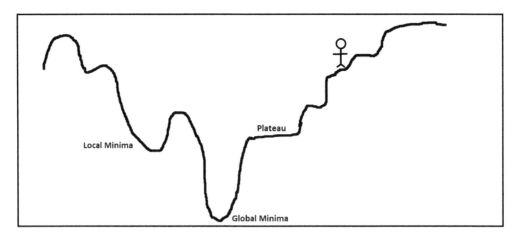

To understand it better, visualize a landscape full of hills, plateaus, and pits. The goal is to come to the ground (global minima of the objective function). If you are standing on top and you have to come down, it is an obvious choice that you will move down the hill, that is, toward the negative slope (or negative gradient). In the same manner, the weights in the Perceptron are changed proportionally to the negative of the gradient of the objective function.

The higher the value of the gradient, the larger will be the change in weight values and vice versa. Now, all this is quite fine, but we can land up with problems when we reach plateaus as the gradient is zero and hence there is no change in weights. We can also land in problems when we enter a small pit (local minima) because when we try to move to either side, the gradient will increase, forcing the network to stay in the pit.

As discussed in `Chapter 2`, *Regression*, there are various variants of gradient descent aimed at increasing convergence and that avoid the problem of getting stuck at local minima or plateaus (adding momentum, variable learning rate).

TensorFlow calculates these gradients automatically with the help of different optimizers. The important thing to note, however, is that as TensorFlow will calculate gradients, which will involve derivatives of the activation functions as well, it is important that the activation function you choose is differentiable and preferably has a non-zero gradient throughout the training scenario.

One of the major ways gradient descent for perceptrons differ from Chapter 2, *Regression,* applications is that the objective function is defined for the output layer, but is used to find the weight change of the neurons of the hidden layers as well. This is done using the **backpropagation (BPN)** algorithm, where the error at the output is propagated backwards to the hidden layers and used to determine the weight change. You will learn more about it soon.

Activation functions

Every neuron must have an activation function. They are what gives the neuron the nonlinear property necessary to model the complex nonlinear datasets. The function takes the weighted sum of all the inputs and generates an output signal. You can think of it as a transform between input and output. Using the proper activation function, we can bound our output values in a defined range.

If x_j is the jth input, W_j the weight connecting j^{th} input to our neuron, and b the bias of our neuron, the output of the neuron (in biological terms, firing of the neuron) is decided by the activation function, and mathematically it is expressed as follows:

$$Y_{hat} = g\left(\sum_{j=1}^{N} W_j x_j + b\right)$$

Here, g represents the activation function. The argument to the activation function $\sum W_j x_j + b$ is called **activity of the neuron**.

Getting ready

Our response to a given input stimulus is governed by the activation function of our neurons. Sometimes our response is a binary yes or no; for example, when presented with a joke, we either laugh or do not laugh. At other times, the response seems linear, for example, crying due to pain. At times, the response seems to be bounded within a range.

Mimicking similar behavior, many different activation functions are used by artificial neurons. In this recipe, you will learn how to define and use some of the common activation functions in TensorFlow.

How to do it...

We proceed with activation functions as follows:

1. **Threshold activation function**: this is the simplest activation function. Here, the neuron fires if the activity of the neuron is greater than zero; otherwise, it does not fire. Here is the plot of the threshold activation function as the activity of the neuron changes along with the code to implement the threshold activation function in TensorFlow:

    ```python
    import tensorflow as tf
    import numpy as np
    import matplotlib.pyplot as plt

    # Threshold Activation function
    def threshold (x):
        cond = tf.less(x, tf.zeros(tf.shape(x), dtype = x.dtype))
        out = tf.where(cond, tf.zeros(tf.shape(x)),
    tf.ones(tf.shape(x)))
        return out
    # Plotting Threshold Activation Function
    h = np.linspace(-1,1,50)
    out = threshold(h)
    init = tf.global_variables_initializer()
    with tf.Session() as sess:
        sess.run(init)
        y = sess.run(out)
        plt.xlabel('Activity of Neuron')
        plt.ylabel('Output of Neuron')
        plt.title('Threshold Activation Function')
        plt.plot(h, y)
    ```

Following is the output of the preceding code:

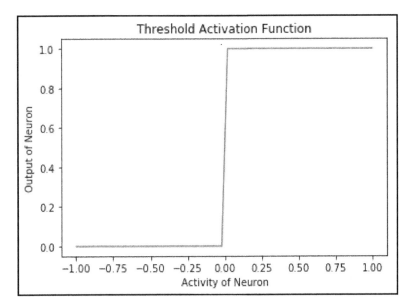

2. **Sigmoidal activation function**: In this case, the output of the neuron is specified by the function $g(x) = 1 / (1 + \exp(-x))$. In TensorFlow, there is a method, `tf.sigmoid`, which provides Sigmoid activation. The range of this function is between 0 and 1. In shape, it looks like the alphabet **S**, hence the name Sigmoid:

```
# Plotting Sigmoidal Activation function
h = np.linspace(-10,10,50)
out = tf.sigmoid(h)
init = tf.global_variables_initializer()
with tf.Session() as sess:
    sess.run(init)
    y = sess.run(out)
    plt.xlabel('Activity of Neuron')
    plt.ylabel('Output of Neuron')
    plt.title('Sigmoidal Activation Function')
    plt.plot(h, y)
```

Following is the output of the following code:

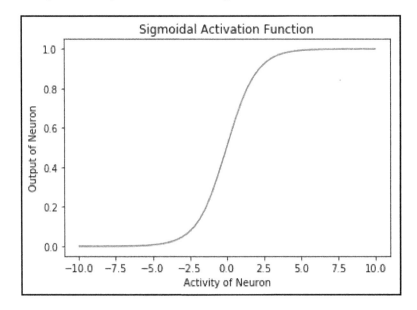

3. **Hyperbolic tangent activation function**: Mathematically, it is *(1 - exp(-2x)/(1+exp(-2x))).* In shape, it resembles the sigmoid function, but it is centred at 0 and its range is from -1 to 1. TensorFlow has a built-in function, `tf.tanh`, for the hyperbolic tangent activation function:

```
# Plotting Hyperbolic Tangent Activation function
h = np.linspace(-10,10,50)
out = tf.tanh(h)
init = tf.global_variables_initializer()
with tf.Session() as sess:
    sess.run(init)
    y = sess.run(out)
    plt.xlabel('Activity of Neuron')
    plt.ylabel('Output of Neuron')
    plt.title('Hyperbolic Tangent Activation Function')
    plt.plot(h, y)
```

Following is the output of the preceding code:

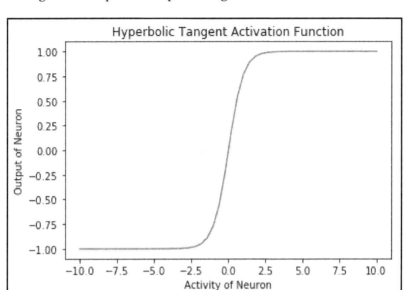

4. **Linear activation function**: In this case, the output of the neuron is the same as the activity of the neuron. This function is not bounded on either side:

```
# Linear Activation Function
b = tf.Variable(tf.random_normal([1,1], stddev=2))
w = tf.Variable(tf.random_normal([3,1], stddev=2))
linear_out = tf.matmul(X_in, w) + b
init = tf.global_variables_initializer()
with tf.Session() as sess:
    sess.run(init)
    out = sess.run(linear_out)
print(out)
```

5. **Rectified linear units (ReLU)** activation function is again built-in with the TensorFlow library. The activation function is similar to the linear activation function, but with one big change--for a negative value of the activity, the neuron does not fire (zero output), and for a positive value of the activity, the output of the neuron is the same as the given activity:

```
# Plotting ReLU Activation function
h = np.linspace(-10,10,50)
out = tf.nn.relu(h)
init = tf.global_variables_initializer()
```

```
with tf.Session() as sess:
    sess.run(init)
    y = sess.run(out)
plt.xlabel('Activity of Neuron')
plt.ylabel('Output of Neuron')
plt.title('ReLU Activation Function')
plt.plot(h, y)
```

Following is the output of the ReLu activation function:

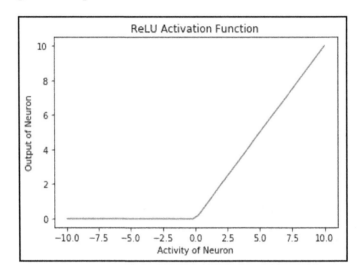

6. **Softmax activation function** is a normalized exponential function. The output of one neuron depends not only on its own activity but the sum of the activity of all other neurons present in that layer. One advantage of this is that it keeps the output of the neurons small and thus the gradients never blow up. Mathematically, it is $y_i = exp(x_i)/ \sum_j exp(x_j)$:

```
# Plotting Softmax Activation function
h = np.linspace(-5,5,50)
out = tf.nn.softmax(h)
init = tf.global_variables_initializer()
with tf.Session() as sess:
    sess.run(init)
    y = sess.run(out)
    plt.xlabel('Activity of Neuron')
    plt.ylabel('Output of Neuron')
    plt.title('Softmax Activation Function')
    plt.plot(h, y)
```

Following is the output of the preceding code:

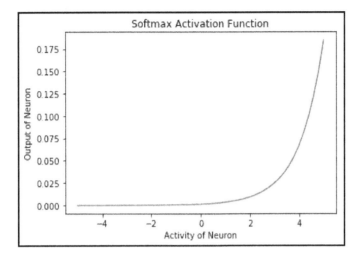

How it works...

Following are the explanations of the functions:

- **Threshold activation function** was used by McCulloch Pitts Neuron and initial Perceptrons. It is not differentiable and is discontinuous at $x=0$. Therefore, it is not possible to use this activation function to train using gradient descent or its variants.
- **Sigmoid activation function** was very popular at one time. If you look at the curve, it looks like a continuous version of the threshold activation function. It suffers from the vanishing gradient problem, that is, the gradient of the function becomes zero near the two edges. This makes training and optimization difficult.
- **Hyperbolic Tangent activation function** is again sigmoidal in shape and has nonlinear properties. The function is centered at zero and has steeper derivatives compared to sigmoid. Like sigmoid, this also suffers from the vanishing gradient problem.
- **Linear activation function** is, as the name suggests, linear in nature. The function is unbounded from both sides *[-inf, inf]*. Its linearity is its major problem. The sum of linear functions will be a linear function and the linear function of a linear function too is a linear function. Thus, using this function, one cannot grasp the non-linearities present in complex datasets.

- **ReLU activation function** is the rectified version of the linear activation function, and this rectification allows it to capture non-linearities when used in multiple layers. One of the major advantages of using ReLU is that it leads to sparse activation; at any instant, all the neurons with negative activity are not firing. This makes the network lighter in terms of computation. ReLU neurons suffer from the dying ReLU problem, that is, neurons that do not fire will have their gradients zero and, hence, will not be able to undergo any training and stay off (dead). Despite this problem, ReLU today is one of the most used activation functions for hidden layers.
- **Softmax activation function** is popularly used as the activation function of the output layer. The function is bounded in the range [0,1]. It is used to represent the probability of a class in a multiclass classification problem. The sum of the output of all the units will always be 1.

There's more...

Neural networks have been employed in a variety of tasks. These tasks can be broadly classified into two categories: function approximation (regression) and classification. Depending on the task at hand, one activation function may be better than the other. Generally, it is better to use ReLU neuron for hidden layers. For classification tasks, softmax is normally a better choice, and for regression problems, it is better to use sigmoid or hyperbolic tangent.

See also

- This link provides details of the activation functions defined in TensorFlow and how to use them: https://www.tensorflow.org/versions/r0.12/api_docs/python/nn/activation_functions_
- A nice summary on activation functions:
  https://en.wikipedia.org/wiki/Activation_function

Single layer perceptron

A simple perceptron is a single-layered neural network. It uses the threshold activation function and, as proved by the Marvin Minsky paper, can solve only linearly separable problems. While this limits the applications of single layer perceptron to only linearly separable problems, it is still always amazing to see it learn.

Getting ready

As perceptron uses the threshold activation function, we cannot use the TensorFlow optimizers to update weights. We will have to use the weight update rule:

$$\Delta W = \eta X^T \left(Y - Y_{hat} \right)$$

Here is the learning rate. For programming simplicity, bias can be added as one additional weight with input fixed to +1. Then the preceding equation can be used to update both weights and biases simultaneously.

How to do it...

Here is how we proceed with the single layer perceptron:

1. Import the modules needed:

```
import tensorflow as tf
import numpy as np
```

2. Define the hyperparameters to be used:

```
# Hyper parameters
eta = 0.4  # learning rate parameter
epsilon = 1e-03 # minimum accepted error
max_epochs = 100 # Maximum Epochs
```

3. Define the `threshold` function:

```
# Threshold Activation function
def threshold (x):
    cond = tf.less(x, tf.zeros(tf.shape(x), dtype = x.dtype))
    out = tf.where(cond, tf.zeros(tf.shape(x)),
tf.ones(tf.shape(x)))
    return out
```

4. Specify the training data. In this example, we take a three input neuron (A,B,C) and train it to learn the logic AB + BC:

```
# Training Data  Y = AB + BC, sum of two linear functions.
T, F = 1., 0.
X_in = [
    [T, T, T, T],
    [T, T, F, T],
```

```
        [T,  F,  T,  T],
        [T,  F,  F,  T],
        [F,  T,  T,  T],
        [F,  T,  F,  T],
        [F,  F,  T,  T],
        [F,  F,  F,  T],
        ]
Y = [
        [T],
        [T],
        [F],
        [F],
        [T],
        [F],
        [F],
        [F]
    ]
```

5. Define the variables to be used, the computational graph to compute updates, and finally, execute the computational graph:

```
W = tf.Variable(tf.random_normal([4,1], stddev=2, seed = 0))
h = tf.matmul(X_in, W)
Y_hat = threshold(h)
error = Y - Y_hat
mean_error = tf.reduce_mean(tf.square(error))
dW =  eta * tf.matmul(X_in, error, transpose_a=True)
train = tf.assign(W, W+dW)
init = tf.global_variables_initializer()
err = 1
epoch = 0
with tf.Session() as sess:
    sess.run(init)
    while err > epsilon and epoch < max_epochs:
        epoch += 1
        err, _ = sess.run([mean_error, train])
        print('epoch: {0}  mean error: {1}'.format(epoch, err))
    print('Training complete')
```

The following is the output of the preceding code:

```
epoch: 1   mean error: 0.625
epoch: 2   mean error: 0.125
epoch: 3   mean error: 0.125
epoch: 4   mean error: 0.375
epoch: 5   mean error: 0.125
epoch: 6   mean error: 0.125
epoch: 7   mean error: 0.375
epoch: 8   mean error: 0.125
epoch: 9   mean error: 0.125
epoch: 10  mean error: 0.125
epoch: 11  mean error: 0.125
epoch: 12  mean error: 0.0
Training complete
```

There's more...

What do you think will happen if, instead of the threshold activation function, we use the sigmoid activation function?

You guessed right; firstly, we can use the TensorFlow optimizer to update weights. Secondly, the network will behave like the logistic regressor.

Calculating gradients of backpropagation algorithm

The BPN algorithm is one of the most studied and most used algorithms in neural networks. It is used to propagate the errors from the output layers to the neurons of the hidden layer, which are then used to update the weights. The whole learning can be broken into two passes--forward pass and backward pass.

Forward pass: The inputs are fed to the network and the signal is propagated from the input layer via the hidden layers, finally to the output layer. At the output layer, the error and the loss function are computed.

Backward pass: In backward pass, the gradient of the loss function is computed first for the output layer neurons and then for the hidden layer neurons. The gradients are then used to update the weights.

The two passes are repeatedly iterated till convergence is reached.

Getting ready

The network is first presented with M training pairs (X, Y), with X as the input and Y the desired output. The input is propagated from input via the activation function $g(h)$ through the hidden layers, up to the output layers. The output Y_{hat} is the output of the network, giving the error $= Y - Y_{hat}$.

The `loss` function $J(W)$ is as follows:

$$J(W) = \frac{1}{2M} \sum_{i=1}^{N} (Y_i - Y_{hat_i})^2$$

Here, i varies over all the neurons of the output layer (1 to N). The change in weights W_{ij}, connecting i^{th} output layer neuron to j^{th} hidden layer neuron, can then be determined using the gradient of $J(W)$ and employing the chain rule for differentiation:

$$\Delta W_{ij} = -\eta \frac{\partial J}{\partial W_{ij}} = \eta \frac{1}{M} \frac{\partial (Y_i - Y_{hat_i})^2}{\partial Y_{hat_i}} \frac{\partial Y_{hat_i}}{\partial h_i} \frac{\partial h_i}{\partial W_{ij}} = \eta \frac{1}{M} (Y_i - Y_{hat_i}) g'(h_i) O_j$$

Here, O_j is the output of the hidden layer neuron, j and h represent activity. This was easy, but now how do we find the update for weights W_{jk} connecting the neuron k from n^{th} hidden layer to the neuron j of $n+1^{th}$ hidden layer? The process is the same--we will use the gradient of the `loss` function and chain rule for differentiation, but we will be calculating it for W_{jk} this time:

$$\Delta W_{jk} = -\eta \frac{\partial J}{\partial W_{jk}} = \eta \frac{1}{M} \sum_i \left\{ \frac{\partial (Y_i - Y_{hat_i})^2}{\partial Y_{hat_i}} \frac{\partial Y_{hat_i}}{\partial h_i} \frac{\partial h_i}{\partial O_j} \right\} \frac{\partial O_j}{\partial W_{jk}}$$

$$= \eta \frac{1}{M} \sum_i \left\{ (Y_i - Y_{hat_i}) g'(h_i) W_{ij} \right\} g'(h_k) O_k$$

Now that the equations are in place, let's see how to do it in TensorFlow. In this recipe, we work with our same old the MNIST dataset (http://yann.lecun.com/exdb/mnist/).

How to do it...

Let us now get started on the backpropagation algorithm:

1. Import the modules:

```
import tensorflow as tf
from tensorflow.examples.tutorials.mnist import input_data
```

2. Load the dataset; we use one-hot encoded labels by setting one_hot = True:

```
mnist = input_data.read_data_sets("MNIST_data/", one_hot=True)
```

3. Define hyperparameters and other constants. Here, each handwritten digit is of the size 28 x 28 = 784 pixels. The dataset is classified into 10 categories, as digits can be any number between 0 to 9. These two are fixed. The learning rate, the maximum number of epochs, the batch size of the mini batch to be trained, and the number of neurons in the hidden layer are the hyperparameters. One can play around with them to see how they affect the network behaviour:

```
# Data specific constants
n_input = 784 # MNIST data input (img shape: 28*28)
n_classes = 10 # MNIST total classes (0-9 digits)

# Hyperparameters
max_epochs = 10000
learning_rate = 0.5
batch_size = 10
seed = 0
n_hidden = 30   # Number of neurons in the hidden layer
```

4. We will require the derivative of the sigmoid function for weight update, so we define it:

```
def sigmaprime(x):
      return tf.multiply(tf.sigmoid(x),
tf.subtract(tf.constant(1.0), tf.sigmoid(x)))
```

5. Create placeholders for the training data:

```
x_in = tf.placeholder(tf.float32, [None, n_input])
y = tf.placeholder(tf.float32, [None, n_classes])
```

6. Create the model:

```
def multilayer_perceptron(x, weights, biases):
    # Hidden layer with RELU activation
    h_layer_1 = tf.add(tf.matmul(x, weights['h1']), biases['h1'])
    out_layer_1 = tf.sigmoid(h_layer_1)
    # Output layer with linear activation
    h_out = tf.matmul(out_layer_1, weights['out']) + biases['out']
    return tf.sigmoid(h_out), h_out, out_layer_1, h_layer_1
```

7. Define variables for `weights` and `biases`:

```
weights = {
    'h1': tf.Variable(tf.random_normal([n_input, n_hidden], seed =
seed)),
    'out': tf.Variable(tf.random_normal([n_hidden, n_classes],
seed = seed)) }

 biases = {
    'h1': tf.Variable(tf.random_normal([1, n_hidden], seed =
seed)),
    'out': tf.Variable(tf.random_normal([1, n_classes], seed =
seed))}
```

8. Create the computation graph for the forward pass, error, gradient, and update calculations:

```
# Forward Pass
 y_hat, h_2, o_1, h_1 = multilayer_perceptron(x_in, weights,
biases)

 # Error
 err = y_hat - y

 # Backward Pass
 delta_2 = tf.multiply(err, sigmaprime(h_2))
 delta_w_2 = tf.matmul(tf.transpose(o_1), delta_2)

 wtd_error = tf.matmul(delta_2, tf.transpose(weights['out']))
 delta_1 = tf.multiply(wtd_error, sigmaprime(h_1))
 delta_w_1 = tf.matmul(tf.transpose(x_in), delta_1)

 eta = tf.constant(learning_rate)

 # Update weights
 step = [
     tf.assign(weights['h1'],tf.subtract(weights['h1'],
```

```
tf.multiply(eta, delta_w_1)))
    , tf.assign(biases['h1'],tf.subtract(biases['h1'],
tf.multiply(eta, tf.reduce_mean(delta_1, axis=[0]))))
    , tf.assign(weights['out'], tf.subtract(weights['out'],
tf.multiply(eta, delta_w_2)))
    , tf.assign(biases['out'], tf.subtract(biases['out'],
tf.multiply(eta,tf.reduce_mean(delta_2, axis=[0])))))
    ]
```

9. Define ops for `accuracy`:

```
acct_mat = tf.equal(tf.argmax(y_hat, 1), tf.argmax(y, 1))
accuracy = tf.reduce_sum(tf.cast(acct_mat, tf.float32))
```

10. Initialize the variables:

```
init = tf.global_variables_initializer()
```

11. Execute the graph:

```
with tf.Session() as sess:
    sess.run(init)
    for epoch in range(max_epochs):
        batch_xs, batch_ys = mnist.train.next_batch(batch_size)
        sess.run(step, feed_dict = {x_in: batch_xs, y : batch_ys})
        if epoch % 1000 == 0:
            acc_test = sess.run(accuracy, feed_dict =
                     {x_in: mnist.test.images,
                      y : mnist.test.labels})
            acc_train = sess.run(accuracy, feed_dict=
            {x_in: mnist.train.images,
             y: mnist.train.labels})
            print('Epoch: {0}  Accuracy Train%: {1}   Accuracy
Test%: {2}'
                     .format(epoch,acc_train/600,(acc_test/100)))
```

The result is as follows:

How it works...

Here, we are training the network for a batch size of 10. If we increase it, the network performance decreases. Also, the accuracy of the trained network is checked on the test data; the size of the test data on which it is tested is 1,000.

There's more...

Our one hidden layer multilayered perceptron gave an accuracy of 84.45 on training data and 92.1 on test data. It is good but not good enough. The MNIST database is used as a benchmark for classification problems in machine learning. Next, we see how using TensorFlow's built-in optimizer affects network performance.

See also

- The MNIST database: http://yann.lecun.com/exdb/mnist/
- A simplified explanation of backpropagation algorithm: http://neuralnetworksanddeeplearning.com/chap2.html
- Another intuitive explanation of backpropagation algorithm: http://cs231n.github.io/optimization-2/
- One more on backpropagation algorithm, it gives detailed information, along with derivation and how it can be applied to different neyworks: https://page.mi.fu-berlin.de/rojas/neural/chapter/K7.pdf

MNIST classifier using MLP

TensorFlow supports auto-differentiation; we can use TensorFlow optimizer to calculate and apply gradients. It automatically updates the tensors defined as variables using the gradients. In this recipe, we will use the TensorFlow optimizer to train the network.

Getting ready

In the backpropagation algorithm recipe, we defined layers, weights, loss, gradients, and update through gradients manually. It is a good idea to do it manually with equations for better understanding but this can be quite cumbersome as the number of layers in the network increases.

In this recipe, we will use powerful TensorFlow features such as Contrib (Layers) to define neural network layers and TensorFlow's own optimizer to compute and apply gradients. We saw in `Chapter 2`, *Regression*, how to use different TensorFlow optimizers. The contrib can be used to add various layers to the neural network model like adding building blocks. The one method that we use here is `tf.contrib.layers.fully_connected`, defined in TensorFlow documentation as follows:

```
fully_connected(
    inputs,
    num_outputs,
    activation_fn=tf.nn.relu,
    normalizer_fn=None,
    normalizer_params=None,
    weights_initializer=initializers.xavier_initializer(),
    weights_regularizer=None,
    biases_initializer=tf.zeros_initializer(),
    biases_regularizer=None,
    reuse=None,
    variables_collections=None,
    outputs_collections=None,
    trainable=True,
    scope=None
)
```

This adds a fully connected layer.

> `fully_connected` creates a variable called weights, representing a fully connected weight matrix, which is multiplied by the inputs to produce a tensor of hidden units. If a `normalizer_fn` is provided (such as `batch_norm`), it is then applied. Otherwise, if `normalizer_fn` is None and a `biases_initializer` is provided then a biases variable would be created and added to the hidden units. Finally, if `activation_fn` is not None, it is applied to the hidden units as well.

How to do it...

We proceed with the recipe as follows:

1. The first step is to change the `loss` function; though for classification, it is better to use the cross-entropy `loss` function. We presently continue with the **mean square error (MSE)**:

   ```
   loss = tf.reduce_mean(tf.square(y - y_hat, name='loss'))
   ```

2. Next, we use the `GradientDescentOptimizer`:

```
optimizer = tf.train.GradientDescentOptimizer(learning_rate=
learning_rate)
 train = optimizer.minimize(loss)
```

3. With just these two changes, we get an accuracy of only 61.3 percent for the test dataset for the same set of hyperparameters. Increasing the `max_epoch`, we can increase the accuracy, but that will not be an efficient use of TensorFlow abilities.

4. This is a classification problem, so it will be better to use cross-entropy loss, ReLU activation function for hidden layers, and softmax for the output layer. Making the required changes, the full code is as follows:

```
import tensorflow as tf
 import tensorflow.contrib.layers as layers

 from tensorflow.python import debug as tf_debug

 # Network Parameters
 n_hidden = 30
 n_classes = 10
 n_input = 784

 # Hyperparameters
 batch_size = 200
 eta = 0.001
 max_epoch = 10

 # MNIST input data
 from tensorflow.examples.tutorials.mnist import input_data
 mnist = input_data.read_data_sets("/tmp/data/", one_hot=True)

 def multilayer_perceptron(x):
     fc1 = layers.fully_connected(x, n_hidden,
 activation_fn=tf.nn.relu, scope='fc1')
     #fc2 = layers.fully_connected(fc1, 256,
 activation_fn=tf.nn.relu, scope='fc2')
     out = layers.fully_connected(fc1, n_classes,
 activation_fn=None, scope='out')
     return out

 # build model, loss, and train op
 x = tf.placeholder(tf.float32, [None, n_input],
 name='placeholder_x')
 y = tf.placeholder(tf.float32, [None, n_classes],
 name='placeholder_y')
```

```
y_hat = multilayer_perceptron(x)

loss =
tf.reduce_mean(tf.nn.softmax_cross_entropy_with_logits(logits=y_hat
, labels=y))
train = tf.train.AdamOptimizer(learning_rate= eta).minimize(loss)
init = tf.global_variables_initializer()




with tf.Session() as sess:
    sess.run(init)
    for epoch in range(10):
        epoch_loss = 0.0
        batch_steps = int(mnist.train.num_examples / batch_size)
        for i in range(batch_steps):
            batch_x, batch_y = mnist.train.next_batch(batch_size)
            _, c = sess.run([train, loss],
                                feed_dict={x: batch_x, y: batch_y})
            epoch_loss += c / batch_steps
        print ('Epoch %02d, Loss = %.6f' % (epoch, epoch_loss))

    # Test model
    correct_prediction = tf.equal(tf.argmax(y_hat, 1),
tf.argmax(y, 1))
    accuracy = tf.reduce_mean(tf.cast(correct_prediction,
tf.float32))
    print ("Accuracy%:", accuracy.eval({x: mnist.test.images, y:
mnist.test.labels}))
```

How it works...

The modified MNIST MLP classifier gives us ~ 96 percent accuracy on the test dataset, with only one hidden layer and within 10 epochs. Only in a few lines of code we got ~96 percent accuracy, this is the power of TensorFlow:

```
Epoch 00, Loss = 0.319405
Epoch 01, Loss = 0.178234
Epoch 02, Loss = 0.139035
Epoch 03, Loss = 0.116732
Epoch 04, Loss = 0.103431
Epoch 05, Loss = 0.093936
Epoch 06, Loss = 0.085003
Epoch 07, Loss = 0.076824
Epoch 08, Loss = 0.071777
Epoch 09, Loss = 0.065691
Accuracy%: 96.5300142765

Process finished with exit code 0
```

Function approximation using MLP-predicting Boston house prices

The work by Hornik *et al* (`http://www.cs.cmu.edu/~bhiksha/courses/deeplearning/Fall.2016/notes/Sonia_Hornik.pdf`) proved the following:

> *"multilayer feedforward networks with as few as one hidden layer are indeed capable of universal approximation in a very precise and satisfactory sense."*

In this recipe, we will show you how to use MLP for function approximation; specifically, we will be predicting Boston house prices. We are already familiar with the dataset; in `Chapter 2`, *Regression*, we used regression techniques for the house price prediction, now we will do the same using MLPs.

Getting ready

For function approximation, the `loss` function should be the MSE. The inputs should be normalized and, while the hidden layer can be ReLU, the output layer should preferably be sigmoid.

How to do it...

Here is how we start with function approximation using MLP:

1. Import the modules needed--`sklearn` for datasets, preprocessing data, and splitting it into train and test; Pandas to understand the dataset; and `matplotlib` and `seaborn` to visualize:

```
import tensorflow as tf
import tensorflow.contrib.layers as layers
from sklearn import datasets
import matplotlib.pyplot as plt
from sklearn.model_selection  import train_test_split
from sklearn.preprocessing import MinMaxScaler
import pandas as pd
import seaborn as sns
%matplotlib inline
```

2. Load the dataset and create a Pandas dataframe to understand the data:

```
# Data
boston = datasets.load_boston()
df = pd.DataFrame(boston.data, columns=boston.feature_names)
df['target'] = boston.target
```

3. Let us get some details about the data:

```
#Understanding Data
df.describe()
```

The following image gives a good idea of the concept:

	CRIM	ZN	INDUS	CHAS	NOX	RM	AGE	DIS	RAD	TAX	PTRATIO	B	LSTAT	target
count	506	506	506	506	506	506	506	506	506	506	506	506	506	506
mean	3.59376	11.3636	11.1368	0.06917	0.5547	6.28463	68.5749	3.79504	9.54941	408.237	18.4555	356.674	12.6531	22.5328
std	8.59678	23.3225	6.86035	0.25399	0.11588	0.70262	28.1489	2.10571	8.70726	168.537	2.16495	91.2949	7.14106	9.1971
min	0.00632	0	0.46	0	0.385	3.561	2.9	1.1296	1	187	12.6	0.32	1.73	5
25%	0.08205	0	5.19	0	0.449	5.8855	45.025	2.10018	4	279	17.4	375.378	6.95	17.025
50%	0.25651	0	9.69	0	0.538	6.2085	77.5	3.20745	5	330	19.05	391.44	11.36	21.2
75%	3.64742	12.5	18.1	0	0.624	6.6235	94.075	5.18843	24	666	20.2	396.225	16.955	25
max	88.9762	100	27.74	1	0.871	8.78	100	12.1265	24	711	22	396.9	37.97	50

4. Find correlation between different input features and the target:

```
# Plotting correlation
color map _ , ax = plt.subplots( figsize =( 12 , 10 ) )
corr = df.corr(method='pearson')
cmap = sns.diverging_palette( 220 , 10 , as_cmap = True )
_ = sns.heatmap( corr, cmap = cmap, square=True, cbar_kws={
'shrink' : .9 }, ax=ax, annot = True, annot_kws = { 'fontsize' : 12
})
```

Following is the output of the preceding code:

	CRIM	ZN	INDUS	CHAS	NOX	RM	AGE	DIS	RAD	TAX	PTRATIO	B	LSTAT	target
CRIM	1	-0.2	0.4	-0.055	0.42	-0.22	0.35	-0.38	0.62	0.58	0.29	-0.38	0.45	-0.39
ZN	-0.2	1	-0.53	-0.043	-0.52	0.31	-0.57	0.66	-0.31	-0.31	-0.39	0.18	-0.41	0.36
INDUS	0.4	-0.53	1	0.063	0.76	-0.39	0.64	-0.71	0.6	0.72	0.38	-0.36	0.6	-0.48
CHAS	-0.055	-0.043	0.063	1	0.091	0.091	0.087	-0.099	0.0074	0.036	-0.12	0.049	-0.054	0.18
NOX	0.42	-0.52	0.76	0.091	1	-0.3	0.73	-0.77	0.61	0.67	0.19	-0.38	0.59	-0.43
RM	-0.22	0.31	-0.39	0.091	-0.3	1	-0.24	0.21	-0.21	-0.29	-0.36	0.13	-0.61	0.7
AGE	0.35	-0.57	0.64	0.087	0.73	-0.24	1	-0.75	0.46	0.51	0.26	-0.27	0.6	-0.38
DIS	-0.38	0.66	-0.71	-0.099	-0.77	0.21	-0.75	1	-0.49	-0.53	-0.23	0.29	-0.5	0.25
RAD	0.62	-0.31	0.6	-0.0074	0.61	-0.21	0.46	-0.49	1	0.91	0.46	-0.44	0.49	-0.38
TAX	0.58	-0.31	0.72	-0.036	0.67	-0.29	0.51	-0.53	0.91	1	0.46	-0.44	0.54	-0.47
PTRATIO	0.29	-0.39	0.38	-0.12	0.19	-0.36	0.26	-0.23	0.46	0.46	1	-0.18	0.37	-0.51
B	-0.38	0.18	-0.36	0.049	-0.38	0.13	-0.27	0.29	-0.44	-0.44	-0.18	1	-0.37	0.33
LSTAT	0.45	-0.41	0.6	-0.054	0.59	-0.61	0.6	-0.5	0.49	0.54	0.37	-0.37	1	-0.74
target	-0.39	0.36	-0.48	0.18	-0.43	0.7	-0.38	0.25	-0.38	-0.47	-0.51	0.33	-0.74	1

5. From the preceding code, we can see that three parameters--RM, PTRATIO, and LSTAT--have a correlation greater than 0.5 in magnitude. We choose them for the training. Split the dataset into Train and Test datasets. We also use MinMaxScaler to normalize our data set. One important change to note is that since our neural network is using the Sigmoid activation function (output of sigmoid can be between 0-1 only), we will have to normalize the target value Y as well:

```
# Create Test Train Split
X_train, X_test, y_train, y_test = train_test_split(df [['RM',
```

```
'LSTAT', 'PTRATIO']], df[['target']], test_size=0.3,
random_state=0)
# Normalize data
X_train = MinMaxScaler().fit_transform(X_train)
y_train = MinMaxScaler().fit_transform(y_train)
X_test = MinMaxScaler().fit_transform(X_test)
y_test = MinMaxScaler().fit_transform(y_test)
```

6. Define the constants and hyperparameters:

```
#Network Parameters
m = len(X_train)
n = 3 # Number of features
n_hidden = 20 # Number of hidden neurons
# Hyperparameters
batch_size = 200
eta = 0.01
max_epoch = 1000
```

7. Create a multilayer perceptron model with one hidden layer:

```
def multilayer_perceptron(x):
    fc1 = layers.fully_connected(x, n_hidden,
activation_fn=tf.nn.relu, scope='fc1')
    out = layers.fully_connected(fc1, 1, activation_fn=tf.sigmoid,
scope='out')
    return out
```

8. Declare the placeholders for the training data and define the loss and optimizer:

```
# build model, loss, and train op
x = tf.placeholder(tf.float32, name='X', shape=[m,n])
y = tf.placeholder(tf.float32, name='Y')
y_hat = multilayer_perceptron(x)
correct_prediction = tf.square(y - y_hat)
mse = tf.reduce_mean(tf.cast(correct_prediction, "float"))
train = tf.train.AdamOptimizer(learning_rate= eta).minimize(mse)
init = tf.global_variables_initializer()
```

9. Execute the computational graph:

```
# Computation Graph
with tf.Session() as sess: # Initialize variables
    sess.run(init) writer = tf.summary.FileWriter('graphs',
sess.graph)
# train the model for 100 epcohs
    for i in range(max_epoch):
```

```
        _, l, p = sess.run([train, loss, y_hat], feed_dict={x:
X_train, y: y_train})
        if i%100 == 0:
            print('Epoch {0}: Loss {1}'.format(i, l))
    print("Training Done")
print("Optimization Finished!")
# Test model correct_prediction = tf.square(y - y_hat)
# Calculate accuracy
accuracy = tf.reduce_mean(tf.cast(correct_prediction, "float"))
print(" Mean Error:", accuracy.eval({x: X_train, y: y_train}))
plt.scatter(y_train, p)
writer.close()
```

How it works...

With only one hidden layer, the model predicts the prices on the training dataset with a mean error of 0.0071. The figure below shows the relationship between estimated and actual price of the house:

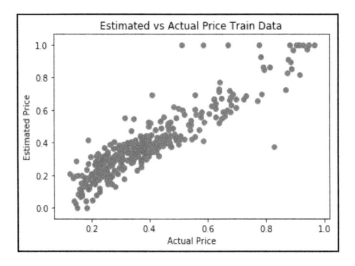

There's more...

Here, we used TensorFlow ops Layers (Contrib) to build neural network layers. It made our work slightly easier as we were saved from declaring weights and biases for each layer separately. The work can be further simplified if we use an API like Keras. Here is the code for the same in Keras with TensorFlow as the backend:

```
#Network Parameters
m = len(X_train)
n = 3 # Number of features
n_hidden = 20 # Number of hidden neurons

# Hyperparameters
batch = 20
eta = 0.01
max_epoch = 100
# Build Model
model = Sequential()
model.add(Dense(n_hidden, input_dim=n, activation='relu'))
model.add(Dense(1, activation='sigmoid'))
model.summary()
# Summarize the model
#Compile model
model.compile(loss='mean_squared_error', optimizer='adam')
#Fit the model
model.fit(X_train, y_train, validation_data=(X_test,
y_test),epochs=max_epoch, batch_size=batch, verbose=1)
#Predict the values and calculate RMSE and R2 score
y_test_pred = model.predict(X_test)
y_train_pred = model.predict(X_train)
r2 = r2_score( y_test, y_test_pred )
rmse = mean_squared_error( y_test, y_test_pred )
print( "Performance Metrics R2 : {0:f}, RMSE : {1:f}".format( r2, rmse ) )
```

The preceding code gives the following result between predicted and actual values. We can see that the result can be improved by removing the outliers (some houses with max price irrespective of other parameters, the points at the right extreme):

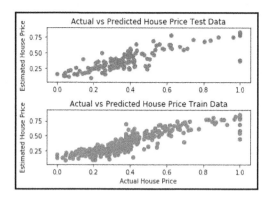

Tuning hyperparameters

The neural network performance, as you must have observed by now, depends on a lot on hyperparameters. Thus, it becomes important that one gains an understanding as to how these parameters affect the network. Common examples of hyperparameters are learning rate, regularizers, regularizing coefficient, dimensions of hidden layers, initial weight values, and even the optimizer selected to optimize weights and biases.

How to do it...

Here is how we proceed with the recipe:

1. The first step in tuning hyperparameters is building the model. Build the model in TensorFlow, exactly the way we have been.
2. Add a way to save the model in `model_file`. In TensorFlow, this can be done using a `Saver` object. Then save it in the session:

```
... saver = tf.train.Saver() ... with tf.Session() as sess: ... #Do
the training steps ... save_path = saver.save(sess,
"/tmp/model.ckpt") print("Model saved in file: %s" % save_path)
```

3. Next, identify the hyperparameters that you want to tune.

4. Choose possible values for the hyperparameters. Here, you can make a random choice, constant spaced choice, or manual choice. The three are respectively known as random search, grid search, or manual search for optimized hyperparameters. For example, this is for the learning rate:

```
# Random Choice: generate 5 random values of learning rate
# lying between 0 and 1
learning_rate = np.random.rand(5)
#Grid Search: generate 5 values starting from 0, separated by
# 0.2
learning_rate = [i for i in np.arange(0,1,0.2)]
#Manual Search: give any values you seem plausible manually
learning_rate = [0.5, 0.6, 0.32, 0.7, 0.01]
```

5. We choose the parameters that give the best response to our chosen `loss` function. So, we can define a maximum value of `loss` function at the start as `best_loss` (in the case of accuracy, you will choose the minimum accuracy you desire from your model):

```
best_loss = 2
# It can be any number, but it would be better if you keep it same
as the loss you achieved from your base model defined in steps 1
and 2
```

6. Wrap your model in a for loop for the learning rate; any model that gives a better estimate of loss is then saved:

```
...  # Load and preprocess data
...  # Hyperparameters
Tuning epochs = [50, 60, 70]
batches = [5, 10, 20]
rmse_min = 0.04
for epoch in epochs:
    for batch in batches:
        model = get_model()
        model.compile(loss='mean_squared_error', optimizer='adam')
        model.fit(X_train, y_train, validation_data=(X_test,
y_test),epochs=epoch, batch_size=batch, verbose=1)
        y_test_pred = model.predict(X_test)
        rmse = mean_squared_error( y_test, y_test_pred )
        if rmse < rmse_min:
            rmse_min = rmse
            # serialize model to JSON
            model_json = model.to_json()
```

```
with open("model.json", "w") as json_file:
    json_file.write(model_json)
    # serialize weights to HDF5
    model.save_weights("model.hdf5")
    print("Saved model to disk")
```

There's more...

There is another approach called **Bayesian optimization**, which can also be used to tune hyperparameters. In it, we define an acquisition function along with a Gaussian process. The Gaussian process uses a set of previously evaluated parameters and resulting accuracy to assume about unobserved parameters. The acquisition function using this information suggests the next set of parameters. There is a wrapper available for even gradient-based hyperparameter optimization https://github.com/lucfra/RFHO.

See also

- Good introduction to different two excellent open-source packages for hyperparameter optimization, Hyperopt and scikit-optimize: https://roamanalytics.com/2016/09/15/optimizing-the-hyperparameter-of-which-hyperparameter-optimizer-to-use/
- Another one on Hyperopt: http://fastml.com/optimizing-hyperparams-with-hyperopt/
- A detailed paper by Bengio and others on various algorithms for hyperparameter optimization:https://papers.nips.cc/paper/4443-algorithms-for-hyper-parameter-optimization.pdf

Higher-level APIs-Keras

Keras is a higher-level API used with TensorFlow as the backend. Adding layers to it is as easy as adding a single line of code. After the model architecture, using one line of code, you can compile and fit the model. Later, it can be used for prediction. Declaration of variables, placeholders, and even the session is managed by the API.

How to do it...

We proceed with Keras as follows:

1. As the first step, we define the type of our model. Keras offers two types of models: sequential and Model class API. Keras offers various types of neural network layers:

```
# Import the model and layers needed
from keras.model import Sequential
from keras.layers import Dense

model = Sequential()
```

2. Add the layers to the model with the help of `model.add()`. Keras offers the option of a dense layer--for a densely connected neural network, `layer Dense(units, activation=None, use_bias=True, kernel_initializer='glorot_uniform', bias_initializer='zeros', kernel_regularizer=None, bias_regularizer=None, activity_regularizer=None, kernel_constraint=None, bias_constraint=None)`. According to Keras documentation:

> Dense implements the operation: `output = activation(dot(input, kernel) + bias)` where activation is the element-wise activation function passed as the activation argument, kernel is a weights matrix created by the layer, and bias is a bias vector created by the layer (only applicable if `use_bias` is `True`).

3. We can use it to add as many layers as we want, with each hidden layer being fed by the previous layer. We need to specify the input dimension only for the first layer:

```
#This will add a fully connected neural network layer with 32
neurons, each taking 13 inputs, and with activation function ReLU
mode.add(Dense(32, input_dim=13, activation='relu')) ))
model.add(10, activation='sigmoid')
```

4. Once the model is defined, we need to choose a `loss` function and optimizers. Keras offers a variety
   of `loss_functions`: `mean_squared_error`, `mean_absolute_error`, `mean_ab solute_percentage_error`, `categorical_crossentropy`; and
   optimizers: sgd, RMSprop, Adagrad, Adadelta, Adam, and so on. With these two decided, we can configure the learning process using `compile(self, optimizer, loss, metrics=None, sample_weight_mode=None)`:

```
model.compile(optimizer='rmsprop',
        loss='categorical_crossentropy',
        metrics=['accuracy'])
```

5. Next, the model is trained using the `fit` method:

```
model.fit(data, labels, epochs=10, batch_size=32)
```

6. Lastly, prediction can be performed with the help
   of the `predict` method `predict(self, x, batch_size=32, verbose=0)`:

```
model.predict(test_data, batch_size=10)
```

There's more...

Keras offers options to add convolutional layers, pooling layers, recurrent layers, and even locally connected layers. The detailed description of each method is available in Keras documentation at `https://keras.io/models/sequential/`.

See also

- McCulloch, Warren S., and Walter Pitts. *A logical calculus of the ideas immanent in nervous activity* The bulletin of mathematical biophysics 5.4 (1943): 115-133. `http://vordenker.de/ggphilosophy/mcculloch_a-logical-calculus.pdf`
- Rosenblatt, Frank (1957), The Perceptron--a perceiving and recognizing automaton. Report 85-460-1, Cornell Aeronautical Laboratory. `https://blogs.umass.edu/brain-wars/files/2016/03/rosenblatt-1957.pdf`
- *The Thinking Machine*, CBS Broadcast `https://www.youtube.com/watch?v=jPHUlQiwD9Y`
- Hornik, Kurt, Maxwell Stinchcombe, and Halbert White. *Multilayer feedforward networks are universal approximators. Neural networks 2.5 (1989): 359-366.*

4
Convolutional Neural Networks

Convolutional Neural Networks (**CNNs** or sometimes referred to as **ConvNets**) are fascinating. Over a short period of time, they became a disruptive technology, breaking all the state-of-the-art results in multiple domains from text, to video, to speech--going well beyond their original use for image processing. In this chapter, we will present a number of recipes as follows:

- Creating a ConvNet to classify handwritten MNIST numbers
- Creating a ConvNet to classify CIFAR-10
- Transferring style with VGG19 for image repainting
- Using a pretrained VGG16 net for transfer learning
- Creating a DeepDream network

Introduction

A CNN consists of many neural network layers. Two different types of layers, convolutional and pooling, are typically alternated. The depth of each filter increases from left to right in the network. The last stage is typically made of one or more fully connected layers:

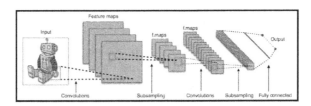

An example of Convolutional Neural Network as seen is https://commons.wikimedia.org/wiki/File:Typical_cnn.png

There are three key intuitions behind convnets: **local receptive fields**, **shared weights**, and **pooling**. Let's review them together.

Local receptive fields

If we want to preserve the spatial information typically found in images, then it is convenient to represent each image with a matrix of pixels. Then, a simple way to encode the local structure is to connect a submatrix of adjacent input neurons into one single hidden neuron belonging to the next layer. That single hidden neuron represents one local receptive field. Note that this operation is named **Convolution** and it provides the name to this type of network.

Of course, we can encode more information by having overlapping submatrices. For instance, let's suppose that the size of every single submatrix is 5 x 5 and that those submatrices are used with MNIST images of 28 x 28 pixels. Then we will be able to generate 23 x 23 local receptive field neurons in the next hidden layer. In fact, it is possible to slide the submatrices by only 23 positions before touching the borders of the images.

Let's define the feature map from one layer to another. Of course, we can have multiple feature maps that learn independently from each hidden layer. For instance, we can start with 28 x 28 input neurons to process MNIST images, and then recall *k* feature maps of size 23 x 23 neurons each (again with a stride of 5 x 5) in the next hidden layer.

Shared weights and bias

Let's suppose that we want to move away from the raw pixel representation by gaining the ability to detect the same feature independently from the location where it is placed in the input image. A simple intuition is to use the same set of weights and bias for all the neurons in the hidden layers. In this way, each layer will learn a set of position-independent latent features derived from the image.

A mathematical example

One simple way to understand convolution is to think about a sliding window function applied to a matrix. In the following example, given the input matrix **I** and the kernel **K**, we get the convolved output. The 3 x 3 kernel **K** (sometimes called **filter** or **feature detector**) is multiplied element-wise with the input matrix to get one cell in the output convolved matrix. All the other cells are obtained by sliding the window on **I**:

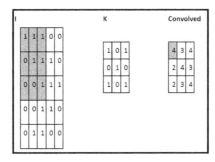

An example of convolutional operation: in bold the cells involved in the computation

In this example, we decided to stop the sliding window as soon as we touch the borders of **I** (so the output is 3 x 3). Alternatively, we could have chosen to pad the input with zeros (so that the output would have been 5 x 5). This decision relates to the **padding** choice adopted.

Another choice is about the **stride** which is about the type of shift adopted by our sliding windows. This can be one or more. A larger stride generates fewer applications of the kernel and a smaller output size, while a smaller stride generates more output and retains more information.

The size of the filter, the stride, and the type of padding are hyperparameters that can be fine-tuned during the training of the network.

ConvNets in TensorFlow

In TensorFlow, if we want to add a convolutional layer, we will write the following:

```
tf.nn.conv2d(input, filter, strides, padding, use_cudnn_on_gpu=None,
data_format=None, name=None)
```

The following are the arguments:

- `input`: A tensor, must be one of the following types: half, `float32`, `float64`.
- `filter`: A tensor, must have the same type as input.
- `strides`: A list of ints. 1D of length 4. The stride of the sliding window for each dimension of input. Must be in the same order as the dimension specified with format.
- `padding`: A string from: `SAME`, `VALID`. The type of padding algorithm to use.
- `use_cudnn_on_gpu`: An optional bool. Defaults to `True`.

- `data_format`: An optional string from: `NHWC` and `NCHW`. Defaults to `NHWC`. Specifies the data format of the input and output data. With the default format `NHWC`, the data is stored in the order of: [`batch, in_height, in_width,` and `in_channels`]. Alternatively, the format could be `NCHW`, the data storage order of: [`batch, in_channels, in_height, in_width`].
- `name`: A name for the operation (optional).

An example of convolution is provided in the following image:

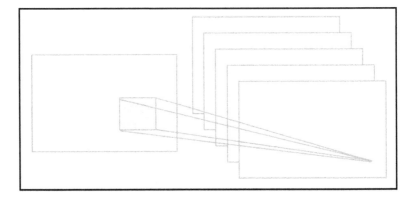

An example of convolutional operation

Pooling layers

Let's suppose that we want to summarize the output of a feature map. Again, we can use the spatial contiguity of the output produced from a single feature map and aggregate the values of a sub-matrix into one single output value synthetically describing the meaning associated with that physical region.

Max pooling

One easy and common choice is the so-called **max-pooling operator**, which simply outputs the maximum activation as observed in the region. In TensorFlow, if we want to define a max pooling layer of size 2 x 2, we will write the following:

```
tf.nn.max_pool(value, ksize, strides, padding, data_format='NHWC',
name=None)
```

These are the arguments:

- `value`: A 4-D Tensor with shape [`batch`, `height`, `width`, `channels`]and type `tf.float32`.
- `ksize`: A list of ints that has length >= 4. The size of the window for each dimension of the input tensor.
- `strides`: A list of ints that has length >= 4. The stride of the sliding window for each dimension of the input tensor.
- `padding`: A string, either `VALID` or `SAME`.
- `data_format`: A string. `NHWC` and `NCHW` are supported.
- `name`: Optional name for the operation.

An example of the max pooling operation is given in the following image:

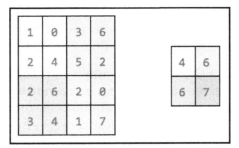

An example of pooling operation

Average pooling

Another choice is average-pooling, which simply aggregates a region into the average values of the activation observed in that region.

TensorFlow implements a large number of pooling layers and a complete list is available online. (`https://www.tensorflow.org/api_guides/python/nn#Pooling`) In short, all the pooling operations are nothing more than a summary operation on a given region.

ConvNets summary

CNNs are basically several layers of convolutions with nonlinear activation functions and pooling layers applied to the results. Each layer applies different filters (hundreds or thousands). The key observation to understand is that the filters are not pre-assigned, but instead, they are learned during the training phase in such a way that a suitable loss function is minimized. It has been observed that lower layers will learn to detect basic features, while the higher layers detect progressively more sophisticated features such as shapes or faces. Note that, thanks to pooling, individual neurons in later layers see more of the original image, hence they are able to compose basic features learned in the earlier layers.

So far we have described the basic concepts of ConvNets. CNNs apply convolution and pooling operations in one dimension for audio and text data along the time dimension, in two dimensions for images along the (height x width) dimensions, and in three dimensions for videos along the (height x width x time) dimensions. For images, sliding the filter over an input volume produces a map that provides the responses of the filter for each spatial position.

 In other words, a ConvNet has multiple filters stacked together that learn to recognize specific visual features independently of the location in the image. Those visual features are simple in the initial layers of the network and then more and more sophisticated deeper in the network.

Creating a ConvNet to classify handwritten MNIST numbers

In this recipe, you will learn how to create a simple three-layer convolutional network to predict the MNIST digits. The deep network consists of two convolutional layers with ReLU and maxpool and two fully connected final layers.

Getting ready

MNIST is a set of 60,000 images representing handwritten numbers. The goal of this recipe is to recognize those numbers with high accuracy.

How to do it...

Let us start with the recipe:

1. Import `tensorflow`, `matplotlib`, `random`, and `numpy`. Then, import the `minst` data and perform one-hot encoding. Note the TensorFlow has some built-in libraries to deal with `MNIST` and we are going to use them:

```
from __future__ import  division, print_function
import tensorflow as tf
import matplotlib.pyplot as plt
import numpy as np
# Import MNIST data
from tensorflow.examples.tutorials.mnist import input_data
mnist = input_data.read_data_sets("MNIST_data/", one_hot=True)
```

2. Introspect some data to understand what `MNIST` is. This gives us an idea of how many images are in the training dataset and how many are in the test dataset. We are also going to visualize a few numbers just to understand how they are represented. The multi-flat output can give us a visual sense of how difficult it can be to recognize a handwritten number, even for humans.

```
def train_size(num):
    print ('Total Training Images in Dataset = ' +
str(mnist.train.images.shape))
    print ('--------------------------------------------------')
    x_train = mnist.train.images[:num,:]
    print ('x_train Examples Loaded = ' + str(x_train.shape))
    y_train = mnist.train.labels[:num,:]
    print ('y_train Examples Loaded = ' + str(y_train.shape))
    print('')
    return x_train, y_train
def test_size(num):
    print ('Total Test Examples in Dataset = ' +
str(mnist.test.images.shape))
    print ('--------------------------------------------------')
    x_test = mnist.test.images[:num,:]
    print ('x_test Examples Loaded = ' + str(x_test.shape))
    y_test = mnist.test.labels[:num,:]
    print ('y_test Examples Loaded = ' + str(y_test.shape))
    return x_test, y_test
def display_digit(num):
    print(y_train[num])
    label = y_train[num].argmax(axis=0)
    image = x_train[num].reshape([28,28])
    plt.title('Example: %d  Label: %d' % (num, label))
```

```
        plt.imshow(image, cmap=plt.get_cmap('gray_r'))
        plt.show()
def display_mult_flat(start, stop):
    images = x_train[start].reshape([1,784])
    for i in range(start+1,stop):
        images = np.concatenate((images,
x_train[i].reshape([1,784])))
    plt.imshow(images, cmap=plt.get_cmap('gray_r'))
    plt.show()
x_train, y_train = train_size(55000)
display_digit(np.random.randint(0, x_train.shape[0]))
display_mult_flat(0,400)
```

Let us look at the output of the preceding code:

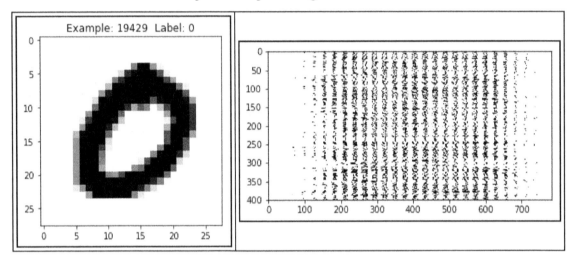

An example of MNIST handwritten numbers

3. Set up the learning parameter, the `batch_size`, and the `display_step`. In addition, set up `n_input = 784` given that the MNIST images share 28 x 28 pixels, output `n_classes = 10` representing the output digits [0-9], and the dropout probability = 0.85:

```
# Parameters
learning_rate = 0.001
training_iters = 500
batch_size = 128
display_step = 10
# Network Parameters
n_input = 784
```

```
# MNIST data input (img shape: 28*28)
n_classes = 10
# MNIST total classes (0-9 digits)
dropout = 0.85
# Dropout, probability to keep units
```

4. Set up the TensorFlow computation graph input. Let's define two placeholders to store predictions and true labels:

```
x = tf.placeholder(tf.float32, [None, n_input])
y = tf.placeholder(tf.float32, [None, n_classes])
keep_prob = tf.placeholder(tf.float32)
```

5. Define a convolutional layer with input x, weight W, bias b, and a given stride. The activation function is ReLU and padding is SAME:

```
def conv2d(x, W, b, strides=1):
    x = tf.nn.conv2d(x, W, strides=[1, strides, strides, 1],
padding='SAME')
    x = tf.nn.bias_add(x, b)
    return tf.nn.relu(x)
```

6. Define a maxpool layer with input x, with ksize and padding SAME:

```
def maxpool2d(x, k=2):
    return tf.nn.max_pool(x, ksize=[1, k, k, 1], strides=[1, k, k,
1], padding='SAME')
```

7. Define convnet with two convolutional layers followed by a fully connected layer, a dropout layer, and a final output layer:

```
def conv_net(x, weights, biases, dropout):
    # reshape the input picture
    x = tf.reshape(x, shape=[-1, 28, 28, 1])
    # First convolution layer
    conv1 = conv2d(x, weights['wc1'], biases['bc1'])
    # Max Pooling used for downsampling
    conv1 = maxpool2d(conv1, k=2)
    # Second convolution layer
    conv2 = conv2d(conv1, weights['wc2'], biases['bc2'])
    # Max Pooling used for downsampling
    conv2 = maxpool2d(conv2, k=2)
    # Reshape conv2 output to match the input of fully connected
layer
    fc1 = tf.reshape(conv2, [-1,
weights['wd1'].get_shape().as_list()[0]])
    # Fully connected layer
```

```
fc1 = tf.add(tf.matmul(fc1, weights['wd1']), biases['bd1'])
fc1 = tf.nn.relu(fc1)
# Dropout
fc1 = tf.nn.dropout(fc1, dropout)
# Output the class prediction
out = tf.add(tf.matmul(fc1, weights['out']), biases['out'])
return out
```

8. Define the layers weights and the bias. The first conv layer has a 5 x 5 convolution, 1 input, and 32 outputs. The second conv layer has 5 x 5 convolutions, 32 inputs, and 64 outputs. The fully connected layer has 7 x 7 x 64 inputs and 1,024 outputs, while the second layer has 1,024 inputs and 10 outputs corresponding to the final digit classes. All the weights and bias are initialized with `randon_normal` distribution:

```
weights = {
    # 5x5 conv, 1 input, and 32 outputs
    'wc1': tf.Variable(tf.random_normal([5, 5, 1, 32])),
    # 5x5 conv, 32 inputs, and 64 outputs
    'wc2': tf.Variable(tf.random_normal([5, 5, 32, 64])),
    # fully connected, 7*7*64 inputs, and 1024 outputs
    'wd1': tf.Variable(tf.random_normal([7*7*64, 1024])),
    # 1024 inputs, 10 outputs for class digits
    'out': tf.Variable(tf.random_normal([1024, n_classes]))
}
biases = {
    'bc1': tf.Variable(tf.random_normal([32])),
    'bc2': tf.Variable(tf.random_normal([64])),
    'bd1': tf.Variable(tf.random_normal([1024])),
    'out': tf.Variable(tf.random_normal([n_classes]))
}
```

9. Build the convnet with the given weights and bias. Define the `loss` function based on `cross_entropy` with `logits` and use the Adam optimizer for cost minimization. After optimization, compute the accuracy:

```
pred = conv_net(x, weights, biases, keep_prob)
cost =
tf.reduce_mean(tf.nn.softmax_cross_entropy_with_logits(logits=pred,
labels=y))
optimizer =
tf.train.AdamOptimizer(learning_rate=learning_rate).minimize(cost)
correct_prediction = tf.equal(tf.argmax(pred, 1), tf.argmax(y, 1))
accuracy = tf.reduce_mean(tf.cast(correct_prediction, tf.float32))
init = tf.global_variables_initializer()
```

10. Launch the graph and iterate for `training_iterats` times where each time a `batch_size` is taken in the input to run the optimizer. Note that we train by using the `mnist.train` data, which is separated from `minst`. Each `display_step`, the current partial accuracy is computed. At the end, the accuracy is computed on 2,048 test images with no dropout.

```
train_loss = []
train_acc = []
test_acc = []
with tf.Session() as sess:
    sess.run(init)
    step = 1
    while step <= training_iters:
        batch_x, batch_y = mnist.train.next_batch(batch_size)
        sess.run(optimizer, feed_dict={x: batch_x, y: batch_y,
                                        keep_prob: dropout})
        if step % display_step == 0:
            loss_train, acc_train = sess.run([cost, accuracy],
                                            feed_dict={x: batch_x,
                                                y: batch_y,
                                                keep_prob:
1.})
            print "Iter " + str(step) + ", Minibatch Loss= " + \
                "{:.2f}".format(loss_train) + ", Training
Accuracy= " + \
                "{:.2f}".format(acc_train)
            # Calculate accuracy for 2048 mnist test images.
            # Note that in this case no dropout
            acc_test = sess.run(accuracy,
                                feed_dict={x: mnist.test.images,
                                    y: mnist.test.labels,
                                    keep_prob: 1.})
            print "Testing Accuracy:" + \
                "{:.2f}".format(acc_train)
            train_loss.append(loss_train)
            train_acc.append(acc_train)
            test_acc.append(acc_test)
        step += 1
```

11. Plot the Softmax loss per iteration, together with train and test accuracy:

```
eval_indices = range(0, training_iters, display_step)
# Plot loss over time
plt.plot(eval_indices, train_loss, 'k-')
plt.title('Softmax Loss per iteration')
plt.xlabel('Iteration')
```

```
plt.ylabel('Softmax Loss')
plt.show()
# Plot train and test accuracy
plt.plot(eval_indices, train_acc, 'k-', label='Train Set Accuracy')
plt.plot(eval_indices, test_acc, 'r--', label='Test Set Accuracy')
plt.title('Train and Test Accuracy')
plt.xlabel('Generation')
plt.ylabel('Accuracy')
plt.legend(loc='lower right')
plt.show()
```

Following is the output of the preceding code. We first look at Softmax per iteration:

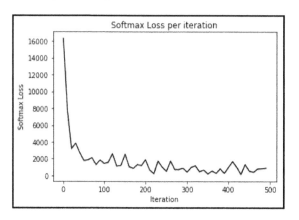

An example of loss decrease

We look at the train and text accuracy next:

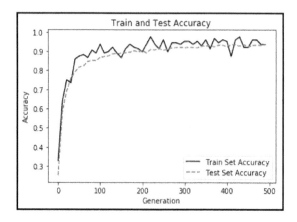

An example of train and test accuracy increase

How it works...

Using ConvNets, we increased our performance on the MNIST dataset reaching almost 95 percent accuracy. Our ConvNet consists of two layers combining convolutions, ReLU, and maxpooling, followed by two fully connected layers with dropout. Training happens in batches of size 128 with Adam used as an optimizer, a learning rate of 0.001, and a maximum number of 500 iterations.

Creating a ConvNet to classify CIFAR-10

In this recipe, you will learn how to do classify images taken from CIFAR-10. The CIFAR-10 dataset consists of 60,000 32 x 32 color images in 10 classes, with 6,000 images per class. There are 50,000 training images and 10,000 test images. The following image is taken from `https://www.cs.toronto.edu/~kriz/cifar.html`:

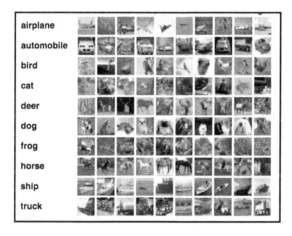

Examples of CIFAR images

Getting ready

In this recipe, we use `tflearn`--a higher-level framework--which abstracts some of the TensorFlow internals and allows us to focus on the definition of deep networks. TFLearn is available at `http://tflearn.org/` and this code is part of the standard distribution. (`https://github.com/tflearn/tflearn/tree/master/examples`)

How to do it...

We proceed with the recipe as follows:

1. Import a few `utils` and core layers for ConvNets, `dropout`, `fully_connected`, and `max_pool`. In addition, import a few modules useful for image processing and image augmentation. Note that TFLearn provides some already defined higher-level layers for ConvNets and this allows us to focus on the definition of our code:

```
from __future__ import division, print_function, absolute_import
import tflearn
from tflearn.data_utils import shuffle, to_categorical
from tflearn.layers.core import input_data, dropout,
fully_connected
from tflearn.layers.conv import conv_2d, max_pool_2d
from tflearn.layers.estimator import regression
from tflearn.data_preprocessing import ImagePreprocessing
from tflearn.data_augmentation import ImageAugmentation
```

2. Load the CIFAR-10 data and separate it into X train data, Y train labels, `X_test` for test, and `Y_test` for test labels. It might be useful to shuffle X and Y to avoid depending on a particular data configuration. The last step is to perform one-hot encoding for both X and Y:

```
# Data loading and preprocessing
from tflearn.datasets import cifar10
(X, Y), (X_test, Y_test) = cifar10.load_data()
X, Y = shuffle(X, Y)
Y = to_categorical(Y, 10)
Y_test = to_categorical(Y_test, 10)
```

3. Use `ImagePreprocessing()` for Zero Center (with mean computed over the whole dataset) and for STD Normalization (with std computed over the whole dataset). The TFLearn data stream is designed to speed up training by preprocessing data on CPU while GPU is performing model training.

```
# Real-time data preprocessing
img_prep = ImagePreprocessing()
img_prep.add_featurewise_zero_center()
img_prep.add_featurewise_stdnorm()
```

4. Augment the dataset by performing random flip right and left and by random rotation. This step is a simple trick used to increase the data available for the training:

```
# Real-time data augmentation
img_aug = ImageAugmentation()
img_aug.add_random_flip_leftright()
img_aug.add_random_rotation(max_angle=25.)
```

5. Create the convolutional network with the images preparation and augmentation defined earlier. The network consists of three convolutional layers. The first one uses 32 convolutional filters, with size of filters 3 and activation function ReLU. After that, there is a max_pool layer for the downsizing. Then there are two convolutional filters in cascade with 64 convolutional filters, with size of filters 3 and activation function ReLU. After that, there is a max_pool for the downsizing and a fully connected network with 512 neurons with activation function ReLU followed by a dropout with probability 50 percent. The last layer is a fully connected network with 10 neurons and activation function softmax to determine the category of the handwritten digits. Note that this particular type of ConvNet is known to be very effective with CIFAR-10. In this particular case, we use the Adam optimizer with categorical_crossentropy and learning rate 0.001:

```
# Convolutional network building
network = input_data(shape=[None, 32, 32, 3],
                     data_preprocessing=img_prep,
                     data_augmentation=img_aug)
network = conv_2d(network, 32, 3, activation='relu')
network = max_pool_2d(network, 2)
network = conv_2d(network, 64, 3, activation='relu')
network = conv_2d(network, 64, 3, activation='relu')
network = max_pool_2d(network, 2)
network = fully_connected(network, 512, activation='relu')
network = dropout(network, 0.5)
network = fully_connected(network, 10, activation='softmax')
network = regression(network, optimizer='adam',
                     loss='categorical_crossentropy',
                     learning_rate=0.001)
```

6. Instantiate the ConvNet and run the train for 50 epochs with `batch_size=96`:

```
# Train using classifier
model = tflearn.DNN(network, tensorboard_verbose=0)
model.fit(X, Y, n_epoch=50, shuffle=True, validation_set=(X_test,
Y_test),
          show_metric=True, batch_size=96, run_id='cifar10_cnn')
```

How it works...

TFLearn hides many of the implementation details exposed by TensorFlow and, in many cases, it allows us to focus on the definition of the ConvNet with a higher level of abstraction. Our pipeline reaches an accuracy of 88 percent in 50 iterations. The following image is a snapshot of the execution in a Jupyter notebook:

```
In [4]:   # Convolutional network building
          network = input_data(shape=[None, 32, 32, 3],
                               data_preprocessing=img_prep,
                               data_augmentation=img_aug)
          network = conv_2d(network, 32, 3, activation='relu')
          network = max_pool_2d(network, 2)
          network = conv_2d(network, 64, 3, activation='relu')
          network = conv_2d(network, 64, 3, activation='relu')
          network = max_pool_2d(network, 2)
          network = fully_connected(network, 512, activation='relu')
          network = dropout(network, 0.5)
          network = fully_connected(network, 10, activation='softmax')
          network = regression(network, optimizer='adam',
                               loss='categorical_crossentropy',
                               learning_rate=0.001)


In [5]:   # Train using classifier
          model = tflearn.DNN(network, tensorboard_verbose=0)
          model.fit(X, Y, n_epoch=50, shuffle=True, validation_set=(X_test, Y_test),
                    show_metric=True, batch_size=96, run_id='cifar10_cnn')

          Training Step: 26049  | total loss: 0.32852 | time: 119.623s
          | Adam | epoch: 050 | loss: 0.32852 - acc: 0.8853 -- iter: 49920/50000
          Training Step: 26050  | total loss: 0.32454 | time: 127.685s
          | Adam | epoch: 050 | loss: 0.32454 - acc: 0.8853 | val_loss: 0.64020 - v
          al_acc: 0.8192 -- iter: 50000/50000
          --
```

An example of Jupyter execution for CIFAR10 classification

There's more...

To install TFLearn, see the Installation Guide (`http://tflearn.org/installation`) and if you want to see more examples, there is a long list of already cooked solutions available online (`http://tflearn.org/examples/`).

Transferring style with VGG19 for image repainting

In this recipe, you will teach a computer how to paint. The key idea is to have a painting model image from which the neural network infers the painting style. This style is then transferred to a another picture that is repainted accordingly. The recipe is a modification of the code developed by log0 and available online (`https://github.com/log0/neural-style-painting/blob/master/TensorFlow%20Implementation%20of%20A%20Neural%20Algorithm%20of%20Artistic%20Style.ipynb`).

Getting ready

We are going to implement the algorithm described in the paper, *A Neural Algorithm of Artistic Style* (`https://arxiv.org/abs/1508.06576`) by Leon A. Gatys, Alexander S. Ecker, and Matthias Bethge. So, it would be good to read the paper first (`https://arxiv.org/abs/1508.06576`). This recipe will reuse a pretrained model VGG19 available online (`http://www.vlfeat.org/matconvnet/models/beta16/imagenet-vgg-verydeep-19.mat`), which should be downloaded locally. Our style image will be a famous painting of Van Gogh available online (`https://commons.wikimedia.org/wiki/File:VanGogh-starry_night.jpg`), and our content image is a picture of Marilyn Monroe downloaded from Wikipedia (`https://commons.wikimedia.org/wiki/File:Marilyn_Monroe_in_1952.jpg`). The content image will be repainted according to the *Van Gogh* style.

How to do it...

Let us start with the recipe:

1. Import a few modules such as numpy, scipy, tensorflow, and matplotlib. Then import PIL to manipulate images. Note that as this code runs on a Jupyter notebook that you can download from online, the fragment %matplotlib inline has been added:

```
import os
import sys
import numpy as np
import scipy.io
import scipy.misc
import tensorflow as tf
import matplotlib.pyplot as plt
from matplotlib.pyplot
import imshow
from PIL
import Image %matplotlib inline from __future__
import division
```

2. Then, set the input path for the image used to learn the style and for the content image to be repainted according to the style:

```
OUTPUT_DIR = 'output/'
# Style image
STYLE_IMAGE = 'data/StarryNight.jpg'
# Content image to be repainted
CONTENT_IMAGE = 'data/Marilyn_Monroe_in_1952.jpg'
```

3. Then we set up the noise ratio used during the image generation and the emphasis we would like to put on content loss and on style loss when repainting the content image. In addition to that, we store the path to the pretrained VGG model and the mean computed during the VGG pretraining. This mean is already known and it is subtracted from the input to the VGG model:

```
# how much noise is in the image
NOISE_RATIO = 0.6
# How much emphasis on content loss.
BETA = 5
# How much emphasis on style loss.
ALPHA = 100
# the VGG 19-layer pre-trained model
VGG_MODEL = 'data/imagenet-vgg-verydeep-19.mat'
```

```
# The mean used when the VGG was trained
# It is subtracted from the input to the VGG model. MEAN_VALUES =
np.array([123.68, 116.779, 103.939]).reshape((1,1,1,3))
```

4. Show the content image just to understand how it is:

```
content_image = scipy.misc.imread(CONTENT_IMAGE)
imshow(content_image)
```

Here is the output of the preceding code (note that this image is in `https://commons.wikimedia.org/wiki/File:Marilyn_Monroe_in_1952.jpg`):

5. Resize the style image and show it just to understand how it is. Note that the content image and the style image have now the same size and the same number of color channels:

```
style_image = scipy.misc.imread(STYLE_IMAGE)
# Get shape of target and make the style image the same
target_shape = content_image.shape
print "target_shape=", target_shape
print "style_shape=", style_image.shape
#ratio = target_shape[1] / style_image.shape[1]
#print "resize ratio=", ratio
style_image = scipy.misc.imresize(style_image, target_shape)
scipy.misc.imsave(STYLE_IMAGE, style_image)
imshow(style_image)
```

Here is the output of the preceding code:

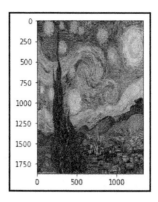

An example of Vicent Van Gogh painting as seen in https://commons.wikimedia.org/wiki/File:VanGogh-starry_night_ballance1.jpg

6. The next step is to define the VGG model as described in the original paper. Note that the deep learning network is rather complex as it combines multiple ConvNet layers with ReLU activation function and max pooling. An additional note is that in the original paper for Transfer Styling (*A Neural Algorithm of Artistic Style* by Leon A. Gatys, Alexander S. Ecker, and Matthias Bethge), many experiments show that average pooling is actually outperforming max pooling. So, we will use average pooling instead:

```
def load_vgg_model(path, image_height, image_width,
color_channels):
    """
    Returns the VGG model as defined in the paper
        0 is conv1_1 (3, 3, 3, 64)
        1 is relu
        2 is conv1_2 (3, 3, 64, 64)
        3 is relu
        4 is maxpool
        5 is conv2_1 (3, 3, 64, 128)
        6 is relu
        7 is conv2_2 (3, 3, 128, 128)
        8 is relu
        9 is maxpool
        10 is conv3_1 (3, 3, 128, 256)
        11 is relu
        12 is conv3_2 (3, 3, 256, 256)
        13 is relu
        14 is conv3_3 (3, 3, 256, 256)
        15 is relu
```

```
            16 is conv3_4 (3, 3, 256, 256)
            17 is relu
            18 is maxpool
            19 is conv4_1 (3, 3, 256, 512)
            20 is relu
            21 is conv4_2 (3, 3, 512, 512)
            22 is relu
            23 is conv4_3 (3, 3, 512, 512)
            24 is relu
            25 is conv4_4 (3, 3, 512, 512)
            26 is relu
            27 is maxpool
            28 is conv5_1 (3, 3, 512, 512)
            29 is relu
            30 is conv5_2 (3, 3, 512, 512)
            31 is relu
            32 is conv5_3 (3, 3, 512, 512)
            33 is relu
            34 is conv5_4 (3, 3, 512, 512)
            35 is relu
            36 is maxpool
            37 is fullyconnected (7, 7, 512, 4096)        38 is relu
            39 is fullyconnected (1, 1, 4096, 4096)
            40 is relu
            41 is fullyconnected (1, 1, 4096, 1000)
            42 is softmax
    """
    vgg = scipy.io.loadmat(path)
    vgg_layers = vgg['layers']

    def _weights(layer, expected_layer_name):
        """        Return the weights and bias from the VGG model for
a given layer.
    """
        W = vgg_layers[0][layer][0][0][0][0][0]
        b = vgg_layers[0][layer][0][0][0][0][1]
        layer_name = vgg_layers[0][layer][0][0][-2]
        assert layer_name == expected_layer_name
        return W, b
    def _relu(conv2d_layer):
        """
        Return the RELU function wrapped over a TensorFlow layer.
Expects a
        Conv2d layer input.
        """
        return tf.nn.relu(conv2d_layer)

    def _conv2d(prev_layer, layer, layer_name):
```

```
        """
        Return the Conv2D layer using the weights, biases from the
VGG
        model at 'layer'.
        """
        W, b = _weights(layer, layer_name)
        W = tf.constant(W)
        b = tf.constant(np.reshape(b, (b.size)))
        return tf.nn.conv2d(
            prev_layer, filter=W, strides=[1, 1, 1, 1],
padding='SAME') + b

    def _conv2d_relu(prev_layer, layer, layer_name):
        """
        Return the Conv2D + RELU layer using the weights, biases
from the VGG
        model at 'layer'.
        """
        return _relu(_conv2d(prev_layer, layer, layer_name))

    def _avgpool(prev_layer):
        """
        Return the AveragePooling layer.
        """
        return tf.nn.avg_pool(prev_layer, ksize=[1, 2, 2, 1],
strides=[1, 2, 2, 1], padding='SAME')

    # Constructs the graph model.
    graph = {}
    graph['input']   = tf.Variable(np.zeros((1,
                                             image_height,
image_width, color_channels)),
                                   dtype = 'float32')
    graph['conv1_1'] = _conv2d_relu(graph['input'], 0, 'conv1_1')
    graph['conv1_2'] = _conv2d_relu(graph['conv1_1'], 2, 'conv1_2')
    graph['avgpool1'] = _avgpool(graph['conv1_2'])
    graph['conv2_1'] = _conv2d_relu(graph['avgpool1'], 5,
'conv2_1')
    graph['conv2_2'] = _conv2d_relu(graph['conv2_1'], 7, 'conv2_2')
    graph['avgpool2'] = _avgpool(graph['conv2_2'])
    graph['conv3_1'] = _conv2d_relu(graph['avgpool2'], 10,
'conv3_1')
    graph['conv3_2'] = _conv2d_relu(graph['conv3_1'], 12,
'conv3_2')
    graph['conv3_3'] = _conv2d_relu(graph['conv3_2'], 14,
'conv3_3')
    graph['conv3_4'] = _conv2d_relu(graph['conv3_3'], 16,
'conv3_4')
```

```
    graph['avgpool3'] = _avgpool(graph['conv3_4'])
    graph['conv4_1'] = _conv2d_relu(graph['avgpool3'], 19,
'conv4_1')
    graph['conv4_2'] = _conv2d_relu(graph['conv4_1'], 21,
'conv4_2')
    graph['conv4_3'] = _conv2d_relu(graph['conv4_2'], 23,
'conv4_3')
    graph['conv4_4'] = _conv2d_relu(graph['conv4_3'], 25,
'conv4_4')
    graph['avgpool4'] = _avgpool(graph['conv4_4'])
    graph['conv5_1'] = _conv2d_relu(graph['avgpool4'], 28,
'conv5_1')
    graph['conv5_2'] = _conv2d_relu(graph['conv5_1'], 30,
'conv5_2')
    graph['conv5_3'] = _conv2d_relu(graph['conv5_2'], 32,
'conv5_3')
    graph['conv5_4'] = _conv2d_relu(graph['conv5_3'], 34,
'conv5_4')
    graph['avgpool5'] = _avgpool(graph['conv5_4'])
    return graph
```

7. Define the content `loss` function as it has been described in the original paper:

```
def content_loss_func(sess, model):
""" Content loss function as defined in the paper. """

def _content_loss(p, x):
# N is the number of filters (at layer l).
N = p.shape[3]
# M is the height times the width of the feature map (at layer l).
M = p.shape[1] * p.shape[2] return (1 / (4 * N * M)) *
tf.reduce_sum(tf.pow(x - p, 2))
return _content_loss(sess.run(model['conv4_2']), model['conv4_2'])
```

8. Define which VGG layers we are going to reuse. If we would like to have softer features, we will need to increase the weight of higher layers (`conv5_1`) and decrease the weight of the lower layers (`conv1_1`). If we would like to have harder features, we need to do the opposite:

```
STYLE_LAYERS = [
('conv1_1', 0.5),
('conv2_1', 1.0),
('conv3_1', 1.5),
('conv4_1', 3.0),
('conv5_1', 4.0),
]
```

9. Define the style loss function as it has been described in the original paper:

```
def style_loss_func(sess, model):
    """
    Style loss function as defined in the paper.
    """

    def _gram_matrix(F, N, M):
        """
        The gram matrix G.
        """
        Ft = tf.reshape(F, (M, N))
        return tf.matmul(tf.transpose(Ft), Ft)

    def _style_loss(a, x):
        """
        The style loss calculation.
        """
        # N is the number of filters (at layer l).
        N = a.shape[3]
        # M is the height times the width of the feature map (at layer l).
        M = a.shape[1] * a.shape[2]
        # A is the style representation of the original image (at layer l).
        A = _gram_matrix(a, N, M)
        # G is the style representation of the generated image (at layer l).
        G = _gram_matrix(x, N, M)
        result = (1 / (4 * N**2 * M**2)) * tf.reduce_sum(tf.pow(G - A, 2))
        return result
    E = [_style_loss(sess.run(model[layer_name]), model[layer_name])
            for layer_name, _ in STYLE_LAYERS]
    W = [w for _, w in STYLE_LAYERS]
    loss = sum([W[l] * E[l] for l in range(len(STYLE_LAYERS))])
    return loss
```

10. Define a function to generate a noise image and intermix it with the content image with a given ratio. Define two auxiliary methods to preprocess and save images:

```
def generate_noise_image(content_image, noise_ratio = NOISE_RATIO):
    """   Returns a noise image intermixed with the content image at a certain
ratio.
    """
    noise_image = np.random.uniform(
            -20, 20,
            (1,
            content_image[0].shape[0],
            content_image[0].shape[1],
```

```
        content_image[0].shape[2])).astype('float32')
    # White noise image from the content representation. Take a weighted
average
    # of the values
    input_image = noise_image * noise_ratio + content_image * (1 -
noise_ratio)
    return input_image

def process_image(image):
    # Resize the image for convnet input, there is no change but just
    # add an extra dimension.
    image = np.reshape(image, ((1,) + image.shape))
    # Input to the VGG model expects the mean to be subtracted.
    image = image - MEAN_VALUES
    return image

def save_image(path, image):
    # Output should add back the mean.
    image = image + MEAN_VALUES
    # Get rid of the first useless dimension, what remains is the image.
    image = image[0]
    image = np.clip(image, 0, 255).astype('uint8')
    scipy.misc.imsave(path, image)
```

11. Start a TensorFlow interactive session:

```
    sess = tf.InteractiveSession()
```

12. Load the processed content image and show it:

```
    content_image = load_image(CONTENT_IMAGE) imshow(content_image[0])
```

We get the output of the preceding code as follows (note that we used an image from
https://commons.wikimedia.org/wiki/File:Marilyn_Monroe_in_1952.jpg) :

13. Load the processed style image and show it:

```
style_image = load_image(STYLE_IMAGE) imshow(style_image[0])
```

The out is as follows:

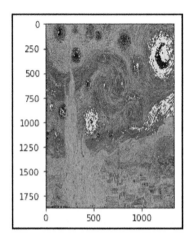

14. Load the `model` and show it:

```
model = load_vgg_model(VGG_MODEL, style_image[0].shape[0],
style_image[0].shape[1], style_image[0].shape[2]) print(model)
```

15. Generate a random noise image that is used to bootstrap the repainting:

```
input_image = generate_noise_image(content_image)
imshow(input_image[0])
```

16. Run TensorFlow sessions:

```
sess.run(tf.initialize_all_variables())
```

17. Construct the `content_loss` and `sytle_loss` with respective images:

```
# Construct content_loss using content_image.
sess.run(model['input'].assign(content_image))
content_loss = content_loss_func(sess, model)
# Construct style_loss using style_image.
sess.run(model['input'].assign(style_image))
style_loss = style_loss_func(sess, model)
```

18. Construct the `total_loss` as weighted combination of `content_loss` and `sytle_loss`:

```
# Construct total_loss as weighted combination of content_loss and
sytle_loss
total_loss = BETA * content_loss + ALPHA * style_loss
```

19. Build an optimizer to minimize the total loss. In this case, we adopt the Adam optimizer:

```
# The content is built from one layer, while the style is from five
# layers. Then we minimize the total_loss
optimizer = tf.train.AdamOptimizer(2.0)
train_step = optimizer.minimize(total_loss)
```

20. Bootstrap the network with the input image:

```
sess.run(tf.initialize_all_variables())
sess.run(model['input'].assign(input_image))
```

21. Run the model for a fixed number of iterations and produce intermediate repainted images:

```
sess.run(tf.initialize_all_variables())
sess.run(model['input'].assign(input_image))
print "started iteration"
for it in range(ITERATIONS):
   sess.run(train_step)
   print it , " "
   if it%100 == 0:
       # Print every 100 iteration.
       mixed_image = sess.run(model['input'])
       print('Iteration %d' % (it))
       print('sum : ',
sess.run(tf.reduce_sum(mixed_image)))
       print('cost: ', sess.run(total_loss))
       if not os.path.exists(OUTPUT_DIR):
           os.mkdir(OUTPUT_DIR)
       filename = 'output/%d.png' % (it)
       save_image(filename, mixed_image)
```

22. In this image, we show how the content image has been repainted after 200, 400, and 600 iterations:

An example of style transfer

How it works...

In this recipe, we have seen how to use style transfer to repaint a content image. A style image has been provided as input to a neural network, which learned the key aspects defining the style adopted by the painter. These aspects have been used to transfer the style to the content image.

There's more...

Style transfer has been an area of active research since the original proposal in 2015. Many new ideas have been proposed to accelerate the computation and extend the style transfer to video analysis. Among many, two results are worth mentioning

The article, fast style transfer by Logan Engstrom `https://github.com/lengstrom/fast-style-transfer/`, introduced a very fast implementation that works out of the box also with videos.

The website, `https://deepart.io/`, allows you to play with your own images and repaint your picture in the style of your favorite artist. An android app, an iPhone app, and a web app are also available.

Using a pretrained VGG16 net for transfer learning

In this recipe, we will discuss transfer learning, a very powerful deep learning technique that has many applications in different domains. The intuition is very simple and can be explained with an analogy. Suppose you want to learn a new language, say Spanish, then it could be useful to start from what you already know in a different language, say English.

Following this line of thinking, computer vision researchers now commonly use pretrained CNNs to generate representations for novel tasks, where the dataset may not be large enough to train an entire CNN from scratch. Another common tactic is to take the pretrained ImageNet network and then to fine-tune the entire network to the novel task. The example proposed here has been inspired by Francois Chollet in a famous blog posting for Keras. (`https://blog.keras.io/building-powerful-image-classification-models-using-very-little-data.html`)

Getting ready

The idea is to use the VGG16 network pretrained on a large dataset such as ImageNet. Note that training could be rather computationally expensive and therefore makes sense to reuse an already pretrained network:

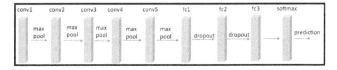

A VGG16 Network

So, how to use a VGG16? Keras makes it easy as the library has a standard VGG16 application available as a library and precomputed weights are automatically downloaded. Note that we explicitly omit the last layer and replace it with our custom layer, which will be fine-tuned on the top of the prebuilt VGG16. In this example, you will learn how to classify dogs and cats images available from Kaggle.

How to do it...

We proceed with the recipe as follows:

1. Download the dogs and cats data from Kaggle
   (https://www.kaggle.com/c/dogs-vs-cats/data) and create a data directory
   containing two subdirectories, train and validation, each of which has two
   additional subdirectory, dogs and cats respectively.

2. Import the Keras modules that will be used later for our computation and save a
   few useful constants:

```
from keras import applications
from keras.preprocessing.image import ImageDataGenerator
from keras import optimizers
from keras.models import Sequential, Model
from keras.layers import Dropout, Flatten, Dense
from keras import optimizers
img_width, img_height = 256, 256
batch_size = 16
epochs = 50
train_data_dir = 'data/dogs_and_cats/train'
validation_data_dir = 'data/dogs_and_cats/validation'
#OUT CATEGORIES
OUT_CATEGORIES=1
#number of train, validation samples
nb_train_samples = 2000
nb_validation_samples =
```

3. Load the pretrained on the ImageNet VGG16 network and omit the last layer
   because we will add a custom classification network on the top of the prebuilt
   VGG16 and replace the last classification layer:

```
# load the VGG16 model pretrained on imagenet
base_model = applications.VGG16(weights = "imagenet",
include_top=False, input_shape = (img_width, img_height, 3))
base_model.summary()
```

Here is the output of the preceding code:

```
Layer (type)                    Output Shape              Param #
=================================================================
input_1 (InputLayer)            (None, 256, 256, 3)       0

block1_conv1 (Conv2D)           (None, 256, 256, 64)      1792

block1_conv2 (Conv2D)           (None, 256, 256, 64)      36928

block1_pool (MaxPooling2D)      (None, 128, 128, 64)      0

block2_conv1 (Conv2D)           (None, 128, 128, 128)     73856

block2_conv2 (Conv2D)           (None, 128, 128, 128)     147584

block2_pool (MaxPooling2D)      (None, 64, 64, 128)       0

block3_conv1 (Conv2D)           (None, 64, 64, 256)       295168

block3_conv2 (Conv2D)           (None, 64, 64, 256)       590080

block3_conv3 (Conv2D)           (None, 64, 64, 256)       590080

block3_pool (MaxPooling2D)      (None, 32, 32, 256)       0

block4_conv1 (Conv2D)           (None, 32, 32, 512)       1180160

block4_conv2 (Conv2D)           (None, 32, 32, 512)       2359808

block4_conv3 (Conv2D)           (None, 32, 32, 512)       2359808

block4_pool (MaxPooling2D)      (None, 16, 16, 512)       0

block5_conv1 (Conv2D)           (None, 16, 16, 512)       2359808

block5_conv2 (Conv2D)           (None, 16, 16, 512)       2359808

block5_conv3 (Conv2D)           (None, 16, 16, 512)       2359808

block5_pool (MaxPooling2D)      (None, 8, 8, 512)         0
=================================================================
Total params: 14,714,688
Trainable params: 14,714,688
Non-trainable params: 0
```

4. Freeze a certain number of lower layers for the pretrained VGG16 network. In this case, we decide to freeze the initial 15 layers:

```
# Freeze the 15 lower layers for layer in base_model.layers[:15]:
layer.trainable = False
```

5. Add a custom set of top layers for classification:

```
# Add custom to layers # build a classifier model to put on top of
the convolutional model top_model = Sequential()
top_model.add(Flatten(input_shape=base_model.output_shape[1:]))
```

```
top_model.add(Dense(256, activation='relu'))
top_model.add(Dropout(0.5)) top_model.add(Dense(OUT_CATEGORIES,
activation='sigmoid'))
```

6. The custom network should be pretrained separately and here, we omit this part for the sake of simplicity, leaving this task to the reader:

```
#top_model.load_weights(top_model_weights_path)
```

7. Create a new network that is the juxtaposition of the pretrained VGG16 network and our pretrained custom network:

```
# creating the final model, a composition of
# pre-trained and
model = Model(inputs=base_model.input,
outputs=top_model(base_model.output))
# compile the model
model.compile(loss = "binary_crossentropy", optimizer =
optimizers.SGD(lr=0.0001, momentum=0.9), metrics=["accuracy"])
```

8. Retrain the juxtaposed new model still keeping the 15 lowest layers of VGG16 frozen. In this particular example, we also use an Image Augmentator to increase our training set:

```
# Initiate the train and test generators with data Augmentation
train_datagen = ImageDataGenerator(
rescale = 1./255,
horizontal_flip = True)
test_datagen = ImageDataGenerator(rescale=1. / 255)
train_generator = train_datagen.flow_from_directory(
    train_data_dir,
    target_size=(img_height, img_width),
    batch_size=batch_size,
    class_mode='binary')
validation_generator = test_datagen.flow_from_directory(
    validation_data_dir,
    target_size=(img_height, img_width),
    batch_size=batch_size,
    class_mode='binary', shuffle=False)
model.fit_generator(
    train_generator,
    steps_per_epoch=nb_train_samples // batch_size,
    epochs=epochs,
    validation_data=validation_generator,
    validation_steps=nb_validation_samples // batch_size,
    verbose=2, workers=12)
```

9. Evaluate the results on the juxtaposed network:

```
score = model.evaluate_generator(validation_generator,
nb_validation_samples/batch_size)
scores = model.predict_generator(validation_generator,
nb_validation_samples/batch_size)
```

How it works...

A standard VGG16 network has been pretrained on the whole ImageNet with precomputed weights downloaded from the Internet. This network has been then juxtaposed with a custom network that has been also trained separately. Then, the juxtaposed network has been retrained as a whole, keeping 15 lower layers of the VGG16 frozen.

This combination is very effective. It allows us to save significant computational power and reuse the work already performed for VGG16 by performing a transfer learning of what the network has learned on ImageNet, apply this learning to our new specific domain, and therefore perform a fine-tuning classification task.

There's more...

There are a few rules of thumb to consider according to the specific classification task:

- If the new dataset is small and similar to the ImageNet dataset, then we can freeze all the VGG16 networks and retrain only the custom network. In this way, we also minimize the risk of overfitting for the juxtaposed network:

  # Freeze all lower layers for layer in `base_model.layers: layer.trainable = False`

- If the new dataset is large and similar to the ImageNet dataset, then we can retrain the whole juxtaposed network. We have still maintained the precomputed weights as a starting point and perform a few iterations for the fine-tuning:

  # UnFreeze all lower layers for layer in `model.layers: layer.trainable = True`

- If the new dataset is very different from the ImageNet dataset, in practice it might be still good to initialize with weights from a pretrained model. In this case, we would have enough data and confidence to fine-tune through the entire network. More information can be found online at `http://cs231n.github.io/transfer-learning/`.

Creating a DeepDream network

Google trained a neural network on **ImageNet for the Large Scale Visual Recognition Challenge (ILSVRC)** in 2014 and made it open source in July 2015. The original algorithm is presented in *Going Deeper with Convolutions, Christian Szegedy, Wei Liu, Yangqing Jia, Pierre Sermanet, Scott Reed, Dragomir Anguelov, Dumitru Erhan, Vincent Vanhoucke e Andrew Rabinovich (https://arxiv.org/abs/1409.4842)* . The network learned a representation of each image. The lower layers learned low-level features, such as lines and edges, while the higher layers learned more sophisticated patterns such as eyes, noses, mouths, and so on. Therefore, if we try to represent a higher level in the network, we will see a mix of different features extracted from the original ImageNet such as the eyes of a bird and the mouth of a dog. With this in mind, if we take a new image and try to maximize the similarity with an upper layer of the network, then the result is a new visionary image. In this visionary image, some of the patterns learned by the higher layers are dreamt (for example, imagined) in the original image. Here is an example of such visionary images:

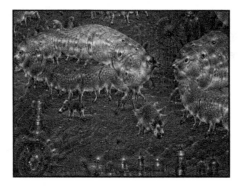

An example of Google Deep Dreams as seen in `https://commons.wikimedia.org/wiki/File:Aurelia-aurita-3-0009.jpg`

Getting ready

Download the pretrained Inception model from online (`https://github.com/martinwicke/
tensorflow-tutorial/blob/master/tensorflow_inception_graph.pb`).

How to do it...

We proceed with the recipes as follows:

1. Import `numpy` for numerical computation, `functools` to define partial functions
   with one or more argument already filled in, Pillow for image manipulation, and
   `matplotlib` to render images:

   ```
   import numpy as np from functools
   import partial import PIL.Image
   import tensorflow as tf
   import matplotlib.pyplot as plt
   ```

2. Set up the path for the content image and the pretrained model. Start with a seed
   image that is just random noise:

   ```
   content_image = 'data/gulli.jpg'
   # start with a gray image with a little noise
   img_noise = np.random.uniform(size=(224,224,3)) + 100.0
   model_fn = 'data/tensorflow_inception_graph.pb'
   ```

3. Load the Inception network downloaded from the internet in a graph. Initialize a
   TensorFlow session, load the graph with `FastGFile(..)`, and parse the graph
   with `ParseFromstring(..)`. After that, create an input as placeholder with the
   `placeholder(..)` method. The `imagenet_mean` is a precomputed constant that
   will be removed from our content image to normalize the data. In fact, this is the
   mean value observed during training and the normalization allows faster
   convergence. The value will be subtracted from the input and stored in a
   `t_preprocessed` variable, which is then used to load the graph definition:

```
# load the graph
graph = tf.Graph()
sess = tf.InteractiveSession(graph=graph)
with tf.gfile.FastGFile(model_fn, 'rb') as f:
        graph_def = tf.GraphDef()
        graph_def.ParseFromString(f.read())
t_input = tf.placeholder(np.float32, name='input') # define
```

```
the input tensor
imagenet_mean = 117.0
t_preprocessed = tf.expand_dims(t_input-imagenet_mean, 0)
tf.import_graph_def(graph_def, {'input':t_preprocessed})
```

4. Define some `util` functions to visualize the image and transform the TF-graph generating function into regular Python functions (see the following example to resize):

```
# helper
#pylint: disable=unused-variable
def showarray(a):
    a = np.uint8(np.clip(a, 0, 1)*255)
    plt.imshow(a)
    plt.show()
def visstd(a, s=0.1):
    '''Normalize the image range for visualization'''
    return (a-a.mean())/max(a.std(), 1e-4)*s + 0.5

def T(layer):
    '''Helper for getting layer output tensor'''
    return graph.get_tensor_by_name("import/%s:0"%layer)

def tffunc(*argtypes):
    '''Helper that transforms TF-graph generating function into a regular
one.
    See "resize" function below.
    '''
    placeholders = list(map(tf.placeholder, argtypes))
    def wrap(f):
        out = f(*placeholders)
        def wrapper(*args, **kw):
            return out.eval(dict(zip(placeholders, args)),
session=kw.get('session'))
        return wrapper
    return wrap

def resize(img, size):
    img = tf.expand_dims(img, 0)
    return tf.image.resize_bilinear(img, size)[0,:,:,:]
resize = tffunc(np.float32, np.int32)(resize)
```

5. Compute the gradient ascent over the image. To increase the efficiency, apply a tiled computation in which separate gradient ascents are computed on different tiles. Random shifts are applied to the image to blur tile boundaries over multiple iterations:

```
def calc_grad_tiled(img, t_grad, tile_size=512):
    '''Compute the value of tensor t_grad over the image in a tiled way.
    Random shifts are applied to the image to blur tile boundaries over
    multiple iterations.'''
    sz = tile_size
    h, w = img.shape[:2]
    sx, sy = np.random.randint(sz, size=2)
    img_shift = np.roll(np.roll(img, sx, 1), sy, 0)
    grad = np.zeros_like(img)
    for y in range(0, max(h-sz//2, sz),sz):
        for x in range(0, max(w-sz//2, sz),sz):
            sub = img_shift[y:y+sz,x:x+sz]
            g = sess.run(t_grad, {t_input:sub})
            grad[y:y+sz,x:x+sz] = g

    return np.roll(np.roll(grad, -sx, 1), -sy, 0)
```

6. Define the optimization object to reduce the mean of our input layer. The `gradient` function allows us to compute the symbolic gradient of our optimized tensor by considering the input tensor. For efficiency, the image is split in a number of octaves, which are then resized and added to an array of octaves. Then, for each octave, we use the `calc_grad_tiled` function:

```
def render_deepdream(t_obj, img0=img_noise,
                     iter_n=10, step=1.5, octave_n=4, octave_scale=1.4):
    t_score = tf.reduce_mean(t_obj) # defining the optimization objective
    t_grad = tf.gradients(t_score, t_input)[0] # behold the power of automatic
differentiation!
    # split the image into a number of octaves
    img = img0
    octaves = []
    for _ in range(octave_n-1):
        hw = img.shape[:2]
        lo = resize(img,
np.int32(np.float32(hw)/octave_scale))
        hi = img-resize(lo, hw)
        img = lo
        octaves.append(hi)
    # generate details octave by octave
    for octave in range(octave_n):
        if octave>0:
```

```
        hi = octaves[-octave]
        img = resize(img, hi.shape[:2])+hi
    for _ in range(iter_n):
        g = calc_grad_tiled(img, t_grad)
        img += g*(step / (np.abs(g).mean()+1e-7))
        #this will usually be like 3 or 4 octaves
        #Step 5 output deep dream image via matplotlib
    showarray(img/255.0)
```

7. Load a specific content image and start dreaming. In this example, the face of the author has been transformed into something resembling a wolf:

An example of Deep Dream transformation. One of the authors transformed into a wolf

How it works...

Neural networks store abstractions of the training images: lower layers memorize features such as lines and edges, while higher layers memorize more sophisticated images features such as eyes, faces, and noses. By applying a gradient ascent process, we maximize the loss function and facilitate the discovery of a content image of patterns similar to the ones memorized by higher layers. This results into a dreaming where the network sees trippy images.

There's more...

Many websites allow you to play directly with DeepDreaming. Among others, I really like DeepArt.io (https://deepart.io/), which allows you to upload a content image and a style image and perform the learning on the cloud.

See also

After the initial results presented in 2015, many new additional papers and blog postings were presented about DeepDreaming:

- *DeepDream: A code example to visualize Neural Networks*--https://research.googleblog.com/2015/07/deepdream-code-example-for-visualizing.html
- When Robots Hallucinate, LaFrance, Adrienne--https://www.theatlantic.com/technology/archive/2015/09/robots-hallucinate-dream/403498/

   In addition, it might be interesting to understand how to visualize each layer of a pretrained network and get a better intuition of how the net memorizes basic features in lower layers and more complex features in higher layers. An interesting blog posting about this topic is available online:

- How convolutional neural networks see the world--https://blog.keras.io/category/demo.html

5
Advanced Convolutional Neural Networks

In this chapter, we will discuss how **Convolutional Neural Networks** (**CNNs**) are used for deep learning in domains other than images. Our attention will be initially devoted to text analysis and **natural language processing** (**NLP**). In this chapter, we will present a number of recipes for:

- Creating a ConvNet for sentiment analysis
- Inspecting what filters a VGG pre-built network has learned
- Classifying images with VGGNet, ResNet, Inception, and Xception
- Recycling pre-built deep learning models for extracting features
- Very deep Inception-v3 net used for transfer learning
- Generating music with dilated ConvNets, WaveNet, and NSynth
- Answering questions about images (Visual Q&A)
- Classifying videos with pre-trained nets in six different ways

Introduction

In the previous chapter, we saw how to apply ConvNets to images. During this chapter, we will apply similar ideas to texts.

What do a text and an image have in common? At first glance, very little. However, if we represent sentences or documents as a matrix then this matrix is not different from an image matrix where each cell is a pixel. So, the next question is, how can we represent a text as a matrix? Well, it is pretty simple: each row of a matrix is a vector which represents a basic unit of the text. Of course, now we need to define what a basic unit is. A simple choice could be to say that the basic unit is a character. Another choice would be to say that a basic unit is a word, yet another choice is to aggregate similar words together and then denote each aggregation (sometimes called cluster or embedding) with a representative symbol.

 Note that regardless of the specific choice adopted for our basic units, we need to have a 1:1 map from basic units into integer IDs so that a text can be seen as a matrix. For instance, if we have a document with 10 lines of text and each line is a 100-dimensional embedding, then we will represent our text with a matrix 10 x 100. In this very particular *image*, a *pixel* is turned on if that sentence x contains the embedding represented by position y. You might also notice that a text is not really a matrix but more a vector because two words located in adjacent rows of text have very little in common. Indeed, there is a major difference with images where two pixels located in adjacent columns most likely have some correlation.

Now you might wonder: I understand that you represent the text as a vector but, in doing so, we lose the position of the words and this position should be important, shouldn't it?

Well, it turns out that in many real applications knowing whether a sentence contains a particular basic unit (a char, a word, or an aggregate) or not is pretty accurate information, even if we don't memorize where exactly in the sentence this basic unit is located.

Creating a ConvNet for Sentiment Analysis

In this recipe, we will use TFLearn for creating a sentiment analysis deep learning network based on CNNs. As discussed in the previous section, our CNN will be in one dimension. We are going to use the IMDb dataset, a collection of 45,000 highly popular movie reviews for training, and 5,000 for testing.

Getting ready

TFLearn has libraries for automatically downloading the dataset from the network and for facilitating the creation of the ConvNet, so let's go directly to the code.

How to do it...

We proceed with the recipe as follows:

1. Import TensorFlow, `tflearn`, and the modules needed for building our network. Then, Import IMDb libraries and perform one-hot encoding and padding:

```
import tensorflow as tf
import tflearn
from tflearn.layers.core import input_data, dropout, fully_connected
from tflearn.layers.conv import conv_1d, global_max_pool
from tflearn.layers.merge_ops import merge
from tflearn.layers.estimator import regression
from tflearn.data_utils import to_categorical, pad_sequences
from tflearn.datasets import imdb
```

2. Load the dataset, pad the sentences to maxlength with 0s, and perform one-hot encoding on the labels with two values corresponding to the true and one false value. Note that the parameter `n_words` is the number of words to keep in the vocabulary. All extra words are set to unknown. Also, note that trainX and trainY are sparse vectors because each review will most likely contain a subset of the whole set of words:

```
# IMDb Dataset loading
train, test, _ = imdb.load_data(path='imdb.pkl', n_words=10000,
valid_portion=0.1)
trainX, trainY = train
testX, testY = test
#pad the sequence
trainX = pad_sequences(trainX, maxlen=100, value=0.)
testX = pad_sequences(testX, maxlen=100, value=0.)
#one-hot encoding
trainY = to_categorical(trainY, nb_classes=2)
testY = to_categorical(testY, nb_classes=2)
```

3. Print a few dimensions to inspect the just-processed data and understand what the dimension of the problem is:

```
print ("size trainX", trainX.size)
print ("size testX", testX.size)
print ("size testY:", testY.size)
print ("size trainY", trainY.size)
size trainX 2250000
 size testX 250000
 size testY: 5000
 site trainY 45000
```

4. Build an embedding for the text contained in the dataset. Just for now, consider this step as a black box which takes the words and maps them into aggregates (clusters) so that similar words are likely to appear in the same cluster. Note that the vocabulary for the previous steps is discrete and sparse. With the embedding, we will create a map which will embed each word into a continuous dense vector space. Using this vector space representation will give us a continuous, distributed representation of our vocabulary words. How to build embeddings is something that will be discussed in detail when we talk about RNNs:

```
# Build an embedding
network = input_data(shape=[None, 100], name='input')
network = tflearn.embedding(network, input_dim=10000, output_dim=128)
```

5. Build a suitable convnet. We have three convolutional layers. Since we are dealing with a text, we will use one-dimension ConvNets and the layers will act in parallel. Each layer takes a tensor of size 128 (the output of the embeddings) and applies a number of filters (respectively 3, 4, 5) with valid padding, the activation function ReLU, and an L2 regularizer. Then the output of each layer is concatenated with a merge operation. After that, a max pool layer is added, followed by a dropout with a probability of 50%. The final layer is a fully connected one with softmax activation:

```
#Build the convnet
branch1 = conv_1d(network, 128, 3, padding='valid', activation='relu',
regularizer="L2")
branch2 = conv_1d(network, 128, 4, padding='valid', activation='relu',
regularizer="L2")
branch3 = conv_1d(network, 128, 5, padding='valid', activation='relu',
regularizer="L2")
network = merge([branch1, branch2, branch3], mode='concat', axis=1)
network = tf.expand_dims(network, 2)
network = global_max_pool(network)
network = dropout(network, 0.5)
network = fully_connected(network, 2, activation='softmax')
```

6. The learning phase implies the Adam optimizer with `categorical_crossentropy` used as a loss function:

```
network = regression(network, optimizer='adam', learning_rate=0.001,
loss='categorical_crossentropy', name='target')
```

7. Then we run the training with batch_size=32 and observe what is the accuracy reached on the training and validation set. As you can see, we are able to get an accuracy of 79% in predicting what is the sentiment expressed for movie reviews:

```
# Training
model = tflearn.DNN(network, tensorboard_verbose=0)
model.fit(trainX, trainY, n_epoch = 5, shuffle=True, validation_set=(testX,
testY), show_metric=True, batch_size=32)
Training Step: 3519 | total loss: 0.09738 | time: 85.043s
 | Adam | epoch: 005 | loss: 0.09738 - acc: 0.9747 -- iter: 22496/22500
 Training Step: 3520 | total loss: 0.09733 | time: 86.652s
 | Adam | epoch: 005 | loss: 0.09733 - acc: 0.9741 | val_loss: 0.58740 -
val_acc: 0.7944 -- iter: 22500/22500
 --
```

How it works...

One-dimension ConvNets for sentiment analysis are discussed in detail in the paper *Convolutional Neural Networks for Sentence Classification*, Yoon Kim, EMNLP 2014 (https://arxiv.org/abs/1408.5882). Note that the model proposed by the paper retains some pieces of information about the position, thanks to the filter windows operating over consecutive words. The following image extracted from the paper graphically represents the key intuitions beyond the network. At the beginning the text is represented as a vector based on standard embeddings, providing us a compact representation in a one-dimensional dense space. Then the matrix is processed with multiple standard one-dimensional convolutional layers.

 Note that the model uses multiple filters (with varying window sizes) to obtain multiple features. After that, there is a max pool operation where the idea is to capture the most important feature-the one with the highest value for each feature map. For regularization, the article proposed to adopt a dropout on the penultimate layer with a constraint on L2-norms of the weight vectors. The final layer will output the sentiment as positive or negative.

A couple of observations for better understanding the model are as follows:

- Filters are typically convolving on a continuous space. For images, this space is the pixel matrix representation which is spatially continuous over height and width. For texts, the continuous space is nothing more than the continuous dimension naturally induced by continuous words. If we use only words represented with one-hot encoding then space is sparse, if we use embedding then the resulting space is dense because similar words are aggregated.

- Images typically have three channels (RGB), while text naturally has only one channel because we have no need to represent colors.

There is more...

The paper *Convolutional Neural Networks for Sentence Classification*, Yoon Kim, EMNLP 2014 (https://arxiv.org/abs/1408.5882) performs an extensive set of experiments. Despite little tuning of hyperparameters, a simple CNN with one layer of convolution performs remarkably well for sentence classification. The paper shows that adopting a set of static embedding - which will be discussed when we talk about RNNs - and building a very simple ConvNet on the top of it, can actually improve the performance of sentiment analysis significantly:

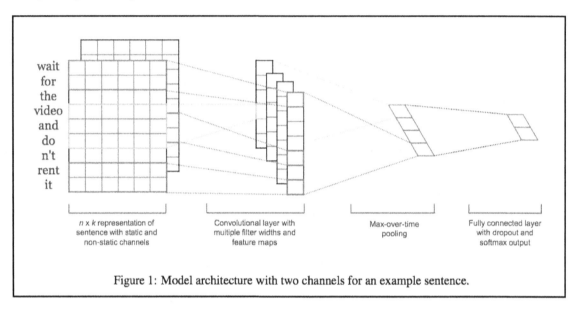

Figure 1: Model architecture with two channels for an example sentence.

An example of model architecture as seen in https://arxiv.org/pdf/1408.5882.pdf

The use of CNNs for text analysis is an active field of research. I suggest having a look at the following article:

- *Text Understanding from Scratch*, Xiang Zhang, Yann LeCun (https://arxiv.org/abs/1502.01710). This article demonstrates that we can apply deep learning to text understanding from character-level inputs all the way up to abstract text concepts, using CNNs. The authors apply CNNs to various large-scale datasets, including ontology classification, sentiment analysis, and text categorization, and show that they can achieve astonishing performance without the knowledge of words, phrases, sentences, or any other syntactic or semantic structures with regards to a human language. The models work for both English and Chinese.

Inspecting what filters a VGG pre-built network has learned

In this recipe, we will use keras-vis (`https://raghakot.github.io/keras-vis/`), an external Keras package for visually inspecting what a pre-built VGG16 network has learned in different filters. The idea is to pick a specific ImageNet category and understand 'how' the VGG16 network has learned to represent it.

Getting ready

The first step is to select a specific category used for training the VGG16 on ImageNet. Let's say that we take the category 20, which corresponds to the *American Dipper* bird shown in the following picture:

An example of American Dipper as seen on `https://commons.wikimedia.org/wiki/File:American_Dipper.jpg`

ImageNet mapping can be found online (`https://gist.github.com/yrevar/6135f1bd8dcf2e0cc683`) as a python pickle dictionary where the ImageNet 1000 class ID is mapped to human-readable labels.

How to do it...

We proceed with the recipe as follows:

1. Import matplotlib and the modules used by keras-vis. In addition, also import the pre-built VGG16 module. Keras makes it easy to deal with this pre-built network:

```
from matplotlib import pyplot as plt
from vis.utils import utils
from vis.utils.vggnet import VGG16
from vis.visualization import visualize_class_activation
```

2. Access the VGG16 network by using the pre-built layers included in Keras and trained with ImageNet weights:

```
# Build the VGG16 network with ImageNet weights
model = VGG16(weights='imagenet', include_top=True)
model.summary()
print('Model loaded.')
```

3. This is how the VGG16 network looks internally. We have many ConvNets, alternated with maxpool2D. Then, we have a Flatten layer followed by three Dense layers. The last one is called **predictions**, and this layer should be able to detect high-level features such as faces or, in our case, the shape of a bird. Note that the top layer is explicitly included in our network because we want to visualize what it learned:

```
Layer (type) Output Shape Param #
=================================================================
input_2 (InputLayer) (None, 224, 224, 3) 0

block1_conv1 (Conv2D) (None, 224, 224, 64) 1792

block1_conv2 (Conv2D) (None, 224, 224, 64) 36928

block1_pool (MaxPooling2D) (None, 112, 112, 64) 0

block2_conv1 (Conv2D) (None, 112, 112, 128) 73856

block2_conv2 (Conv2D) (None, 112, 112, 128) 147584

block2_pool (MaxPooling2D) (None, 56, 56, 128) 0

block3_conv1 (Conv2D) (None, 56, 56, 256) 295168
```

```
block3_conv2 (Conv2D) (None, 56, 56, 256) 590080

block3_conv3 (Conv2D) (None, 56, 56, 256) 590080

block3_pool (MaxPooling2D) (None, 28, 28, 256) 0

block4_conv1 (Conv2D) (None, 28, 28, 512) 1180160

block4_conv2 (Conv2D) (None, 28, 28, 512) 2359808

block4_conv3 (Conv2D) (None, 28, 28, 512) 2359808

block4_pool (MaxPooling2D) (None, 14, 14, 512) 0

block5_conv1 (Conv2D) (None, 14, 14, 512) 2359808

block5_conv2 (Conv2D) (None, 14, 14, 512) 2359808

block5_conv3 (Conv2D) (None, 14, 14, 512) 2359808

block5_pool (MaxPooling2D) (None, 7, 7, 512) 0

flatten (Flatten) (None, 25088) 0

fc1 (Dense) (None, 4096) 102764544

fc2 (Dense) (None, 4096) 16781312

predictions (Dense) (None, 1000) 4097000
=================================================================
Total params: 138,357,544
Trainable params: 138,357,544
Non-trainable params: 0

Model loaded.
```

Visually, the network can be represented as shown in the following figure:

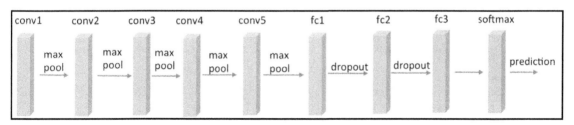

A VGG16 Network

4. Now let's focus on inspecting how the last prediction layer looks internally by focusing on American Dipper, which is the ID 20:

```
layer_name = 'predictions'
layer_idx = [idx for idx, layer in enumerate(model.layers) if layer.name ==
layer_name][0]
# Generate three different images of the same output index.
vis_images = []
for idx in [20, 20, 20]:
img = visualize_class_activation(model, layer_idx, filter_indices=idx,
max_iter=500)
img = utils.draw_text(img, str(idx))
vis_images.append(img)
```

5. Let's display the generated images for the specific layer given the features and observe how the concept of the *American Dipper* bird is internally *seen* by the network:

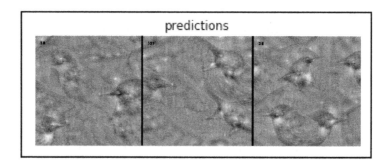

So, this is how a bird is internally represented by a neural network. It is a kind of trippy image, but I swear that no particular kind of artificial drug has been given to the network itself! This is just what this particular kind of artificial network has naturally learned.

6. Are you are still curious to understand a bit more? Well, let's pick an earlier layer and represent how the network is internally seeing this same American Dipper training class:

```
layer_name = 'block3_conv1'
layer_idx = [idx for idx, layer in enumerate(model.layers) if layer.name ==
layer_name][0]
vis_images = []
for idx in [20, 20, 20]:
img = visualize_class_activation(model, layer_idx, filter_indices=idx,
max_iter=500)
img = utils.draw_text(img, str(idx))
```

```
vis_images.append(img)
stitched = utils.stitch_images(vis_images)
plt.axis('off')
plt.imshow(stitched)
plt.title(layer_name)
plt.show()
```

The following is the output of the preceding code:

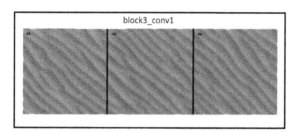

As expected, this particular layer is learning very basic features such as curves. However, the true power of ConvNets is that the network infers more and more sophisticated features the deeper we go into the models.

How it works...

The key idea of keras-vis visualization for Dense layers is to generate an input image that maximizes the final Dense layer output corresponding to the bird class. So in reality what the module does is reverse the problem. Given a specific trained Dense layer with its weight, a new synthetic image is generated which *best* fits the layer itself.

A similar idea is used for each conv filter. In this case, note that the first ConvNet layer is interpretable by simply visualizing its weights, as it is operating over raw pixels. Subsequent conv filters operate over the outputs of previous conv filters, and therefore visualizing them directly is not necessarily very interpretable. However, if we consider each layer independently we can focus on generating only a synthetic input image which maximizes the filter output.

There is more...

The keras-vis repository on GitHub (`https://github.com/raghakot/keras-vis`) has a good set of visualization examples of how to inspect a network internally, including the very recent idea of attention maps, where the goal is to detect which part of an image contributed the most to the training of a specific category (for example, tigers) when images frequently contain other elements (for example, grass). The seed article is *Deep Inside Convolutional Networks: Visualising Image Classification Models and Saliency Maps*, Karen Simonyan, Andrea Vedaldi, Andrew Zisserman (`https://arxiv.org/abs/1312.6034`), and an example extracted from the Git repository is reported below where the network understands by itself what the most salient part in an image to *define* a tiger is:

An example of saliency maps as seen on `https://github.com/raghakot/keras-vis`

Classifying images with VGGNet, ResNet, Inception, and Xception

Image classification is a typical deep learning application. This task had an initial increase of interest thanks to the ImageNet (`http://image-net.org/`) image database organized according to the WordNet (`http://wordnet.princeton.edu/`) hierarchy (currently only the nouns), in which each node of the hierarchy is depicted by hundreds and thousands of images. More precisely, ImageNet aimed to label and categorize images into almost 22,000 separate object categories. In the context of deep learning, ImageNet refers generally to the work contained in the paper *ImageNet Large Scale Visual Recognition Challenge* (`http://www.image-net.org/challenges/LSVRC/`), or ILSVRC for short. In this case, the goal is to train a model that can classify an input image into 1,000 separate object categories. In this recipe, we will use pre-trained models over 1.2 million training images with 50,000 validation images and 100,000 testing images.

VGG16 and VGG19

VGG16 and VGG19 have been introduced in *Very Deep Convolutional Networks for Large Scale Image Recognition*, Karen Simonyan, Andrew Zisserman, 2014, `https://arxiv.org/abs/1409.1556`. The network used 3×3 convolutional layers stacked and alternated with max pooling, two 4096 fully-connected layers, followed by a softmax classifier. The **16** and **19** stand for the number of weight layers in the network (columns D and E):

ConvNet Configuration					
A	A-LRN	B	C	D	E
11 weight layers	11 weight layers	13 weight layers	16 weight layers	16 weight layers	19 weight layers
input (224 × 224 RGB image)					
conv3-64	conv3-64	conv3-64	conv3-64	conv3-64	conv3-64
	LRN	**conv3-64**	conv3-64	conv3-64	conv3-64
maxpool					
conv3-128	conv3-128	conv3-128	conv3-128	conv3-128	conv3-128
		conv3-128	conv3-128	conv3-128	conv3-128
maxpool					
conv3-256	conv3-256	conv3-256	conv3-256	conv3-256	conv3-256
conv3-256	conv3-256	conv3-256	conv3-256	conv3-256	conv3-256
			conv1-256	**conv3-256**	conv3-256
					conv3-256
maxpool					
conv3-512	conv3-512	conv3-512	conv3-512	conv3-512	conv3-512
conv3-512	conv3-512	conv3-512	conv3-512	conv3-512	conv3-512
			conv1-512	**conv3-512**	conv3-512
					conv3-512
maxpool					
conv3-512	conv3-512	conv3-512	conv3-512	conv3-512	conv3-512
conv3-512	conv3-512	conv3-512	conv3-512	conv3-512	conv3-512
			conv1-512	**conv3-512**	conv3-512
					conv3-512
maxpool					
FC-4096					
FC-4096					
FC-1000					
soft-max					

An example of very deep network configurations as seen in `https://arxiv.org/pdf/1409.1556.pdf`

In 2015, having 16 or 19 layers was enough to consider the network deep, while today (2017) we arrive at hundreds of layers. Note that VGG networks are very slow to train and they require large weight space due to the depth and the number of fully-connected layers at the end.

ResNet

ResNet has been introduced in *Deep Residual Learning for Image Recognition*, Kaiming He, Xiangyu Zhang, Shaoqing Ren, Jian Sun, 2015, `https://arxiv.org/abs/1512.03385`. This network is very deep and can be trained using a standard stochastic descent gradient by using a standard network component called the residual module, which is then used to compose more complex networks (the composition is called *network in network*).

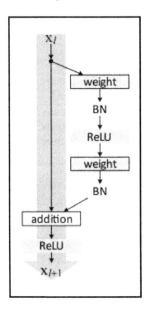

In comparison to VGG, ResNet is deeper, but the size of the model is smaller because a global average pooling operation is used instead of full-dense layers.

Inception

Inception has been introduced in *Rethinking the Inception Architecture for Computer Vision*, Christian Szegedy, Vincent Vanhoucke, Sergey Ioffe, Jonathon Shlens, Zbigniew Wojna, 2015, `https://arxiv.org/abs/1512.00567` and the key idea is to have multiple sizes of convolutions acting as feature extraction and computing 1×1, 3×3, and 5×5 convolutions within the same module. The outputs of these filters are then stacked along the channel dimension and sent into the next layer in the network. This is described in the following image:

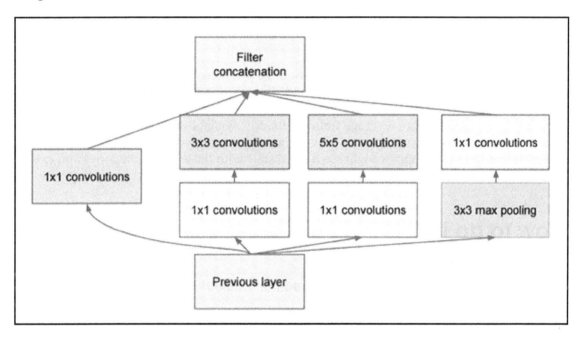

Inception-v3 is described in *Rethinking the Inception Architecture for Computer Vision*, while Inception-v4 is described in *Inception-v4, Inception-ResNet and the Impact of Residual Connections on Learning*, Christian Szegedy, Sergey Ioffe, Vincent Vanhoucke, Alex Alemi, 2016, `https://arxiv.org/abs/1602.07261`.

Xception

Xception is an extension of Inception, introduced in *Xception: Deep Learning with Depthwise Separable Convolutions*, François Chollet, 2016, https://arxiv.org/abs/1610.02357. Xception uses a new concept called depthwise separable convolution operation which allows it to outperform Inception-v3 on a large image classification dataset comprising 350 million images and 17,000 classes. Since the Xception architecture has the same number of parameters as Inception-v3, the performance gains are not due to increased capacity but rather to a more efficient use of model parameters.

Getting ready

This recipe uses Keras because the framework has a pre-cooked implementation of the above modules. Keras automatically downloads the weights of each network the first time it is used and stores these weights on your local disk. In other words, you don't need to retrain the networks but can leverage training already available on the internet. This is true under the assumption that you would like to classify your network on the 1,000 predefined categories. In the next recipe, we will see how to start with these 1,000 categories and extend them to a customized set with a process known as transfer learning.

How to do it...

We proceed with the recipe as follows:

1. Import the pre-built models and additional modules needed for processing and showing images:

```
from keras.applications import ResNet50
from keras.applications import InceptionV3
from keras.applications import Xception # TensorFlow ONLY
from keras.applications import VGG16
from keras.applications import VGG19
from keras.applications import imagenet_utils
from keras.applications.inception_v3 import preprocess_input
from keras.preprocessing.image import img_to_array
from keras.preprocessing.image import load_img
import numpy as np
import matplotlib.pyplot as plt
from matplotlib.pyplot import imshow
from PIL import Image
%matplotlib inline
```

2. Define a map used for memorizing the size of images used for training the networks. These are well-known constants for each model:

```
MODELS = {
"vgg16": (VGG16, (224, 224)),
"vgg19": (VGG19, (224, 224)),
"inception": (InceptionV3, (299, 299)),
"xception": (Xception, (299, 299)), # TensorFlow ONLY
"resnet": (ResNet50, (224, 224))
}
```

3. Define an auxiliary function used for loading and converting each image. Note that the pre-trained networks have been trained on a tensor with a shape that also includes an additional dimension for `batch_size`. Therefore, we need to add this dimension to our image for compatibility:

```
def image_load_and_convert(image_path, model):
pil_im = Image.open(image_path, 'r')
imshow(np.asarray(pil_im))
# initialize the input image shape
# and the pre-processing function (this might need to be changed
inputShape = MODELS[model][1]
preprocess = imagenet_utils.preprocess_input
image = load_img(image_path, target_size=inputShape)
image = img_to_array(image)
# the original networks have been trained on an additional
# dimension taking into account the batch size
# we need to add this dimension for consistency
# even if we have one image only
image = np.expand_dims(image, axis=0)
image = preprocess(image)
return image
```

4. Define an auxiliary function used for classifying the image and loop over the predictions and display the rank-5 predictions along with the probabilities:

```
def classify_image(image_path, model):
img = image_load_and_convert(image_path, model)
Network = MODELS[model][0]
model = Network(weights="imagenet")
preds = model.predict(img)
P = imagenet_utils.decode_predictions(preds)
# loop over the predictions and display the rank-5 predictions
# along with probabilities
for (i, (imagenetID, label, prob)) in enumerate(P[0]):
print("{}. {}: {:.2f}%".format(i + 1, label, prob * 100))
```

5. Then start to test different types of pre-trained networks:

```
classify_image("images/parrot.jpg", "vgg16")
```

Following you will see a list of predictions with respective probabilities:
1. macaw: 99.92%
2. jacamar: 0.03%
3. lorikeet: 0.02%
4. bee_eater: 0.02%
5. toucan: 0.00%

An example of macaw as seen in https://commons.wikimedia.org/wiki/File:Blue-and-Yellow-Macaw.jpg

```
classify_image("images/parrot.jpg", "vgg19")
```

1. macaw: 99.77%
2. lorikeet: 0.07%
3. toucan: 0.06%
4. hornbill: 0.05%
5. jacamar: 0.01%

```
classify_image("images/parrot.jpg", "resnet")
```

1. macaw: 97.93%
2. peacock: 0.86%
3. lorikeet: 0.23%
4. jacamar: 0.12%
5. jay: 0.12%

```
classify_image("images/parrot_cropped1.jpg", "resnet")
```

1. macaw: 99.98%
2. lorikeet: 0.00%
3. peacock: 0.00%
4. sulphur-crested_cockatoo: 0.00%
5. toucan: 0.00%

```
classify_image("images/incredible-hulk-180.jpg", "resnet")
```

1. comic_book: 99.76%
2. book_jacket: 0.19%
3. jigsaw_puzzle: 0.05%
4. menu: 0.00%
5. packet: 0.00%

An example of comic classification as seen in `https://comicvine.gamespot.com/the-incredible-hulk-180-and-the-wind-howls-wendigo/4000-14667/`

```
classify_image("images/cropped_panda.jpg", "resnet")
```

giant_panda: 99.04%
2. indri: 0.59%
3. lesser_panda: 0.17%
4. gibbon: 0.07%
5. titi: 0.05%

```
classify_image("images/space-shuttle1.jpg", "resnet")
```

1. space_shuttle: 92.38%
2. triceratops: 7.15%
3. warplane: 0.11%
4. cowboy_hat: 0.10%
5. sombrero: 0.04%

```
classify_image("images/space-shuttle2.jpg", "resnet")
```

1. space_shuttle: 99.96%
2. missile: 0.03%
3. projectile: 0.00%
4. steam_locomotive: 0.00%
5. warplane: 0.00%

```
classify_image("images/space-shuttle3.jpg", "resnet")
```

1. space_shuttle: 93.21%
2. missile: 5.53%
3. projectile: 1.26%
4. mosque: 0.00%
5. beacon: 0.00%

```
classify_image("images/space-shuttle4.jpg", "resnet")
```

1. space_shuttle: 49.61%
2. castle: 8.17%
3. crane: 6.46%
4. missile: 4.62%
5. aircraft_carrier: 4.24%

Note that some errors are possible. For instance:

```
classify_image("images/parrot.jpg", "inception")
```

1. stopwatch: 100.00%
2. mink: 0.00%
3. hammer: 0.00%
4. black_grouse: 0.00%
5. web_site: 0.00%

```
classify_image("images/parrot.jpg", "xception")
```

1. backpack: 56.69%
2. military_uniform: 29.79%
3. bib: 8.02%
4. purse: 2.14%
5. ping-pong_ball: 1.52%

6. Define an auxiliary function used for showing the internal architecture of each pre-built and pre-trained network:

```
def print_model(model):
print ("Model:",model)
Network = MODELS[model][0]
model = Network(weights="imagenet")
model.summary()
print_model('vgg19')

('Model:', 'vgg19')
```

Layer (type)	Output Shape	Param #
input_14 (InputLayer)	(None, 224, 224, 3)	0
block1_conv1 (Conv2D)	(None, 224, 224, 64)	1792
block1_conv2 (Conv2D)	(None, 224, 224, 64)	36928
block1_pool (MaxPooling2D)	(None, 112, 112, 64)	0
block2_conv1 (Conv2D)	(None, 112, 112, 128)	73856
block2_conv2 (Conv2D)	(None, 112, 112, 128)	147584
block2_pool (MaxPooling2D)	(None, 56, 56, 128)	0
block3_conv1 (Conv2D)	(None, 56, 56, 256)	295168

```
block3_conv2 (Conv2D) (None, 56, 56, 256) 590080

block3_conv3 (Conv2D) (None, 56, 56, 256) 590080

block3_conv4 (Conv2D) (None, 56, 56, 256) 590080

block3_pool (MaxPooling2D) (None, 28, 28, 256) 0

block4_conv1 (Conv2D) (None, 28, 28, 512) 1180160

block4_conv2 (Conv2D) (None, 28, 28, 512) 2359808

block4_conv3 (Conv2D) (None, 28, 28, 512) 2359808

block4_conv4 (Conv2D) (None, 28, 28, 512) 2359808

block4_pool (MaxPooling2D) (None, 14, 14, 512) 0

block5_conv1 (Conv2D) (None, 14, 14, 512) 2359808

block5_conv2 (Conv2D) (None, 14, 14, 512) 2359808

block5_conv3 (Conv2D) (None, 14, 14, 512) 2359808

block5_conv4 (Conv2D) (None, 14, 14, 512) 2359808

block5_pool (MaxPooling2D) (None, 7, 7, 512) 0

flatten (Flatten) (None, 25088) 0

fc1 (Dense) (None, 4096) 102764544

fc2 (Dense) (None, 4096) 16781312

predictions (Dense) (None, 1000) 4097000
=================================================================
Total params: 143,667,240
Trainable params: 143,667,240
Non-trainable params: 0
```

How it works...

We have used Keras Applications, pre-trained Keras learning models that are made available alongside pre-trained weights. These models can be used for prediction, feature extraction, and fine-tuning. In this case, we have used the model for prediction. We will see in the next recipe how to use the model for fine-tuning and for building customized classifiers on datasets that were originally not available when the models were originally trained.

There is more...

Inception-v4 is not directly available in Keras as of July 2017, but it can be downloaded as a separate module online (`https://github.com/kentsommer/keras-inceptionV4`). Once installed, the module will automatically download the weights the first time it is used.

AlexNet was one of the first stacked deep networks and it contained only eight layers, the first five were convolutional layers followed by fully-connected layers. The network was proposed in 2012 and significantly outperformed the second runner-up (top five error of 16% compared to runner-up with 26% error).

Recent research on deep neural networks has focused primarily on improving accuracy. With equivalent accuracy, smaller DNN architectures offer at least three advantages:

- Smaller CNNs require less communication across servers during distributed training.
- Smaller CNNs require less bandwidth to export a new model from the cloud to the place where the model is served.
- Smaller CNNs are more feasible to deploy on FPGAs and other hardware with limited memory. To provide all of these advantages, SqueezeNet has been proposed in the paper *SqueezeNet: AlexNet-level accuracy with 50x fewer parameters and <0.5MB model size*, Forrest N. Iandola, Song Han, Matthew W. Moskewicz, Khalid Ashraf, William J. Dally, Kurt Keutzer, 2016, `https://arxiv.org/abs/1602.07360`. SqueezeNet achieves AlexNet-level accuracy on ImageNet with 50x fewer parameters. Additionally, with model compression techniques we are able to compress SqueezeNet to less than 0.5 MB (510x smaller than AlexNet). Keras implements SqueezeNet as a separate module available online (`https://github.com/DT42/squeezenet_demo`).

Recycling pre-built Deep Learning models for extracting features

In this recipe, we will see how to use Deep Learning for extracting relevant features

Getting ready

One very simple idea is to use VGG16, and DCNN in general, for feature extraction. This code implements the idea by extracting features from a specific layer.

How to do it...

We proceed with the recipe as follows:

1. Import the pre-built models and additional modules needed for processing and showing images:

```
from keras.applications.vgg16 import VGG16
from keras.models import Model
from keras.preprocessing import image
from keras.applications.vgg16 import preprocess_input
import numpy as np
```

2. Select a specific layer from the network and get the features produced as output:

```
# pre-built and pre-trained deep learning VGG16 model
base_model = VGG16(weights='imagenet', include_top=True)
for i, layer in enumerate(base_model.layers):
print (i, layer.name, layer.output_shape)
# extract features from block4_pool block
model =
Model(input=base_model.input,
output=base_model.get_layer('block4_pool').output)
```

3. Extract the features for a given image, as in the following code snippet:

```
img_path = 'cat.jpg'
img = image.load_img(img_path, target_size=(224, 224))
x = image.img_to_array(img)
x = np.expand_dims(x, axis=0)
x = preprocess_input(x)
# get the features from this block
features = model.predict(x)
```

How it works...

Now, you might wonder why we want to extract the features from an intermediate layer in a CNN. The key intuition is that: as the network learns to classify images into categories, each layer learns to identify the features that are necessary to do the final classification.

Lower layers identify lower order features such as colors and edges, and higher layers compose these lower order features into higher order features such as shapes or objects. Hence the intermediate layer has the capability to extract important features from an image, and these features are more likely to help with different kinds of classification.

This has multiple advantages. First, we can rely on publicly available large-scale training and transfer this learning to novel domains. Second, we can save time for expensive large training. Third, we can provide reasonable solutions even when we don't have a large number of training examples for our domain. We also get a good starting network shape for the task at hand, instead of guessing it.

Very deep InceptionV3 Net used for Transfer Learning

Transfer learning is a very powerful deep learning technique which has more applications in different domains. The intuition is very simple and can be explained with an analogy. Suppose you want to learn a new language, say Spanish, then it could be useful to start from what you already know in a different language, say English.

Following this line of thinking, computer vision researchers now commonly use pre-trained CNNs to generate representations for new tasks, where the dataset may not be large enough to train an entire CNN from scratch. Another common tactic is to take the pre-trained ImageNet network and then fine-tune the entire network to the novel task.

InceptionV3 Net is a very deep ConvNet developed by Google. Keras implements the full network, shown in the following figure, and it comes pre-trained on ImageNet. The default input size for this model is 299x299 on three channels:

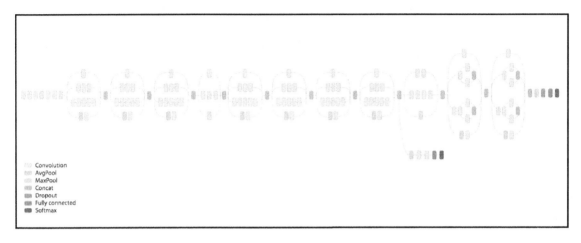

An example of ImageNet v3

Getting ready

This skeleton example is inspired by a scheme available online (`https://keras.io/applications/`) on the Keras website. We suppose to have a training dataset D in a domain, different from ImageNet. D has 1,024 features in input and 200 categories in output.

How to do it...

We can proceed with the recipe as follows:

1. Import the pre-built models and additional modules needed for processing:

```
from keras.applications.inception_v3 import InceptionV3
from keras.preprocessing import image
from keras.models import Model
from keras.layers import Dense, GlobalAveragePooling2D
from keras import backend as K
# create the base pre-trained model
base_model = InceptionV3(weights='imagenet', include_top=False)
```

2. We use a trained Inception-v3 but we do not include the top model because we want to fine-tune on D. The top level is a Dense layer with 1,024 inputs and the last output level is a softmax Dense layer with 200 classes of output. `x = GlobalAveragePooling2D()(x)` is used to convert the input to the correct shape for the Dense layer to handle. In fact, `base_model.output tensor` has the shape (samples, channels, rows, cols) for `dim_ordering="th"` or (samples, rows, cols, channels) for `dim_ordering="tf"`, but Dense needs them as (samples, channels) `GlobalAveragePooling2D` averages across (rows, cols). So if you look at the last four layers (where `include_top=True`), you see these shapes:

```
# layer.name, layer.input_shape, layer.output_shape
('mixed10', [(None, 8, 8, 320), (None, 8, 8, 768), (None, 8, 8, 768),
(None, 8, 8, 192)], (None, 8, 8, 2048))
('avg_pool', (None, 8, 8, 2048), (None, 1, 1, 2048))
('flatten', (None, 1, 1, 2048), (None, 2048))
('predictions', (None, 2048), (None, 1000))
```

3. When you include `_top=False`, you are removing the last three layers and exposing the `mixed_10` layer, so the `GlobalAveragePooling2D` layer converts the `(None, 8, 8, 2048)` to `(None, 2048)`, where each element in the `(None, 2048)` tensor is the average value for each corresponding (8,8) subtensor in the `(None, 8, 8, 2048)` tensor:

```
# add a global spatial average pooling layer
x = base_model.output
x = GlobalAveragePooling2D()(x)
# let's add a fully-connected layer as first layer
x = Dense(1024, activation='relu')(x)
# and a logistic layer with 200 classes as last layer
predictions = Dense(200, activation='softmax')(x)
# model to train
model = Model(input=base_model.input, output=predictions)
```

4. All the convolutional levels are pre-trained so we freeze them during the training of the full model.

```
# i.e. freeze all convolutional Inception-v3 layers
for layer in base_model.layers:
layer.trainable = False
```

5. The model is then compiled and trained for a few epochs so that the top layers are trained:

```
# compile the model (should be done *after* setting layers to non-
trainable)
 model.compile(optimizer='rmsprop', loss='categorical_crossentropy')
# train the model on the new data for a few epochs
 model.fit_generator(...)
```

6. Then we freeze the top layers in Inception and fine-tune the Inception layer. In this example, we freeze the first 172 layers (a hyperparameter to tune):

```
# we chose to train the top 2 inception blocks, i.e. we will freeze
# the first 172 layers and unfreeze the rest:
for layer in model.layers[:172]:
layer.trainable = False
for layer in model.layers[172:]:
layer.trainable = True
```

7. The model is then recompiled for fine-tune optimization. We need to recompile the model for these modifications to take effect:

```
# we use SGD with a low learning rate
 from keras.optimizers import SGD
 model.compile(optimizer=SGD(lr=0.0001, momentum=0.9),
loss='categorical_crossentropy')

 # we train our model again (this time fine-tuning the top 2 inception
blocks
 # alongside the top Dense layers
 model.fit_generator(...)
```

How it works...

Now we have a new deep network which re-uses the standard Inception-v3 network but it is trained on a new domain D via transfer learning. Of course, there are many parameters to fine-tune for achieving good accuracy. However, we are now re-using a very large pre-trained network as a starting point via transfer learning. In doing so, we can save the need for training on our machines by re-using what is already available in Keras.

There is more...

As of 2017, the problem of "computer vision" meant that the problem of finding patterns in an image can be considered as solved, and this problem has an impact on our lives. For instance:

- The paper *Dermatologist-level classification of skin cancer with deep neural networks*, Andre Esteva, Brett Kuprel, Roberto A. Novoa, Justin Ko, Susan M. Swetter, Helen M. Blau & Sebastian Thrun, 2017 `https://www.nature.com/nature/journal/v542/n7639/full/nature21056.html` trains a CNN using a dataset of 129,450 clinical images consisting of 2,032 different diseases. They test the results against 21 board-certified dermatologists on biopsy-proven clinical images with two critical binary classification use cases: keratinocyte carcinomas versus benign seborrheic keratoses; and malignant melanomas versus benign nevi. The CNN achieves performance on par with all tested experts across both tasks, demonstrating an artificial intelligence capable of classifying skin cancer with a level of competence comparable to dermatologists.

- The paper *High-Resolution Breast Cancer Screening with Multi-View Deep Convolutional Neural Networks*, Krzysztof J. Geras, Stacey Wolfson, S. Gene Kim, Linda Moy, Kyunghyun Cho, `https://arxiv.org/abs/1703.07047` promises to improve the breast cancer screening process through its innovative architecture, which can handle the four standard views, or angles, without sacrificing a high resolution. As opposed to the commonly used DCN architectures for natural images, which work with images of 224 x 224 pixels, the MV-DCN is also capable of using a resolution of 2600 x 2000 pixels.

Generating music with dilated ConvNets, WaveNet, and NSynth

WaveNet is a deep generative model for producing raw audio waveforms. This breakthrough technology has been introduced (`https://deepmind.com/blog/wavenet-generative-model-raw-audio/`) by Google DeepMind(`https://deepmind.com/`) for teaching how to speak to computers. The results are truly impressive and online you can find examples of synthetic voices where the computer learns how to talk with the voice of celebrities, such as Matt Damon.

So, you might wonder why learning to synthesize audio is so difficult. Well, each digital sound we hear is based on 16,000 samples per second (sometimes 48,000 or more) and building a predictive model where we learn to reproduce a sample based on all the previous ones is a very difficult challenge. Nevertheless, there are experiments showing that WaveNet has improved the current state-of-the-art **Text-to-Speech** (TTS) systems, reducing the difference with human voices by 50 percent for both US English and Mandarin Chinese.

What is even cooler is that DeepMind proved that WaveNet can be also used to teach to computers how to generate the sound of musical instruments, such as piano music.

Now for some definitions. TTS systems are typically divided into two different classes:

- Concatenative TTS, where single speech voice fragments are first memorized and then recombined when the voice has to be reproduced. However, this approach does not scale because it is possible to reproduce only the memorized voice fragments and it is not possible to reproduce new speakers or different types of audio without memorizing the fragments from the beginning.
- Parametric TTS, where a model is created for storing all the characteristic features of the audio to be synthesized. Before WaveNet, the audio generated with parametric TTS was less natural than concatenative TTS. WaveNet improved the state of the art by modeling directly the production of audio sounds, instead of using intermediate signal processing algorithms used in the past.

In principle, WaveNet can be seen as a stack of 1D convolutional layers (we have seen 2D convolution for images in Chapter 4) with a constant stride of one and with no pooling layers. Note that the input and the output have by construction the same dimension, so the ConvNets are well suited to model sequential data such as audio sounds. However, it has been shown that in order to reach a large size for the receptive field in the output neuron it is necessary to either use a massive number of large filters or prohibitively increase the depth of the network. Remember that the receptive field of a neuron in a layer is the cross-section of the previous layer from which neurons provide inputs. For this reason, pure ConvNets are not so effective in learning how to synthesize audio.

The key intuition beyond WaveNet is the so-called dilated causal convolutions (sometimes known as atrous convolutions), which simply means that some input values are skipped when the filter of a convolutional layer is applied. Atrous is the *bastardization* of the French expression *à trous*, meaning *with holes*. So an AtrousConvolution is a convolution with holes As an example, in one dimension a filter w of size 3 with dilatation 1 would compute the following sum.

So in short, in a D-dilated convolution, usually the stride is 1, but nothing prevents you from using other strides. An example is given in the following figure with increased dilatation (hole) sizes = 0, 1, 2:

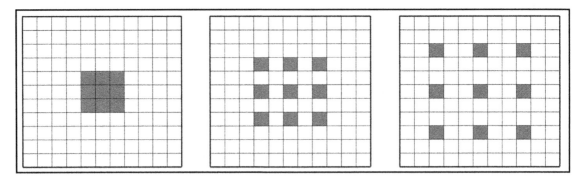

An example of dilated network

Thanks to this simple idea of introducing 'holes', it is possible to stack multiple dilated convolutional layers with exponentially increasing filters and learn long range input dependencies without having an excessively deep network.

A WaveNet is, therefore, a ConvNet where the convolutional layers have various dilation factors allowing the receptive field to grow exponentially with depth, and therefore efficiently cover thousands of audio timesteps.

When we train, the inputs are sounds recorded from human speakers. The waveforms are quantized to a fixed integer range. A WaveNet defines an initial convolutional layer accessing only the current and previous input. Then, there is a stack of dilated ConvNet layers, still accessing only current and previous inputs. At the end, there is a series of Dense layers which combines previous results, followed by a softmax activation function for categorical outputs.

At each step, a value is predicted from the network and fed back into the input. At the same time, a new prediction for the next step is computed. The loss function is the cross-entropy between the output for the current step and the input at the next step.

NSynth (https://magenta.tensorflow.org/nsynth) is an evolution of WaveNet recently released by the Google Brain group, which instead of being causal, aims at seeing the entire context of the input chunk. The neural network is truly, complex as depicted in the following image, but for the sake of this introductory discussion it is sufficient to know that the network learns how to reproduce its input by using an approach based on reducing the error during the encoding/decoding phases:

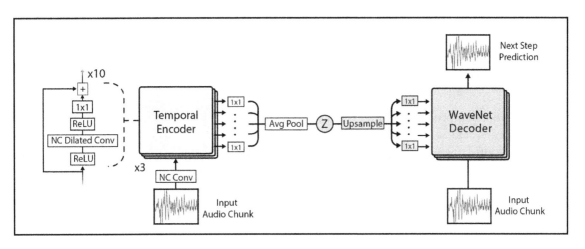

An example of NSynth architecture as seen in `https://magenta.tensorflow.org/nsynth`

Getting ready

For this recipe, we are not going to write code, instead, I'll show you how to use some code available online (`https://github.com/tensorflow/magenta/tree/master/magenta/models/nsynth`) and some cool demos you can find from Google Brain (`https://aiexperiments.withgoogle.com/sound-maker`). The interested reader can also have a look the the paper *Neural Audio Synthesis of Musical Notes with WaveNet Autoencoders*, Jesse Engel, Cinjon Resnick, Adam Roberts, Sander Dieleman, Douglas Eck, Karen Simonyan, Mohammad Norouzi, 5 Apr 2017. `https://arxiv.org/abs/1704.01279`

How to do it...

We proceed with the recipe as follows:

1. Install NSynth by creating a separate conda environment. Create and activate a Magenta conda environment using Python 2.7 with Jupyter Notebook support:

```
conda create -n magenta python=2.7 jupyter
source activate magenta
```

2. Install the Magenta pip package and the librosa, which is used for reading audio formats:

```
pip install magenta
pip install librosa
```

3. Install a pre-built model from the internet http://download.magenta. tensorflow.org/models/nsynth/wavenet-ckpt.tar and download a sample sound https://www.freesound.org/people/MustardPlug/sounds/395058/. Then run the notebook contained in the demo directory (in my case http:// localhost:8888/notebooks/nsynth/Exploring_Neural_Audio_Synthesis_with_ NSynth.ipynb). The first part is about including modules that will be used later in our computations:

```
import os
import numpy as np
import matplotlib.pyplot as plt
from magenta.models.nsynth import utils
from magenta.models.nsynth.wavenet import fastgen
from IPython.display import Audio
%matplotlib inline
%config InlineBackend.figure_format = 'jpg'
```

4. Then we load the demo sound downloaded from the internet and put it in the same directory as the notebook. This will load 40,000 samples in about 2.5 seconds into the machine:

```
# from https://www.freesound.org/people/MustardPlug/sounds/395058/
fname = '395058__mustardplug__breakbeat-hiphop-a4-4bar-96bpm.wav'
sr = 16000
audio = utils.load_audio(fname, sample_length=40000, sr=sr)
sample_length = audio.shape[0]
print('{} samples, {} seconds'.format(sample_length, sample_length /
float(sr)))
```

5. The next step is to encode the audio samples in a very compact representation using a pre-trained NSynth model downloaded from the internet. This will give us a 78 x 16 dimension encoding for every four seconds of audio, which we can then decode or resynthesize. Our encoding is a tensor (#files=1 x 78 x 16):

```
%time encoding = fastgen.encode(audio, 'model.ckpt-200000', sample_length)
INFO:tensorflow:Restoring parameters from model.ckpt-200000
 CPU times: user 1min 4s, sys: 2.96 s, total: 1min 7s
 Wall time: 25.7 s
print(encoding.shape)
```

```
(1, 78, 16)
```

6. Let's save the encoding that will be used later for re-synthesizing. In addition, let's have a quick view of what the encoding shape is with a graphical representation and compare it with the original audio signal. As you can see, the encoding follows the beat presented in the original audio signal:

```
np.save(fname + '.npy', encoding)
fig, axs = plt.subplots(2, 1, figsize=(10, 5))
axs[0].plot(audio);
axs[0].set_title('Audio Signal')
axs[1].plot(encoding[0]);
axs[1].set_title('NSynth Encoding')
```

We observe the following audio signal and Nsynth Encoding:

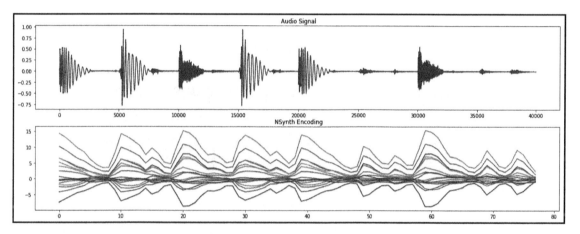

7. Now let's do a decoding of the encoding we just produced. In other words, we try to reproduce the original audio from the compact representation with the intent of understanding if the re-synthesized sound is similar to the original one. Indeed, if you run the experiment and listen to the original audio and the re-synthesized one, they sound very similar:

```
%time fastgen.synthesize(encoding, save_paths=['gen_' + fname],
samples_per_save=sample_length)
```

How it works...

A WaveNet is a ConvNet where the convolutional layers have various dilation factors, allowing the receptive field to grow exponentially with depth and therefore efficiently cover thousands of audio timesteps. NSynth is an evolution of WaveNet where the original audio is encoded using WaveNet-like processing for learning a compact representation. Then, this compact representation is used to reproduce the original audio.

There is more...

As soon as we learn how to create a compact representation of audio via dilated convolutions, we can play with these learnings and have fun. You will find very cool demos on the internet:

1. For instance, you can see how the model learns the sound of different musical instruments: (https://magenta.tensorflow.org/nsynth)

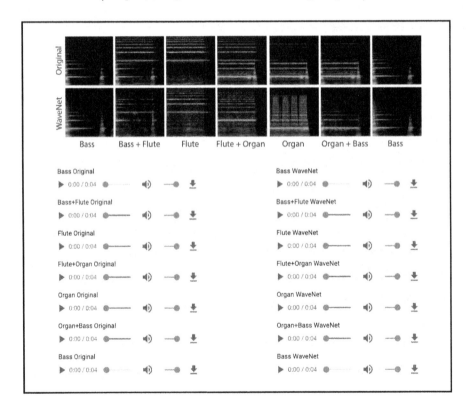

2. Then, you can see how one model learned in one context can be *re-mixed* in another context. For instance, by changing the speaker identity, we can use WaveNet to say the same thing in different voices (`https://deepmind.com/blog/wavenet-generative-model-raw-audio/`).

3. Another very interesting experiment is to learn models for musical instruments and then re-mix them in a such a way that we can create new musical instruments that have never been heard before. This is really cool, and it opens the path to a new range of possibilities that the ex-radio DJ sitting in me cannot resist being super excited about. For instance, in this example, we combine a sitar with an electric guitar, and this is a kind of cool new musical instrument. Not excited enough? So what about combining a bowed bass with a dog's bark? (`https://aiexperiments.withgoogle.com/sound-maker/view/`) Have fun!:

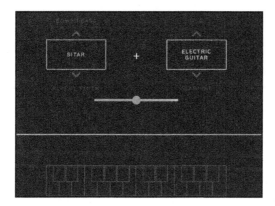

Answering questions about images (Visual Q&A)

In this recipe, we will learn how to answer questions about the content of a specific image. This is a powerful form of Visual Q&A based on a combination of visual features extracted from a pre-trained VGG16 model together with word clustering (embedding). These two sets of heterogeneous features are then combined into a single network where the last layers are made up of an alternating sequence of Dense and Dropout. This recipe works on Keras 2.0+.

Therefore, this recipe will teach you how to:

- Extract features from a pre-trained VGG16 network.
- Use pre-built word embeddings for mapping words into a space where similar words are adjacent.
- Use LSTM layers for building a language model. LSTM will be discussed in Chapter 6 and for now we will use them as black boxes.
- Combine different heterogeneous input features to create a combined feature space. For this task, we will use the new Keras 2.0 functional API.
- Attach a few additional Dense and Dropout layers for creating a multi-layer perceptron and increasing the power of our deep learning network.

For the sake of simplicity we will not re-train the combined network in 5 but, instead, will use a pre-trained set of weights already available online (`https://avisingh599.github.io/deeplearning/visual-qa/`). The interested reader can re-train the network on his own train dataset made up of N images, N questions, and N answers. This is left as an optional exercise. The network is inspired by the paper *VQA: Visual Question Answering*, Aishwarya Agrawal, Jiasen Lu, Stanislaw Antol, Margaret Mitchell, C. Lawrence Zitnick, Dhruv Batra, Devi Parikh, 2015. (`http://arxiv.org/pdf/1505.00468v4.pdf`):

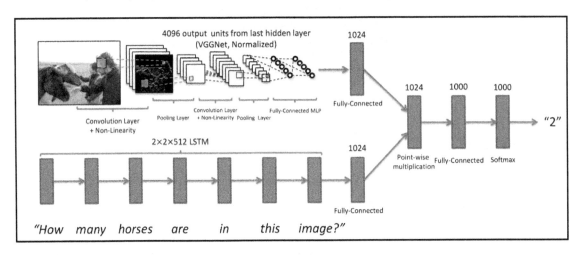

An example of Visual Q&A as seen in *Visual Question Answering* paper

The only difference in our case is that we will concatenate the features produced by the image layer with the features produced by the language layer.

How to do it...

We can proceed with the recipe as follows:

1. Load all the Keras modules needed by the recipe. These include spaCy for word embedding, VGG16 for image features extraction, and LSTM for language modeling. The remaining few additional modules are pretty standard:

```
%matplotlib inline
import os, argparse
import numpy as np
import cv2 as cv2
import spacy as spacy
import matplotlib.pyplot as plt
from keras.models import Model, Input
from keras.layers.core import Dense, Dropout, Reshape
from keras.layers.recurrent import LSTM
from keras.layers.merge import concatenate
from keras.applications.vgg16 import VGG16
from keras.preprocessing import image
from keras.applications.vgg16 import preprocess_input
from sklearn.externals import joblib
import PIL.Image
```

2. Define a few constants. Note that we assume that our corpus of questions has max_length_questions = 30 and we know that we are going to use VGG16 to extract 4,096 features describing our input image. In addition, we know that the word embeddings are in a space of length_feature_space = 300. Note that we are going to use a set of pre-trained weights downloaded from the internet (https://github.com/iamaaditya/VQA_Demo):

```
# mapping id -> labels for categories
label_encoder_file_name =
'/Users/gulli/Books/TF/code/git/tensorflowBook/Chapter5/FULL_labelencoder_t
rainval.pkl'
# max length across corpus
max_length_questions = 30
# VGG output
length_vgg_features = 4096
# Embedding outout
length_feature_space = 300
# pre-trained weights
VQA_weights_file =
'/Users/gulli/Books/TF/code/git/tensorflowBook/Chapter5/VQA_MODEL_WEIGHTS.h
df5'
```

3. Use VGG16 for extracting features. Note that we explicitly extract them from the layer fc2. This function returns 4,096 features given an input image:

```
'''image features'''
def get_image_features(img_path, VGG16modelFull):
'''given an image returns a tensor with (1, 4096) VGG16 features'''
# Since VGG was trained as a image of 224x224, every new image
# is required to go through the same transformation
img = image.load_img(img_path, target_size=(224, 224))
x = image.img_to_array(img)
# this is required because of the original training of VGG was batch
# even if we have only one image we need to be consistent
x = np.expand_dims(x, axis=0)
x = preprocess_input(x)
features = VGG16modelFull.predict(x)
model_extractfeatures = Model(inputs=VGG16modelFull.input,
outputs=VGG16modelFull.get_layer('fc2').output)
fc2_features = model_extractfeatures.predict(x)
fc2_features = fc2_features.reshape((1, length_vgg_features))
return fc2_features
```

Note that VGG16 is defined as follows:

```
Layer (type) Output Shape Param #
=======================================================================
input_5 (InputLayer) (None, 224, 224, 3) 0
_____
block1_conv1 (Conv2D) (None, 224, 224, 64) 1792
_____
block1_conv2 (Conv2D) (None, 224, 224, 64) 36928
_____
block1_pool (MaxPooling2D) (None, 112, 112, 64) 0
_____
block2_conv1 (Conv2D) (None, 112, 112, 128) 73856
_____
block2_conv2 (Conv2D) (None, 112, 112, 128) 147584
_____
block2_pool (MaxPooling2D) (None, 56, 56, 128) 0
_____
block3_conv1 (Conv2D) (None, 56, 56, 256) 295168
_____
block3_conv2 (Conv2D) (None, 56, 56, 256) 590080
_____
block3_conv3 (Conv2D) (None, 56, 56, 256) 590080
_____
block3_pool (MaxPooling2D) (None, 28, 28, 256) 0
_____
block4_conv1 (Conv2D) (None, 28, 28, 512) 1180160
```

```
block4_conv2 (Conv2D) (None, 28, 28, 512) 2359808

block4_conv3 (Conv2D) (None, 28, 28, 512) 2359808

block4_pool (MaxPooling2D) (None, 14, 14, 512) 0

block5_conv1 (Conv2D) (None, 14, 14, 512) 2359808

block5_conv2 (Conv2D) (None, 14, 14, 512) 2359808

block5_conv3 (Conv2D) (None, 14, 14, 512) 2359808

block5_pool (MaxPooling2D) (None, 7, 7, 512) 0

flatten (Flatten) (None, 25088) 0

fc1 (Dense) (None, 4096) 102764544

fc2 (Dense) (None, 4096) 16781312

predictions (Dense) (None, 1000) 4097000
=================================================================
Total params: 138,357,544
Trainable params: 138,357,544
Non-trainable params: 0
```

4. Use spaCy to get a word embedding and map the input question into a space (`max_length_questions, 300`) where `max_length_questions` is the max length of questions in our corpus, and 300 is the dimension of embeddings produced by spaCy. Internally, spaCy uses an algorithm called gloVe (http://nlp.stanford.edu/projects/glove/). gloVe reduces a given token to a 300-dimensional representation. Note that the question is padded to the `max_lengh_questions` with right 0 paddings:

```
'''embedding'''
def get_question_features(question):
''' given a question, a unicode string, returns the time series vector
with each word (token) transformed into a 300 dimension representation
calculated using Glove Vector '''
word_embeddings = spacy.load('en', vectors='en_glove_cc_300_1m_vectors')
tokens = word_embeddings(question)
ntokens = len(tokens)
if (ntokens > max_length_questions) :
ntokens = max_length_questions
```

```
question_tensor = np.zeros((1, max_length_questions, 300))
for j in xrange(len(tokens)):
question_tensor[0,j,:] = tokens[j].vector
return question_tensor
```

5. Load an image and get its salient features by using the previously defined image feature extractor:

```
image_file_name = 'girl.jpg'
img0 = PIL.Image.open(image_file_name)
img0.show()
#get the salient features
model = VGG16(weights='imagenet', include_top=True)
image_features = get_image_features(image_file_name, model)
print image_features.shape
```

6. Write a question and get its salient features by using the previously defined sentence feature extractor:

```
question = u"Who is in this picture?"
language_features = get_question_features(question)
print language_features.shape
```

7. Combine the two heterogeneous sets of features into one. In this network, we have three LSTM layers which will take the creation of our language model into account. Note that the LSTM will be discussed in detail in Chapter 6 and for now we only use them as black boxes. The last LSTM returns 512 features which are then used as inputs to a sequence of Dense and Dropout layers. The last layer is a Dense one with a softmax activation function in a probability space of 1,000 potential answers:

```
'''combine'''
def build_combined_model(
number_of_LSTM = 3,
number_of_hidden_units_LSTM = 512,
number_of_dense_layers = 3,
number_of_hidden_units = 1024,
activation_function = 'tanh',
dropout_pct = 0.5
):
#input image
input_image = Input(shape=(length_vgg_features,),
name="input_image")
model_image = Reshape((length_vgg_features,),
input_shape=(length_vgg_features,))(input_image)
#input language
```

```
input_language = Input(shape=(max_length_questions,length_feature_space,),
name="input_language")
#build a sequence of LSTM
model_language = LSTM(number_of_hidden_units_LSTM,
return_sequences=True,
name = "lstm_1")(input_language)
model_language = LSTM(number_of_hidden_units_LSTM,
return_sequences=True,
name = "lstm_2")(model_language)
model_language = LSTM(number_of_hidden_units_LSTM,
return_sequences=False,
name = "lstm_3")(model_language)
#concatenate 4096+512
model = concatenate([model_image, model_language])
#Dense, Dropout
for _ in xrange(number_of_dense_layers):
model = Dense(number_of_hidden_units,
kernel_initializer='uniform')(model)
model = Dropout(dropout_pct)(model)
model = Dense(1000,
activation='softmax')(model)
#create model from tensors
model = Model(inputs=[input_image, input_language], outputs = model)
return model
```

8. Build the combined network and show its summary just to understand how it
   looks internally. Load the pre-trained weights and compile the model by using
   the `categorical_crossentropy` loss function, with the rmsprop optimizer:

```
combined_model = build_combined_model()
combined_model.summary()
combined_model.load_weights(VQA_weights_file)
combined_model.compile(loss='categorical_crossentropy',
optimizer='rmsprop')
```

```
Layer (type) Output Shape Param # Connected to
=================================================================================
=============================
input_language (InputLayer) (None, 30, 300) 0


lstm_1 (LSTM) (None, 30, 512) 1665024 input_language[0][0]


input_image (InputLayer) (None, 4096) 0

```

```
lstm_2 (LSTM) (None, 30, 512) 2099200 lstm_1[0][0]

reshape_3 (Reshape) (None, 4096) 0 input_image[0][0]

lstm_3 (LSTM) (None, 512) 2099200 lstm_2[0][0]

concatenate_3 (Concatenate) (None, 4608) 0 reshape_3[0][0]
lstm_3[0][0]

dense_8 (Dense) (None, 1024) 4719616 concatenate_3[0][0]

dropout_7 (Dropout) (None, 1024) 0 dense_8[0][0]

dense_9 (Dense) (None, 1024) 1049600 dropout_7[0][0]

dropout_8 (Dropout) (None, 1024) 0 dense_9[0][0]

dense_10 (Dense) (None, 1024) 1049600 dropout_8[0][0]

dropout_9 (Dropout) (None, 1024) 0 dense_10[0][0]

dense_11 (Dense) (None, 1000) 1025000 dropout_9[0][0]
============================================================================
==========================
Total params: 13,707,240
Trainable params: 13,707,240
Non-trainable params: 0
```

9. Use the pre-trained combined network for making the prediction. Note that in this case we use weights already available online for this network, but the interested reader can re-train the combined network on their own training set:

```
y_output = combined_model.predict([image_features, language_features])
# This task here is represented as a classification into a 1000 top answers
# this means some of the answers were not part of training and thus would
# not show up in the result.
# These 1000 answers are stored in the sklearn Encoder class
```

```
labelencoder = joblib.load(label_encoder_file_name)
for label in reversed(np.argsort(y_output)[0,-5:]):
    print str(round(y_output[0,label]*100,2)).zfill(5), "% ",
    labelencoder.inverse_transform(label)
```

How it works...

The task of Visual Question Answering is tackled by using a combination of different deep neural networks. A pre-trained VGG16 has been used to extract features from images, and a sequence of LSTM has been used to extract features from questions previously mapped into an embedding space. VGG16 is a CNN used for image feature extraction, while LSTM is an RNN used for extracting temporal features representing the sequences. The combination of these two is currently the state of the art for dealing with this type of network. A multi-layered perceptron with dropout is then added on top of the combined models in order to form our deep network.

There is more...

On the internet, you can find more experiments performed by Avi Singh (https://avisingh599.github.io/deeplearning/visual-qa/) where different models are compared, including a simple 'bag-of-words' for language together with CNN for images, an LSTM-only model, and an LSTM+CNN model - similar to the one discussed in this recipe. The blog posting also discusses different training strategies for each model.

In addition to that, interested readers can find on the internet (https://github.com/anujshah1003/VQA-Demo-GUI) a nice GUI built on the top of Avi Singh's demo which allows you to interactively load images and ask related questions. A YouTube video is also available (https://www.youtube.com/watch?v=7FB9PvzOuQY).

Classifying videos with pre-trained nets in six different ways

Classifying videos is an area of active research because of a large amount of data needed for processing this type of media. Memory requirements are frequently reaching the limits of modern GPUs and a distributed form of training on multiple machines might be required. Research is currently exploring different directions with increased levels of complexity, let's review them.

The first approach consists of classifying one video frame at a time by considering each of them as a separate image processed with a 2D CNN. This approach simply reduces the video classification problem to an image classification problem. Each video frame *emits* a classification output, and the video is classified by taking into account the more frequently chosen category for each frame.

The second approach consists of creating one single network where a 2D CNN is combined with an RNN. The idea is that the CNN will take into account the image components and the RNN will take into account the sequence information for each video. This type of network can be very difficult to train because of the very high number of parameters to optimize.

The third approach is to use a 3D ConvNet, where 3D ConvNets are an extension of 2D ConvNets operating on a 3D tensor (`time`, `image_width`, `image_height`). This approach is another natural extension of image classification, but again, 3D ConvNets might be hard to train.

The fourth approach is based on smart intuition. Instead of using CNNs directly for classification, they can be used for storing offline features for each frame in the video. The idea is that feature extraction can be made very efficient with transfer learning, as shown in a previous recipe. After all of the features are extracted, they can be passed as a set of inputs into an RNN which will learn sequences across multiple frames and emit the final classification.

The fifth approach is a simple variant of the fourth, where the final layer is an MLP instead of an RNN. In certain situations, this approach can be simpler and less expensive in terms of computational requirements.

The sixth approach is a variant of the fourth, where the phase of feature extraction is realized with a 3D CNN which extracts spatial and visual features. These features are then passed to either an RNN or an MLP.

Deciding on the best approach is strictly dependant on your specific application and there is no definitive answer. The first three approaches are generally more computationally expensive, while the last three approaches are less expensive and frequently achieve better performance.

In this recipe, we show how to use the sixth approach by describing the results presented in the paper *Temporal Activity Detection in Untrimmed Videos with Recurrent Neural Networks*, Montes, Alberto and Salvador, Amaia and Pascual, Santiago and Giro-i-Nieto, Xavier, 2016 (`https://arxiv.org/abs/1608.08128`). This work aims at solving the ActivityNet Challenge `http://activity-net.org/challenges/2016/`. This challenge focuses on recognizing high-level and goal-oriented activities from user-generated videos, similar to those found in internet portals. The challenge is tailored to 200 activity categories in two different tasks:

- Untrimmed Classification Challenge: Given a long video, predict the labels of the activities present in the video
- Detection Challenge: Given a long video, predict the labels and temporal extents of the activities present in the video

The architecture presented consists of two stages, as depicted in the following figure. The first stage encodes the video information into a single vector representation for small video clips. To achieve that, the C3D network is used. The C3D network uses 3D convolutions to extract spatiotemporal features from the videos, which previously have been split into 16-frame clips.

The second stage, once the video features are extracted, is that the activity on each clip is to be classified. To perform this classification an RNN is used, more specifically an LSTM network which tries to exploit long-term correlations and perform a prediction of the video sequence. This stage is the one which has been trained:

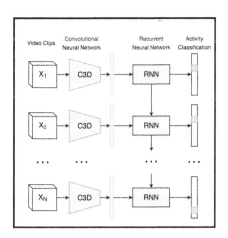

An example of C3D+RNN as seen in `https://imatge-upc.github.io/activitynet-2016-cvprw/`

How to do it...

For this recipe, we simply summarize the results presented online (https://github.com/imatge-upc/activitynet-2016-cvprw/blob/master/misc/step_by_step_guide.md):

1. The first step is to clone the git repository from

```
git clone https://github.com/imatge-upc/activitynet-2016-cvprw.git
```

2. Then we need to download the ActivityNet v1.3 dataset, which has a size of 600 GB:

```
cd dataset
 # This will download the videos on the default directory
 sh download_videos.sh username password
 # This will download the videos on the directory you specify
 sh download_videos.sh username password /path/you/want
```

3. The next step is to download the pre-trained weights for both the CNN3d and the RNN:

```
cd data/models
 sh get_c3d_sports_weights.sh
 sh get_temporal_location_weights.sh
```

4. The last step consists of classifying the videos:

```
python scripts/run_all_pipeline.py -i path/to/test/video.mp4
```

How it works...

If you are interested in training the CNN3D and the RNN on your machines, then you can find the specific commands used by this machine pipeline on the internet.

The intent is to present a high-level view of different approaches available for video classification. Again, there is not only one single recipe, but instead multiple options, which should be carefully chosen for your specific needs.

There is more...

CNN-LSTM architectures are a new RNN layer where the input of input transformations and recurrent transformations are both convolutional. Despite the very similar name, CNN-LSTM layers are therefore different from the combination of CNN and LSTM, as described above. The model is described in the paper *Convolutional LSTM Network: A Machine Learning Approach for Precipitation Nowcasting*, Xingjian Shi, Zhourong Chen, Hao Wang, Dit-Yan Yeung, Wai-kin Wong, Wang-chun Woo, 2015,(`https://arxiv.org/abs/1506.04214`) and in 2017 some people are starting to experiment using this module for video, but this is still an area of active research.

6
Recurrent Neural Networks

In this chapter, we will present a number of recipes covering the following topics:

- Neural machine translation - training a seq2seq RNN
- Neural machine translation - inference on a seq2seq RNN
- All you need is attention - another example of a seq2seq RNN
- Learning to write as Shakespeare with RNNs
- Learning to predict future Bitcoin value with RNNs
- Many-to-one and many-to-many RNN examples

Introduction

In this chapter, we will discuss how **Recurrent Neural Networks** (**RNNs**) are used for deep learning in domains where maintaining a sequential order is important. Our attention will be mainly devoted to text analysis and **natural language processing** (**NLP**), but we will also see examples of sequences used to predict the value of Bitcoins.

Many real-time situations can be described by adopting a model based on temporal sequences. For instance, if you think about writing a document, the order of words is important and the current word certainly depends on the previous ones. If we still focus on text writing, it is clear that the next character in a word depends on the previous characters (for example, *The quick brown f...* there is a very high probability that the next letter will be the letter *o*), as illustrated in the following figure. The key idea is to produce a distribution of next characters given the current context, and then to sample from the distribution to produce the next candidate character:

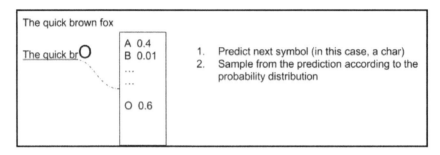

An example of prediction with "The quick brown fox" sentence

A simple variant is to store more than one prediction and therefore create a tree of possible expansions as illustrated in the following figure:

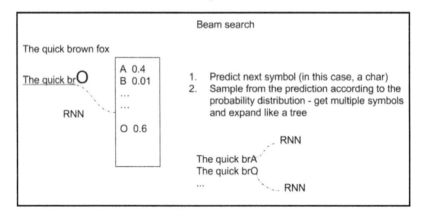

An example of tree prediction with "The quick brown fox" sentence

However, a model based on sequences can be used in a very large number of additional domains. In music, the next note in a composition will certainly depend on the previous notes, and in a video, the next frame in a movie is certainly related to the previous frames. Moreover, in certain situations, the current video frame, word, character, or musical note will not only depend on the previous but also on the following ones.

A model based on a temporal sequence can be described with an RNN where for a given input X_i at time i producing the output Y_i, a memory of previous states at time $[0, i-1]$ is fed back to the network. This idea of feeding back previous states is depicted by a recurrent loop, as shown in the following figures:

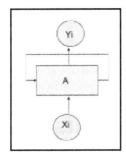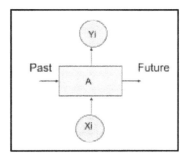

An example of feeding back

The recurrent relation can be conveniently expressed by *unfolding* the network, as illustrated in the following figure:

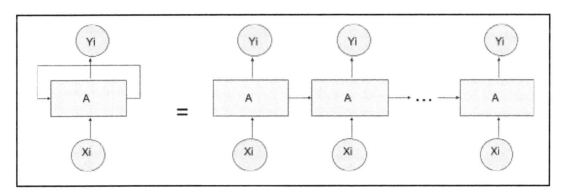

An example of unfolding a recurrent cell

The simplest RNN cell consists of a simple *tanh* function, the hyperbolic tangent function, as represented in the following figures:

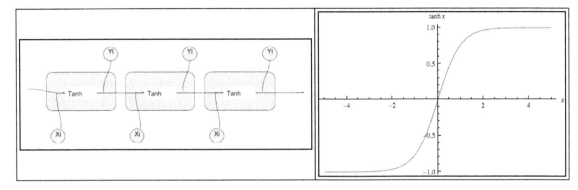

An example of simple tanh cell

Vanishing and exploding gradients

Training an RNN is hard because of two stability problems. Due to the feedback loop, the gradient can quickly diverge to infinity, or it can rapidly to 0. In both cases, as illustrated in the following figure, the network will stop learning anything useful. The problem of an exploding gradient can be tackled with a relatively simple solution based on **gradient clipping**. The problem of a vanishing gradient is more difficult to solve and it involves the definition of more complex RNN basic cells, such as **Long Short Term Memory (LSTM)**, or **Gated Recurrent Units (GRUs)**. Let's first discuss exploding gradients and gradient clipping:

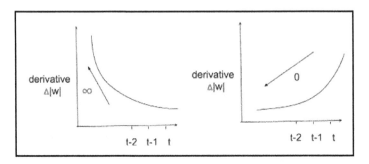

Examples of gradient

Gradient clipping consists of imposing a maximum value to the the gradient so that it cannot grow boundless. This simple solution, illustrated in the following figure, offers a simple solution to the problem of **exploding gradients:**

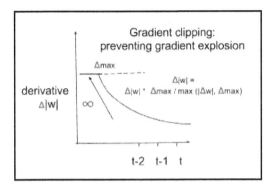

An example of gradient clipping

Solving the problem of a vanishing gradient requires a more complex model for memory which allows it to selectively forget previous states and remember only the one that really matters. Considering the following figure, the input is written in a memory M with a probability p in $[0,1]$, which is multiplied to weight the input.

In a similar way, the output is read with a probability p in $[0,1]$, which is multiplied to weight the output. One more probability is used to decide what to remember or forget:

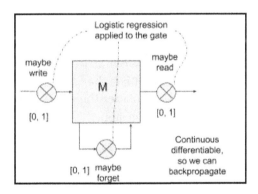

An example of memory cell

Long Short Term Memory (LSTM)

An LSTM network can control when to let the input enter the neuron, when to remember what has been learned in the previous time step, and when to let the output pass on to the next timestamp. All these decisions are self-tuned and only based on the input. At first glance, an LSTM looks difficult to understand but it is not. Let's use the following figure to explain how it works:

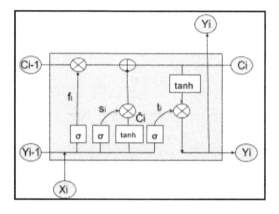

An example of an LSTM cell

First, we need a logistic function σ (see `Chapter 2`, *Regression*) to compute a value between 0 and 1 and control which piece of information flows through the LSTM *gates*. Remember that the logistic function is differentiable and therefore it allows backpropagation. Then, we need an operator ⊗ that takes two matrices of the same dimensions and produces another matrix where each element *ij* is the product of the elements *ij* of the original two matrices. Similarly, we need an operator ⊕ that takes two matrices of the same dimensions and produces another matrix where each element *ij* is the sum of the elements *ij* of the original two matrices. With these basic blocks, we consider the input X_i at time i and simply juxtapose it with output Y_{i-1} from the previous step.

The equation $f_t = \sigma(W_f.[y_{i-1}, x_i] + b_f$ is implements a logistic regression which controls the activation gate ⊗ and it is used to decide how much information from the *previous* candidate value C_{i-1} should be passed to the next candidate value C_i (here, W_f and b_f are the weight matrix and the bias used for the logistic regression). If the logistic outputs 1, this would mean *don't forget* the previous cell state C_{i-1}; if it outputs 0, this would mean *forget* the previous cell state C_{i-1}. Any number in (0,1) will represent the amount of information to be passed.

Then we have two equations: $s_i = \sigma(W_s[Y_{i-1},x_i]+b_s)$ used to control via $\otimes$ how much of the information $\hat{C}_i = tanh(W_C.[Y_{i-1},x_i] + b_c$ produced by the *current* cell should be added to the next candidate value C_i via the operator $\oplus$ according to the scheme represented in the preceding figure.

To implement what has discussed with the operators $\oplus$ and $\otimes$, we need another equation where the actual sums + and multiplications * take place: $C_i = f_i{}^*C_{i-1} + s_i{}^*\hat{C}_i$

Finally, we need to decide which part of the current cell should be sent to the Y_i output. This is simple: we take a logistic regression equation one more time and use this to control via an $\otimes$ operation which part of the candidate value should go to the output. Here, there is a little piece that deserves care and it is the use of the *tanh* function to squash the output into [-1, 1]. This latest step is described by the equation: $Y_i = t_i * \tanh(C_i)$

Now, I understand that this looks like a lot of math but there are two pieces of good news. First, the math part is not so difficult after all if you understand what the goal is that we want to achieve. Second, you can use LSTM cells as a blackbox drop-in replacement of standard RNN cells and immediately get the benefit of solving the problem of a vanishing gradient. For this reason, you really don't need to know all the math. You just take the TensorFlow LSTM implementation from the library and use it.

Gated Recurrent Units (GRUs) and Peephole LSTM

There have been a number of variants of LSTM cells proposed during recent years. Two of them are really popular. Peephole LSTM allows the gate layers to look at the cell state, as depicted in the following figure with dotted lines, while **Gated Recurrent Units (GRUs)** merge the hidden state and the cell state into one single channel of information.

Again, both GRUs and Peephole LSTM can be used as a blackbox drop-in for standard RNN cells with no need to know the underlying math. Both cells can be used for solving the problem of vanishing gradients and can be used for building deep neural networks:

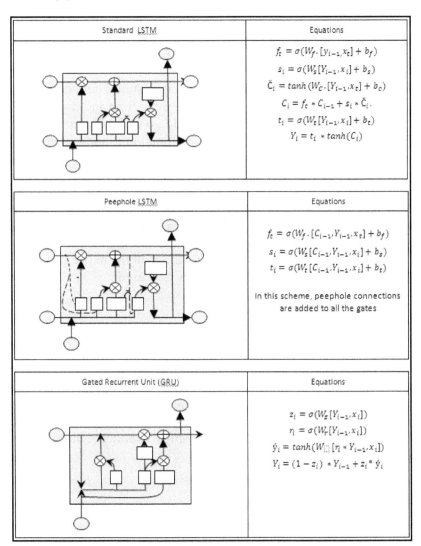

Standard LSTM	Equations
	$f_t = \sigma(W_f \cdot [y_{i-1}, x_t] + b_f)$
	$s_i = \sigma(W_s [Y_{i-1}, x_i] + b_s)$
	$\check{C}_i = \tanh(W_C \cdot [Y_{i-1}, x_t] + b_c)$
	$C_i = f_t * C_{i-1} + s_i * \check{C}_i$
	$t_i = \sigma(W_t [Y_{i-1}, x_i] + b_t)$
	$Y_i = t_i * \tanh(C_i)$
Peephole LSTM	Equations
	$f_t = \sigma(W_f \cdot [C_{i-1}, Y_{i-1}, x_t] + b_f)$
	$s_i = \sigma(W_s [C_{i-1}, Y_{i-1}, x_i] + b_s)$
	$t_i = \sigma(W_t [C_{i-1}, Y_{i-1}, x_i] + b_t)$
	In this scheme, peephole connections are added to all the gates
Gated Recurrent Unit (GRU)	Equations
	$z_i = \sigma(W_z [Y_{i-1}, x_i])$
	$r_i = \sigma(W_r [Y_{i-1}, x_i])$
	$\hat{y}_i = \tanh(W_\square [r_i * Y_{i-1}, x_i])$
	$Y_i = (1 - z_i) * Y_{i-1} + z_i * \hat{y}_i$

Examples of Standard LSTM, PeepHole LSTM, and GRU

Operating on sequences of vectors

What really makes RNNs powerful is the ability to operate over sequences of vectors, where both the input to an RNN and/or the output of an RNN can be a sequence. This is well represented by the following figure, where the leftmost example is a traditional (non-recursive) network, followed by an RNN with a sequence in output, followed by an RNN with a sequence in input, followed by an RNN with sequences both in input and in output where the sequences are not synced, followed by an RNN with sequences both in input and in output where the sequences are synced:

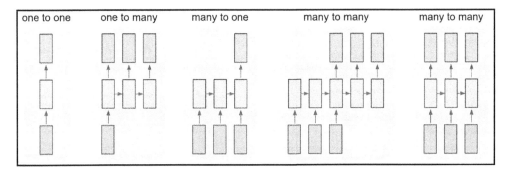

An example of RNN sequences as seen in http://karpathy.github.io/2015/05/21/rnn-effectiveness/

Machine translation is an example of non-synced sequences both in input and output: the network reads the input text as a sequence and *after* reading the full text, it outputs the target language.

Video classification is an example of synced sequences both in input and output: a video input is a sequence of frames and for each frame, a classification label is provided in output.

Andrej Karpathy's blog posting at `http://karpathy.github.io/2015/05/21/rnn-effectiveness/` is a must-read if you want to know more about fun applications of RNNs. He trained networks to write essays in Shakespeare's style (in Karpathy's words: *can barely recognize these samples from actual Shakespeare*), for writing realistic Wikipedia articles on imaginary subjects, for writing realistic theorem proofs of silly and unrealistic problems (in Karpathy's words: *More hallucinated algebraic geometry*) , and to write realistic fragments of Linux code (in Karpathy's words: *the model first recites the GNU license character by character, samples a few includes, generates some macros and then dives into the code*).

The following example is taken from `http://karpathy.github.io/2015/05/21/rnn-effectiveness/`:

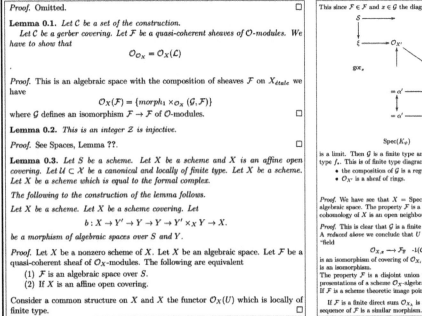
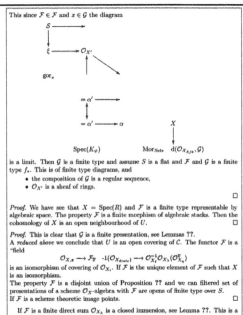

An example of text generated with RNNs

Neural machine translation - training a seq2seq RNN

Sequence to sequence (seq2seq) is a particular kind of RNN with successful applications in neural machine translation, text summarization, and speech recognition. In this recipe, we will discuss how to implement a neural machine translation with results similar to the one achieved by the Google Neural Machine Translation system (`https://research.googleblog.com/2016/09/a-neural-network-for-machine.html`). The key idea is to input a whole sequence of text, understand the entire meaning, and then output the translation as another sequence. The idea of reading an entire sequence is very different from the previous architectures, where a fixed set of words was translated from one source language into a destination language.

This section is inspired by the 2016 PhD thesis, *Neural Machine Translation*, by Minh-Thang Luong (`https://github.com/lmthang/thesis/blob/master/thesis.pdf`). The first key concept is the presence of an encoder-decoder architecture, where an encoder transforms a source sentence into a vector representing the meaning. This vector is then passed through a decoder to produce a translation. Both the encoders and the decoders are RNNs that can capture long-range dependencies in languages, for example, gender agreements and syntax structures, without knowing them a priori and with no need to have a 1:1 mapping across languages. This is a powerful capacity which enables very fluent translations:

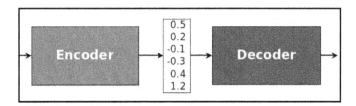

An example of encoder-decoder as seen in https://github.com/lmthang/thesis/blob/master/thesis.pdf

Let's see an example of an RNN translating the sentence **She loves cute cats** into **Elle aime les chats mignons**.

There are two RNNs: one that acts as the encoder, and one that acts as the decoder. The source sentence **She loves cute cats** is followed by a separator sign - and by the target sentence **Elle aime les chats mignons**. These two concatenated sentences are given in input to the encoder for training, and the decoder will produce the target **Elle aime les chats mignons**. Of course, we need multiple examples like this one for achieving good training:

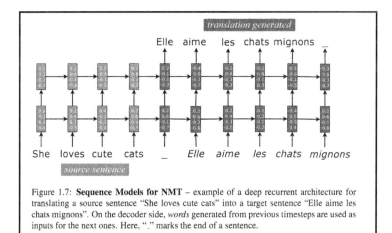

Figure 1.7: **Sequence Models for NMT** – example of a deep recurrent architecture for translating a source sentence "She loves cute cats" into a target sentence "Elle aime les chats mignons". On the decoder side, *words* generated from previous timesteps are used as inputs for the next ones. Here, "_" marks the end of a sentence.

An example of sequence models for NMT as seen in https://github.com/lmthang/thesis/blob/master/thesis.pdf

Now there is a number of RNNs variants we can have. Let's look at some of them:

- RNNs can be unidirectional or bidirectional. The latter will capture long-term relations in both directions.
- RNNs can have multiple hidden layers. The choice is a matter of optimization: on one hand, a deeper network can learn more; on the other hand, it might require a long time to be trained and might overfit.
- RNNs can have an embedding layer which maps words into an embedding space where similar words happen to be mapped very close.
- RNNs can use simple either recurrent cells, or LSTM, or PeepHole LSTM, or GRUs.

Still considering the PhD thesis, *Neural Machine Translation* (`https://github.com/lmthang/thesis/blob/master/thesis.pdf`), we can use embedding layers to map the input sentences into an embedding space. Then, there are two RNNs *stuck together* - the encoder for the source language and the decoder for the target language. As you can see, there are multiple hidden layers, and two flows: the feed-forward vertical direction connects the hidden layers, and the horizontal direction is the recurrent part transferring knowledge from the previous step to the next one:

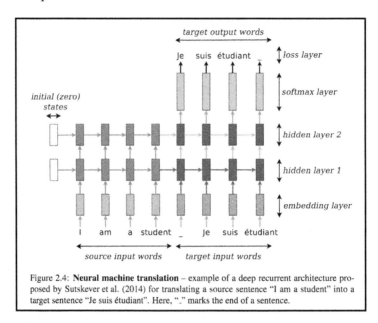

Figure 2.4: **Neural machine translation** – example of a deep recurrent architecture proposed by Sutskever et al. (2014) for translating a source sentence "I am a student" into a target sentence "Je suis étudiant". Here, "_" marks the end of a sentence.

An example of Neural machine translation as seen in https://github.com/lmthang/thesis/blob/master/thesis.pdf

In this recipe, we use NMT (Neural Machine Translation), a demo package for translation available online on top of TensorFlow.

Getting ready

NMT is available at `https://github.com/tensorflow/nmt/` and the code is on GitHub.

How to do it...

We proceed with the recipe as follows:

1. Clone NMT from GitHub:

```
git clone https://github.com/tensorflow/nmt/
```

2. Download a training dataset. In this case, we will use the training set for translating from Vietnamese to English. Other datasets are available at `https://nlp.stanford.edu/projects/nmt/` for additional languages, such as German and Czech:

```
nmt/scripts/download_iwslt15.sh /tmp/nmt_data
```

3. Considering `https://github.com/tensorflow/nmt/`, we are going to define the first embedding layer. The embedding layer takes an input, the vocabulary size V, and the desired size of the output embedding space. The vocabulary size is such that only the most frequent words in V are considered for embedding, while all the others are mapped to a common *unknown* term. In our case, the input is time-major, which means that the max time is the first input parameter (`https://www.tensorflow.org/api_docs/python/tf/nn/dynamic_rnn`):

```
# Embedding
embedding_encoder = variable_scope.get_variable(
"embedding_encoder", [src_vocab_size, embedding_size], ...)
# Look up embedding:
# encoder_inputs: [max_time, batch_size]
# encoder_emb_inp: [max_time, batch_size, embedding_size]
encoder_emb_inp = embedding_ops.embedding_lookup(
embedding_encoder, encoder_inputs)
```

4. Still considering `https://github.com/tensorflow/nmt/`, we define a simple encoder which uses `tf.nn.rnn_cell.BasicLSTMCell(num_units)` as a basic RNN cell. This is pretty simple but it is important to notice that given the basic RNN cell, we create the RNN by using `tf.nn.dynamic_rnn` (as specified in `https://www.tensorflow.org/api_docs/python/tf/nn/dynamic_rnn`):

```
# Build RNN cell
encoder_cell = tf.nn.rnn_cell.BasicLSTMCell(num_units)

# Run Dynamic RNN
# encoder_outpus: [max_time, batch_size, num_units]
# encoder_state: [batch_size, num_units]
encoder_outputs, encoder_state = tf.nn.dynamic_rnn(
encoder_cell, encoder_emb_inp,
sequence_length=source_sequence_length, time_major=True)
```

5. After that, we need to define the decoder. So the first thing is to have a basic RNN cell with `tf.nn.rnn_cell.BasicLSTMCell`, which is then used to create a basic sampling decoder `tf.contrib.seq2seq.BasicDecoder`, which is used to perform dynamic decoding with the decoder `tf.contrib.seq2seq.dynamic_decode`:

```
# Build RNN cell
decoder_cell = tf.nn.rnn_cell.BasicLSTMCell(num_units)
# Helper
helper = tf.contrib.seq2seq.TrainingHelper(
decoder_emb_inp, decoder_lengths, time_major=True)
# Decoder
decoder = tf.contrib.seq2seq.BasicDecoder(
decoder_cell, helper, encoder_state,
output_layer=projection_layer)
# Dynamic decoding
outputs, _ = tf.contrib.seq2seq.dynamic_decode(decoder, ...)
logits = outputs.rnn_output
```

6. The last stage in the network is a softmax dense stage to transform the top hidden states into a logit vector:

```
projection_layer = layers_core.Dense(
tgt_vocab_size, use_bias=False)
```

7. Of course, we need to define the cross-entropy function and the loss used during the training phase :

```
crossent = tf.nn.sparse_softmax_cross_entropy_with_logits(
 labels=decoder_outputs, logits=logits)
 train_loss = (tf.reduce_sum(crossent * target_weights) /
 batch_size)
```

8. The next step is to define the steps needed for backpropagation, and use an appropriate optimizer (in this case, Adam). Note that the gradient has been clipped and that Adam uses a predefined learning rate:

```
# Calculate and clip gradients
 params = tf.trainable_variables()
 gradients = tf.gradients(train_loss, params)
 clipped_gradients, _ = tf.clip_by_global_norm(
 gradients, max_gradient_norm)
# Optimization
 optimizer = tf.train.AdamOptimizer(learning_rate)
 update_step = optimizer.apply_gradients(
 zip(clipped_gradients, params))
```

9. So now we can run the code and understand what the different executed steps are. First, the training graph is created. Then the training iterations start. The metric used for evaluations is **bilingual evaluation understudy** (BLEU). This metric is the standard for evaluating the quality of text which has been machine-translated from one natural language to another. Quality is considered to be the correspondence between a machine and a human output. As you can see, this value grows over time:

```
python -m nmt.nmt --src=vi --tgt=en --vocab_prefix=/tmp/nmt_data/vocab --
train_prefix=/tmp/nmt_data/train --dev_prefix=/tmp/nmt_data/tst2012 --
test_prefix=/tmp/nmt_data/tst2013 --out_dir=/tmp/nmt_model --
num_train_steps=12000 --steps_per_stats=100 --num_layers=2 --num_units=128
--dropout=0.2 --metrics=bleu
# Job id 0
[...]
# creating train graph ...
num_layers = 2, num_residual_layers=0
cell 0 LSTM, forget_bias=1 DropoutWrapper, dropout=0.2 DeviceWrapper,
device=/gpu:0
cell 1 LSTM, forget_bias=1 DropoutWrapper, dropout=0.2 DeviceWrapper,
device=/gpu:0
cell 0 LSTM, forget_bias=1 DropoutWrapper, dropout=0.2 DeviceWrapper,
device=/gpu:0
cell 1 LSTM, forget_bias=1 DropoutWrapper, dropout=0.2 DeviceWrapper,
```

```
device=/gpu:0
start_decay_step=0, learning_rate=1, decay_steps 10000,decay_factor 0.98
[...]
# Start step 0, lr 1, Thu Sep 21 12:57:18 2017
# Init train iterator, skipping 0 elements
global step 100 lr 1 step-time 1.65s wps 3.42K ppl 1931.59 bleu 0.00
global step 200 lr 1 step-time 1.56s wps 3.59K ppl 690.66 bleu 0.00
[...]
global step 9100 lr 1 step-time 1.52s wps 3.69K ppl 39.73 bleu 4.89
global step 9200 lr 1 step-time 1.52s wps 3.72K ppl 40.47 bleu 4.89
global step 9300 lr 1 step-time 1.55s wps 3.62K ppl 40.59 bleu 4.89
[...]
# External evaluation, global step 9000
decoding to output /tmp/nmt_model/output_dev.
done, num sentences 1553, time 17s, Thu Sep 21 17:32:49 2017.
bleu dev: 4.9
saving hparams to /tmp/nmt_model/hparams
# External evaluation, global step 9000
decoding to output /tmp/nmt_model/output_test.
done, num sentences 1268, time 15s, Thu Sep 21 17:33:06 2017.
bleu test: 3.9
saving hparams to /tmp/nmt_model/hparams
[...]
global step 9700 lr 1 step-time 1.52s wps 3.71K ppl 38.01 bleu 4.89
```

How it works...

All the preceding code has been defined in `https://github.com/tensorflow/nmt/blob/master/nmt/model.py`. The key idea is to have two RNNs *packed together*. The first one is the encoder which works into an embedding space, mapping similar words very closely. The encoder *understands* the meaning of training examples and it produces a tensor as output. This tensor is then passed to the decoder simply by connecting the last hidden layer of the encoder to the initial layer of the decoder. Note that the learning happens because of our loss function based on cross-entropy with `labels=decoder_outputs`.

The code learns how to translate and the progress is tracked through iterations by the BLEU metric, as shown in the following figure:

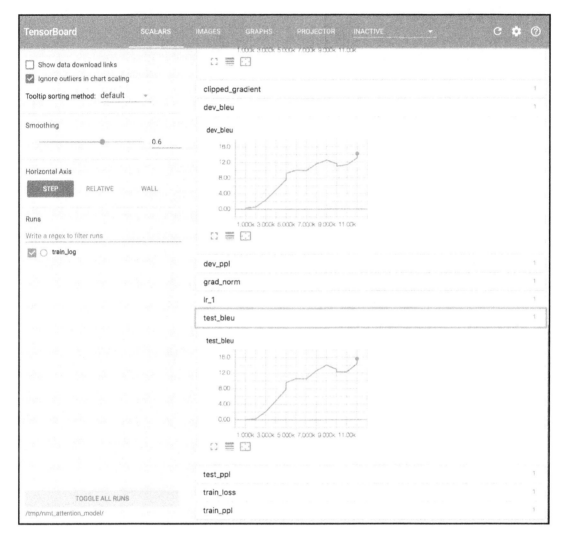

An example of BLEU metric in Tensorboard

Neural machine translation - inference on a seq2seq RNN

In this recipe, we use the results of the previous recipe to translate from a source language into a target language. The idea is very simple: a source sentence is given the two combined RNNs (encoder + decoder) as input . As soon as the sentence concludes, the decoder will emit logit values and we *greedily* emit the word associated with the maximum value. As an example, the word *moi* is emitted as the first token from the decoder because this word has the maximum logit value. After that, the word *suis* is emitted, and so on:

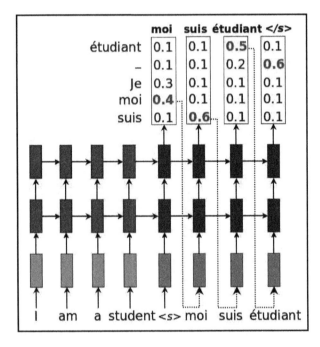

An example of sequence models for NMT with probabilities as seen in https://github.com/lmthang/thesis/blob/master/thesis.pdf

There are multiple strategies for using the output of a decoder:

- **Greedy:** The word corresponding to the maximum logit is emitted
- **Sampling:** A word is emitted by sampling the logit emitted by logits
- **Beam Search**: More than one prediction and therefore a tree of possible expansions is created

How to do it...

We proceed with the recipe as follows:

1. Define the greedy strategy for sampling the decoder. This is easy because we can use the library defined in `tf.contrib.seq2seq.GreedyEmbeddingHelper`. Since we don't know the exact length of the target sentence, we use a heuristic by limiting it to be a maximum of twice the length of the source sentence:

```
# Helper
helper = tf.contrib.seq2seq.GreedyEmbeddingHelper(
embedding_decoder,
tf.fill([batch_size], tgt_sos_id), tgt_eos_id)

# Decoder
decoder = tf.contrib.seq2seq.BasicDecoder(
decoder_cell, helper, encoder_state,
output_layer=projection_layer)
# Dynamic decoding
outputs, _ = tf.contrib.seq2seq.dynamic_decode(
decoder, maximum_iterations=maximum_iterations)
translations = outputs.sample_id
maximum_iterations = tf.round(tf.reduce_max(source_sequence_length) * 2)
```

2. We can now run the net, giving as input a sentence never seen before (`inference_input_file=/tmp/my_infer_file`) and letting the network translate the outcome (`inference_output_file=/tmp/nmt_model/output_infer`):

```
python -m nmt.nmt \
 --out_dir=/tmp/nmt_model \
 --inference_input_file=/tmp/my_infer_file.vi \
 --inference_output_file=/tmp/nmt_model/output_infer
```

How it works...

Two RNNs are *packed together* to form an encoder-decoder RNN network. The decoder emits logits, which are greedily transformed into words of the target language. As an example, an automatic translation from Vietnamese into English is shown here:

- **Input sentence in Vietnamese:** Khi tôi còn nhỏ , Tôi nghĩ rằng BắcTriều Tiên là đất nước tốt nhất trên thế giới và tôi thường hát bài " Chúng ta chẳng có gì phải ghen tị.

- **Output sentence translated into English:** When I'm a very good , I'm going to see the most important thing about the most important and I'm not sure what I'm going to say.

All you need is attention - another example of a seq2seq RNN

In this recipe, we present the **attention** methodology, a state-of-the-art solution for neural network translation. The idea behind attention was introduced in 2015 in the paper, *Neural Machine Translation by Jointly Learning to Align and Translate*, by Dzmitry Bahdanau, Kyunghyun Cho, and Yoshua Bengio (ICLR, 2015, https://arxiv.org/abs/1409.0473) and it consists of adding additional connections between the encoder and the decoder RNNs. Indeed, connecting the decoder only with the latest layer of the encoder imposes an information bottleneck and does not necessarily allow the passing of the information acquired by the previous encoder layers. The solution adopted with attention is illustrated in the following figure:

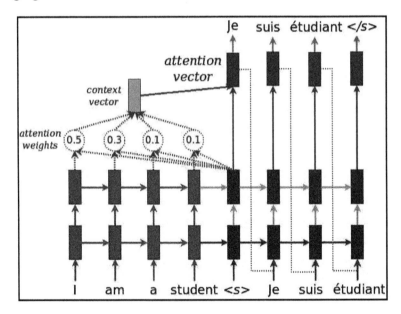

An example of attention model for NMT as seen in https://github.com/lmthang/thesis/blob/master/thesis.pdf

There are three aspects to consider:

- First, the current target hidden state is used together with all previous source states to derive attention weights which are used to pay more or less attention to tokens previously seen in the sequence
- Second, a context vector is created to summarize the results of the attention weights
- Third, the context vector is combined with the current target hidden state to obtain the attention vector

How to do it...

We proceed with the recipe as follows:

1. Define an attention mechanism by using the library `tf.contrib.seq2seq.LuongAttention`, which implements the attention model defined in *Effective Approaches to Attention-based Neural Machine Translation* by Minh-Thang Luong, Hieu Pham, and Christopher D. Manning (2015):

```
# attention_states: [batch_size, max_time, num_units]
attention_states = tf.transpose(encoder_outputs, [1, 0, 2])

# Create an attention mechanism
attention_mechanism = tf.contrib.seq2seq.LuongAttention(
num_units, attention_states,
memory_sequence_length=source_sequence_length)
```

2. Use the defined attention mechanism as a wrapper around the decoder cell by means of an attention wrapper:

```
decoder_cell = tf.contrib.seq2seq.AttentionWrapper(
decoder_cell, attention_mechanism,
attention_layer_size=num_units)
```

3. Run the code to see the results. We immediately notice that the attention mechanism produces a significant improvement in terms of the BLEU score:

```
python -m nmt.nmt \
> --attention=scaled_luong \
> --src=vi --tgt=en \
> --vocab_prefix=/tmp/nmt_data/vocab \
> --train_prefix=/tmp/nmt_data/train \
> --dev_prefix=/tmp/nmt_data/tst2012 \
```

```
>  --test_prefix=/tmp/nmt_data/tst2013 \
>  --out_dir=/tmp/nmt_attention_model \
>  --num_train_steps=12000 \
>  --steps_per_stats=100 \
>  --num_layers=2 \
>  --num_units=128 \
>  --dropout=0.2 \
>  --metrics=bleu
[...]
# Start step 0, lr 1, Fri Sep 22 22:49:12 2017
# Init train iterator, skipping 0 elements
global step 100 lr 1 step-time 1.71s wps 3.23K ppl 15193.44 bleu 0.00
[...]
# Final, step 12000 lr 0.98 step-time 1.67 wps 3.37K ppl 14.64, dev ppl
14.01, dev bleu 15.9, test ppl 12.58, test bleu 17.5, Sat Sep 23 04:35:42
2017
# Done training!, time 20790s, Sat Sep 23 04:35:42 2017.
# Start evaluating saved best models.
[..]
loaded infer model parameters from
/tmp/nmt_attention_model/best_bleu/translate.ckpt-12000, time 0.06s
# 608
src: nhưng bạn biết điều gì không ?
ref: But you know what ?
nmt: But what do you know ?
[...]
# Best bleu, step 12000 step-time 1.67 wps 3.37K, dev ppl 14.01, dev bleu
15.9, test ppl 12.58, test bleu 17.5, Sat Sep 23 04:36:35 2017
```

How it works...

Attention is a mechanism for using the information acquired by the inner states of the encoder RNN and combining this information with the final state of the decoder. The key idea is that, in this way, it is possible to pay more or less attention to some tokens in the source sequence. The gain obtained with attention is shown in the following figure representing the BLEU score.

We notice a significant gain with respect to the same diagram given in our first recipe, where no attention was used:

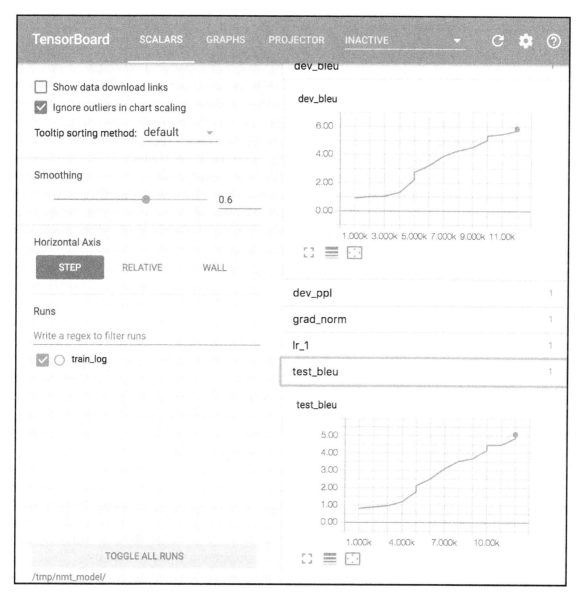

An example of BLEU metrics with attention in Tensorboard

There's more...

It is worth remembering that seq2seq can be used for more than just Machine Translation. Let's see some examples:

- Lukasz Kaiser, in *Grammar as a Foreign Language* (https://arxiv.org/abs/1412. 7449), uses the seq2seq model to build a constituency parser. A constituency parse tree breaks text into subphrases. Non-terminals in the tree are types of phrases, the terminals are the words in the sentence, and the edges are unlabeled.
- Another application of seq2seq is SyntaxNet, aka Parsey McParserFace, (a syntactic parser; https://research.googleblog.com/2016/05/announcing-syntaxnet-worlds-most.html), which is a key first component in many NLU systems. Given a sentence as input, it tags each word with a **part-of-speech** (POS) tag that describes the word's syntactic function, and it determines the syntactic relationships between words in the sentence, represented in the dependency parse tree. These syntactic relationships are directly related to the underlying meaning of the sentence in question.

The following figure gives us a good idea of the concept:

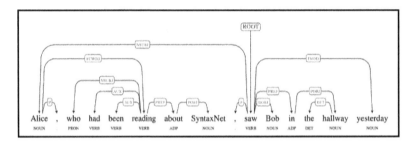

An example of SyntaxNet as seen in https://research.googleblog.com/2016/05/announcing-syntaxnet-worlds-most.html

Learning to write as Shakespeare with RNNs

In this recipe, we will learn how to generate text similar to that written by William Shakespeare. The key idea is very simple: we take as input a real text written by Shakespeare and we give it as input to an RNN which will learn the sequences. This learning is then used to generate new text which looks like that written by the greatest writer in the English language.

For the sake of simplicity, we will use the framework TFLearn (`http://tflearn.org/`), which runs on top of TensorFlow. This example is part of the standard distribution and it is available at `https://github.com/tflearn/tflearn/blob/master/examples/nlp/lstm_generator_shakespeare.py`. The model developed one is an RNN character-level language model where the sequences considered are sequences of characters and not words.

How to do it...

We proceed with the recipe as follows:

1. Install TFLearn with `pip`:

```
pip install -I tflearn
```

2. Import a number of useful modules and download an example of text written by Shakespeare. In this case, we use one available at `https://raw.githubusercontent.com/tflearn/tflearn.github.io/master/resources/shakespeare_input.txt`:

```
import os
import pickle
from six.moves import urllib
import tflearn
from tflearn.data_utils import *
path = "shakespeare_input.txt"
char_idx_file = 'char_idx.pickle'
if not os.path.isfile(path):
urllib.request.urlretrieve("https://raw.githubusercontent.com/tflearn/tflearn.github.io/master/resources/shakespeare_input.txt", path)
```

3. Transform the input text into a vector and return the parsed sequences and targets, along with the associated dictionary, by using `string_to_semi_redundant_sequences()`, which returns a tuple (inputs, targets, dictionary):

```
maxlen = 25
char_idx = None
if os.path.isfile(char_idx_file):
print('Loading previous char_idx')
char_idx = pickle.load(open(char_idx_file, 'rb'))
X, Y, char_idx = \
```

```
textfile_to_semi_redundant_sequences(path, seq_maxlen=maxlen, redun_step=3,
pre_defined_char_idx=char_idx)
pickle.dump(char_idx, open(char_idx_file,'wb'))
```

4. Define an RNN made up of three LSTMs, each of which has 512 nodes and returns the full sequence instead of the last sequence output only. Note that we use drop-out modules with a probability of 50% for connecting the LSTM modules. The last layer is a dense layer applying a softmax with length equal to the dictionary size. The loss function is `categorical_crossentropy` and the optimizer is Adam:

```
g = tflearn.input_data([None, maxlen, len(char_idx)])
g = tflearn.lstm(g, 512, return_seq=True)
g = tflearn.dropout(g, 0.5)
g = tflearn.lstm(g, 512, return_seq=True)
g = tflearn.dropout(g, 0.5)
g = tflearn.lstm(g, 512)
g = tflearn.dropout(g, 0.5)
g = tflearn.fully_connected(g, len(char_idx), activation='softmax')
g = tflearn.regression(g, optimizer='adam',
loss='categorical_crossentropy',
learning_rate=0.001)
```

5. Given the network defined in step 4, we can now generate the sequence with the library `flearn.models.generator.SequenceGenerator(network, dictionary=char_idx, seq_maxlen=maxle, clip_gradients=5.0, checkpoint_path='model_shakespeare')`:

```
m = tflearn.SequenceGenerator(g, dictionary=char_idx,
seq_maxlen=maxlen,
clip_gradients=5.0,
checkpoint_path='model_shakespeare')
```

6. For 50 iterations, we take a random sequence from the input text and we generate a new text. Temperature is controlling the novelty of the created sequence; a temperature close to 0 will look like samples used for training, while the higher the temperature, the more the novelty:

```
for i in range(50):
seed = random_sequence_from_textfile(path, maxlen)
m.fit(X, Y, validation_set=0.1, batch_size=128,
n_epoch=1, run_id='shakespeare')
print("-- TESTING...")
print("-- Test with temperature of 1.0 --")
print(m.generate(600, temperature=1.0, seq_seed=seed))
```

```
print("-- Test with temperature of 0.5 --")
print(m.generate(600, temperature=0.5, seq_seed=seed))
```

How it works...

When a new unknown or forgotten work of art is about to be attributed to an author, there are eminent academics who compare this work with other pieces of work attributed to the author. What the academics do is to find common patterns in the text sequence of the well-known works, hoping to find similar patterns in the unknown work.

This recipe works in a similar way: an RNN learns what the most peculiar patterns in Shakespeare's writing are and then these patterns are used to generate new, never-seen-before texts which well represent the style of the greatest English author.

Let's see a few examples of execution:

```
python shakespeare.py
Loading previous char_idx
Vectorizing text...
Text total length: 4,573,338
Distinct chars : 67
Total sequences : 1,524,438
---------------------------------
Run id: shakespeare
Log directory: /tmp/tflearn_logs/
```

First iteration

Here, the network is learning some basic structure, including the need to have dialog about fictional characters (DIA, SURYONT, HRNTLGIPRMAR, and ARILEN). However, the English is still very poor and lots of words are not really in proper English:

```
---------------------------------
Training samples: 1371994
Validation samples: 152444
--
Training Step: 10719 | total loss: 2.22092 | time: 22082.057s
| Adam | epoch: 001 | loss: 2.22092 | val_loss: 2.12443 -- iter:
1371994/1371994
-- TESTING...
-- Test with temperature of 1.0 --
'st thou, malice?
If thou caseghough memet oud mame meard'ke. Afs weke wteak, Dy ny wold' as
to of my tho gtroy ard has seve, hor then that wordith gole hie, succ,
```

```
caight fom?
DIA:
A gruos ceen, I peey
by my
Wiouse rat Sebine would.
waw-this afeean.
SURYONT:
Teeve nourterong a oultoncime bucice'is furtutun
Ame my sorivass; a mut my peant?
Am:
Fe, that lercom ther the nome, me, paatuy corns wrazen meas ghomn'ge const
pheale,
As yered math thy vans:
I im foat worepoug and thit mije woml!
HRNTLGIPRMAR:
I'd derfomquesf thiy of doed ilasghele hanckol, my corire-hougangle!
Kiguw troll! you eelerd tham my fom Inow lith a
-- Test with temperature of 0.5 --
'st thou, malice?
If thou prall sit I har, with and the sortafe the nothint of the fore the
fir with with the ceme at the ind the couther hit yet of the sonsee in
solles and that not of hear fore the hath bur.
ARILEN:
More you a to the mare me peod sore,
And fore string the reouck and and fer to the so has the theat end the
dore; of mall the sist he the bot courd wite be the thoule the to nenge ape
and this not the the ball bool me the some that dears,
The be to the thes the let the with the thear tould fame boors and not to
not the deane fere the womour hit muth so thand the e meentt my to the
treers and woth and wi
```

After a few iterations

Here, the network is starting to learn the proper structure for dialog, and the written English looks like more correct with sentences such as `Well, there shall the things to need the offer to our heart` and `There is not that be so then to the death To make the body and all the mind:`

```
--------------------------------
Training samples: 1371994
Validation samples: 152444
--
Training Step: 64314 | total loss: 1.44823 | time: 21842.362s
| Adam | epoch: 006 | loss: 1.44823 | val_loss: 1.40140 -- iter:
1371994/1371994
--
```

```
-- Test with temperature of 0.5 --
in this kind.
THESEUS:
There is not that be so then to the death
To make the body and all the mind.
BENEDICK:
Well, there shall the things to need the offer to our heart,
To not are he with him: I have see the hands are to true of him that I am
not,
The whom in some the fortunes,
Which she were better not to do him?
KING HENRY VI:
I have some a starter, and and seen the more to be the boy, and be such a
plock and love so say, and I will be his entire,
And when my masters are a good virtues,
That see the crown of our worse,
This made a called grace to hear him and an ass,
And the provest and stand,
```

There's more...

The blog post *The Unreasonable Effectiveness of Recurrent Neural Networks* (`http://karpathy.github.io/2015/05/21/rnn-effectiveness/`) describes a fascinating set of examples of RNN character-level language models, including the following:

- Shakespeare text generation similar to this example
- Wikipedia text generation similar to this example, but based on different training text
- Algebraic geometry (LaTex) text generation similar to this example, but based on different training text
- Linux source code text generation similar to this example, but based on different training text
- Baby names text generation similar to this example, but based on different training text

Learning to predict future Bitcoin value with RNNs

In this recipe, we will learn how to predict future Bitcoin value with an RNN. The key idea is that the temporal sequence of values observed in the past is a good predictor of future values. For this recipe, we will use the code available at `https://github.com/guillaume-chevalier/seq2seq-signal-prediction` under the MIT license. The Bitcoin value for a given temporal interval is downloaded via an API from `https://www.coindesk.com/api/`. Here is a piece of the API documentation:

> *We offer historical data from our Bitcoin Price Index through the following endpoint:*
> *https://api.coindesk.com/v1/bpi/historical/close.json*
> *By default, this will return the previous 31 days' worth of data. This endpoint accepts the following optional parameters:*
> *?index=[USD/CNY]The index to return data for. Defaults to USD.*
> *?currency=<VALUE>The currency to return the data in, specified in ISO 4217 format. Defaults to USD.*
> *?start=<VALUE>&end=<VALUE> Allows data to be returned for a specific date range. Must be listed as a pair of start and end parameters, with dates supplied in the YYYY-MM-DD format, e.g. 2013-09-01 for September 1st, 2013.*
> *?for=yesterday Specifying this will return a single value for the previous day. Overrides the start/end parameter.*
> *Sample Request:*
> `https://api.coindesk.com/v1/bpi/historical/close.json?start=2013-09-01&end=2013-09-05`
> *Sample JSON Response:*
> *{"bpi":{"2013-09-01":128.2597,"2013-09-02":127.3648,"2013-09-03":127.5915,"2013-09-04":120.5738,"2013-09-05":120.5333},"disclaimer":"This data was produced from the CoinDesk Bitcoin Price Index. BPI value data returned as USD.","time":{"updated":"Sep 6, 2013 00:03:00 UTC","updatedISO":"2013-09-06T00:03:00+00:00"}}*

How to do it...

Here is how we proceed with the recipe:

1. Clone the following GitHub repository. This is a project to encourage users to try and experiment with the seq2seq neural network architecture:

```
git clone
https://github.com/guillaume-chevalier/seq2seq-signal-prediction.git
```

2. Given the preceding repository, consider the following functions which load and normalize the Bitcoin historical data for the USD or EUR Bitcoin value. The functions are defined in `dataset.py`. Training and testing data are separated according to the 80/20 rule. As a consequence, 20 percent of the testing data is the most recent historical Bitcoin values. Every example contains 40 data points of USD and then EUR data in the feature axis/dimension. Data is normalized according to the mean and standard deviation. The function `generate_x_y_data_v4` generates random samples of the training data (respectively, the testing data) of size `batch_size`:

```python
def loadCurrency(curr, window_size):
    """
    Return the historical data for the USD or EUR bitcoin value. Is done
with an web API call.
    curr = "USD" | "EUR"
    """
    # For more info on the URL call, it is inspired by :
    # https://github.com/Levino/coindesk-api-node
    r = requests.get(
"http://api.coindesk.com/v1/bpi/historical/close.json?start=2010-07-17&end=
2017-03-03&currency={}".format(
        curr
    )
    )
    data = r.json()
    time_to_values = sorted(data["bpi"].items())
    values = [val for key, val in time_to_values]
    kept_values = values[1000:]
    X = []
    Y = []
    for i in range(len(kept_values) - window_size * 2):
        X.append(kept_values[i:i + window_size])
        Y.append(kept_values[i + window_size:i + window_size * 2])
    # To be able to concat on inner dimension later on:
    X = np.expand_dims(X, axis=2)
    Y = np.expand_dims(Y, axis=2)
    return X, Y
def normalize(X, Y=None):
    """
    Normalise X and Y according to the mean and standard
deviation of the X values only.
    """
    # # It would be possible to normalize with last rather than mean, such
as:
    # lasts = np.expand_dims(X[:, -1, :], axis=1)
    # assert (lasts[:, :] == X[:, -1, :]).all(), "{}, {}, {}.
```

```
{}".format(lasts[:, :].shape, X[:, -1, :].shape, lasts[:, :], X[:, -1, :])
    mean = np.expand_dims(np.average(X, axis=1) + 0.00001, axis=1)
    stddev = np.expand_dims(np.std(X, axis=1) + 0.00001, axis=1)
    # print (mean.shape, stddev.shape)
    # print (X.shape, Y.shape)
    X = X - mean
    X = X / (2.5 * stddev)
    if Y is not None:
        assert Y.shape == X.shape, (Y.shape, X.shape)
        Y = Y - mean
        Y = Y / (2.5 * stddev)
        return X, Y
    return X


def fetch_batch_size_random(X, Y, batch_size):
    """
    Returns randomly an aligned batch_size of X and Y among all examples.
    The external dimension of X and Y must be the batch size
(eg: 1 column = 1 example).
    X and Y can be N-dimensional.
    """
    assert X.shape == Y.shape, (X.shape, Y.shape)
    idxes = np.random.randint(X.shape[0], size=batch_size)
    X_out = np.array(X[idxes]).transpose((1, 0, 2))
    Y_out = np.array(Y[idxes]).transpose((1, 0, 2))
    return X_out, Y_out
X_train = []
Y_train = []
X_test = []
Y_test = []


def generate_x_y_data_v4(isTrain, batch_size):
    """
    Return financial data for the bitcoin.
    Features are USD and EUR, in the internal dimension.
    We normalize X and Y data according to the X only to not
    spoil the predictions we ask for.
    For every window (window or seq_length), Y is the prediction following
X.
    Train and test data are separated according to the 80/20
rule.
    Therefore, the 20 percent of the test data are the most
    recent historical bitcoin values. Every example in X contains
    40 points of USD and then EUR data in the feature axis/dimension.
    It is to be noted that the returned X and Y has the same shape
    and are in a tuple.
    """
    # 40 pas values for encoder, 40 after for decoder's predictions.
```

```
    seq_length = 40
    global Y_train
    global X_train
    global X_test
    global Y_test
    # First load, with memoization:
    if len(Y_test) == 0:
        # API call:
        X_usd, Y_usd = loadCurrency("USD",
window_size=seq_length)
        X_eur, Y_eur = loadCurrency("EUR",
window_size=seq_length)
        # All data, aligned:
        X = np.concatenate((X_usd, X_eur), axis=2)
        Y = np.concatenate((Y_usd, Y_eur), axis=2)
        X, Y = normalize(X, Y)
        # Split 80-20:
        X_train = X[:int(len(X) * 0.8)]
        Y_train = Y[:int(len(Y) * 0.8)]
        X_test = X[int(len(X) * 0.8):]
        Y_test = Y[int(len(Y) * 0.8):]
    if isTrain:
        return fetch_batch_size_random(X_train, Y_train, batch_size)
    else:
        return fetch_batch_size_random(X_test, Y_test, batch_size)
```

3. Generate the training, validation, and testing data, and define a number of hyperparameters such as `batch_size`, `hidden_dim` (the number of hidden neurons in the RNN), and `layers_stacked_count` (the number of stacked recurrent cells). In addition, define a number of parameters for fine-tuning the optimizer, such as the optimizer's learning rate, number of iterations, `lr_decay` for the optimizer's simulated annealing, the optimizer's momentum, and L2 regularization for avoiding overfitting. Note that the GitHub repository has the default `batch_size` = 5 and `nb_iters` = 150 but I've obtained better results with `batch_size` = 1000 and `nb_iters` = 100000:

```
from datasets import generate_x_y_data_v4
generate_x_y_data = generate_x_y_data_v4
import tensorflow as tf
import numpy as np
import matplotlib.pyplot as plt
%matplotlib inline
sample_x, sample_y = generate_x_y_data(isTrain=True, batch_size=3)
print("Dimensions of the dataset for 3 X and 3 Y training
examples : ")
print(sample_x.shape)
```

```
print(sample_y.shape)
print("(seq_length, batch_size, output_dim)")
print sample_x, sample_y
# Internal neural network parameters
seq_length = sample_x.shape[0]  # Time series will have the same past and
future (to be predicted) lenght.
batch_size = 5  # Low value used for live demo purposes - 100 and 1000
would be possible too, crank that up!
output_dim = input_dim = sample_x.shape[-1]  # Output dimension (e.g.:
multiple signals at once, tied in time)
hidden_dim = 12  # Count of hidden neurons in the recurrent units.
layers_stacked_count = 2  # Number of stacked recurrent cells, on the
neural depth axis.
# Optmizer:
learning_rate = 0.007  # Small lr helps not to diverge during training.
nb_iters = 150  # How many times we perform a training step (therefore how
many times we show a batch).
lr_decay = 0.92  # default: 0.9 . Simulated annealing.
momentum = 0.5  # default: 0.0 . Momentum technique in weights update
lambda_l2_reg = 0.003  # L2 regularization of weights - avoids overfitting
```

4. Define the network as an encoder-decoder made up of basic GRU cells. The network is made up of `layers_stacked_count=2` RNNs, and we will visualize the network with TensorBoard. Note that `hidden_dim = 12` are the hidden neurons in the recurrent units:

```
tf.nn.seq2seq = tf.contrib.legacy_seq2seq
tf.nn.rnn_cell = tf.contrib.rnn
tf.nn.rnn_cell.GRUCell = tf.contrib.rnn.GRUCell
tf.reset_default_graph()
# sess.close()
sess = tf.InteractiveSession()
with tf.variable_scope('Seq2seq'):
    # Encoder: inputs
    enc_inp = [
        tf.placeholder(tf.float32, shape=(None, input_dim),
name="inp_{}".format(t))
            for t in range(seq_length)
    ]
    # Decoder: expected outputs
    expected_sparse_output = [
        tf.placeholder(tf.float32, shape=(None, output_dim),
name="expected_sparse_output_".format(t))
            for t in range(seq_length)
    ]
    # Give a "GO" token to the decoder.
    # You might want to revise what is the appended value "+ enc_inp[:-1]".
```

```
    dec_inp = [ tf.zeros_like(enc_inp[0], dtype=np.float32, name="GO") ] +
enc_inp[:-1]
    # Create a `layers_stacked_count` of stacked RNNs (GRU cells here).
    cells = []
    for i in range(layers_stacked_count):
        with tf.variable_scope('RNN_{}'.format(i)):
            cells.append(tf.nn.rnn_cell.GRUCell(hidden_dim))
            # cells.append(tf.nn.rnn_cell.BasicLSTMCell(...))
    cell = tf.nn.rnn_cell.MultiRNNCell(cells)
    # For reshaping the input and output dimensions of the seq2seq RNN:
    w_in = tf.Variable(tf.random_normal([input_dim, hidden_dim]))
    b_in = tf.Variable(tf.random_normal([hidden_dim], mean=1.0))
    w_out = tf.Variable(tf.random_normal([hidden_dim, output_dim]))
    b_out = tf.Variable(tf.random_normal([output_dim]))
reshaped_inputs = [tf.nn.relu(tf.matmul(i, w_in) + b_in) for i in enc_inp]
# Here, the encoder and the decoder uses the same cell, HOWEVER,
    # the weights aren't shared among the encoder and decoder, we have two
    # sets of weights created under the hood according to that function's
def.

    dec_outputs, dec_memory = tf.nn.seq2seq.basic_rnn_seq2seq(
        enc_inp,
        dec_inp,
        cell
    )

output_scale_factor = tf.Variable(1.0, name="Output_ScaleFactor")
    # Final outputs: with linear rescaling similar to batch norm,
    # but without the "norm" part of batch normalization hehe.
    reshaped_outputs = [output_scale_factor*(tf.matmul(i, w_out) + b_out)
for i in dec_outputs]
    # Merge all the summaries and write them out to /tmp/bitcoin_logs (by
default)
    merged = tf.summary.merge_all()
    train_writer = tf.summary.FileWriter('/tmp/bitcoin_logs',
sess.graph)
```

5. Now let's run the TensorBoard and visualize the network consisting of an RNN encoder and an RNN decoder:

```
tensorboard --logdir=/tmp/bitcoin_logs
```

The following is the flow of the code:

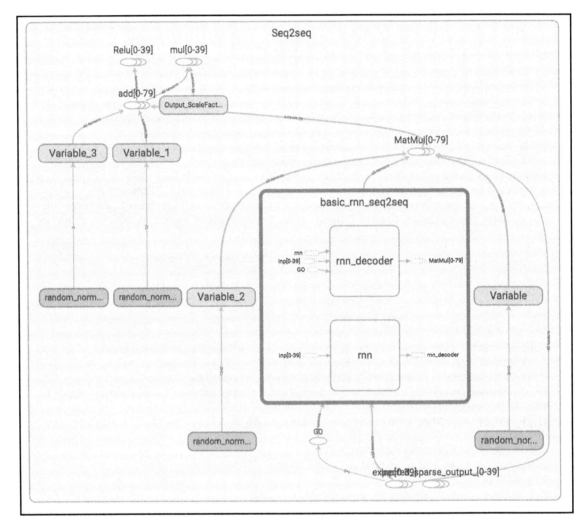

An example of code for Bitcoin value prediction as seen in Tensorboard

6. Now let's define the loss function as an L2 loss with regularization to avoid overfitting and to have a better generalization. The chosen optimizer is RMSprop with the value of `learning_rate`, decay, and momentum as defined at step 3:

```
# Training loss and optimizer
with tf.variable_scope('Loss'):
    # L2 loss
    output_loss = 0
    for _y, _Y in zip(reshaped_outputs, expected_sparse_output):
        output_loss += tf.reduce_mean(tf.nn.l2_loss(_y - _Y))
    # L2 regularization (to avoid overfitting and to have a  better
generalization capacity)
    reg_loss = 0
    for tf_var in tf.trainable_variables():
        if not ("Bias" in tf_var.name or "Output_" in tf_var.name):
            reg_loss += tf.reduce_mean(tf.nn.l2_loss(tf_var))
    loss = output_loss + lambda_l2_reg * reg_loss

with tf.variable_scope('Optimizer'):
    optimizer = tf.train.RMSPropOptimizer(learning_rate, decay=lr_decay,
momentum=momentum)
    train_op = optimizer.minimize(loss)
```

7. Prepare for training in batch by generating the training data and by running the optimizer on `batch_size` examples from the dataset. Similarly, prepare for test by generating test data on `batch_size` examples from the dataset. Training runs for `nb_iters+1` iterations, and one iteration out of ten is used to test the results:

```
def train_batch(batch_size):
    """
    Training step that optimizes the weights
    provided some batch_size X and Y examples from the dataset.
    """
    X, Y = generate_x_y_data(isTrain=True, batch_size=batch_size)
    feed_dict = {enc_inp[t]: X[t] for t in range(len(enc_inp))}
    feed_dict.update({expected_sparse_output[t]: Y[t] for t in
range(len(expected_sparse_output))})
    _, loss_t = sess.run([train_op, loss], feed_dict)
    return loss_t

def test_batch(batch_size):
    """
    Test step, does NOT optimizes. Weights are frozen by not
    doing sess.run on the train_op.
    """
    X, Y = generate_x_y_data(isTrain=False, batch_size=batch_size)
```

```
   feed_dict = {enc_inp[t]: X[t] for t in range(len(enc_inp))}
   feed_dict.update({expected_sparse_output[t]: Y[t] for t in
range(len(expected_sparse_output))})
   loss_t = sess.run([loss], feed_dict)
   return loss_t[0]

# Training
train_losses = []
test_losses = []
sess.run(tf.global_variables_initializer())

for t in range(nb_iters+1):
   train_loss = train_batch(batch_size)
   train_losses.append(train_loss)
   if t % 10 == 0:
       # Tester
       test_loss = test_batch(batch_size)
       test_losses.append(test_loss)
       print("Step {}/{}, train loss: {}, \tTEST loss: {}".format(t,
nb_iters, train_loss, test_loss))
print("Fin. train loss: {}, \tTEST loss: {}".format(train_loss, test_loss))
```

8. Visualize the `n_predictions` results. We will visualize `nb_predictions` = 5 predictions in yellow and the actual value ix in blue with an x. Note that the prediction starts with the last blue dot in the histogram and, visually, you can observe that even this simple model is pretty accurate:

```
# Test
nb_predictions = 5
print("Let's visualize {} predictions with our
signals:".format(nb_predictions))
X, Y = generate_x_y_data(isTrain=False, batch_size=nb_predictions)
feed_dict = {enc_inp[t]: X[t] for t in range(seq_length)}
outputs = np.array(sess.run([reshaped_outputs], feed_dict)[0])
for j in range(nb_predictions):
   plt.figure(figsize=(12, 3))
   for k in range(output_dim):
       past = X[:,j,k]
       expected = Y[:,j,k]
       pred = outputs[:,j,k]
       label1 = "Seen (past) values" if k==0 else "_nolegend_"
       label2 = "True future values" if k==0 else "_nolegend_"
       label3 = "Predictions" if k==0 else "_nolegend_"
       plt.plot(range(len(past)), past, "o--b", label=label1)
       plt.plot(range(len(past), len(expected)+len(past)), expected, "x--
b", label=label2)
       plt.plot(range(len(past), len(pred)+len(past)), pred, "o--y",
```

```
        label=label3)
    plt.legend(loc='best')
    plt.title("Predictions v.s. true values")
    plt.show()
```

We get the results as follows:

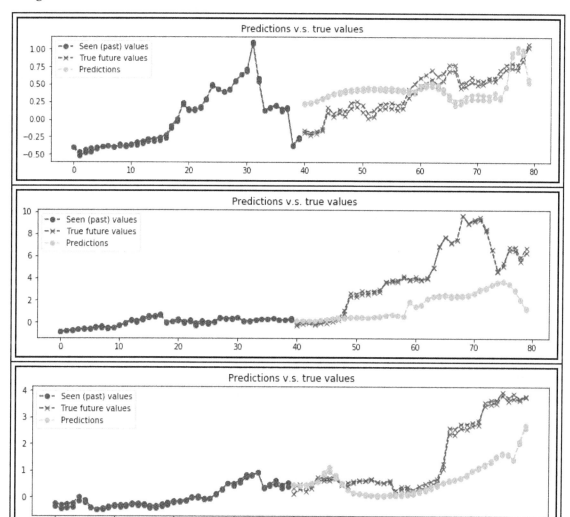

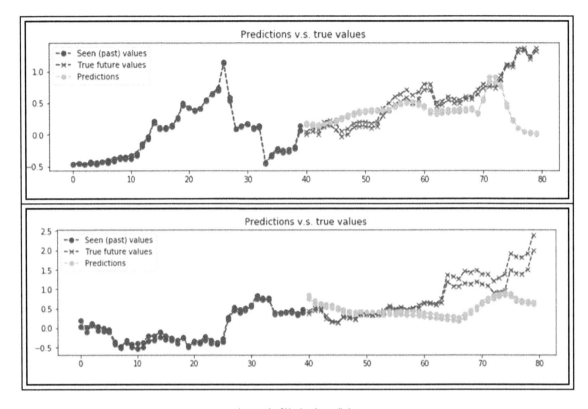

An example of bitcoin value prediction

How it works...

An encoder-decoder layer stacked RNN with GRU basic cells is used to predict Bitcoin value. RNNs are very good at learning sequences, and indeed the Bitcoin prediction is reasonably accurate even with a simple model based on 2 layers and 12 GRU cells. Of course, this prediction code is not an encouragement to invest in Bitcoin but only to discuss a deep learning methodology. Moreover, more experiments are needed in order to verify whether or not we have a situation of data overfitting.

There's more...

Predicting stock market values is a cool RNN application and there are a number of handy packages available, for instance:

- Drnns-prediction implements deep RNNs using the Keras neural networks library on the Daily News for Stock Market Prediction dataset from Kaggle. The dataset task is to predict future movement of the DJIA using the current and previous day's news headlines as features. The open source code is available at `https://github.com/jvpoulos/drnns-prediction`.

- Michael Luk wrote an interesting blog posting on how to predict Coca Cola stock volume based on RNNs: `https://sflscientific.com/data-science-blog/2017/2/10/predicting-stock-volume-with-lstm`.

- Jakob Aungiers wrote another interesting blog posting on *LSTM Neural Network for Time Series Prediction*: `http://www.jakob-aungiers.com/articles/a/LSTM-Neural-Network-for-Time-Series-Prediction`.

Many-to-one and many-to-many RNN examples

In this recipe, we summarize what has been discussed with RNNs by providing various examples of RNN mapping. For the sake of simplicity, we will adopt Keras and will show how to write one-to-one, one-to-many, many-to-one, and many-to-many mappings as represented in the following figure:

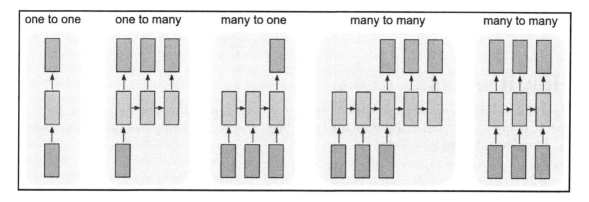

An example of RNN sequences as seen in http://karpathy.github.io/2015/05/21/rnn-effectiveness/

How to do it...

We proceed with the recipe as follows:

1. If you want to create a **one-to-one** mapping, this is not an RNN but instead a dense layer. Suppose to have a model already defined and you want to add a Dense network. Then this is easily implemented in Keras:

```
model = Sequential()
model.add(Dense(output_size, input_shape=input_shape))
```

2. If you want to create a **one-to-many** option, this can be achieved with `RepeatVector(...)`. Note that `return_sequences` is a boolean to decide whether to return the last output in the output sequence, or the full sequence:

```
model = Sequential()
model.add(RepeatVector(number_of_times,input_shape=input_shape))
model.add(LSTM(output_size, return_sequences=True))
```

3. If you want to create a **many-to-one** option, this can be achieved with the following LSTM code snippet:

```
model = Sequential()
model.add(LSTM(1, input_shape=(timesteps, data_dim)))
```

4. If you want to create a **many-to-many** option, this can be achieved with the following LSTM code snippet when length of input and output matches the number of recurrent steps:

```
model = Sequential()
model.add(LSTM(1, input_shape=(timesteps, data_dim),
return_sequences=True))
```

How it works...

Keras allows you to easily write various shapes of RNNs, including one-to-one, one-to-many, many-to-one, and many-to-many mappings. The above examples explain how easy is to implement them with Keras.

7
Unsupervised Learning

All the models that we have covered in this book up to now were based on the supervised learning paradigm; the training dataset included the input and the desired label of that input. This chapter, in contrast, focuses on the unsupervised learning paradigm. The chapter will include the following topics:

- Principal component analysis
- k-means clustering
- Self-organizing maps
- Restricted Boltzmann Machine
- Recommender system using RBM
- DBN for Emotion Detection

Introduction

In machine learning, there are three different learning paradigms: supervised learning, unsupervised learning, and reinforcement learning.

In **supervised learning**, also known as learning with a teacher, the network is provided with both the inputs and the respective desired outputs. For example, in the MNIST dataset, each image of the handwritten digit has a label signifying the digit value associated with it.

In **reinforcement learning**, also known as learning with a critic, the network is not provided with the desired output; instead, the environment provides a feedback in terms of reward or punishment. When its output is correct, the environment rewards the network, and when the output is not correct, the environment punishes it.

In **unsupervised learning,** also known as learning without a teacher, no information is provided to the network about its output. The network receives the input, but is neither provided with desired outputs nor with rewards from the environment; the network learns the hidden structure of the input by itself. Unsupervised learning can be very useful because data available normally is unlabeled. It can be used for tasks such as pattern recognition, feature extraction, data clustering, and dimensionality reduction. In this, and the next chapter, you will learn about different machine learning and NN techniques based on unsupervised learning.

Principal component analysis

Principal component analysis (PCA) is the most popular multivariate statistical technique for dimensionality reduction. It analyzes the training data consisting of several dependent variables, which are, in general, intercorrelated, and extracts important information from the training data in the form of a set of new orthogonal variables called **principal components.** We can perform PCA using two methods--**eigen decomposition** or **singular value decomposition (SVD).**

Getting ready

PCA reduces the n-dimensional input data to r-dimensional input data, where $r<n$. In simpler terms, PCA involves translating the origin and performing rotation of the axis such that one of the axes (the principal axis) has the least variance with data points. A reduced dimension dataset is obtained from the original dataset by performing this transformation and then dropping (removing) the orthogonal axes with high variance. Here, we employ the SVD method for PCA dimensionality reduction. Consider X, the n-dimensional data, with p points $X_{p,n}$. Any real ($p \times n$) matrix can be decomposed as follows:

$$X = U \, \Sigma \, V^T$$

Here, U and V are orthonormal matrices (that is, $U.U^T = V^T.V = 1$) of size $p \times n$ and $n \times n$ respectively. Σ is a diagonal matrix of size $n \times n$. Next, slice the Σ matrix to r columns resulting in Σ_r; using U and V, we find the reduced dimension data points Y_r:

$$Y_r = U\Sigma_r$$

The code presented here has been adapted from this GitHub link:
`https://github.com/eliorc/Medium/blob/master/PCA-tSNE-AE.ipynb`

How to do it...

We proceed with the recipes as follows:

1. Import the modules that are required. We will be definitely using TensorFlow; we will also need numpy for some elementary matrix calculation, and matplotlib, mpl_toolkit, and seaborn for the plotting:

   ```
   import tensorflow as tf
   import numpy as np
   import matplotlib.pyplot as plt
   from mpl_toolkits.mplot3d import Axes3D
   import seaborn as sns
   %matplotlib inline
   ```

2. We load the dataset--we will use our favorite MNIST dataset:

   ```
   from tensorflow.examples.tutorials.mnist import input_data
   mnist = input_data.read_data_sets("MNIST_data/")
   ```

3. We define a class, TF_PCA, which will implement all our work. The class is initialized as follows:

   ```
   def __init__(self, data,  dtype=tf.float32):
           self._data = data
           self._dtype = dtype
           self._graph = None
           self._X = None
           self._u = None
           self._singular_values = None
           self._sigma = None)
   ```

4. The SVD of the given input data is calculated in the fit method. The method defines the computational graph and executes it to calculate the singular values and the orthonormal matrix U. It takes self.data to feed the placeholder self._X. tf.svd returns s (singular_values) in shape [..., p] in descending order of magnitude. We use tf.diag to convert it to a diagonal matrix:

   ```
   def fit(self):
           self._graph = tf.Graph()
           with self._graph.as_default():
               self._X = tf.placeholder(self._dtype,
   shape=self._data.shape)
   ```

```
# Perform SVD
singular_values, u, _ = tf.svd(self._X)
# Create sigma matrix
sigma = tf.diag(singular_values)
with tf.Session(graph=self._graph) as session:
    self._u, self._singular_values, self._sigma =
session.run([u, singular_values, sigma], feed_dict={self._X:
self._data})
```

5. Now that we have the sigma matrix, the orthonormal U matrix, and the singular values, we calculate the reduced dimension data by defining the `reduce` method. The method requires one of the two input arguments, `n_dimensions` or `keep_info`. The `n_dimensions` argument represents the number of dimensions we want to keep in the reduced dimension dataset. The `keep_info` argument, on the other hand, decides the percentage of the information that we intend to keep (a value of 0.8 means that we want to keep 80 percent of the original data). The method creates a graph that slices the Sigma matrix and calculates the reduced dimension dataset Y_r:

```
def reduce(self, n_dimensions=None, keep_info=None):
    if keep_info:
        # Normalize singular values
        normalized_singular_values = self._singular_values /
sum(self._singular_values)
        # information per dimension
        info = np.cumsum(normalized_singular_values)
# Get the first index which is above the given information
threshold
        it = iter(idx for idx, value in enumerate(info) if value
>= keep_info)
        n_dimensions = next(it) + 1
    with self.graph.as_default():
        # Cut out the relevant part from sigma
        sigma = tf.slice(self._sigma, [0, 0],
[self._data.shape[1], n_dimensions])
        # PCA
        pca = tf.matmul(self._u, sigma)

    with tf.Session(graph=self._graph) as session:
        return session.run(pca, feed_dict={self._X:
self._data})
```

6. Our `TF_PCA` class is ready. Now, we will use it to reduce the MNIST data from each input being of dimension 784 (28 x 28) to new data with each point of dimension 3. Here, we retained only 10 percent of the information for better viewing, but normally you would need to retain roughly 80 percent of the information:

```
tf_pca.fit()
pca = tf_pca.reduce(keep_info=0.1)   # The reduced dimensions
dependent upon the % of information
print('original data shape', mnist.train.images.shape)
print('reduced data shape', pca.shape)
```

Following is the output of the following code:

```
original data shape (55000, 784)
reduced data shape (55000, 3)
```

7. Let's now plot the 55,000 data points in the three-dimensional space:

```
Set = sns.color_palette("Set2", 10)
color_mapping = {key:value for (key,value) in enumerate(Set)}
colors = list(map(lambda x: color_mapping[x], mnist.train.labels))
fig = plt.figure()
ax = Axes3D(fig)
ax.scatter(pca[:, 0], pca[:, 1],pca[:, 2], c=colors)
```

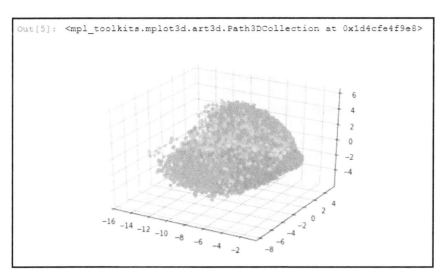

```
Out[5]: <mpl_toolkits.mplot3d.art3d.Path3DCollection at 0x1d4cfe4f9e8>
```

How it works...

The preceding code performs dimensionality reduction on the MNIST images. Each original image is of size 28 x 28; using the PCA method, we can reduce it to a smaller size. Normally, for image data, dimensionality reduction is necessary. This is so because images are large in size and contain a significant amount of redundant data.

There's more...

TensorFlow provides a technique called **embeddings**, which is a mapping of objects into vectors. Embedding Projector of TensorBoard allows us to interactively visualize embeddings from our model. Embedding Projector provides three ways for dimensionality reduction: PCA, t-SNE, and Custom. We can use the Embedding Projector of TensorBoard to achieve a similar result as the previous one. We will need to import the `projector` class from `tensorflow.contrib.tensorboard.plugins` to do the same from `tensorflow.contrib.tensorboard.plugins` import `projector`. We can do it in three simple steps:

1. Load the data whose embeddings you want to explore:

```
mnist = input_data.read_data_sets('MNIST_data')
images = tf.Variable(mnist.test.images, name='images')
```

2. Create a `metadata` file a (`metadata` file is a tab-separated value `.tsv` file):

```
with open(metadata, 'w') as metadata_file:
    for row in mnist.test.labels:
        metadata_file.write('%d\n' % row)
```

3. Save the embeddings in the desired `Log_DIR`:

```
with tf.Session() as sess:
    saver = tf.train.Saver([images])

    sess.run(images.initializer)
    saver.save(sess, os.path.join(LOG_DIR, 'images.ckpt'))

    config = projector.ProjectorConfig()
    # One can add multiple embeddings.
    embedding = config.embeddings.add()
    embedding.tensor_name = images.name
    # Link this tensor to its metadata file (e.g. labels).
```

```
embedding.metadata_path = metadata
# Saves a config file that TensorBoard will read during
startup.
projector.visualize_embeddings(tf.summary.FileWriter(LOG_DIR),
config)
```

The embeddings are ready and can now be seen using TensorBoard. Launch TensorBoard through CLI `tensorboard --logdir=log`, open TensorBoard in your web browser, and go to the **EMBEDDINGS** tab. Here is the TensorBoard projection using PCA with the first three principal components as the axis:

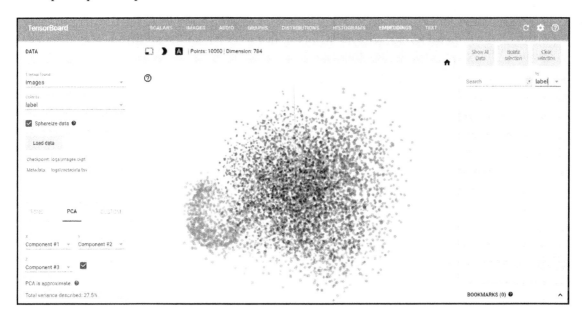

See also

- https://arxiv.org/abs/1404.1100
- http://www.cs.otago.ac.nz/cosc453/student_tutorials/principal_components.pdf
- http://mplab.ucsd.edu/tutorials/pca.pdf
- http://projector.tensorflow.org/

k-means clustering

The k-means clustering, as the name suggests, is a technique to cluster data, that is, partition data into a specified number of data points. It is an unsupervised learning technique. It works by identifying patterns in the given data. Remember the sorting hat from Harry Potter fame? What it is doing in the book is clustering--dividing new (unlabeled) students into four different clusters: Gryffindor, Ravenclaw, Hufflepuff, and Slytherin.

Humans are very good at grouping objects together; clustering algorithms try to give a similar capability to computers. There are many clustering techniques available such as Hierarchical, Bayesian, or Partional. The k-means clustering belongs to Partional clustering; it partitions the data into k clusters. Each cluster has a center, called **centroid**. The number of clusters k has to be specified by the user.

The k-means algorithm works in the following manner:

1. Randomly choose k data points as the initial centroids (cluster centers)
2. Assign each data point to the closest centroid; there can be different measures to find closeness, the most common being the Euclidean distance
3. Recompute the centroids using current cluster membership, such that the sum of squared distance decreases
4. Repeat the last two steps until convergence is met

Getting ready

We will use TensorFlow `KmeansClustering` Estimator class to implement k-means. It is defined in `https://github.com/tensorflow/tensorflow/blob/r1.3/tensorflow/contrib/learn/python/learn/estimators/kmeans.py`. It creates a model to run k-means and inference. According to the TensorFlow docs, once a `KmeansClustering` class object is created, it is instantiated with the following __init__ method:

```
__init__(
num_clusters,
model_dir=None,
initial_clusters=RANDOM_INIT,
distance_metric=SQUARED_EUCLIDEAN_DISTANCE,
random_seed=0,
use_mini_batch=True,
mini_batch_steps_per_iteration=1,
kmeans_plus_plus_num_retries=2,
relative_tolerance=None,
```

```
config=None
)
```

TensorFlow Docs define these arguments as follows:

> **Args:**
> **num_clusters**: The number of clusters to train.
> **model_dir:** The directory to save the model results and log files.
> **initial_clusters:** Specifies how to initialize the clusters for training. See clustering_ops.kmeans for the possible values.
> **distance_metric:** The distance metric used for clustering. See clustering_ops.kmeans for the possible values.
> **random_seed**: Python integer. Seed for PRNG used to initialize centers.
> **use_mini_batch**: If true, use the mini-batch k-means algorithm. Or else assume full batch.
> **mini_batch_steps_per_iteration**: The number of steps after which the updated cluster centers are synced back to a master copy. See clustering_ops.py for more details.
> **kmeans_plus_plus_num_retries:** For each point that is sampled during kmeans++ initialization, this parameter specifies the number of additional points to draw from the current distribution before selecting the best. If a negative value is specified, a heuristic is used to sample O(log(num_to_sample)) additional points.
> **relative_tolerance**: A relative tolerance of change in the loss between iterations. Stops learning if the loss changes less than this amount. Note that this may not work correctly if use_mini_batch=True.
> **config**: See Estimator.

TensorFlow supports Euclidean distance and cosine distance as the measure of the centroid. TensorFlow KmeansClustering provides various methods to interact with the KmeansClustering object. In the present recipe, we will use fit(), clusters(), and predict_clusters_idx() methods:

```
fit(
  x=None,
  y=None,
  input_fn=None,
  steps=None,
  batch_size=None,
  monitors=None,
  max_steps=None
)
```

According to TensorFlow docs, for `KmeansClustering` Estimator, we need to provide `input_fn()` to `fit()`. The `cluster` method returns cluster centres and the `predict_cluster_idx` method returns predicted cluster indices.

How to do it...

Here is how we proceed with the recipe:

1. As before, we start by loading the necessary modules. We will require TensorFlow, NumPy, and Matplotlib as usual. In this recipe, we are working with the Iris dataset, which contains three classes of 50 instances each, where each class refers to a type of Iris plant. We can either download the data from `https://archive.ics.uci.edu/ml/datasets/iris` as a `.csv` file or we can use the dataset module of sklearn (scikit-learn)to do the task:

```
import numpy as np
import tensorflow as tf
import matplotlib.pyplot as plt
from matplotlib.colors import ListedColormap
# dataset Iris
from sklearn import datasets

%matplotlib inline
```

2. We load the dataset:

```
# import some data to play with
iris = datasets.load_iris()
x = iris.data[:, :2] # we only take the first two features.
y = iris.target
```

3. Let's see how this dataset looks:

```
# original data without clustering
plt.scatter(hw_frame[:,0], hw_frame[:,1])
plt.xlabel('Sepia Length')
plt.ylabel('Sepia Width')
```

Following is the output of the following code:

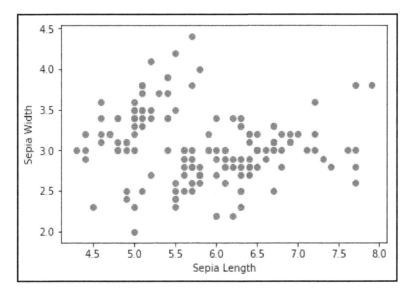

4. We can see that there are no clusters obviously visible in the data. Now we define `input_fn`, which will be used to feed the `fit` method. Our input function returns a TensorFlow constant, which is assigned the value and shape of x, and is of the type `float`:

```
def input_fn():
    return tf.constant(np.array(x), tf.float32, x.shape), None
```

5. Now we use the `KmeansClustering` class; here, we already know the number of classes as 3, so we set `num_clusters=3`. Normally, we are not aware of what the number of clusters should be; in that case, a common methodology is the **elbow method**:

```
kmeans = tf.contrib.learn.KMeansClustering(num_clusters=3,
relative_tolerance=0.0001, random_seed=2)
kmeans.fit(input_fn=input_fn)
```

6. We find the clusters using the `clusters()` method and, to each input point, we assign the cluster index using the `predict_cluster_idx()` method:

```
clusters = kmeans.clusters()
assignments = list(kmeans.predict_cluster_idex(input_fn=input_fn))
```

7. Let's now visualize the clusters created by k-means. To do this, we create a
   wrapper function `ScatterPlot` that takes the `X` and `Y` values along with the
   clusters and cluster index of each data point:

```
def ScatterPlot(X, Y, assignments=None, centers=None):
if assignments is None:
assignments = [0] * len(X)
fig = plt.figure(figsize=(14,8))
cmap = ListedColormap(['red', 'green', 'blue'])
plt.scatter(X, Y, c=assignments, cmap=cmap)
if centers is not None:
plt.scatter(centers[:, 0], centers[:, 1], c=range(len(centers)),
marker='+', s=400, cmap=cmap)
plt.xlabel('Sepia Length')
plt.ylabel('Sepia Width')
```

We use it to plot our `clusters`:

```
ScatterPlot(x[:,0], x[:,1], assignments, clusters)
```

The plot is as follows:

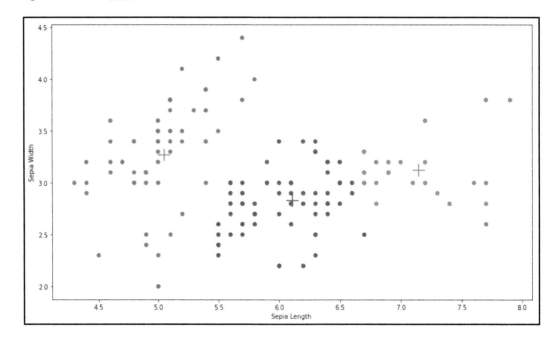

The **+** marks are the centroids of the three clusters.

How it works...

The preceding recipe used the k-means clustering estimator of TensorFlow to cluster the given data into clusters. Here, as we know the number of clusters, we decided to keep `num_clusters=3`, but in most cases with unlabeled data, one is never sure how many clusters exist. One can determine the optimal number of clusters using the elbow method. The method is based on the principle that we should choose the cluster number that reduces that **sum of squared error (SSE)** distance. If k is the number of clusters, then as k increases, the SSE decreases, with SSE = 0; when k is equal to the number of data points, each point is its own cluster. We want a low value of k such that SSE is also low. In TensorFlow, we can find the SSE using the `score()` method defined in the `KmeansClustering` class; the method returns the total sum of distances to the nearest clusters:

```
sum_distances = kmeans.score(input_fn=input_fn, steps=100)
```

For Iris data, if we plot SSE for different k values, we see that for $k=3$, the variance in SSE is the highest; after that, it starts reducing, thus the elbow point is $k=3$:

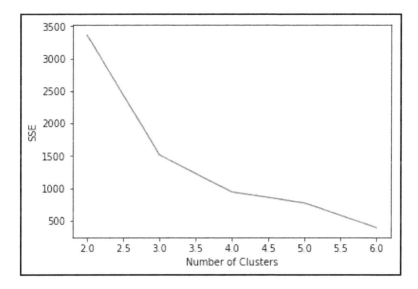

There's more...

K-means clustering is very popular because it is fast, simple, and robust. It also has some disadvantages: the biggest being that the user has to specify the number of clusters. Second, the algorithm does not guarantee global optima. Third, it is very sensitive to outliers.

See also

- Kanungo, Tapas, et al. *An efficient k-means clustering algorithm: Analysis and implementation.* IEEE transactions on pattern analysis and machine intelligence 24.7 (2002): 881-892.

- Ortega, Joaquín Pérez, et al. *Research issues on k-means algorithm: An experimental trial using matlab.* CEUR Workshop Proceedings: Semantic Web and New Technologies.

- http://home.deib.polimi.it/matteucc/Clustering/tutorial_html/kmeans.html

- Chen, Ke. *On coresets for k-median and k-means clustering in metric and euclidean spaces and their applications.* SIAM Journal on Computing 39.3 (2009): 923-947.

- https://en.wikipedia.org/wiki/Determining_the_number_of_clusters_in_a_data_set

Self-organizing maps

Self-organized maps (SOM), sometimes known as **Kohonen networks** or **Winner take all units (WTU)**, are a very special kind of neural network, motivated by a distinctive feature of the human brain. In our brain, different sensory inputs are represented in a topologically ordered manner. Unlike other neural networks, neurons are not all connected to each other via weights, instead, they influence each other's learning. The most important aspect of SOM is that neurons represent the learned inputs in a topographic manner.

In SOM, neurons are usually placed at nodes of a (1D or 2D) lattice. Higher dimensions are also possible but are rarely used in practice. Each neuron in the lattice is connected to all the input units via weight matrix. Here, you can see a SOM with 3 x 4 (12 neurons) and seven inputs. For clarity, only the weight vectors connecting all inputs to one neuron are shown. In this case, each neuron will have seven elements, resulting in a combined weight matrix of size (12 x 7):

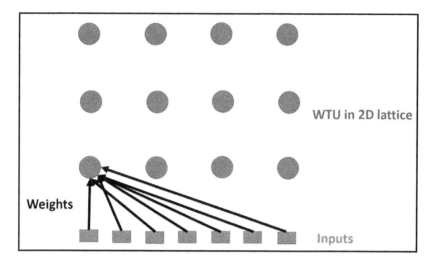

SOM learns via competitive learning. It can be considered as a nonlinear generalization of PCA and thus, like PCA, can be employed for dimensionality reduction.

Getting ready

In order to implement SOM, let's first understand how it works. As the first step, the weights of the network are initialized to either some random value or by taking random samples from the input. Each neuron occupying a space in the lattice will be assigned specific locations. Now as an input is presented, the neuron with the least distance from the input is declared Winner (WTU). This is done by measuring the distance between weight vector (W) and input vectors (X) of all neurons:

$$d_j = \sqrt{\sum_{i=1}^{N}\left(W_{ji} - X_i\right)^2}$$

Here, d_j is the distance of weights of neuron j from input X. The neuron with minimum d value is the winner.

Next, the weights of the winning neuron and its neighboring neurons are adjusted in a manner to ensure that the same neuron is the winner if the same input is presented next time. To decide which neighboring neurons need to be modified, the network uses a neighborhood function $\Lambda(r)$; normally, the Gaussian Mexican hat function is chosen as a neighborhood function. The neighborhood function is mathematically represented as follows:

$$\Lambda(r) = e^{-\frac{d^2}{2\sigma^2}}$$

Here, σ is a time-dependent radius of influence of a neuron and d is its distance from the winning neuron:

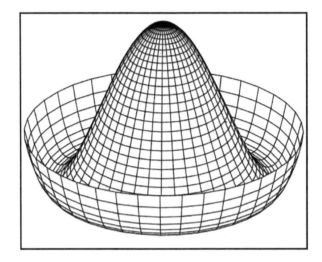

Another important property of the neighborhood function is that its radius reduces with time. As a result, in the beginning, many neighboring neurons' weights are modified, but as the network learns, eventually a few neurons' weights (at times, only one or none) are modified in the learning process. The change in weight is given by the following equation:

$$dW = \eta \Lambda (X\text{-}W)$$

We continue the process for all inputs and repeat it for a given number of iterations. As the iterations progress, we reduce the learning rate and the radius by a factor dependent on the iteration number.

How to do it...

We proceed with the recipe as follows:

1. As always, we start with importing the necessary modules:

```
import tensorflow as tf
import numpy as np
import matplotlib.pyplot as plt
%matplotlib inline
```

2. Next, we declare a class, WTU, which will perform all the tasks. The class is instantiated with m x n the size of the 2D SOM lattice, dim the number of dimensions in the input data, and the total number of iterations:

```
def __init__(self, m, n, dim, num_iterations, eta = 0.5, sigma = None):
    """
    m x n : The dimension of 2D lattice in which neurons are arranged
    dim : Dimension of input training data
    num_iterations: Total number of training iterations
    eta : Learning rate
    sigma: The radius of neighbourhood function.
    """
    self._m = m
    self._n = n
    self._neighbourhood = []
    self._topography = []
    self._num_iterations = int(num_iterations)
    self._learned = False
```

3. In the __init__ itself, we define the computation graph and the session.

4. If the network is not provided with any sigma value, it will take a default value, which is normally half of the maximum dimension of the SOM lattice:

```
if sigma is None:
    sigma = max(m,n)/2.0 # Constant radius
else:
    sigma = float(sigma)
```

5. Next, in the graph, we declare variables for the weight matrix, placeholders for the input, and computational steps to calculate the winner and update its and its neighbors' weight. As SOM provides a topographic map, we also add ops to get the topographic location of neurons:

```
self._graph = tf.Graph()

# Build Computation Graph of SOM
 with self._graph.as_default():
# Weight Matrix and the topography of neurons
    self._W = tf.Variable(tf.random_normal([m*n, dim], seed = 0))
    self._topography =
tf.constant(np.array(list(self._neuron_location(m, n))))

    # Placeholders for training data
    self._X = tf.placeholder('float', [dim])
    # Placeholder to keep track of number of iterations
    self._iter = tf.placeholder('float')

    # Finding the Winner and its location
    d = tf.sqrt(tf.reduce_sum(tf.pow(self._W - tf.stack([self._X
        for i in range(m*n)]),2),1))
    self.WTU_idx = tf.argmin(d,0)
    slice_start = tf.pad(tf.reshape(self.WTU_idx,
[1]),np.array([[0,1]]))
    self.WTU_loc = tf.reshape(tf.slice(self._topography,
slice_start,              [1,2]), [2])
    # Change learning rate and radius as a function of iterations
    learning_rate = 1 - self._iter/self._num_iterations
    _eta_new = eta * learning_rate
    _sigma_new = sigma * learning_rate
    # Calculating Neighbourhood function
    distance_square = tf.reduce_sum(tf.pow(tf.subtract(
    self._topography, tf.stack([self.WTU_loc for i in range(m *
n)])), 2), 1)
    neighbourhood_func = tf.exp(tf.negative(tf.div(tf.cast(
distance_square, "float32"), tf.pow(_sigma_new, 2))))
    # multiply learning rate with neighbourhood func
    eta_into_Gamma = tf.multiply(_eta_new, neighbourhood_func)
    # Shape it so that it can be multiplied to calculate dW
    weight_multiplier = tf.stack([tf.tile(tf.slice(
eta_into_Gamma, np.array([i]), np.array([1])), [dim])
for i in range(m * n)])
    delta_W = tf.multiply(weight_multiplier,
tf.subtract(tf.stack([self._X for i in range(m * n)]),self._W))
    new_W = self._W + delta_W
    self._training = tf.assign(self._W,new_W)
```

```
# Initialize All variables
init = tf.global_variables_initializer()
self._sess = tf.Session()
self._sess.run(init)
```

6. We define a `fit` method for the class, which executes the training op declared in the default graph of the class. The method also calculates centroid grid:

```
def fit(self, X):
    """
    Function to carry out training
    """
    for i in range(self._num_iterations):
        for x in X:
            self._sess.run(self._training, feed_dict= {self._X:x,
self._iter: i})


    # Store a centroid grid for easy retreival
    centroid_grid = [[] for i in range(self._m)]
    self._Wts = list(self._sess.run(self._W))
    self._locations = list(self._sess.run(self._topography))
    for i, loc in enumerate(self._locations):
        centroid_grid[loc[0]].append(self._Wts[i])
    self._centroid_grid = centroid_grid

    self._learned = True
```

7. We define a function to determine the index and the location of the winning neuron in the 2D lattice:

```
def winner(self, x):
    idx = self._sess.run([self.WTU_idx, self.WTU_loc], feed_dict =
{self._X:x})
    return idx
```

8. We define some more helper functions to perform the 2D mapping of neurons in the lattice and to map input vectors to the relevant neurons in the 2D lattice:

```
def _neuron_location(self,m,n):
    """
    Function to generate the 2D lattice of neurons
    """
    for i in range(m):
        for j in range(n):
            yield np.array([i,j])
```

```
def get_centroids(self):
    """
    Function to return a list of 'm' lists, with each inner
    list containing the 'n' corresponding centroid locations      as 1-D
    NumPy arrays.
    """
    if not self._learned:
        raise ValueError("SOM not trained yet")
    return self._centroid_grid

def map_vects(self, X):
    """
    Function to map each input vector to the relevant neuron
    in the lattice
    """
    if not self._learned:
        raise ValueError("SOM not trained yet")
    to_return = []
    for vect in X:
        min_index = min([i for i in range(len(self._Wts))],
        key=lambda x: np.linalg.norm(vect -
self._Wts[x]))
        to_return.append(self._locations[min_index])
    return to_return
```

9. Now that our WTU class is ready, we read data from the `.csv` file and normalize it:

```
def normalize(df):
    result = df.copy()
    for feature_name in df.columns:
        max_value = df[feature_name].max()
        min_value = df[feature_name].min()
        result[feature_name] = (df[feature_name] - min_value) /
(max_value - min_value)
        return result

# Reading input data from file
import pandas as pd
df = pd.read_csv('colors.csv') # The last column of data file is a
label
data = normalize(df[['R', 'G', 'B']]).values
name = df['Color-Name'].values
n_dim = len(df.columns) - 1

# Data for Training
colors = data
```

```
color_names = name
```

10. Finally, we use our class to perform dimensionality reduction and arrange it in a beautiful topographic map:

```
som = WTU(30, 30, n_dim, 400, sigma=10.0)
som.fit(colors)

# Get output grid
image_grid = som.get_centroids()

# Map colours to their closest neurons
mapped = som.map_vects(colors)

# Plot
plt.imshow(image_grid)
plt.title('Color Grid SOM')
for i, m in enumerate(mapped):
        plt.text(m[1], m[0], color_names[i], ha='center', va='center',
bbox=dict(facecolor='white', alpha=0.5, lw=0))
```

The plot is as follows:

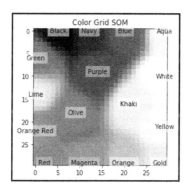

How it works...

SOMs are computationally expensive and thus are not really useful for a very large dataset. Still, they are easy to understand and they can very nicely find the similarity between input data. Thus, they have been employed for image segmentation and to determine word similarity maps in NLP.

See also

- This is a very good blog post, explaining SOM in simple language: `http://www.ai-junkie.com/ann/som/som1.html`
- A brief introduction on SOM: `https://en.wikipedia.org/wiki/Self-organizing_map`
- The seminal paper by Kohonen on SOM: "The self-organizing map." Neurocomputing 21.1 (1998): 1-6: `https://pdfs.semanticscholar.org/8c6a/aea3159e9f49283de252d0548b337839ca6f.pdf`

Restricted Boltzmann Machine

Restricted Boltzmann Machine (RBM) is a two-layered neural network--the first layer is called the **visible layer** and the second layer is called the **hidden layer**. They are called **shallow neural networks** because they are only two layers deep. They were first proposed in 1986 by Paul Smolensky (he called them Harmony Networks[1]) and later by Geoffrey Hinton who in 2006 proposed **Contrastive Divergence (CD)** as a method to train them. All neurons in the visible layer are connected to all the neurons in the hidden layer, but there is a **restriction**--no neuron in the same layer can be connected. All neurons are binary in nature:

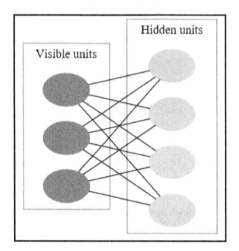

Source: By Qwertyus - Own work, CC BY-SA 3.0, https://commons.wikimedia.org/w/index.php?curid=22717044

RBM can be used for dimensionality reduction, feature extraction, and collaborative filtering. The training in RBMs can be divided into three parts: forward pass, backward pass, and then compare.

Getting ready

Let's see the expressions that we will need to make our RBM:

Forward pass: The information at visible units (V) is passed via weights (W) and biases (c) to the hidden units (h_0). The hidden unit may fire or not depending on the stochastic probability (σ is stochastic probability):

$$p(h_i|v_0) = \sigma(V^T W + c)_i$$

Backward pass: The hidden unit representation (h_0) is then passed back to the visible units through the same weights W, but different bias c, where they reconstruct the input. Again, the input is sampled:

$$p(v_i|h_0) = \sigma(W^T h_0 + b)_i$$

These two passes are repeated for k-steps or till the convergence is reached. According to researchers, $k=1$ gives good results, so we will keep $k = 1$.

The joint configuration of the visible vector V and the hidden vector has an energy given as follows:

$$E(v, h) = -b^T V - c^T h - V^T W h$$

Also associated with each visible vector V is free energy, the energy that a single configuration would need to have in order to have the same probability as all of the configurations that contain V:

$$F(v) = -b^T V - \sum_{j \in hidden} log\left(1 + e^{c_j + V^T w}\right)$$

Using the Contrastive Divergence objective function, that is, $Mean(F(V_{original}))$-$Mean(F(V_{reconstructed}))$, the change in weights is given by:

$$dW = \eta(\{V^T h\}_{input} - \{V^T h\}_{reconstructed})$$

Here, η is the learning rate. Similar expressions exist for the biases b and c.

How to do it...

We proceed with the recipe as follows:

1. Import the modules:

```
import tensorflow as tf
import numpy as np
from tensorflow.examples.tutorials.mnist import input_data
import matplotlib.pyplot as plt
%matplotlib inline
```

2. Declare the class RBM, which will do the major task. The __init__ will build the complete graph, forward and backward pass, and the objective function; we will use the TensorFlow built-in optimizer to update the weights and biases:

```
class RBM(object):
    def __init__(self, m, n):
        """
        m: Number of neurons in visible layer
        n: number of neurons in hidden layer
        """
        self._m = m
        self._n = n
        # Create the Computational graph
        # Weights and biases
        self._W =
tf.Variable(tf.random_normal(shape=(self._m,self._n)))
        self._c = tf.Variable(np.zeros(self._n).astype(np.float32))
#bias for hidden layer
        self._b = tf.Variable(np.zeros(self._m).astype(np.float32))
#bias for Visible layer
        # Placeholder for inputs
        self._X = tf.placeholder('float', [None, self._m])
        # Forward Pass
        _h = tf.nn.sigmoid(tf.matmul(self._X, self._W) + self._c)
        self.h = tf.nn.relu(tf.sign(_h -
tf.random_uniform(tf.shape(_h))))
        #Backward pass
        _v = tf.nn.sigmoid(tf.matmul(self.h, tf.transpose(self._W))
+ self._b)
        self.V = tf.nn.relu(tf.sign(_v -
tf.random_uniform(tf.shape(_v))))
```

```
        # Objective Function
        objective = tf.reduce_mean(self.free_energy(self._X)) -
tf.reduce_mean(
self.free_energy(self.V))
        self._train_op =
tf.train.GradientDescentOptimizer(1e-3).minimize(objective)
        # Cross entropy cost
        reconstructed_input = self.one_pass(self._X)
        self.cost =
tf.reduce_mean(tf.nn.sigmoid_cross_entropy_with_logits(
labels=self._X, logits=reconstructed_input))
```

3. We define the `fit()` method in the RBM class. After declaring all the ops in
   `__init__`, training is simply calling the `train_op` within the session. We use
   batch training:

```
def fit(self, X, epochs = 1, batch_size = 100):
    N, D = X.shape
    num_batches = N // batch_size
    obj = []
    for i in range(epochs):
        #X = shuffle(X)
        for j in range(num_batches):
            batch = X[j * batch_size: (j * batch_size +
batch_size)]
            _, ob = self.session.run([self._train_op,self.cost
], feed_dict={self._X: batch})
            if j % 10 == 0:
                print('training epoch {0} cost
{1}'.format(j,ob))
        obj.append(ob)
    return obj
```

4. There are other helper functions to calculate the logit error and return
   reconstructed images from the network:

```
def set_session(self, session):
    self.session = session

def free_energy(self, V):
    b = tf.reshape(self._b, (self._m, 1))
    term_1 = -tf.matmul(V,b)
    term_1 = tf.reshape(term_1, (-1,))
    term_2 = -tf.reduce_sum(tf.nn.softplus(tf.matmul(V,self._W) +
        self._c))
    return term_1 + term_2
```

```
def one_pass(self, X):
    h = tf.nn.sigmoid(tf.matmul(X, self._W) + self._c)
    return tf.matmul(h, tf.transpose(self._W)) + self._b

def reconstruct(self,X):
    x = tf.nn.sigmoid(self.one_pass(X))
    return self.session.run(x, feed_dict={self._X: X})
```

5. We load the MNIST dataset:

```
mnist = input_data.read_data_sets("MNIST_data/", one_hot=True)
trX, trY, teX, teY = mnist.train.images, mnist.train.labels,
mnist.test.images, mnist.test.labels
```

6. Next, we train our RBM on the MNIST dataset:

```
Xtrain = trX.astype(np.float32)
Xtest = teX.astype(np.float32)
_, m = Xtrain.shape
rbm = RBM(m, 100)
#Initialize all variables
init = tf.global_variables_initializer()
with tf.Session() as sess:
    sess.run(init)
    rbm.set_session(sess)
    err = rbm.fit(Xtrain)
    out = rbm.reconstruct(Xest[0:100])  # Let us reconstruct Test
Data
```

7. The error as a function of **epochs**:

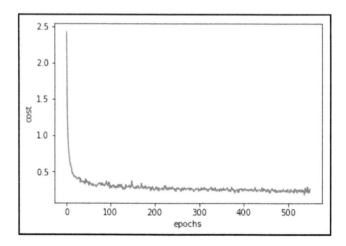

How it works...

Due to its ability to reconstruct images, RBM can be used to generate more data from the existing data. We can see the original and reconstructed MNIST images by making a small helper plotting code:

```
row, col = 2, 8
idx = np.random.randint(0, 100, row * col // 2)
f, axarr = plt.subplots(row, col, sharex=True, sharey=True, figsize=(20,4))
for fig, row in zip([Xtest_noisy,out], axarr):
    for i,ax in zip(idx,row):
        ax.imshow(fig[i].reshape((28, 28)), cmap='Greys_r')
        ax.get_xaxis().set_visible(False)
        ax.get_yaxis().set_visible(False)
```

We get the result as follows:

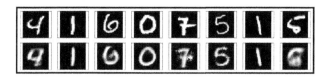

See also

- Smolensky, Paul. *Information processing in dynamical systems: Foundations of harmony theory*. No. CU-CS-321-86. COLORADO UNIV AT BOULDER DEPT OF COMPUTER SCIENCE, 1986. (Link)

- Salakhutdinov, Ruslan, Andriy Mnih, and Geoffrey Hinton. *Restricted Boltzmann machines for collaborative filtering*. Proceedings of the 24th international conference on Machine learning. ACM, 2007.(Link)

- Hinton, Geoffrey. *A practical guide to training restricted Boltzmann machines.* Momentum 9.1 (2010): 926.(Link)

- If you are interested in math, this is a good tutorial: http://deeplearning.net/tutorial/rbm.html#rbm

Recommender system using RBM

Recommender systems are widely used by web retailers to suggest products to their customers; for example, Amazon tells you what other customers who purchased this item were interested in or Netflix suggests TV serials and movies based on what you have watched and what other Netflix users with the same interest have watched. These recommender systems work on the basis of collaborative filtering. In collaborative filtering, the system builds a model from a user's past behavior. We will use the RBM, made in the previous recipe, to build a recommender system using collaborative filtering to recommend movies. An important challenge in this work is that most users will not rate all products/movies, thus most data is missing. If there are M products and N users, then we need to build an array, N x M, which contains the known ratings of the users and makes all unknown values zero.

Getting ready

To make a recommender system using collaborative filtering, we need to modify our data. As an illustration, we will use the movie dataset taken from `https://grouplens.org/datasets/movielens/`. The data consists of two `.dat` files: `movies.dat` and `ratings.dat`. The `movies.dat` file contains three columns: MovieID, Title, and Genre for 3,883 movies. The `ratings.dat` file contains four columns: UserID, MovieID, Rating, and Time. We need to merge these two data files such that we are able to build an array, where, for each user, we have a rating for all the 3,883 movies. The problem is that users normally do not rate all movies, so we have non-zero (normalized) ratings only for some movies. The rest is made zero and hence will not contribute to the hidden layer.

How to do it...

1. We will use the `RBM` class created in the previous recipe. Let's define our RBM network; the number of visible units will be the number of movies, in our case, 3,883 (`movies_df` is the data frame containing data from the `movies.dat` file):

```
m = len(movies_df)  # Number of visible units
n = 20  # Number of Hidden units
recommender = rbm.RBM(m,n)
```

2. We created a list, `trX`, of about 1,000 users with their normalized movie ratings using Pandas merge and `groupby` commands. The list is of size 1000 x 3883. We use this to train our RBM:

```
Xtrain = np.array(trX)
init = tf.global_variables_initializer()
with tf.Session() as sess:
  sess.run(init)
  recommender.set_session(sess)
  err = recommender.fit(Xtrain, epochs=10)
```

3. The cross-logit error per epoch decreases:

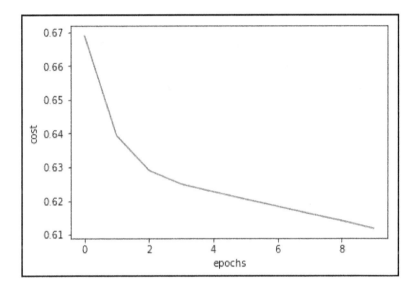

4. The network is now trained; we use it get the recommendation for a random user with index 150 (it could be any existing user):

```
user_index = 150
x = np.array([Xtrain[user_index, :]])
init = tf.global_variables_initializer()
with tf.Session() as sess:
  sess.run(init)
  recommender.set_session(sess)
  out = recommender.reconstruct(x.astype(np.float32))
```

5. The result is merged with the existing data frame and we can see the recommendation score for this user:

```
Out[13]:
```

	MovieID	Title	Genre	List_Index	Recommendation_Score
0	1	Toy Story (1995)	Animation|Children's|Comedy	0	0.560319
1	2	Jumanji (1995)	Adventure|Children's|Fantasy	1	0.699984
2	3	Grumpier Old Men (1995)	Comedy|Romance	2	0.751833
3	4	Waiting to Exhale (1995)	Comedy|Drama	3	0.894270
4	5	Father of the Bride Part II (1995)	Comedy	4	0.238415

There's more...

Prof Geoffrey Hinton led the University of Toronto team that won the Netflix competition for the best collaborative filtering to predict user ratings for movies using RBM (https://en.wikipedia.org/wiki/Netflix_Prize). The detail of their work can be accessed from their paper: http://www.cs.toronto.edu/~hinton/absps/netflixICML.pdf.

The output from the hidden units of one RBM can be fed to visible units of another RBM, the process can be repeated to form a stack of RBMs. This results in **Stacked RBMs**. Each stacked RBM is trained independently assuming that others do not exist. A large number of stacked RBMs form **Deep Belief Networks (DBN)**. DBNs can be trained using both supervised or unsupervised training. You will learn more about them in the next recipe.

DBN for Emotion Detection

In this recipe, we will learn how to first stack RBMs to make a DBN, and then train it to detect emotions. The interesting part of the recipe is that we employ two different learning paradigms: first, we pretrain RBMs one by one using unsupervised learning, and then, in the end, we have an MLP layer, which is trained using supervised learning.

Getting ready

We use the RBM class we have already created in the recipe *Restricted Boltzmann Machine*, with just one change, we do not need to reconstruct the image after training now. Instead, our stacked RBMs will be only forward passing the data up to the last MLP layer of DBN. This is achieved by removing the `reconstruct()` function from the class, and replacing it with the `rbm_output()` function:

```
def rbm_output(self,X):
    x = tf.nn.sigmoid(tf.matmul(X, self._W) + self._c)
    return self.session.run(x, feed_dict={self._X: X})
```

For the data, we consider the Kaggle Face Emotion Recognition data, available at `https://www.kaggle.com/c/challenges-in-representation-learning-facial-expression-recognition-challenge`. The data description given there is:

> *The data consists of 48 x 48 pixel grayscale images of faces. The faces have been automatically registered so that the face is more or less centered and occupies about the same amount of space in each image. The task is to categorize each face based on the emotion shown in the facial expression into one of seven categories (0=Angry, 1=Disgust, 2=Fear, 3=Happy, 4=Sad, 5=Surprise, 6=Neutral).*
>
> *train.csv contains two columns, "emotion" and "pixels". The "emotion" column contains a numeric code ranging from 0 to 6, inclusive, for the emotion that is present in the image. The "pixels" column contains a string surrounded in quotes for each image. The contents of this string are space-separated pixel values in row major order. test.csv contains only the "pixels" column and your task is to predict the emotion column.*
>
> *The training set consists of 28,709 examples. The public test set used for the leaderboard consists of 3,589 examples. The final test set, which was used to determine the winner of the competition, consists of another 3,589 examples.*
>
> *This dataset was prepared by Pierre-Luc Carrier and Aaron Courville, as part of an ongoing research project. They have graciously provided the workshop organizers with a preliminary version of their dataset to use for this contest.*

The complete data is in one `.csv` file called `fer2013.csv`. We separate out training, validation, and test data from this:

```
data = pd.read_csv('data/fer2013.csv')
tr_data = data[data.Usage == "Training"]
test_data = data[data.Usage == "PublicTest"]
mask = np.random.rand(len(tr_data)) < 0.8
train_data = tr_data[mask]
val_data = tr_data[~mask]
```

We will need to preprocess the data, that is, separate the pixels and emotion labels. For this we make two function dense_to_one_hot (), it performs the one hot encoding for labels. The second function is preprocess_data(), which separates out individual pixels as an array. With the help of these two functions, we generate the input feature and label of the training, validation, and test dataset:

```python
def dense_to_one_hot(labels_dense, num_classes):
    num_labels = labels_dense.shape[0]
    index_offset = np.arange(num_labels) * num_classes
    labels_one_hot = np.zeros((num_labels, num_classes))
    labels_one_hot.flat[index_offset + labels_dense.ravel()] = 1
    return labels_one_hot
def preprocess_data(dataframe):
    pixels_values = dataframe.pixels.str.split(" ").tolist()
    pixels_values = pd.DataFrame(pixels_values, dtype=int)
    images = pixels_values.values
    images = images.astype(np.float32)
    images = np.multiply(images, 1.0/255.0)
    labels_flat = dataframe["emotion"].values.ravel()
    labels_count = np.unique(labels_flat).shape[0]
    labels = dense_to_one_hot(labels_flat, labels_count)
    labels = labels.astype(np.uint8)
    return images, labels
```

Using the functions defined in the preceding code, we get the data in the format required for training. We build the emotion detection DBN, based on the similar principle as mentioned in this paper for MNIST: https://www.cs.toronto.edu/~hinton/absps/fastnc.pdf.

How to do it...

We proceed with the recipe as follows:

1. We need to import the standard modules, TensorFlow, NumPy, and Pandas, for reading the .csv file, and Matplolib:

```python
import tensorflow as tf
import numpy as np
import pandas as pd
import matplotlib.pyplot as plt
```

2. The training, validation, and testing data is obtained using the helper functions:

```
X_train, Y_train = preprocess_data(train_data)
X_val, Y_val = preprocess_data(val_data)
X_test, Y_test = preprocess_data(test_data)
```

3. Let us explore our data a little. We plot the mean image and find the number of images in each training, validation, and testing dataset:

```
# Explore Data
mean_image = X_train.mean(axis=0)
std_image = np.std(X_train, axis=0)
print("Training Data set has {} images".format(len(X_train)))
print("Validation Data set has {} images".format(len(X_val)))
print("Test Data set has {} images".format(len(X_test)))
plt.imshow(mean_image.reshape(48,48), cmap='gray')
```

We get the result as follows:

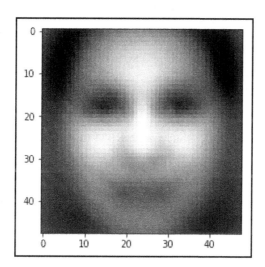

4. We also see the images from the training sample and their respective label:

```
classes =
['angry','disgust','fear','happy','sad','surprise','neutral']
num_classes = len(classes)
samples_per_class = 7
for y,cls in enumerate(classes):
    idxs = np.flatnonzero(np.argmax(Y_train, axis =1) == y)
    idxs = np.random.choice(idxs, samples_per_class,
replace=False)
```

```
        for i, idx in enumerate(idxs):
            plt_idx = i * num_classes + y + 1
            plt.subplot(samples_per_class, num_classes, plt_idx)
            plt.imshow(X_train[idx].reshape(48,48), cmap='gray')
#pixel height and width
            plt.axis('off')
            if i == 0:
                plt.title(cls)
plt.show()
```

The plot is as follows:

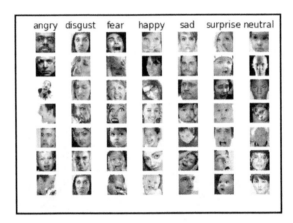

5. Next, we define the RBM stack; each RBM takes the output of the previous RBM as its input:

```
RBM_hidden_sizes = [1500, 700, 400] #create 4 layers of RBM with
size 1500, 700, 400 and 100
#Set input as training data
inpX = X_train
#Create list to hold our RBMs
rbm_list = []
#Size of inputs is the number of inputs in the training set
input_size = inpX.shape[1]
#For each RBM we want to generate
for i, size in enumerate(RBM_hidden_sizes):
    print ('RBM: ',i,' ',input_size,'->', size)
    rbm_list.append(RBM(input_size, size))
    input_size = size
```

This generates three RBMs: the first RBM with 2,304 (48 × 48) input and 1,500 hidden units, the second RBM with 1,500 input and 700 hidden units, and finally the third RBM with 700 input and 400 hidden units.

6. We train each RBM one by one. The technique is also called **greedy wise training**. In the original paper the number of epochs for training each RBM on MNIST was 30, so here, too, increasing the epochs should improve the performance of the network:

```
# Greedy wise training of RBMs
init = tf.global_variables_initializer()
for rbm in rbm_list:
    print ('New RBM:')
    #Train a new one
    with tf.Session() as sess:
        sess.run(init)
        rbm.set_session(sess)
        err = rbm.fit(inpX, 5)
        inpX_n = rbm.rbm_output(inpX)
        print(inpX_n.shape)
        inpX = inpX_n
```

7. We define a DBN class. In the class, we build the complete DBN with the three layers of RBM and two additional MLP layers. The weights of RBM layers are loaded from the pre-trained RBMs. We also declare methods to train and predict the DBN; for fine-tuning, the network tries to minimize the mean square loss function:

```
class DBN(object):

    def __init__(self, sizes, X, Y, eta = 0.001, momentum = 0.0,
epochs = 10, batch_size = 100):
        #Initialize hyperparameters
        self._sizes = sizes
        print(self._sizes)
        self._sizes.append(1000) # size of the first FC layer
        self._X = X
        self._Y = Y
        self.N = len(X)
        self.w_list = []
        self.c_list = []
        self._learning_rate = eta
        self._momentum = momentum
        self._epochs = epochs
        self._batchsize = batch_size
        input_size = X.shape[1]
```

```
            #initialization loop
            for size in self._sizes + [Y.shape[1]]:
                #Define upper limit for the uniform distribution range
                max_range = 4 * math.sqrt(6. / (input_size + size))

                #Initialize weights through a random uniform
distribution
                self.w_list.append(
                np.random.uniform( -max_range, max_range, [input_size,
size]).astype(np.float32))

                #Initialize bias as zeroes
                self.c_list.append(np.zeros([size], np.float32))
                input_size = size


            # Build DBN
            #Create placeholders for input, weights, biases, output
            self._a = [None] * (len(self._sizes) + 2)
            self._w = [None] * (len(self._sizes) + 1)
            self._c = [None] * (len(self._sizes) + 1)
            self._a[0] = tf.placeholder("float", [None,
self._X.shape[1]])
            self.y = tf.placeholder("float", [None, self._Y.shape[1]])

            #Define variables and activation function
            for i in range(len(self._sizes) + 1):
                self._w[i] = tf.Variable(self.w_list[i])
                self._c[i] = tf.Variable(self.c_list[i])
            for i in range(1, len(self._sizes) + 2):
                self._a[i] = tf.nn.sigmoid(tf.matmul(self._a[i - 1],
self._w[i - 1]) + self._c[i - 1])

            #Define the cost function
            cost =
tf.reduce_mean(tf.nn.softmax_cross_entropy_with_logits(labels=self.
y, logits= self._a[-1]))
            #cost = tf.reduce_mean(tf.square(self._a[-1] - self.y))

            #Define the training operation (Momentum Optimizer
minimizing the Cost function)
            self.train_op =
tf.train.AdamOptimizer(learning_rate=self._learning_rate).minimize(
cost)

            #Prediction operation
            self.predict_op = tf.argmax(self._a[-1], 1)
```

```
        #load data from rbm
        def load_from_rbms(self, dbn_sizes,rbm_list):
            #Check if expected sizes are correct
            assert len(dbn_sizes) == len(self._sizes)

            for i in range(len(self._sizes)):
                #Check if for each RBN the expected sizes are correct
                assert dbn_sizes[i] == self._sizes[i]

            #If everything is correct, bring over the weights and
biases
            for i in range(len(self._sizes)-1):
                self.w_list[i] = rbm_list[i]._W
                self.c_list[i] = rbm_list[i]._c


    def set_session(self, session):
        self.session = session

    #Training method
    def train(self, val_x, val_y):
        #For each epoch
        num_batches = self.N // self._batchsize

        batch_size = self._batchsize
        for i in range(self._epochs):
            #For each step
            for j in range(num_batches):
                batch = self._X[j * batch_size: (j * batch_size +
batch_size)]
                batch_label = self._Y[j * batch_size: (j *
batch_size + batch_size)]

                self.session.run(self.train_op,
feed_dict={self._a[0]: batch, self.y: batch_label})

                for j in range(len(self._sizes) + 1):
                    #Retrieve weights and biases
                    self.w_list[j] = sess.run(self._w[j])
                    self.c_list[j] = sess.run(self._c[j])

            train_acc = np.mean(np.argmax(self._Y, axis=1) ==
 self.session.run(self.predict_op, feed_dict={self._a[0]: self._X,
self.y: self._Y}))

            val_acc = np.mean(np.argmax(val_y, axis=1) ==
 self.session.run(self.predict_op, feed_dict={self._a[0]: val_x,
self.y: val_y}))
```

```
            print (" epoch " + str(i) + "/" + str(self._epochs) +
     " Training Accuracy: " +  str(train_acc) + " Validation Accuracy: "
     + str(val_acc))

        def predict(self, X):
            return self.session.run(self.predict_op,
     feed_dict={self._a[0]: X})
```

8. Now, we train instantiate a DBN object and train it. And predict the labels for the test data:

```
nNet = DBN(RBM_hidden_sizes, X_train, Y_train, epochs = 80)
with tf.Session() as sess:
    #Initialize Variables
    sess.run(tf.global_variables_initializer())
    nNet.set_session(sess)
    nNet.load_from_rbms(RBM_hidden_sizes, rbm_list)
    nNet.train(X_val, Y_val)
    y_pred = nNet.predict(X_test)
```

How it works...

The RBMs learn the hidden representations/features of the model using unsupervised learning and then the fully connected layers added along with pre-trained RBMs are finetuned.

The accuracy here varies largely on image representation. In the preceding recipe, we have used no image processing, only grayscale images scaled between 0 to 1. But if we add the image processing as done in the following paper, it increases the accuracy further-http://deeplearning.net/wp-content/uploads/2013/03/dlsvm.pdf. Thus we multiply each image by 100.0/255.0 in the preprocess_data function, and add these few lines of the code to main code:

```
std_image = np.std(X_train, axis=0)
X_train = np.divide(np.subtract(X_train,mean_image), std_image)
X_val = np.divide(np.subtract(X_val,mean_image), std_image)
X_test = np.divide(np.subtract(X_test,mean_image), std_image)
```

There's more...

In the preceding example, without preprocessing, the accuracy of the three data sets is roughly ~40 percent. But when we add preprocessing, the accuracy for the training data increases to 90 percent, but for validation and testing, we still get an accuracy of ~45 percent.

There are many changes which can be introduced to improve the result. First, the dataset that we used in the recipe is the Kaggle dataset with only 22,000 images. If you observe these images you will find the addition of the step of filtering only faces will improve the result. Another strategy, as mentioned in the following paper, is increasing the size of hidden layers instead of reducing them-https://www.cs.swarthmore.edu/~meeden/cs81/s14/papers/KevinVincent.pdf.

Another change that has been found really successful in identifying the emotions is using facial-keypoints instead of training for the whole face, http://cs229.stanford.edu/proj2010/McLaughlinLeBayanbat-RecognizingEmotionsWithDeepBeliefNets.pdf.

With the preceding recipe, you can play around with these changes and explore how performance improves. May the GPU force be with you!

8
Autoencoders

Autoencoders are feed-forward, non-recurrent neural networks, which learn by unsupervised learning. They have an inherent capability to learn a compact representation of data. They are at the centre of deep belief networks and find applications in image reconstruction, clustering, machine translation, and much more. In this chapter, you will learn and implement different variants of autoencoders and eventually learn how to stack autoencoders. The chapter includes the following topics:

- Vanilla autoencoder
- Sparse autoencoder
- Denoising autoencoder
- Convolutional autoencoders
- Stacked autoencoders

Introduction

Autoencoders, also known as **Diabolo networks** or **autoassociators**, was initially proposed in the 1980s by Hinton and the PDP group [1]. They are feedforward networks, without any feedback, and they learn via unsupervised learning. Like multiplayer perceptrons of Chapter 3, *Neural Networks-Perceptrons*, they use the backpropagation algorithm to learn, but with a major difference--the target is the same as the input.

We can think of an autoencoder as consisting of two cascaded networks--the first network is an encoder, it takes the input x, and encodes it using a transformation h to encoded signal y:

$$y = h(x)$$

The second network uses the encoded signal y as its input and performs another transformation f to get a reconstructed signal r:

$$r = f(y) = f(h(x))$$

We define error e as the difference between the original input x and the reconstructed signal r, $e = x - r$. The network then learns by reducing the **mean squared error** (**MSE**), and the error is propagated back to the hidden layers as in the case of MLPs. The following figure shows an autoencoder with encoder and decoder highlighted separately. Autoencoders can have weight sharing, that is, weights of decoder and encoder are simply a transpose of each other, which can help the network learn faster as the number of training parameters is less, but at the same time reduces the degrees of freedom of the network. They are very similar to RBMs of Chapter 7, *Unsupervised Learning*, but with one big difference--the state of the neurons in autoencoders is deterministic, while in RBMs, the state of the neurons is probabilistic:

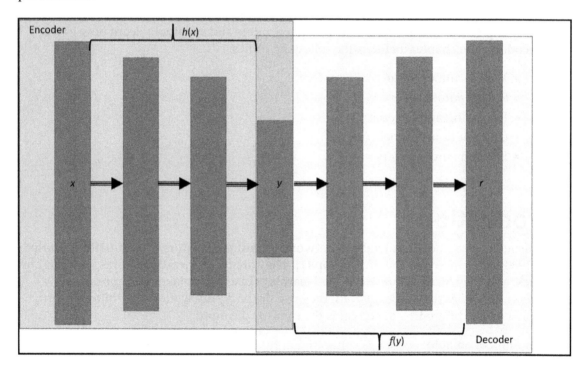

Depending on the size of the hidden layer, autoencoders are classified as **Undercomplete** (hidden layer has fewer neurons than the input layer) or **Overcomplete** (hidden layer has more neurons than the input layer). Depending on the restriction/constraints imposed on the loss, we have various types of autoencoders: Sparse Autoencoders, Denoising Autoencoders, and Convolution Autoencoders. In this chapter, you will learn about these variations in autoencoders and implement them using TensorFlow.

One of the obvious applications of autoencoders is in the field of dimensionality reduction [2]; the results show that autoencoders yield better results as compared to PCA. Autoencoders can also be used for feature extraction [3], document retrieval [2], classification, and anomaly detection.

See Also

- Rumelhart, David E., Geoffrey E. Hinton, and Ronald J. Williams. Learning internal representations by error propagation. No. ICS-8506. California Univ San Diego La Jolla Inst for Cognitive Science, 1985. (http://www.cs.toronto.edu/~fritz/absps/pdp8.pdf)

- Hinton, Geoffrey E., and Ruslan R. Salakhutdinov. *Reducing the dimensionality of data with neural networks*, science 313.5786 (2006): 504-507. (https://pdfs.semanticscholar.org/7d76/b71b700846901ac4ac119403aa737a285e36.pdf)

- Masci, Jonathan, et al. *Stacked convolutional auto-encoders for hierarchical feature extraction*. Artificial Neural Networks and Machine Learning–ICANN 2011 (2011): 52-59. (https://www.researchgate.net/profile/Jonathan_Masci/publication/221078713_Stacked_Convolutional_Auto-Encoders_for_Hierarchical_Feature_Extraction/links/0deec518b9c6ed4634000000/Stacked-Convolutional-Auto-Encoders-for-Hierarchical-Feature-Extraction.pdf)

- Japkowicz, Nathalie, Catherine Myers, and Mark Gluck. *A novelty detection approach to classification*. IJCAI. Vol. 1. 1995. (http://www.ijcai.org/Proceedings/95-1/Papers/068.pdf)

Vanilla autoencoders

The vanilla autoencoder, as proposed by Hinton, consists of only one hidden layer. The number of neurons in the hidden layer is less than the number of neurons in the input (or output) layer. This results in producing a bottleneck effect on the flow of information in the network, and therefore we can think of the hidden layer as a bottleneck layer, restricting the information that would be stored. Learning in the autoencoder consists of developing a compact representation of the input signal at the hidden layer so that the output layer can faithfully reproduce the original input:

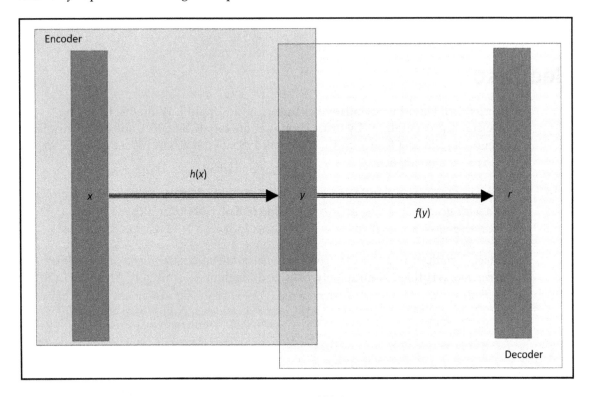

Autoencoder with a single hidden layer

Getting ready

This recipe will use autoencoders for image reconstruction; we will train the autoencoder on MNIST database and use it to reconstruct the test images.

How to do it...

We proceed with the recipe as follows:

1. As always, the first step is to import all the necessary modules:

```
import tensorflow as tf
import numpy as np
from tensorflow.examples.tutorials.mnist import input_data
import matplotlib.pyplot as plt
%matplotlib inline
```

2. Next, we take the MNIST data from the TensorFlow examples--the important thing to note here is that the labels are not one-hot encoded, simply because we are not using labels to train the network. Autoencoders learn via unsupervised learning:

```
mnist = input_data.read_data_sets("MNIST_data/")
trX, trY, teX, teY = mnist.train.images, mnist.train.labels,
mnist.test.images, mnist.test.labels
```

3. Next, we declare a class `AutoEncoder`; the class has the `init` method to initialize weights, biases, and placeholders for the autoencoder. We can also build the complete graph in the `init` method. The class also has methods for `encoder`, `decoder`, setting session (`set_session`), and `fit`. The autoencoder we build here uses the simple MSE as the `loss` function, and we try to optimize it using `AdamOptimizer`:

```
class AutoEncoder(object):
def __init__(self, m, n, eta = 0.01):
"""
m: Number of neurons in input/output layer
n: number of neurons in hidden layer
"""
self._m = m
self._n = n
self.learning_rate = eta
```

```
# Create the Computational graph

# Weights and biases
self._W1 = tf.Variable(tf.random_normal(shape=(self._m,self._n)))
self._W2 = tf.Variable(tf.random_normal(shape=(self._n,self._m)))
self._b1 = tf.Variable(np.zeros(self._n).astype(np.float32)) #bias
for hidden layer
self._b2 = tf.Variable(np.zeros(self._m).astype(np.float32)) #bias
for output layer

# Placeholder for inputs
self._X = tf.placeholder('float', [None, self._m])

self.y = self.encoder(self._X)
self.r = self.decoder(self.y)
error = self._X - self.r

self._loss = tf.reduce_mean(tf.pow(error, 2))
self._opt =
tf.train.AdamOptimizer(self.learning_rate).minimize(self._loss)


def encoder(self, x):
h = tf.matmul(x, self._W1) + self._b1
return tf.nn.sigmoid(h)


def decoder(self, x):
h = tf.matmul(x, self._W2) + self._b2
return tf.nn.sigmoid(h)

def set_session(self, session):
self.session = session


def reduced_dimension(self, x):
h = self.encoder(x)
return self.session.run(h, feed_dict={self._X: x})

def reconstruct(self,x):
h = self.encoder(x)
r = self.decoder(h)
return self.session.run(r, feed_dict={self._X: x})


def fit(self, X, epochs = 1, batch_size = 100):
N, D = X.shape
```

```
num_batches = N // batch_size

obj = []
for i in range(epochs):
#X = shuffle(X)
for j in range(num_batches):
    batch = X[j * batch_size: (j * batch_size + batch_size)]
    _, ob = self.session.run([self._opt,self._loss],
feed_dict={self._X: batch})
    if j % 100 == 0 and i % 100 == 0:
        print('training epoch {0} batch {2} cost {1}'.format(i,ob,
j))
obj.append(ob)
return obj
```

To be able to use the autoencoder after training, we also define two utility functions--reduced_dimension, which gives the output of the encoder network, and reconstruct, which reconstructs the final image.

4. We convert the input data to a float for the training, initialize all the variables, and start the computation session. In computation, we are, at present, only testing the reconstruction power of the autoencoder:

```
Xtrain = trX.astype(np.float32)
Xtest = teX.astype(np.float32)
_, m = Xtrain.shape

autoEncoder = AutoEncoder(m, 256)

#Initialize all variables
init = tf.global_variables_initializer()
with tf.Session() as sess:
    sess.run(init)
    autoEncoder.set_session(sess)
    err = autoEncoder.fit(Xtrain, epochs=10)
    out = autoEncoder.reconstruct(Xtest[0:100])
```

5. We can verify if our network indeed optimized the MSE while training by plotting error versus epoch. For a good training, the error should reduce with epochs:

```
plt.plot(err)
plt.xlabel('epochs')
plt.ylabel('cost')
```

The graph is shown here:

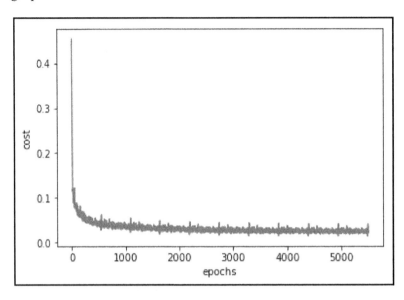

We can see that loss/cost is decreasing as the network learns and by the time we reach 5,000 epochs, it is almost oscillating about a line. This means further increasing epochs will not be useful. If we want to now improve our training, we should change the hyperparameters like learning rate, batch size, and optimizer used.

6. Let's now see the reconstructed images. Here, you can see the original and reconstructed images together as generated by our autoencoder:

```
# Plotting original and reconstructed images
row, col = 2, 8
idx = np.random.randint(0, 100, row * col // 2)
f, axarr = plt.subplots(row, col, sharex=True, sharey=True,
figsize=(20,4))
for fig, row in zip([Xtest,out], axarr):
    for i,ax in zip(idx,row):
        ax.imshow(fig[i].reshape((28, 28)), cmap='Greys_r')
        ax.get_xaxis().set_visible(False)
        ax.get_yaxis().set_visible(False)
```

We the following result:

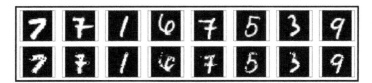

How it works...

It is interesting to note that in the preceding code, we reduced the dimensions of the input from 784 to 256 and our network could still reconstruct the original image. Let's compare our performance with RBM (*Chapter 7, Unsupervised Learning*) with the same dimension of the hidden layer:

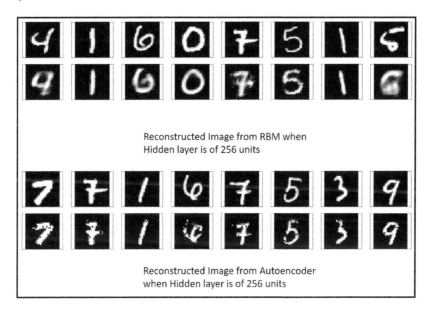

We can see that the images reconstructed by the autoencoder are much crisper than the ones reconstructed by RBM. The reason is that, in the autoencoder, there are additional weights (weights from hidden to decoder output layer) to be trained and hence retain learning. As the autoencoder learns more, it performs better than RBM, even when both compact the information to the same dimensions.

There's more...

Autoencoders like PCA can be used for dimensionality reduction, but while PCA can only represent linear transformations, we can use nonlinear activation functions in autoencoders, thus introducing non-linearities in our encodings. Here is the result reproduced from the Hinton paper, *Reducing the dimensionality of data with Neural Networks*. The result compares the result of a PCA (A) with that of stacked RBMs as autoencoders with architecture consisting of 784-1000-500-250-2:

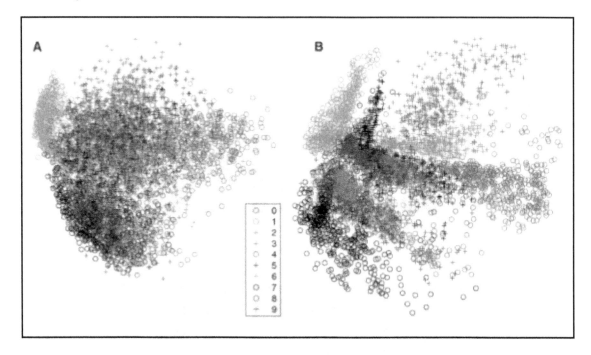

As we will see later when an autoencoder is made using stacked autoencoders, each autoencoder is initially pretrained individually, and then the entire network is fine-tuned for better performance.

Sparse autoencoder

The autoencoder that we saw in the previous recipe worked more like an identity network--they simply reconstruct the input. The emphasis is to reconstruct the image at the pixel level, and the only constraint is the number of units in the bottleneck layer; while it is interesting, pixel-level reconstruction does not ensure that the network will learn abstract features from the dataset. We can ensure that the network learns abstract features from the dataset by adding further constraints.

In sparse autoencoders, a sparse penalty term is added to the reconstruction error, which tries to ensure that fewer units in the bottleneck layer will fire at any given time. If *m* is the total number of input patterns, then we can define a quantity ρ_hat (you can check the mathematical details in Andrew Ng's Lecture at `https://web.stanford.edu/class/cs294a/sparseAutoencoder_2011new.pdf`), which measures the net activity (how many times on an average it fires) for each hidden layer unit. The basic idea is to put a constraint ρ_hat, such that it is equal to the sparsity parameter ρ. This results in adding a regularization term for sparsity in the loss function so that now the `loss` function is as follows:

```
loss = Mean squared error + Regularization for sparsity parameter
```

This regularization term will penalize the network if ρ_hat deviates from ρ; one standard way to do this is to use **Kullback-Leiber (KL)** divergence between ρ and ρ_hat.

Getting Ready...

Before starting with the recipe, let's explore the KL divergence, D_{KL} a little more. It is a non-symmetric measure of the difference between two distributions, in our case, ρ and ρ_hat. When ρ and ρ_hat are equal, then it is zero, otherwise, it increases monotonically as ρ_hat diverges from ϱ. Mathematically, it is expressed as follows:

$$D_{KL}(\rho||\hat{\rho}_j) = \rho log \frac{\rho}{\hat{\rho}_j} + (1-\rho)log \frac{1-\rho}{1-\hat{\rho}_j}$$

Here is the plot of D_{KL} for a fixed $\varrho=0.3$, where we can see that when $\varrho\_hat=0.3$, $D_{KL}=0$; otherwise, it is increasing monotonically on both sides:

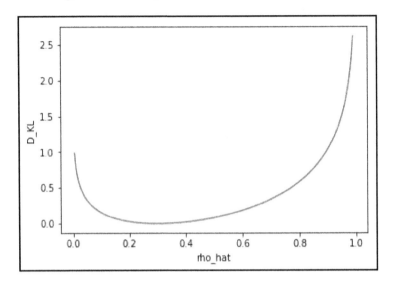

How to do it...

We proceed with the recipe as follows:

1. We import the necessary modules:

```
import tensorflow as tf
import numpy as np
from tensorflow.examples.tutorials.mnist import input_data
import matplotlib.pyplot as plt
%matplotlib inline
```

2. Load the MNIST dataset from TensorFlow examples:

```
mnist = input_data.read_data_sets("MNIST_data/")
trX, trY, teX, teY = mnist.train.images, mnist.train.labels,
mnist.test.images, mnist.test.labels
```

3. Define the `SparseAutoEncoder` class, which is very similar to the autoencoder class in the previous recipe, except for introducing the KL divergence loss:

```
def kl_div(self, rho, rho_hat):
 term2_num = tf.constant(1.) - rho
 term2_den = tf.constant(1.) - rho_hat
 kl = self.logfunc(rho,rho_hat) + self.logfunc(term2_num,
term2_den)
 return kl

def logfunc(self, x1, x2):
 return tf.multiply( x1, tf.log(tf.div(x1,x2)))
```

We add the KL constraint to the loss as follows:

```
alpha = 7.5e-5
kl_div_loss = tf.reduce_sum(self.kl_div(0.02,
tf.reduce_mean(self.y,0)))
loss = self._loss + alpha * kl_div_loss
```

Here, `alpha` is the weightage given to the sparsity constraint. The complete code for the class is as follows:

```
class SparseAutoEncoder(object):
 def __init__(self, m, n, eta = 0.01):
 """
 m: Number of neurons in input/output layer
 n: number of neurons in hidden layer
 """
 self._m = m
 self._n = n
 self.learning_rate = eta

 # Create the Computational graph

 # Weights and biases
 self._W1 = tf.Variable(tf.random_normal(shape=(self._m,self._n)))
 self._W2 = tf.Variable(tf.random_normal(shape=(self._n,self._m)))
 self._b1 = tf.Variable(np.zeros(self._n).astype(np.float32)) #bias
for hidden layer
 self._b2 = tf.Variable(np.zeros(self._m).astype(np.float32)) #bias
for output layer

 # Placeholder for inputs
 self._X = tf.placeholder('float', [None, self._m])

 self.y = self.encoder(self._X)
```

```
self.r = self.decoder(self.y)
error = self._X - self.r

self._loss = tf.reduce_mean(tf.pow(error, 2))
alpha = 7.5e-5
kl_div_loss = tf.reduce_sum(self.kl_div(0.02,
tf.reduce_mean(self.y,0)))
loss = self._loss + alpha * kl_div_loss
self._opt =
tf.train.AdamOptimizer(self.learning_rate).minimize(loss)


def encoder(self, x):
h = tf.matmul(x, self._W1) + self._b1
return tf.nn.sigmoid(h)


def decoder(self, x):
h = tf.matmul(x, self._W2) + self._b2
return tf.nn.sigmoid(h)

def set_session(self, session):
self.session = session


def reduced_dimension(self, x):
h = self.encoder(x)
return self.session.run(h, feed_dict={self._X: x})

def reconstruct(self,x):
h = self.encoder(x)
r = self.decoder(h)
return self.session.run(r, feed_dict={self._X: x})

def kl_div(self, rho, rho_hat):
term2_num = tf.constant(1.)- rho
term2_den = tf.constant(1.) - rho_hat
kl = self.logfunc(rho,rho_hat) + self.logfunc(term2_num,
term2_den)
return kl

def logfunc(self, x1, x2):
return tf.multiply( x1, tf.log(tf.div(x1,x2)))


def fit(self, X, epochs = 1, batch_size = 100):
N, D = X.shape
```

```
    num_batches = N // batch_size

    obj = []
    for i in range(epochs):
        #X = shuffle(X)
        for j in range(num_batches):
            batch = X[j * batch_size: (j * batch_size + batch_size)]
            _, ob = self.session.run([self._opt,self._loss],
feed_dict={self._X: batch})
            if j % 100 == 0:
                print('training epoch {0} batch {2} cost
{1}'.format(i,ob, j))
    obj.append(ob)
    return obj
```

4. Next, we declare an object of the `SparseAutoEncoder` class, perform the fit on the training data, and compute the reconstructed image:

```
Xtrain = trX.astype(np.float32)
Xtest = teX.astype(np.float32)
_, m = Xtrain.shape
sae = SparseAutoEncoder(m, 256)
#Initialize all variables
init = tf.global_variables_initializer()
with tf.Session() as sess:
 sess.run(init)
 sae.set_session(sess)
 err = sae.fit(Xtrain, epochs=10)
 out = sae.reconstruct(Xtest[0:100])
```

5. Let's see the variation of mean squared reconstruction loss as the network learns:

```
plt.plot(err)
plt.xlabel('epochs')
plt.ylabel('Reconstruction Loss (MSE)')
```

The plot is as follows:

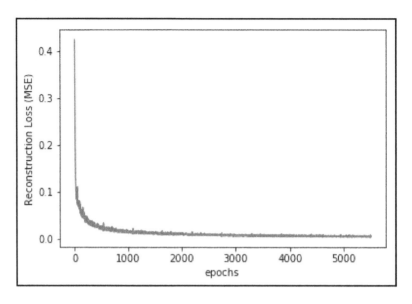

6. Let's see the reconstructed images:

```
# Plotting original and reconstructed images
row, col = 2, 8
idx = np.random.randint(0, 100, row * col // 2)
f, axarr = plt.subplots(row, col, sharex=True, sharey=True,
figsize=(20,4))
for fig, row in zip([Xtest,out], axarr):
    for i,ax in zip(idx,row):
        ax.imshow(fig[i].reshape((28, 28)), cmap='Greys_r')
        ax.get_xaxis().set_visible(False)
        ax.get_yaxis().set_visible(False)
```

We get the folllowing result:

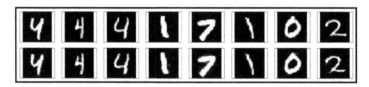

How it works...

The main code of the sparse autoencoder, as you must have noticed, is exactly the same as that of the vanilla autoencoder, which is so because the sparse autoencoder has just one major change--the addition of the KL divergence loss to ensure sparsity of the hidden (bottleneck) layer. However, if you compare the two reconstructions, you can see that the sparse autoencoder is much better than the standard encoder, even with the same number of units in the hidden layer:

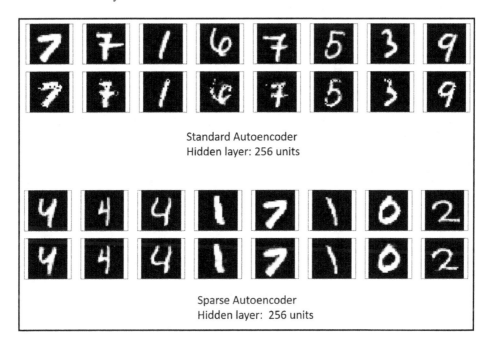

The reconstruction loss after training the vanilla autoencoder for the MNIST dataset is 0.022, while for the sparse autoencoder, it is 0.006. Thus, adding constraint forces the network to learn hidden representations of the data.

There's More...

The compact representation of the inputs is stored in weights; let's visualize the weights learned by the network. Here are the weights of the encoder layer for the standard and sparse autoencoder respectively. We can see that, in the standard autoencoder, many hidden units have their very large weights, suggesting they are overworked:

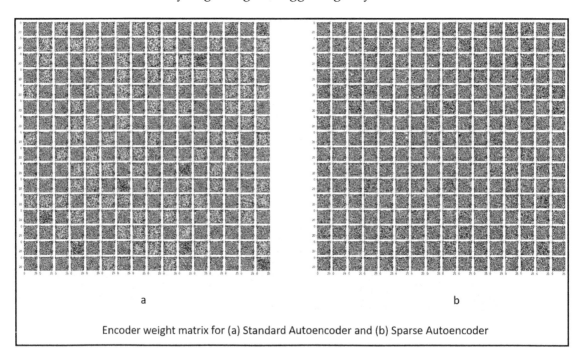

a   b

Encoder weight matrix for (a) Standard Autoencoder and (b) Sparse Autoencoder

See Also

- http://web.engr.illinois.edu/~hanj/cs412/bk3/KL-divergence.pdf
- https://en.wikipedia.org/wiki/Kullback%E2%80%93Leibler_divergence

Denoising autoencoder

The two autoencoders that we have explored in the previous two recipes are examples of **Undercomplete** Autoencoders because the hidden layer in them has a lower dimension as compared to the input (output) layer. Denoising autoencoder belongs to the class of **Overcomplete** Autoencoders because it works better when the dimensions of the hidden layer are more than the input layer.

A denoising autoencoder learns from a corrupted (noisy) input; it feeds its encoder network the noisy input and then the reconstructed image from the decoder is compared with the original input. The idea is that this will help the network learn how to denoise an input. It will no longer just make a pixel-wise comparison, but in order to denoise, it will learn the information of neighbouring pixels as well.

Getting Ready

A denoising autoencoder will also have the KL divergence penalty term; it will differ from the sparse autoencoder of the previous recipe in two main aspects. First, n_hidden, the number of hidden units in the bottleneck layer is more than the number of units in the input layer, m, that is n_hidden > m. Second, the input to the encoder is corrupted input; to do this in TensorFlow, we add the function corrupt, which adds noise to the input:

```
def corruption(x, noise_factor = 0.3): #corruption of the input
    noisy_imgs = x + noise_factor * np.random.randn(*x.shape)
    noisy_imgs = np.clip(noisy_imgs, 0., 1.)
    return noisy_imgs
```

How to do it...

1. Like always, the first step is to import the necessary modules--TensorFlow, numpy to manipulate input data, matplotlib to plot, and so on:

```
import tensorflow as tf
import numpy as np
from tensorflow.examples.tutorials.mnist import input_data
import matplotlib.pyplot as plt
import math
%matplotlib inline
```

2. Load the data from TensorFlow examples. We have used the standard MNIST database for illustration in all the recipes of this chapter to provide you with a benchmark between different autoencoders.

```
mnist = input_data.read_data_sets("MNIST_data/")
trX, trY, teX, teY = mnist.train.images, mnist.train.labels,
mnist.test.images, mnist.test.labels
```

3. Next, we define the main component of this recipe--the `DenoisingAutoEncoder` class. The class is very similar to the `SparseAutoEncoder` class that we made in the previous recipe. Here, we have a placeholder for the noisy image; this noisy input is fed to the encoder. The reconstruction error is now the difference between the original clean image and the output of the decoder when the noisy image is the input. We retain the sparsity penalty term here. The fit function thus takes both the original image and the noisy image as its argument.

```
class DenoisingAutoEncoder(object):
def __init__(self, m, n, eta = 0.01):
"""
m: Number of neurons in input/output layer
n: number of neurons in hidden layer
"""
self._m = m
self._n = n
self.learning_rate = eta

# Create the Computational graph

# Weights and biases
self._W1 = tf.Variable(tf.random_normal(shape=(self._m,self._n)))
self._W2 = tf.Variable(tf.random_normal(shape=(self._n,self._m)))
self._b1 = tf.Variable(np.zeros(self._n).astype(np.float32)) #bias for
hidden layer
self._b2 = tf.Variable(np.zeros(self._m).astype(np.float32)) #bias for
output layer

# Placeholder for inputs
self._X = tf.placeholder('float', [None, self._m])

self._X_noisy = tf.placeholder('float', [None, self._m])

self.y = self.encoder(self._X_noisy)
self.r = self.decoder(self.y)
error = self._X - self.r

self._loss = tf.reduce_mean(tf.pow(error, 2))
```

```
#self._loss = tf.reduce_mean(tf.nn.sigmoid_cross_entropy_with_logits(labels
=self._X, logits = self.r))
alpha = 0.05
kl_div_loss = tf.reduce_sum(self.kl_div(0.02, tf.reduce_mean(self.y,0)))
loss = self._loss + alpha * kl_div_loss
self._opt = tf.train.AdamOptimizer(self.learning_rate).minimize(loss)


def encoder(self, x):
h = tf.matmul(x, self._W1) + self._b1
return tf.nn.sigmoid(h)


def decoder(self, x):
h = tf.matmul(x, self._W2) + self._b2
return tf.nn.sigmoid(h)

def set_session(self, session):
self.session = session

def reconstruct(self,x):
h = self.encoder(x)
r = self.decoder(h)
return self.session.run(r, feed_dict={self._X: x})

def kl_div(self, rho, rho_hat):
term2_num = tf.constant(1.)- rho
term2_den = tf.constant(1.) - rho_hat
kl = self.logfunc(rho,rho_hat) + self.logfunc(term2_num, term2_den)
return kl

def logfunc(self, x1, x2):
return tf.multiply( x1, tf.log(tf.div(x1,x2)))

def corrupt(self,x):
return x * tf.cast(tf.random_uniform(shape=tf.shape(x),
minval=0,maxval=2),tf.float32)

def getWeights(self):
return self.session.run([self._W1, self._W2,self._b1, self._b2])

def fit(self, X, Xorg, epochs = 1, batch_size = 100):
N, D = X.shape
num_batches = N // batch_size

obj = []
for i in range(epochs):
#X = shuffle(X)
```

```
for j in range(num_batches):
batch = X[j * batch_size: (j * batch_size + batch_size)]
batchO = Xorg[j * batch_size: (j * batch_size + batch_size)]
_, ob = self.session.run([self._opt,self._loss], feed_dict={self._X:
batchO, self._X_noisy: batch})
if j % 100 == 0:
print('training epoch {0} batch {2} cost {1}'.format(i,ob, j))
obj.append(ob)
return obj
```

It is also possible to add noise to the autoencoder object. In that case, you will use the corrupt method defined in the class, `self._X_noisy = self.corrupt(self._X) * 0.3 + self._X * (1 - 0.3)`, and the fit method will also change to the following:

```
def fit(self, X, epochs = 1, batch_size = 100):
        N, D = X.shape
        num_batches = N // batch_size
        obj = []
        for i in range(epochs):
            #X = shuffle(X)
            for j in range(num_batches):
                batch = X[j * batch_size: (j * batch_size + batch_size)]
                _, ob = self.session.run([self._opt,self._loss],
feed_dict={self._X: batch})
                if j % 100 == 0:
                    print('training epoch {0} batch {2} cost
{1}'.format(i,ob, j))
                obj.append(ob)
        return obj
```

4. Now, we use the corruption function defined earlier to generate a noisy image and feed it to the session:

```
n_hidden = 800
Xtrain = trX.astype(np.float32)
Xtrain_noisy = corruption(Xtrain).astype(np.float32)
Xtest = teX.astype(np.float32)
#noise = Xtest * np.random.randint(0, 2, Xtest.shape).astype(np.float32)
Xtest_noisy = corruption(Xtest).astype(np.float32) #Xtest * (1-0.3)+ noise
*(0.3)
_, m = Xtrain.shape

dae = DenoisingAutoEncoder(m, n_hidden)

#Initialize all variables
init = tf.global_variables_initializer()
with tf.Session() as sess:
```

```
sess.run(init)
dae.set_session(sess)
err = dae.fit(Xtrain_noisy, Xtrain, epochs=10)
out = dae.reconstruct(Xtest_noisy[0:100])
W1, W2, b1, b2 = dae.getWeights()
red = dae.reduced_dimension(Xtrain)
```

5. The reconstruction loss reduces as the network learns:

```
plt.plot(err)
plt.xlabel('epochs')
plt.ylabel('Reconstruction Loss (MSE)')
```

The plot is as follows:

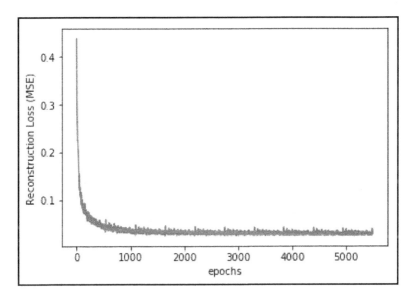

6. The reconstructed images, when noisy images from the test dataset are presented to the trained network, are as follows:

```
# Plotting original and reconstructed images
row, col = 2, 8
idx = np.random.randint(0, 100, row * col // 2)
f, axarr = plt.subplots(row, col, sharex=True, sharey=True, figsize=(20,4))
for fig, row in zip([Xtest_noisy,out], axarr):
 for i,ax in zip(idx,row):
 ax.imshow(fig[i].reshape((28, 28)), cmap='Greys_r')
 ax.get_xaxis().set_visible(False)
 ax.get_yaxis().set_visible(False)
```

We the following result:

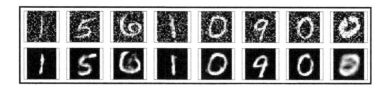

See Also

- https://cs.stanford.edu/people/karpathy/convnetjs/demo/autoencoder.html
- http://blackecho.github.io/blog/machine-learning/2016/02/29/denoising-autoencoder-tensorflow.html

Convolutional autoencoders

Researchers have found that **Convolutional Neural Networks** (**CNN**) work best with images because they can extract the spatial information hidden in the image. It is thus natural to assume that if encoder and decoder network consists of CNN, it will work better than the rest of the autoencoders, and so we have **Convolutional Autoencoders** (**CAE**). In Chapter 4, *Convolutional Neural Networks*, the process of convolution and max-pooling was explained, which we will use as a base to understand how convolutional autoencoders work.

A CAE is one where both the encoder and decoder are CNN networks. The convolutional network of the encoder learns to encode the input as a set of signals and then the decoder CNN tries to reconstruct the input from them. They work as general purpose feature extractors and learn the optimal filters needed to capture the features from the input.

Getting Ready...

From Chapter 4, *Convolutional Neural Network,* you had learned that, as convolutional layers are added, the information passed to the next layer reduces in spatial extent, but in an autoencoder, the reconstructed image should be of the same size and depth as the input image. This implies that the decoder should somehow do both image resizing and convolution to reconstruct the original image. One way of increasing the spatial extent along with convolution is with the help of **transposed convolution layers**. These are easily implemented in TensorFlow by `tf.nn.conv2d_transpose`, but it was found that transposed convolution layers result in artefacts in the final image. Augustus Odena et al. [1], in their work, showed that these artefacts can be avoided by resizing the layers using either the nearest neighbour or bilinear interpolation (upsampling) followed by a convolutional layer. They achieved best results with nearest neighbour interpolation, implemented via `tf.image.resize_images`; we will follow the same approach here.

How to do it...

1. The first step, as always, is including the necessary modules:

```
import tensorflow as tf
import numpy as np
from tensorflow.examples.tutorials.mnist import input_data
import matplotlib.pyplot as plt
import math
%matplotlib inline
```

2. Load the input data:

```
mnist = input_data.read_data_sets("MNIST_data/")
trX, trY, teX, teY = mnist.train.images, mnist.train.labels,
mnist.test.images, mnist.test.labels
```

3. Define the network parameters. Here, we also calculate the spatial dimensions of the output of each max-pool layer; we need this information to upsample the image in the decoder network:

```
# Network Parameters
h_in, w_in = 28, 28 # Image size height and width
k = 3 # Kernel size
p = 2 # pool
s = 2 # Strides in maxpool
filters = {1:32,2:32,3:16}
```

```
activation_fn=tf.nn.relu
# Change in dimensions of image after each MaxPool
h_l2, w_l2 = int(np.ceil(float(h_in)/float(s))) ,
int(np.ceil(float(w_in)/float(s))) # Height and width: second
encoder/decoder layer
h_l3, w_l3 = int(np.ceil(float(h_l2)/float(s))) ,
int(np.ceil(float(w_l2)/float(s))) # Height and width: third
encoder/decoder layer
```

4. Create placeholders for input (noisy image) and target (corresponding clear image):

```
X_noisy = tf.placeholder(tf.float32, (None, h_in, w_in, 1), name='inputs')
X = tf.placeholder(tf.float32, (None, h_in, w_in, 1), name='targets')
```

5. Build the Encoder and Decoder networks:

```
### Encoder
conv1 = tf.layers.conv2d(X_noisy, filters[1], (k,k), padding='same',
activation=activation_fn)
# Output size h_in x w_in x filters[1]
maxpool1 = tf.layers.max_pooling2d(conv1, (p,p), (s,s), padding='same')
# Output size h_l2 x w_l2 x filters[1]
conv2 = tf.layers.conv2d(maxpool1, filters[2], (k,k), padding='same',
activation=activation_fn)
# Output size h_l2 x w_l2 x filters[2]
maxpool2 = tf.layers.max_pooling2d(conv2,(p,p), (s,s), padding='same')
# Output size h_l3 x w_l3 x filters[2]
conv3 = tf.layers.conv2d(maxpool2,filters[3], (k,k), padding='same',
activation=activation_fn)
# Output size h_l3 x w_l3 x filters[3]
encoded = tf.layers.max_pooling2d(conv3, (p,p), (s,s), padding='same')
# Output size h_l3/s x w_l3/s x filters[3] Now 4x4x16

### Decoder
upsample1 = tf.image.resize_nearest_neighbor(encoded, (h_l3,w_l3))
# Output size h_l3 x w_l3 x filters[3]
conv4 = tf.layers.conv2d(upsample1, filters[3], (k,k), padding='same',
activation=activation_fn)
# Output size h_l3 x w_l3 x filters[3]
upsample2 = tf.image.resize_nearest_neighbor(conv4, (h_l2,w_l2))
# Output size h_l2 x w_l2 x filters[3]
conv5 = tf.layers.conv2d(upsample2, filters[2], (k,k), padding='same',
activation=activation_fn)
# Output size h_l2 x w_l2 x filters[2]
upsample3 = tf.image.resize_nearest_neighbor(conv5, (h_in,w_in))
# Output size h_in x w_in x filters[2]
```

```
conv6 = tf.layers.conv2d(upsample3, filters[1], (k,k), padding='same',
activation=activation_fn)
# Output size h_in x w_in x filters[1]

logits = tf.layers.conv2d(conv6, 1, (k,k) , padding='same',
activation=None)

# Output size h_in x w_in x 1
decoded = tf.nn.sigmoid(logits, name='decoded')

loss = tf.nn.sigmoid_cross_entropy_with_logits(labels=X, logits=logits)
cost = tf.reduce_mean(loss)
opt = tf.train.AdamOptimizer(0.001).minimize(cost)
```

6. **Start the session:**

```
sess = tf.Session()
```

7. **Fit the model for the given input:**

```
epochs = 10
batch_size = 100
# Set's how much noise we're adding to the MNIST images
noise_factor = 0.5
sess.run(tf.global_variables_initializer())
err = []
for i in range(epochs):
 for ii in range(mnist.train.num_examples//batch_size):
 batch = mnist.train.next_batch(batch_size)
 # Get images from the batch
 imgs = batch[0].reshape((-1, h_in, w_in, 1))

 # Add random noise to the input images
 noisy_imgs = imgs + noise_factor * np.random.randn(*imgs.shape)
 # Clip the images to be between 0 and 1
 noisy_imgs = np.clip(noisy_imgs, 0., 1.)

 # Noisy images as inputs, original images as targets
 batch_cost, _ = sess.run([cost, opt], feed_dict={X_noisy: noisy_imgs,X:
imgs})
 err.append(batch_cost)
 if ii%100 == 0:
 print("Epoch: {0}/{1}... Training loss {2}".format(i, epochs, batch_cost))
```

8. The error of the network as it learns is as follows:

```
plt.plot(err)
plt.xlabel('epochs')
plt.ylabel('Cross Entropy Loss')
```

The plot is as follows:

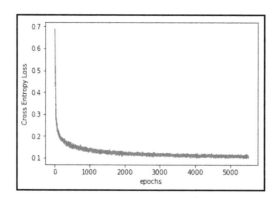

9. Finally, let's see the reconstructed images:

```
fig, axes = plt.subplots(rows=2, cols=10, sharex=True, sharey=True,
figsize=(20,4))
in_imgs = mnist.test.images[:10]
noisy_imgs = in_imgs + noise_factor * np.random.randn(*in_imgs.shape)
noisy_imgs = np.clip(noisy_imgs, 0., 1.)
reconstructed = sess.run(decoded, feed_dict={X_noisy:
noisy_imgs.reshape((10, 28, 28, 1))})
for images, row in zip([noisy_imgs, reconstructed], axes):
 for img, ax in zip(images, row):
 ax.imshow(img.reshape((28, 28)), cmap='Greys_r')
 ax.get_xaxis().set_visible(False)
 ax.get_yaxis().set_visible(False)
```

Here is the output of the preceding code:

10. Close the Session:

```
sess.close()
```

How it Works...

The preceding CAE is a denoising CAE, and we can see that it is better in denoising the image as compared to the simple denoising autoencoder consisting of only one bottleneck layer.

There's More...

CAE has been used by researchers for semantic segmentation. An interesting read is a 2015 paper by Badrinayanan et al, Segnet: *a Deep Convolutional Encoder-Decoder Architecture for Image Segmentation* (`https://arxiv.org/pdf/1511.00561.pdf`). The network uses the convolutional layers of VGG16 as its Encoder Network and contains a hierarchy of decoders, one corresponding to each encoder as its Decoder Network. The decoders use the max-pooling indices received from the corresponding Encoder and perform nonlinear upsampling of the input feature map. The link of the paper is given in the See Also section of this recipe along with the GitHub link.

See Also

1. `https://distill.pub/2016/deconv-checkerboard/`
2. `https://pgaleone.eu/neural-networks/2016/11/24/convolutional-autoencoders/`
3. `https://arxiv.org/pdf/1511.00561.pdf`
4. `https://github.com/arahusky/Tensorflow-Segmentation`

Stacked autoencoder

Autoencoders covered so far (except for CAEs) consisted only of a single-layer encoder and a single-layer decoder. However, it is possible for us to have multiple layers in encoder and decoder networks; using deeper encoder and decoder networks can allow the autoencoder to represent complex features. The structure so obtained is called a Stacked Autoencoder (**Deep Autoencoders**); the features extracted by one encoder are passed on to the next encoder as input. The stacked autoencoder can be trained as a whole network with an aim to minimize the reconstruction error, or each individual encoder/decoder network can be first pretrained using the unsupervised method you learned earlier, and then the complete network is fine-tuned. It has been pointed out that, by pretraining, also called Greedy layer-wise training, the results are better.

Getting Ready

In the recipe we will use the Greedy layer-wise approach to train the stacked autoencoders; to make the task easier, we will use shared weights, thus the corresponding encoder/decoder weights would be the transpose of each other.

How to do it...

We proceed with the recipe as follows:

1. The first step is importing all the necessary modules:

```
import tensorflow as tf
import numpy as np
from tensorflow.examples.tutorials.mnist import input_data
import matplotlib.pyplot as plt
%matplotlib inline
```

2. Load the dataset:

```
mnist = input_data.read_data_sets("MNIST_data/")
trX, trY, teX, teY = mnist.train.images, mnist.train.labels,
mnist.test.images, mnist.test.labels
```

3. Next, we define the class, `StackedAutoencoder`. The class `__init__` method contains a list containing a number of neurons in each autoencoder, starting from the first input autoencoder and the learning rate. As each layer will have different dimensions for input and output, we choose a dictionary data structure to represent weights, biases, and inputs for each layer:

```
class StackedAutoEncoder(object):
 def __init__(self, list1, eta = 0.02):
 """
 list1: [input_dimension, hidden_layer_1, ....,hidden_layer_n]
 """
 N = len(list1)-1
 self._m = list1[0]
 self.learning_rate = eta

 # Create the Computational graph
 self._W = {}
 self._b = {}
 self._X = {}
 self._X['0'] = tf.placeholder('float', [None, list1[0]])

 for i in range(N):
 layer = '{0}'.format(i+1)
 print('AutoEncoder Layer {0}: {1} --> {2}'.format(layer, list1[i],
list1[i+1]))
 self._W['E' + layer] = tf.Variable(tf.random_normal(shape=(list1[i],
list1[i+1])),name='WtsEncoder'+layer)
 self._b['E'+ layer] =
tf.Variable(np.zeros(list1[i+1]).astype(np.float32),name='BiasEncoder'+laye
r)
 self._X[layer] = tf.placeholder('float', [None, list1[i+1]])
 self._W['D' + layer] = tf.transpose(self._W['E' + layer]) # Shared weights
 self._b['D' + layer] =
tf.Variable(np.zeros(list1[i]).astype(np.float32),name='BiasDecoder' +
layer)
 # Placeholder for inputs
 self._X_noisy = tf.placeholder('float', [None, self._m])
```

4. We build a computation graph to define the optimization parameters for each autoencoder while pretraining. It involves defining the reconstruction loss for each autoencoder when the output of the previous autoencoder's Encoder is its input. To do this, we define the class methods, pretrain and one_pass, which return the training ops and output of the Encoder respectively for each stacked autoencoder:

```
self.train_ops = {}
self.out = {}


for i in range(N):
layer = '{0}'.format(i+1)
prev_layer = '{0}'.format(i)
opt = self.pretrain(self._X[prev_layer], layer)
self.train_ops[layer] = opt
self.out[layer] = self.one_pass(self._X[prev_layer], self._W['E'+layer],
self._b['E'+layer], self._b['D'+layer])
```

5. We build the computation graph for the fine-tuning of the complete stacked autoencoder. To do this, we make use of the class methods, encoder and decoder:

```
self.y = self.encoder(self._X_noisy,N)  #Encoder output
self.r = self.decoder(self.y,N)  # Decoder ouput

optimizer = tf.train.AdamOptimizer(self.learning_rate)
error = self._X['0'] - self.r  # Reconstruction Error

self._loss = tf.reduce_mean(tf.pow(error, 2))
self._opt = optimizer.minimize(self._loss)
```

6. Finally, we define the class method, fit, to perform the batch-wise pretraining of each autoencoder, followed by fine-tuning. While pretraining, we use the non-corrupted input, and for fine-tuning, we use the corrupted input. This allows us to use the stacked autoencoder to reconstruct even from the noisy input:

```
def fit(self, Xtrain, Xtr_noisy, layers, epochs = 1, batch_size = 100):
N, D = Xtrain.shape
num_batches = N // batch_size
X_noisy = {}
X = {}
X_noisy ['0'] = Xtr_noisy
X['0'] = Xtrain
```

```
for i in range(layers):
Xin = X[str(i)]
print('Pretraining Layer ', i+1)
for e in range(5):
for j in range(num_batches):
batch = Xin[j * batch_size: (j * batch_size + batch_size)]
self.session.run(self.train_ops[str(i+1)], feed_dict= {self._X[str(i)]:
batch})
print('Pretraining Finished')
X[str(i+1)] = self.session.run(self.out[str(i+1)], feed_dict =
{self._X[str(i)]: Xin})
```

```
obj = []
for i in range(epochs):
for j in range(num_batches):
batch = Xtrain[j * batch_size: (j * batch_size + batch_size)]
batch_noisy = Xtr_noisy[j * batch_size: (j * batch_size + batch_size)]
_, ob = self.session.run([self._opt,self._loss], feed_dict={self._X['0']:
batch, self._X_noisy: batch_noisy})
if j % 100 == 0 :
print('training epoch {0} batch {2} cost {1}'.format(i,ob, j))
obj.append(ob)
return obj
```

7. The different class methods are as follows:

```
def encoder(self, X, N):
 x = X
 for i in range(N):
 layer = '{0}'.format(i+1)
 hiddenE = tf.nn.sigmoid(tf.matmul(x, self._W['E'+layer]) +
self._b['E'+layer])
 x = hiddenE
 return x

def decoder(self, X, N):
 x = X
 for i in range(N,0,-1):
 layer = '{0}'.format(i)
 hiddenD = tf.nn.sigmoid(tf.matmul(x, self._W['D'+layer]) +
self._b['D'+layer])
 x = hiddenD
 return x

def set_session(self, session):
```

```
    self.session = session

def reconstruct(self,x, n_layers):
 h = self.encoder(x, n_layers)
 r = self.decoder(h, n_layers)
 return self.session.run(r, feed_dict={self._X['0']: x})

def pretrain(self, X, layer ):
 y = tf.nn.sigmoid(tf.matmul(X, self._W['E'+layer]) + self._b['E'+layer])
 r =tf.nn.sigmoid(tf.matmul(y, self._W['D'+layer]) + self._b['D'+layer])

 # Objective Function
 error = X - r # Reconstruction Error
  loss = tf.reduce_mean(tf.pow(error, 2))
 opt = tf.train.AdamOptimizer(.001).minimize(loss, var_list =
 [self._W['E'+layer],self._b['E'+layer],self._b['D'+layer]])
  return opt

def one_pass(self, X, W, b, c):
 h = tf.nn.sigmoid(tf.matmul(X, W) + b)
 return h
```

8. We use the corruption function defined in the Denoising autoencoder recipe to corrupt the images and, finally, create a StackAutoencoder and train it:

```
Xtrain = trX.astype(np.float32)
Xtrain_noisy = corruption(Xtrain).astype(np.float32)
Xtest = teX.astype(np.float32)
Xtest_noisy = corruption(Xtest).astype(np.float32)
_, m = Xtrain.shape

list1 = [m, 500, 50] # List with number of neurons in Each hidden layer,
starting from input layer
n_layers = len(list1)-1
autoEncoder = StackedAutoEncoder(list1)

#Initialize all variables
init = tf.global_variables_initializer()


with tf.Session() as sess:
 sess.run(init)
 autoEncoder.set_session(sess)
 err = autoEncoder.fit(Xtrain, Xtrain_noisy, n_layers, epochs=30)
 out = autoEncoder.reconstruct(Xtest_noisy[0:100],n_layers)
```

9. The reconstruction error versus epochs, as the stacked autoencoder is fine-tuned, is given here. You can see that, due to pretraining, we already start from a very low reconstruction loss:

```
plt.plot(err)
plt.xlabel('epochs')
plt.ylabel('Fine Tuning Reconstruction Error')
```

The plot is as follows:

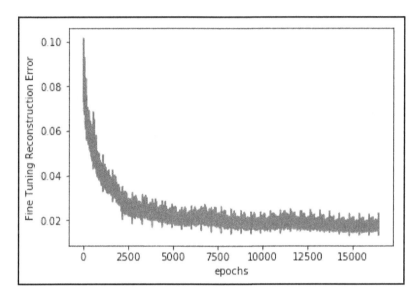

10. Let's now check the performance of our network. Here is the denoised handwritten images, when the network is presented with the noisy test images:

How it works...

The experiments on the stacked autoencoder suggest that pretraining should be done with low values of learning rate. This ensures better convergence and performance during the fine tuning.

There's More...

This whole chapter was about autoencoders, and, while right now they are used only for dimensionality reduction and information retrieval, they generate a lot of interest. Firstly, because they are unsupervised, and secondly because they can be employed along with FCNs. They can help us deal with the curse of dimensionality. Researchers have demonstrated that they can also be used for classification and anomaly detection.

See Also

- A nice tutorial on stacked autoencoders: `http://ufldl.stanford.edu/wiki/index.php/Stacked_Autoencoders`.
- Schwenk, Holger. "The diabolo classifier." Neural Computation 10.8 (1998): 2175-2200.
- Sakurada, Mayu, and Takehisa Yairi. "Anomaly detection using autoencoders with nonlinear dimensionality reduction." Proceedings of the MLSDA 2014 2nd Workshop on Machine Learning for Sensory Data Analysis. ACM, 2014.
- Cool TensorBoard visualization and implementation of stacked autoencoders: `https://github.com/cmgreen210/TensorFlowDeepAutoencoder`

9
Reinforcement Learning

This chapter introduces **reinforcement learning** (RL)—the least explored and yet most promising learning paradigm. The chapter includes the following topics:

- Learning OpenAI Gym
- Implementing neural network agent to play Pac-Man
- Q learning to balance Cart-Pole
- Game of Atari using Deep Q Networks
- Policy gradients to play the game of Pong

Introduction

In March 2016, AlphaGo--the program made by Google's DeepMind--defeated the world's best Go player, 18-time world champion Lee Sedol, by 4 to 1. The match was historic because Go is a notoriously difficult game for computers to play, with:

```
208,168,199,381,979,984,699,478,633,344,862,770,286,522,
453,884,530,548,425,639,456,820,927,419,612,738,015,378,
525,648,451,698,519,643,907,259,916,015,628,128,546,089,
888,314,427, 129,715,319,317,557,736,620,397,247,064,840,935
```

possible legal board positions. Playing and winning Go cannot be done by simple brute force. It requires skill, creativity, and, as professional Go players say, intuition.

This remarkable feat was accomplished by AlphaGo with the help of RL algorithm-based deep neural networks combined with a state-of-the-art tree search algorithm. This chapter introduces RL and some algorithms that we employ to perform RL.

So, the first question that arises is what is RL and how is it different from supervised and unsupervised learning, which we explored in earlier chapters?

Anyone who owns a pet knows that the best strategy to train a pet is rewarding it for desirable behavior and punishing it for bad behavior. The RL, also called **learning with a critic**, is a learning paradigm where the agent learns in the same manner. The Agent here corresponds to our network (program); it can perform a set of **Actions (a)**, which brings about a change in the **State (s)** of the environment and, in turn, the Agent perceives whether it gets a reward or punishment.

For example, in the case of a dog, the dog is our Agent, the voluntary muscle movements that the dog makes are the actions, and the ground is the environment; the dog perceives our reaction to its action in terms of giving it a bone as a reward:

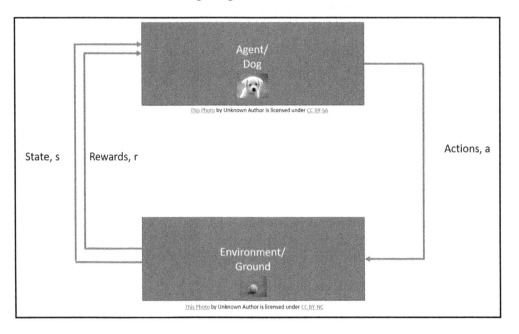

Adapted from Reinforcement Learning: an Introduction by Sutton and Barto

 Even our brain has a group of subcortical nuclei situated at the base of the forebrain called **basal ganglia**, which, according to neuroscience, are responsible for action selection, that is, help us decide which of several possible actions to execute at any given time.

The aim of the agent is to maximize the rewards and reduce the punishments. There are various challenges involved in making this decision, the most important one being how to maximize future rewards, also known as the **temporal credit assignment problem**. The agent decides its action based on some policy (π); the agent learns this policy (π) based on its interaction with the environment. There are various policy learning algorithms; we will explore some of them in this chapter. The agent infers the optimal policy (π^*) by a process of trial and error, and to learn the optimal policy, the agent requires an environment to interact with; we will be using OpenAI Gym, which provides different environments.

We have given here only a review of the basic concepts involved in RL; we assume that you are familiar with the Markov concepts decision process, discount factor, and value function (state value and action value).

In this chapter, and the recipes that follow, we define an episode as one run of the game, for example, solving one sudoku. Typically, an agent will play many episodes to learn an optimal policy, the one which maximizes the rewards.

It is really amazing to see how the RL agent, without any implicit knowledge of the game, learns to play and, not only play, even beat humans in these games.

Learning OpenAI Gym

We will be using OpenAI Gym to provide an environment for our Agent. OpenAI Gym is an open source toolkit to develop and compare RL algorithms. It contains a variety of simulated environments that can be used to train agents and develop new RL algorithms.

Getting ready

The first thing to do is install OpenAI Gym; a minimal installation can be done using `pip install gym`. The OpenAI gym provides a variety of environments, such as Atari, board games, and 2D or 3D physics engines. The minimal installation works on Windows and supports only basic environments--algorithmic, `toy_text`, and `classic_control`--but if you want to explore other environments, they will need more dependencies. The full make is supported in OS X and Ubuntu. Detailed instructions can be read at OpenAI Gym's GitHub link (`https://github.com/openai/gym#installing-dependencies-for-specific-environments`).

How to do it...

Let's start with the recipe:

1. The core interface provided by OpenAI Gym is the Unified Environment Interface. The agent can interact with the environment using three basic methods, that is, reset, step, and render. The `reset` method resets the environment and returns the observation. The `step` method steps the environment by one timestep and returns observation, reward, done, and info. The `render` method renders one frame of the environment, like popping a window.

2. To use OpenAI Gym, you will need to import it first:

```
import gym
```

3. Next, we create our first environment:

```
env_name = 'Breakout-v3'
env = gym.make(env_name)
```

4. We start the environment using the `reset` method:

```
obs = env.reset()
```

5. Let's check the shape of our environment:

```
print(obs.shape)
```

6. The number of actions possible can be checked using the command `actions = env.action_space`. We can see from the result of this that, for Breakout-v4, we have four possible actions: NoOp, Fire, Left, and Right. The total number of actions can be obtained by calling the `env.action_space.n` command.

7. Let's define an agent with a random policy. The agent chooses any of the four possible actions randomly:

```
def random_policy(n):
  action = np.random.randint(0,n)
  return action
```

8. We next allow our random agent to play for 1,000 steps, using `obs, reward, done, info = env.step(action)`:

```
for step in range(1000): # 1000 steps max
  action = random_policy(env.action_space.n)
  obs, reward, done, info = env.step(action)
```

```
env.render()
if done:
    img = env.render(mode='rgb_array')
    plt.imshow(img)
    plt.show()
    print("The game is over in {} steps".format(step))
    break
```

The `obs` tells the agent what the environment looks like; for our environment, it corresponds to an RGB image of size 210 x 160 x 3. The agent is rewarded either 0 or 1 at each step, the `reward` as per the OpenAI Gym wiki is `[-inf, inf]`. Once the game is over, the environment returns `done` as `True`. The `info` can be useful for debugging but is not used by the agent. The `env.render()` command pops up a window that shows the present state of the environment; when you include this command, you can see through the popped-up window how the agent is trying to play and learn. It is better to comment it when the agent is under training to save time.

9. Lastly, close the environment:

```
env.close()
```

How it works...

The preceding code implements a random agent; the agent randomly selects one of the four actions:

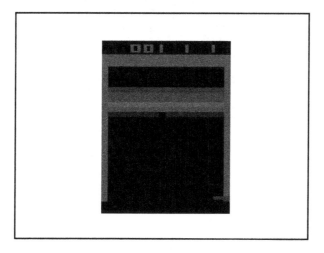

Another important thing to observe is that in this environment, the action space is Discrete, while the observation space is of type Box. The terms Discrete and Box in reference to space (action/observation) in OpenAI refer to the allowed values. The Discrete space allows a fixed range of non-negative numbers, in our case, (0,1,2,3). The Box space, on the other hand, represents an *n*-dimensional box, thus any valid observation would be an array of 210 × 160 × 3 numbers for Pac-Man.

There's more...

OpenAI Gym consists of many different environments and many are added to it by its active contributing community. To get a list of all the existing environments, you can run this simple code (taken from https://github.com/openai/gym):

```
from gym import envs
env_ids = [spec.id for spec in envs.registry.all()]
print("Total Number of environments are", len(env_ids))
for env_id in sorted(env_ids):
    print(env_id)
```

At present, OpenAI Gym has 777 environments in total. Here is the image of Pac-Man using the same random agent as earlier:

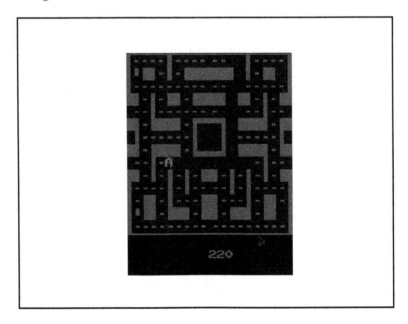

See also

- The details about different environments can be obtained from `https://gym.openai.com/envs`
- Wiki pages are maintained for some environments at `https://github.com/openai/gym/wiki`
- Details regarding installation instructions and dependencies can be obtained from `https://github.com/openai/gym`

Implementing neural network agent to play Pac-Man

Let's first build a simple neural network agent to play the game Pac-Man. We will create an agent with a set of random weights and biases. These agents will then try to play the game; we select the agent that is able to play for the longest average duration, assuming theirs to be the best policy.

Getting ready

The agents in this recipe are not learning any policy; they make their decision based on their initial set of weights (fixed policy). The agent picks the actions based on the probability given by the neural network. The decision that each agent makes is based only on the present observation of the environment.

We implement this by a fully connected neural network. The inputs to the NN are decided by the observation space of the environment; the number of output neurons is decided by the number of possible discrete actions. The Pac-Man game has nine discrete possible actions--NoOp, Turn Right, Turn Left, Turn Up, Turn Down, Move Left, Move Right, Move Up, and Move Down--and so our NN has nine output neurons.

How to do it...

Let's start with the recipe:

1. The first step, as always, is importing modules. Besides the usual modules, in this case, we will import `gym` so that we can use the different environments provided by it:

```
import gym
import numpy as np
import tensorflow as tf
import matplotlib.pyplot as plt
```

2. Next, we create a `RlAgent` class. The class is made with three methods--the `__init__` method initializes the NN size and creates the computational graph. Here, we employed the TensorFlow function, `tf.multinomial`, to make the decision of the possible action to take. The function returns the action based on the sigmoidal values of the nine output neurons of our network. This ensures that the network chooses the final action probabilistically. The `predict` method returns the action predicted by the NN. The `get_weights` method helps us get the weights and biases of the winner agent:

```
class RlAgent(object):
  def __init__(self,m,n,ini=False,W=None, b=None ):
      self._graph = tf.Graph()
      with self._graph.as_default():
      self._X = tf.placeholder(tf.float32,shape=(1,m))
      if ini==False:
          self.W = tf.Variable(tf.random_normal([m,n]),
trainable=False)
          self.bias =
tf.Variable(tf.random_normal([1,n]),trainable=False)
      else:
          self.W = W
          self.bias = b
      out = tf.nn.sigmoid(tf.matmul(self._X,self.W)+ self.bias)
      self._result = tf.multinomial(out,1)
      init = tf.global_variables_initializer()

      self._sess = tf.Session()
      self._sess.run(init)

      def predict(self, X):
          action = self._sess.run(self._result, feed_dict= {self._X:
X})
```

```
        return action

    def get_weights(self):
        W, b = self._sess.run([self.W, self.bias])
        return W, b
```

3. We define some helper functions to play a single complete game, `play_one_episode`:

```
def play_one_episode(env, agent):
    obs = env.reset()
    img_pre = preprocess_image(obs)
    done = False
    t = 0
    while not done and t < 10000:
        env.render()  # This can be commented to speed up
        t += 1
        action = agent.predict(img_pre)
        #print(t,action)
        obs, reward, done, info = env.step(action)
        img_pre = preprocess_image(obs)
        if done:
            break
    return t
```

4. The `play_multiple_episodes` function creates an instance of the agent and plays a number of games with this agent, returning its average duration of play:

```
def play_multiple_episodes(env, T,ini=False, W=None, b=None):
    episode_lengths = np.empty(T)
    obs = env.reset()
    img_pre = preprocess_image(obs)
    if ini== False:
        agent = RlAgent(img_pre.shape[1],env.action_space.n)
    else:
        agent = RlAgent(img_pre.shape[1],env.action_space.n,ini, W,
b)
    for i in range(T):
        episode_lengths[i] = play_one_episode(env, agent)
    avg_length = episode_lengths.mean()
    print("avg length:", avg_length)
    if ini == False:
        W, b = agent.get_weights()
    return avg_length, W, b
```

5. The `random_search` function invokes `play_multiple_episodes`; each time `play_multiple_episodes` is called, a new agent is instantiated with a new set of random weights and biases. One of these randomly created NN agents will outperform others, and this will be the agent that we finally select:

```
def random_search(env):
    episode_lengths = []
    best = 0
    for t in range(10):
        print("Agent {} reporting".format(t))
        avg_length, wts, bias = play_multiple_episodes(env, 10)
        episode_lengths.append(avg_length)
        if avg_length > best:
            best_wt = wts
            best_bias = bias
            best = avg_length
    return episode_lengths, best_wt, best_bias
```

6. The environment returns an observation field each time it progresses a step. This observation is with three color channels; to feed it to the NN, the observation needs to be preprocessed and, at present, the only preprocessing we do is convert it to grayscale, increase the contrast, and reshape it into a row vector:

```
def preprocess_image(img):
    img = img.mean(axis =2) # to grayscale
    img[img==150] = 0  # Bring about a better contrast
    img = (img - 128)/128 - 1 # Normalize image from -1 to 1
    m,n = img.shape
    return img.reshape(1,m*n)
```

7. The NN agents are instantiated one by one and the best is selected. For computational efficiency, we have at present searched only 10 agents, each playing 10 games. The one that can play the longest is considered the best:

```
if __name__ == '__main__':
    env_name = 'Breakout-v0'
    #env_name = 'MsPacman-v0'
    env = gym.make(env_name)
    episode_lengths, W, b = random_search(env)
    plt.plot(episode_lengths)
    plt.show()
    print("Final Run with best Agent")
    play_multiple_episodes(env,10, ini=True, W=W, b=b)
```

The result is as follows:

```
nn credit assignment ny
Run    nn_random_agent                                                                                    ✱ ⌄
▶  ↑   /home/am/Anaconda/envs/tensorflow_VM/bin/python /home/am/PycharmProjects/BookTf/nn_random_agent.py
   ↓   [2017-10-07 23:56:31,409] Making new env: MsPacman-v0
   ✂   Agent 0 reporting
║  ▦   2017-10-07 23:56:31.638924: W tensorflow/core/platform/cpu_feature_guard.cc:45] The TensorFlow library wasn't compiled
▦  ▨   2017-10-07 23:56:31.638941: W tensorflow/core/platform/cpu_feature_guard.cc:45] The TensorFlow library wasn't compiled
↗  ⬚   2017-10-07 23:56:31.638945: W tensorflow/core/platform/cpu_feature_guard.cc:45] The TensorFlow library wasn't compiled
✗  ⬚   avg length: 608.1
?      Agent 1 reporting
       avg length: 663.2
       Agent 2 reporting
       avg length: 594.8
       Agent 3 reporting
       avg length: 621.5
       Agent 4 reporting
       avg length: 758.3
       Agent 5 reporting
       avg length: 669.0
       Agent 6 reporting
       avg length: 745.8
       Agent 7 reporting
       avg length: 612.4
       Agent 8 reporting
       avg length: 631.3
       Agent 9 reporting
       avg length: 591.3
       Final Run with best Agent
       avg length: 615.5

       Process finished with exit code 0

   Packages installed successfully: Installed packages: 'scikit-learn' (yesterday 4:27 PM)          96:30  LF:  UTF-8 :
```

We can see that our random agent too can play the game for an average length of **615.5**. Not bad!

Q learning to balance Cart-Pole

As discussed in the introduction, we have an environment described by a state s ($s \in S$ where S is the set of all possible states) and an agent that can perform an action a ($a \in A$, where A is set of all possible actions) resulting in the movement of the agent from one state to another. The agent is rewarded for its action, and the goal of the agent is to maximize the reward. In Q learning, the agent learns the action to take (policy, π) by calculating the Quantity of a state-action combination that maximizes reward (R). In making the choice of the action, the agent takes into account not only the present but discounted future rewards:

$$Q: S \times A \rightarrow R$$

The agent starts with some arbitrary initial value of Q, and, as the agent selects an action a and receives a reward r, it updates the state s' (which depends on the past state s and action a) and the Q value:

$$Q(s,a) = (1 - \alpha)Q(s,a) + \alpha\,[r + \gamma\,max_{a'}\,Q(s',a')\,]$$

Here, α is the learning rate and γ is the discount factor. The first term preserves the old value of Q, and the second term provides an improved estimate of the Q value (it includes the present reward and discounted rewards for future actions). This will reduce the Q value when the resultant state is undesirable, thus ensuring that the agent will not choose the same action the next time this state is encountered. Similarly, when the resultant state is desirable, the corresponding Q value will increase.

The simplest implementation of Q learning involves maintaining and updating a state-action value lookup table; the size of the table will be N × M where N is the number of all the possible states and M the number of all the possible actions. For most environments, this table will be significantly large; the larger the table, the more time is needed to search and the more memory is needed to store the table and thus it is not a feasible solution. In this recipe, we will use NN implementation of Q learning. Here, the neural networks are employed as a function approximator to predict the value function (Q). NN has output nodes equal to the number of possible actions, and their output signifies the value function of the corresponding action.

Getting ready

We will train a linear neural network to solve the `'CartPole-v0'` environment (https://github.com/openai/gym/wiki/CartPole-v0). The goal here is to balance the pole on the cart; the observation state consists of four continuous-valued parameters: Cart Position [-2.4, 2.4], Cart Velocity [-∞, ∞], Pole Angle [~-41.8º, ~41.8º], and Pole Velocity at Tip [-∞, ∞]. The balancing can be achieved by pushing the cart either to left or right, so the action space consists of two possible actions. You can see the `CartPole-v0` environment space:

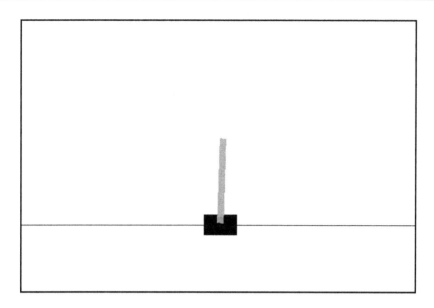

Now, for Q learning, we need to find a way to quantize the continuous-valued observation states. This is achieved using the class `FeatureTransform`; the class first generates 20,000 random samples of observation space examples. The randomly generated observation space examples are standardized using the scikit `StandardScaler` class. Then scikit's `RBFSampler` is employed with different variances to cover different parts of the observation space. The `FeatureTransformer` class is instantiated with the random observation space examples, which are used to train the `RBFSampler` using the `fit_transform` function method.

Later, the `transform` method is employed to transform the continuous observation space to this featurized representation:

```
class FeatureTransformer:
  def __init__(self, env):
    obs_examples = np.random.random((20000, 4))
    print(obs_examples.shape)
    scaler = StandardScaler()
    scaler.fit(obs_examples)

    # Used to converte a state to a featurizes represenation.
    # We use RBF kernels with different variances to cover different parts
of the space
    featurizer = FeatureUnion([
        ("cart_position", RBFSampler(gamma=0.02, n_components=500)),
        ("cart_velocity", RBFSampler(gamma=1.0, n_components=500)),
        ("pole_angle", RBFSampler(gamma=0.5, n_components=500)),
```

```
    ("pole_velocity", RBFSampler(gamma=0.1, n_components=500))
    ])
  feature_examples = 
featurizer.fit_transform(scaler.transform(obs_examples))
  print(feature_examples.shape)

  self.dimensions = feature_examples.shape[1]
  self.scaler = scaler
  self.featurizer = featurizer

def transform(self, observations):
  scaled = self.scaler.transform(observations)
  return self.featurizer.transform(scaled)
```

How to do it...

We proceed with the recipe as follows:

1. The first step is importing the necessary modules. This time, besides our usual TensorFlow, Numpy, and Matplotlib, we will be importing Gym and some classes from scikit:

```
import numpy as np
import tensorflow as tf
import gym
import matplotlib.pyplot as plt
from sklearn.pipeline import FeatureUnion
from sklearn.preprocessing import StandardScaler
from sklearn.kernel_approximation import RBFSampler
```

2. In Q learning, we use NNs as function approximators to estimate the value-function. We define a linear NeuralNetwork class; the NN will take the transformed observation space as input and will predict the estimated Q value. As we have two possible actions, we need two different neural network objects to get the predicted state action value. The class includes methods to train the individual NN and predict the output:

```
class NeuralNetwork:
  def __init__(self, D):
    eta = 0.1
    self.W = tf.Variable(tf.random_normal(shape=(D, 1)), name='w')
    self.X = tf.placeholder(tf.float32, shape=(None, D), name='X')
    self.Y = tf.placeholder(tf.float32, shape=(None,), name='Y')
```

```
    # make prediction and cost
    Y_hat = tf.reshape(tf.matmul(self.X, self.W), [-1])
    err = self.Y - Y_hat
    cost = tf.reduce_sum(tf.pow(err,2))

    # ops we want to call later
    self.train_op =
tf.train.GradientDescentOptimizer(eta).minimize(cost)
    self.predict_op = Y_hat

    # start the session and initialize params
    init = tf.global_variables_initializer()
    self.session = tf.Session()
    self.session.run(init)

def train(self, X, Y):
    self.session.run(self.train_op, feed_dict={self.X: X, self.Y:
Y})

def predict(self, X):
    return self.session.run(self.predict_op, feed_dict={self.X: X})
```

3. The next important class is the `Agent` class that uses the `NeuralNetwork` class to create a learning agent. The class on instantiation creates an agent with two linear NNs, each with 2,000 input neurons and 1 output neuron. (Essentially, this means that the agent has 2 neurons each with 2,000 inputs as the input layer of the NN does not do any processing). The `Agent` class has methods defined to predict the output of the two NNs and update the weights of the two NNs. The agent here uses Epsilon Greedy Policy for exploration during the training phase. At each step, the agent either chooses an action with the highest Q value or a random action, depending on the value of epsilon (`eps`); epsilon is annealed during the training process so that, initially, the agent takes lots of random actions (exploration) but as training progresses, the actions with maximum Q value are taken (exploitation). This is called the **Exploration-Exploitation** trade-off: we allow the agent to explore random actions over the exploited course of actions, which allows the agent to try new random actions and learn from them:

```
class Agent:
 def __init__(self, env, feature_transformer):
 self.env = env
 self.agent = []
 self.feature_transformer = feature_transformer
 for i in range(env.action_space.n):
 model = NeuralNetwork(feature_transformer.dimensions)
 self.agent.append(model)
```

```
def predict(self, s):
 X = self.feature_transformer.transform([s])
 return np.array([m.predict(X)[0] for m in self.agent])

def update(self, s, a, G):
 X = self.feature_transformer.transform([s])
 self.agent[a].train(X, [G])

def sample_action(self, s, eps):
 if np.random.random() < eps:
     return self.env.action_space.sample()
 else:
     return np.argmax(self.predict(s))
```

4. Next, we define a function to play one episode; it is similar to the `play_one` function we used earlier, but now we use Q learning to update the weights of our agent. We start the episode by resetting the environment using `env.reset()`, and then till the game is done (and maximum iterations to ensure the program ends). Like before, the agent chooses an action for the present observation state (`obs`) and implements the action on the environment (`env.step(action)`). The difference now is that, based on the previous state and the state after the action is taken, the NN weights are updated using $G = r + \gamma \, max_{a'} \, Q(s',a')$, such that it can predict an accurate expected value corresponding to an action. For better stability, we have modified the rewards--whenever the pole falls, the agent is given a reward of -400, otherwise for each step, it gets a reward of +1:

```
def play_one(env, model, eps, gamma):
 obs = env.reset()
 done = False
 totalreward = 0
 iters = 0
 while not done and iters < 2000:
 action = model.sample_action(obs, eps)
 prev_obs = obs
 obs, reward, done, info = env.step(action)
 env.render()    # Can comment it to speed up.

 if done:
  reward = -400

 # update the model
 next = model.predict(obs)
 assert(len(next.shape) == 1)
 G = reward + gamma*np.max(next)
 model.update(prev_obs, action, G)
```

```
if reward == 1:
  totalreward += reward
iters += 1
```

5. Now that all the functions and classes are in place, we define our agent and environment (in this case, `'CartPole-v0'`). The agent plays in total 1,000 episodes and learns by interacting with the environment with the help of the value function:

```
if __name__ == '__main__':
    env_name = 'CartPole-v0'
    env = gym.make(env_name)
    ft = FeatureTransformer(env)
    agent = Agent(env, ft)
    gamma = 0.97

    N = 1000
    totalrewards = np.empty(N)
    running_avg = np.empty(N)
    for n in range(N):
        eps = 1.0 / np.sqrt(n + 1)
        totalreward = play_one(env, agent, eps, gamma)
        totalrewards[n] = totalreward
        running_avg[n] = totalrewards[max(0, n - 100):(n +
1)].mean()
        if n % 100 == 0:
            print("episode: {0}, total reward: {1} eps: {2} avg
reward (last 100): {3}".format(n, totalreward, eps,
running_avg[n]), )

    print("avg reward for last 100 episodes:",
totalrewards[-100:].mean())
    print("total steps:", totalrewards.sum())

    plt.plot(totalrewards)
    plt.xlabel('episodes')
    plt.ylabel('Total Rewards')
    plt.show()

    plt.plot(running_avg)

    plt.xlabel('episodes')
    plt.ylabel('Running Average')
    plt.show()
    env.close()
```

```
episode: 0, total reward: 13.0 eps: 1.0 avg reward (last 100): 13.0
episode: 100, total reward: 128.0 eps: 0.09950371902099892 avg reward (last 100): 111.70297029702971
episode: 200, total reward: 181.0 eps: 0.07053456158585983 avg reward (last 100): 171.15841584158414
episode: 300, total reward: 199.0 eps: 0.0576390417704235 avg reward (last 100): 167.23762376237624
episode: 400, total reward: 184.0 eps: 0.04993761694389223 avg reward (last 100): 184.8019801980198
episode: 500, total reward: 199.0 eps: 0.04467670516087703 avg reward (last 100): 186.46534653465346
episode: 600, total reward: 199.0 eps: 0.04079085082240021 avg reward (last 100): 181.5742574257426
episode: 700, total reward: 199.0 eps: 0.0377694787300249 avg reward (last 100): 173.21782178217822
episode: 800, total reward: 199.0 eps: 0.03533326266687867 avg reward (last 100): 194.04950495049505
episode: 900, total reward: 199.0 eps: 0.03331483023263848 avg reward (last 100): 178.47524752475246
avg reward for last 100 episodes: 195.7
total steps: 174300.0

Process finished with exit code 0
```

6. The following is the plot for total rewards and running average reward as the agent learned through the game. According to the Cart-Pole wiki, a reward of 200 means that the agent won the episode after being trained for 1,000 episodes; our agent managed to reach an average reward of 195.7 while playing 100 episodes, which is a remarkable feat:

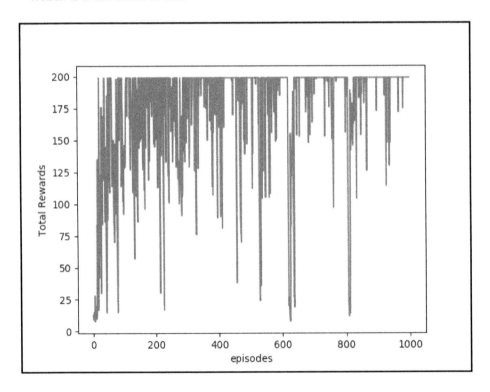

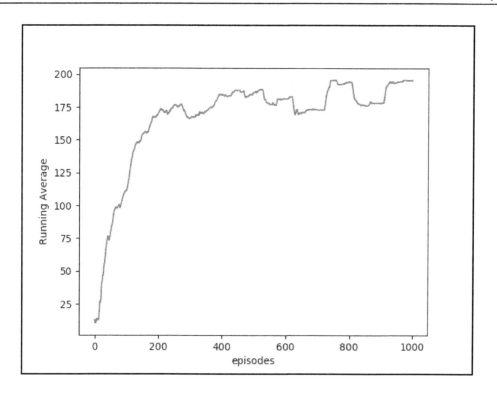

There's more...

The same logic can be used to make an agent for other environments of OpenAI; however, for Atari games such as Breakout or Pac-Man, the observation space is not an array of just four numbers. Instead, it is very large ($210 \times 160 = 33,600$ pixels with 3 RGB values); without some form of quantization, the possible states are infinite and do not yield good results with this simplistic NN. We will resolve this issue using CNN in our deep Q learning recipe.

See also

Although there are a large number of web links on Q learning, some of the useful ones are as follows:

- https://en.wikipedia.org/wiki/Q learning
- http://mnemstudio.org/path-finding-q-learning-tutorial.htm
- http://artint.info/html/ArtInt_265.html
- https://medium.com/emergent-future/simple-reinforcement-learning-with-tensorflow-part-0-q-learning-with-tables-and-neural-networks-d195264329d0

Game of Atari using Deep Q Networks

A **deep Q network (DQN)** is a combination of Q learning with **convolutional neural networks (CNNs)**, first proposed by Mnih and others in 2013 (https://arxiv.org/pdf/1312.5602.pdf). The CNN network, due to its ability to extract spatial information, is able to learn successful control policies from raw pixel data. We have already played with CNNs in Chapter 4, *Convolutional Neural Networks*, and so we start directly with the recipe here.

This recipe is based on the original DQN paper, Playing Atari with Deep Reinforcement Learning by DeepMind. In the paper, they used a concept called **experience replay**, which involved randomly sampling the previous game moves (state, action reward, next state).

Getting ready

As mentioned in the previous recipe, *Q learning to balance CartPole*, for Atari games such as Pac-Man or Breakout, we need to preprocess the observation state space, which consists of 33,600 pixels with 3 RGB values. Each of these pixels can take any value between 0 and 255. Our preprocess function should be able to quantize the pixel possible values and, at the same time, reduce the observation state space.

We make use of Scipy's imresize function to downsample the image. The following functions preprocess the image before it is fed to the DQN:

```
def preprocess(img):
    img_temp = img[31:195]  # Choose the important area of the image
    img_temp = img_temp.mean(axis=2)  # Convert to Grayscale#
```

```
        # Downsample image using nearest neighbour interpolation
        img_temp = imresize(img_temp, size=(IM_SIZE, IM_SIZE),
    interp='nearest')
        return img_temp
```

`IM_SIZE` is a global parameter--in the code, we take its value to be 80. The function has comments describing each process. Here, you can see the observation space before and after the preprocessing:

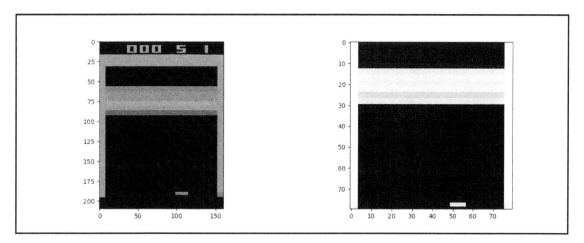

Another important thing to note is that the present observation space does not give a complete picture of the game; for example, seeing the preceding figure, you cannot determine whether the paddle was moving toward left or right. Thus, to completely understand the present state of the game, we need to consider the sequences of actions and observations. In the recipe, we consider four sequences of actions and observations to determine the current situation and train the agent. This is accomplished with the help of the `state_update` function, which appends the present observation state to the previous state, thus generating a sequence of states:

```
def update_state(state, obs):
    obs_small = preprocess(obs)
    return np.append(state[1:], np.expand_dims(obs_small, 0), axis=0)
```

Lastly, to deal with the stability issues while training, we use the concept of `target_network`, which is a copy of the DQN but is not updated as often. We use the target network to generate the target value function for the DQN network, while the DQN is updated at each step/episode and the `target_network` is updated (made the same as DQN) after a regular interval. As all updates take place within the TensorFlow session, we use the name scope to differentiate the `target_network` and DQN network.

How to do it...

1. We import the necessary modules. We are using the `sys` module's `stdout.flush()` to help us force Python to *flush* the data in the standard output (computer monitor in our case). The `random` module is used to derive random samples from the experience replay buffer (the buffer where we store the past experience). The `datetime` module is used to keep track of the time spent in training:

```
import gym
import sys
import random
import numpy as np
import tensorflow as tf
import matplotlib.pyplot as plt
from datetime import datetime
from scipy.misc import imresize
```

2. We define the hyperparameters for the training; you can experiment by changing them. These parameters define the minimum and maximum size of the experience replay buffer and the number of episodes after which the target network is updated:

```
MAX_EXPERIENCES = 500000
MIN_EXPERIENCES = 50000
TARGET_UPDATE_PERIOD = 10000
IM_SIZE = 80
K = 4
```

3. The class `DQN` is defined; its constructor builds the CNN network using the `tf.contrib.layers.conv2d` function and defines the cost and training ops:

```
class DQN:
    def __init__(self, K, scope, save_path= 'models/atari.ckpt'):

        self.K = K
        self.scope = scope
        self.save_path = save_path

        with tf.variable_scope(scope):

            # inputs and targets
            self.X = tf.placeholder(tf.float32, shape=(None, 4,
IM_SIZE, IM_SIZE), name='X')
```

```
            # tensorflow convolution needs the order to be:
            # (num_samples, height, width, "color")
            # so we need to tranpose later
            self.G = tf.placeholder(tf.float32, shape=(None,),
name='G')
            self.actions = tf.placeholder(tf.int32, shape=(None,),
name='actions')

            # calculate output and cost
            # convolutional layers
            Z = self.X / 255.0
            Z = tf.transpose(Z, [0, 2, 3, 1])
            cnn1 = tf.contrib.layers.conv2d(Z, 32, 8, 4,
activation_fn=tf.nn.relu)
            cnn2 = tf.contrib.layers.conv2d(cnn1, 64, 4, 2,
activation_fn=tf.nn.relu)
            cnn3 = tf.contrib.layers.conv2d(cnn2, 64, 3, 1,
activation_fn=tf.nn.relu)

            # fully connected layers
            fc0 = tf.contrib.layers.flatten(cnn3)
            fc1 = tf.contrib.layers.fully_connected(fc0, 512)

            # final output layer
            self.predict_op =
tf.contrib.layers.fully_connected(fc1, K)

            selected_action_values = tf.reduce_sum(self.predict_op
* tf.one_hot(self.actions, K),
                reduction_indices=[1]
            )

            self.cost = tf.reduce_mean(tf.square(self.G -
selected_action_values))
            self.train_op = tf.train.RMSPropOptimizer(0.00025,
0.99, 0.0, 1e-6).minimize(self.cost)
```

4. The class has methods to set the session, `set_session()`, predict the action value function, `predict()`, update the network, `update()`, and select an action using Epsilon Greedy algorithm, `sample_action()`:

```
def set_session(self, session):
    self.session = session

def predict(self, states):
    return self.session.run(self.predict_op, feed_dict={self.X:
states})
```

```
def update(self, states, actions, targets):
    c, _ = self.session.run(
        [self.cost, self.train_op],
        feed_dict={
            self.X: states,
            self.G: targets,
            self.actions: actions
        }
    )
    return c

def sample_action(self, x, eps):
    """Implements epsilon greedy algorithm"""
    if np.random.random() < eps:
        return np.random.choice(self.K)
    else:
        return np.argmax(self.predict([x])[0])
```

5. We also define methods to load and save the network as the training can take time:

```
def load(self):
    self.saver = tf.train.Saver(tf.global_variables())
    load_was_success = True
    try:
        save_dir = '/'.join(self.save_path.split('/')[:-1])
        ckpt = tf.train.get_checkpoint_state(save_dir)
        load_path = ckpt.model_checkpoint_path
        self.saver.restore(self.session, load_path)
    except:
        print("no saved model to load. starting new session")
        load_was_success = False
    else:
        print("loaded model: {}".format(load_path))
        saver = tf.train.Saver(tf.global_variables())
        episode_number = int(load_path.split('-')[-1])


def save(self, n):
    self.saver.save(self.session, self.save_path, global_step=n)
    print("SAVED MODEL #{}".format(n))
```

6. The method to copy the parameters of the main DQN network to the target network is as follows:

```
def copy_from(self, other):
    mine = [t for t in tf.trainable_variables() if
t.name.startswith(self.scope)]
    mine = sorted(mine, key=lambda v: v.name)
    others = [t for t in tf.trainable_variables() if
t.name.startswith(other.scope)]
    others = sorted(others, key=lambda v: v.name)

    ops = []
    for p, q in zip(mine, others):
        actual = self.session.run(q)
        op = p.assign(actual)
        ops.append(op)

    self.session.run(ops)
```

7. We define a function `learn()`, which predicts the value function and updates the original DQN network:

```
def learn(model, target_model, experience_replay_buffer, gamma,
batch_size):
    # Sample experiences
    samples = random.sample(experience_replay_buffer, batch_size)
    states, actions, rewards, next_states, dones = map(np.array,
zip(*samples))

    # Calculate targets
    next_Qs = target_model.predict(next_states)
    next_Q = np.amax(next_Qs, axis=1)
    targets = rewards + np.invert(dones).astype(np.float32) * gamma
* next_Q

    # Update model
    loss = model.update(states, actions, targets)
    return loss
```

8. Now that we have all the ingredients defined in the main code, we use them to build and train a DQN network to play the game of Atari. The code is well commented and is an extension of the previous Q learning code with an addition of the Experience Replay buffer, so you should not have trouble understanding it:

```python
if __name__ == '__main__':
    # hyperparameters
    gamma = 0.99
    batch_sz = 32
    num_episodes = 500
    total_t = 0
    experience_replay_buffer = []
    episode_rewards = np.zeros(num_episodes)
    last_100_avgs = []

    # epsilon for Epsilon Greedy Algorithm
    epsilon = 1.0
    epsilon_min = 0.1
    epsilon_change = (epsilon - epsilon_min) / 500000

    # Create Atari Environment
    env = gym.envs.make("Breakout-v0")


    # Create original and target  Networks
    model = DQN(K=K, gamma=gamma, scope="model")
    target_model = DQN(K=K, gamma=gamma, scope="target_model")

    with tf.Session() as sess:
        model.set_session(sess)
        target_model.set_session(sess)
        sess.run(tf.global_variables_initializer())
        model.load()

        print("Filling experience replay buffer...")
        obs = env.reset()
        obs_small = preprocess(obs)
        state = np.stack([obs_small] * 4, axis=0)

        # Fill experience replay buffer
        for i in range(MIN_EXPERIENCES):

            action = np.random.randint(0,K)
            obs, reward, done, _ = env.step(action)
            next_state = update_state(state, obs)

            experience_replay_buffer.append((state, action, reward,
```

```
next_state, done))

            if done:
                obs = env.reset()
                obs_small = preprocess(obs)
                state = np.stack([obs_small] * 4, axis=0)

            else:
                state = next_state

        # Play a number of episodes and learn
        for i in range(num_episodes):
            t0 = datetime.now()

            # Reset the environment
            obs = env.reset()
            obs_small = preprocess(obs)
            state = np.stack([obs_small] * 4, axis=0)
            assert (state.shape == (4, 80, 80))
            loss = None

            total_time_training = 0
            num_steps_in_episode = 0
            episode_reward = 0

            done = False
            while not done:

                # Update target network
                if total_t % TARGET_UPDATE_PERIOD == 0:
                    target_model.copy_from(model)
                    print("Copied model parameters to target
network. total_t = %s, period = %s" % (
                        total_t, TARGET_UPDATE_PERIOD))

                # Take action
                action = model.sample_action(state, epsilon)
                obs, reward, done, _ = env.step(action)
                obs_small = preprocess(obs)
                next_state = np.append(state[1:],
np.expand_dims(obs_small, 0), axis=0)

                episode_reward += reward

                # Remove oldest experience if replay buffer is full
                if len(experience_replay_buffer) ==
MAX_EXPERIENCES:
                    experience_replay_buffer.pop(0)
```

```
                    # Save the recent experience
                    experience_replay_buffer.append((state, action,
reward, next_state, done))

                    # Train the model and keep measure of time
                    t0_2 = datetime.now()
                    loss = learn(model, target_model,
experience_replay_buffer, gamma, batch_sz)
                    dt = datetime.now() - t0_2

                    total_time_training += dt.total_seconds()
                    num_steps_in_episode += 1

                    state = next_state
                    total_t += 1

                    epsilon = max(epsilon - epsilon_change,
epsilon_min)

                duration = datetime.now() - t0

                episode_rewards[i] = episode_reward
                time_per_step = total_time_training /
num_steps_in_episode

                last_100_avg = episode_rewards[max(0, i - 100):i +
1].mean()
                last_100_avgs.append(last_100_avg)
                print("Episode:", i,"Duration:", duration, "Num
steps:", num_steps_in_episode,
                        "Reward:", episode_reward, "Training time per
step:", "%.3f" % time_per_step,
                        "Avg Reward (Last 100):", "%.3f" %
last_100_avg,"Epsilon:", "%.3f" % epsilon)

                if i % 50 == 0:
                    model.save(i)
                sys.stdout.flush()

        #Plots
        plt.plot(last_100_avgs)
        plt.xlabel('episodes')
        plt.ylabel('Average Rewards')
        plt.show()
        env.close()
```

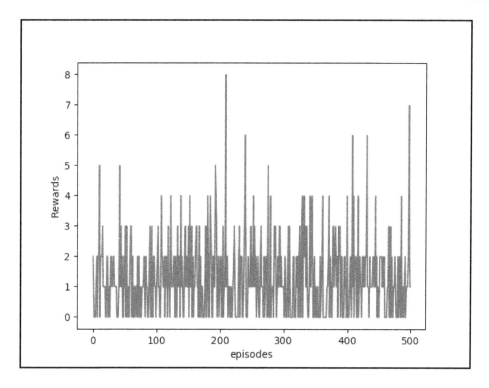

We can see from the preceding figure that the agent is reaching higher rewards with training, and the situation is clearer with the plot of average reward per 100 episodes:

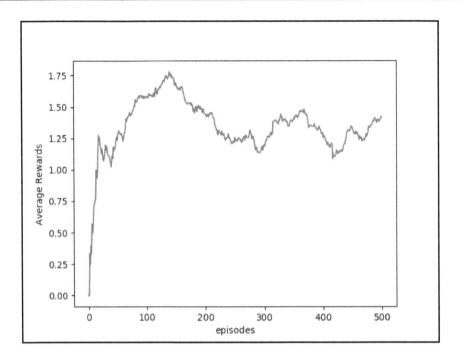

This is only after the first 500 episodes of training; for better results, you will need to train it much longer, ~10,000 episodes.

There's more...

Training the agent takes lots of episodes, which is both time-and memory-consuming. OpenAI Gym provides a wrapper to save the game as a video and so, instead of using render, you can use the wrapper to save videos and later monitor how the agent learned. AI engineers and enthusiasts can upload these videos to show their results. To do so, we need to first import wrappers, then create the environment, and finally use Monitor. By default, it will store the video of 1, 8, 27, 64, ... and then every 1,000th episode (episode numbers with perfect cubes); each training, by default, is saved in one folder. The code to be added for this is as follows:

```
import gym
from gym import wrappers
env = gym.make('Breakout-v0)
env = wrappers.Monitor(env, '/save-path')
```

In case you want to use the same folder in the next training, you can add force=True to Monitor.

See also

- Mnih, Volodymyr, and others, Playing Atari with deep reinforcement learning, arXiv preprint arXiv:1312.5602 (2013) (`https://arxiv.org/pdf/1312.5602.pdf`)
- Mnih, Volodymyr, et al. Human-level control through deep reinforcement learning, Nature 518.7540 (2015): 529-533
- A cool implementation of DQN to play Atari: `https://github.com/devsisters/DQN-tensorflow`

Policy gradients to play the game of Pong

As of today, policy gradient is one of the most used RL algorithms. Research has shown that when properly tuned, they perform better than DQNs and, at the same time, do not suffer from excessive memory and computation disadvantages. Unlike Q learning, policy gradients use a parameterized policy that can select actions without consulting a value function. In policy gradients, we talk about a performance measure $\eta(\theta_p)$; the goal is to maximize the performance and hence the weights of the NN are updated according to the gradient ascent algorithm. However, TensorFlow does not have a `maximum` optimizer, thus we use the negative of the gradient of performance, $-\nabla\eta(\theta_p)$, and minimize it.

Getting ready

The game of Pong is a two-player game, where the goal is to bounce the ball past the other player. The agent can move the paddle up or down (and, yes, the standard NoOp). One of the players in the OpenAI environment is a decent AI player who knows how to play the game well. Our goal is to train the second agent using policy gradients. Our agent gets proficient with each game it plays. While the code has been built to run only for 500 episodes, we should add a provision to save the agent state at specified checkpoints and, in the next run, start by loading the previous checkpoint. We achieve this by first declaring a saver, then using the TensorFlow `saver.save` method to save the present network state (checkpoint), and lastly load the network from the last saved checkpoint. The following methods of the class `PolicyNetwork`, defined in the *How to do it* section of this recipe, perform this work:

```
def load(self):
    self.saver = tf.train.Saver(tf.global_variables())
    load_was_success = True  # yes, I'm being optimistic
    try:
```

```
        save_dir = '/'.join(self.save_path.split('/')[:-1])
        ckpt = tf.train.get_checkpoint_state(save_dir)
        load_path = ckpt.model_checkpoint_path
        self.saver.restore(self.session, load_path)
    except:
        print("no saved model to load. starting new session")
        load_was_success = False
    else:
        print("loaded model: {}".format(load_path))
        saver = tf.train.Saver(tf.global_variables())
        episode_number = int(load_path.split('-')[-1])
```

To save the model after every 50 episodes, we use the following:

```
def save(self):
    self.saver.save(self.session, self.save_path, global_step=n)
    print("SAVED MODEL #{}".format(n))
```

How to do it...

1. The code for this recipe is based on the Andrej Karpathy blog (`http://karpathy.github.io/2016/05/31/rl/`) and a part of it has been adapted from code by Sam Greydanus (`https://gist.github.com/karpathy/a4166c7fe253700972fcbc77e4ea32c5`).

2. We have the usual imports:

   ```
   import numpy as np
   import gym
   import matplotlib.pyplot as plt
   import tensorflow as tf
   ```

3. We define our `PolicyNetwork` class. During the class construction, the model hyperparameters are also initialized. The __init__ method defines the placeholders for input state, `self.tf_x`; predicted action, `self.tf.y`; corresponding reward, `self.tf_epr`; network weights; and ops to predict action value, training, and updating. You can see that the class construction also initiates an interactive TensorFlow session:

   ```
   class PolicyNetwork(object):
       def __init__(self, N_SIZE, h=200, gamma=0.99, eta=1e-3,
   decay=0.99, save_path = 'models2/pong.ckpt' ):

           self.gamma = gamma
   ```

```
        self.save_path = save_path
        # Placeholders for passing state....
        self.tf_x = tf.placeholder(dtype=tf.float32, shape=[None,
N_SIZE * N_SIZE], name="tf_x")
        self.tf_y = tf.placeholder(dtype=tf.float32, shape=[None,
n_actions], name="tf_y")
        self.tf_epr = tf.placeholder(dtype=tf.float32, shape=[None,
1], name="tf_epr")

        # Weights
        xavier_l1 = tf.truncated_normal_initializer(mean=0,
stddev=1. / N_SIZE, dtype=tf.float32)
        self.W1 = tf.get_variable("W1", [N_SIZE * N_SIZE, h],
initializer=xavier_l1)
        xavier_l2 = tf.truncated_normal_initializer(mean=0,
stddev=1. / np.sqrt(h), dtype=tf.float32)
        self.W2 = tf.get_variable("W2", [h, n_actions],
initializer=xavier_l2)

        # Build Computation
        # tf reward processing (need tf_discounted_epr for policy
gradient wizardry)
        tf_discounted_epr = self.tf_discount_rewards(self.tf_epr)
        tf_mean, tf_variance = tf.nn.moments(tf_discounted_epr,
[0], shift=None, name="reward_moments")
        tf_discounted_epr -= tf_mean
        tf_discounted_epr /= tf.sqrt(tf_variance + 1e-6)

        # Define Optimizer, compute and apply gradients
        self.tf_aprob = self.tf_policy_forward(self.tf_x)
        loss = tf.nn.l2_loss(self.tf_y - self.tf_aprob)
        optimizer = tf.train.RMSPropOptimizer(eta, decay=decay)
        tf_grads = optimizer.compute_gradients(loss,
var_list=tf.trainable_variables(), grad_loss=tf_discounted_epr)
        self.train_op = optimizer.apply_gradients(tf_grads)

        # Initialize Variables
        init = tf.global_variables_initializer()
        self.session = tf.InteractiveSession()
        self.session.run(init)
        self.load()
```

4. We define a method to calculate the discounted rewards. This ensures that the agent takes into account not only the present reward, but also future rewards. The discounted reward at any time t is given by $R_t = \sum \gamma^k r_{t+k}$, where the summation is over $k \in [0,\infty]$, and γ is the discount factor with value lying between 0 and 1. In our code, we have used gamma = 0.99:

```
def tf_discount_rewards(self, tf_r):  # tf_r ~ [game_steps,1]
    discount_f = lambda a, v: a * self.gamma + v;
    tf_r_reverse = tf.scan(discount_f, tf.reverse(tf_r, [0]))
    tf_discounted_r = tf.reverse(tf_r_reverse, [0])
    return tf_discounted_r
```

5. We define a `tf_policy_forward` method to provide the probability of moving the paddle UP, given an input observation state. We implement it using a two-layer NN. The network takes the processed image of the state of the game and generates a single number denoting the probability of moving the paddle UP. In TensorFlow, as the network graph is computed only in the TensorFlow session, we therefore define another method, `predict_UP`, to compute the probability:

```
def tf_policy_forward(self, x): #x ~ [1,D]
    h = tf.matmul(x, self.W1)
    h = tf.nn.relu(h)
    logp = tf.matmul(h, self.W2)
    p = tf.nn.softmax(logp)
    return p

def predict_UP(self,x):
    feed = {self.tf_x: np.reshape(x, (1, -1))}
    aprob = self.session.run(self.tf_aprob, feed);
    return aprob
```

6. The `PolicyNetwork` agent updates the weights using the `update` method:

```
def update(self, feed):
    return self.session.run(self.train_op, feed)
```

7. We define a helper function to preprocess the observation state space:

```
# downsampling
def preprocess(I):
    """ prepro 210x160x3 uint8 frame into 6400 (80x80) 1D float
vector """
    I = I[35:195] # crop
    I = I[::2,::2,0] # downsample by factor of 2
    I[I == 144] = 0  # erase background (background type 1)
```

```
    I[I == 109] = 0  # erase background (background type 2)
    I[I != 0] = 1    # everything else (paddles, ball) just set to
1
    return I.astype(np.float).ravel()
```

8. The rest is simple--we create a game environment, define arrays to hold (state, action, reward, state), and make the agent learn for a very large number of episodes (with a break or continuously, depending solely on your computational resources). An important thing to note here is that the agent is not learning per action step. Instead, the agent uses the complete set of (state, action, reward, state) of one episode to correct its policy. This can be memory-expensive:

```
if __name__ == '__main__':
    # Create Game Environment
    env_name = "Pong-v0"
    env = gym.make(env_name)
    env = wrappers.Monitor(env, '/tmp/pong', force=True)
    n_actions = env.action_space.n  # Number of possible actions
    # Initializing Game and State(t-1), action, reward, state(t)
    xs, rs, ys = [], [], []
    obs = env.reset()
    prev_x = None


    running_reward = None
    running_rewards = []
    reward_sum = 0
    n = 0
    done = False
    n_size = 80
    num_episodes = 500

    #Create Agent
    agent = PolicyNetwork(n_size)

    # training loop
    while not done and n< num_episodes:
        # Preprocess the observation
        cur_x = preprocess(obs)
        x = cur_x - prev_x if prev_x is not None else
np.zeros(n_size*n_size)
        prev_x = cur_x

        #Predict the action
        aprob = agent.predict_UP(x) ; aprob = aprob[0,:]
```

```
        action = np.random.choice(n_actions, p=aprob)
        #print(action)
        label = np.zeros_like(aprob) ; label[action] = 1

        # Step the environment and get new measurements
        obs, reward, done, info = env.step(action)
        env.render()
        reward_sum += reward

        # record game history
        xs.append(x) ; ys.append(label) ; rs.append(reward)

        if done:
            # update running reward
            running_reward = reward_sum if running_reward is None
else running_reward * 0.99 + reward_sum * 0.01
            running_rewards.append(running_reward)
            feed = {agent.tf_x: np.vstack(xs), agent.tf_epr:
np.vstack(rs), agent.tf_y: np.vstack(ys)}
            agent.update(feed)
            # print progress console
            if n % 10 == 0:
                print ('ep {}: reward: {}, mean reward:
{:3f}'.format(n, reward_sum, running_reward))
            else:
                print ('\tep {}: reward: {}'.format(n, reward_sum))

            # Start next episode and save model
            xs, rs, ys = [], [], []
            obs = env.reset()
            n += 1 # the Next Episode

            reward_sum = 0
            if n % 50 == 0:
                agent.save()
            done = False

    plt.plot(running_rewards)
    plt.xlabel('episodes')
    plt.ylabel('Running Averge')
    plt.show()
    env.close()
```

The following figure shows the average running reward as the agent learns for the first 500 episodes:

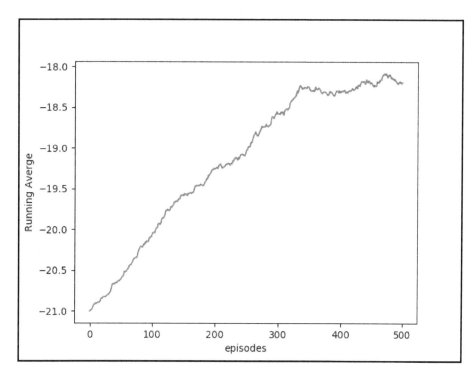

How it works...

Weights were initialized using Xavier initialization, which ensures that our weights are neither too large nor too small; both cases impede the learning of the network. In Xavier initialization, the weights are assigned a value from a distribution with zero mean and a specific variance $2/(n_{in}+n_{out})$, where n_{in} and n_{out} are respectively the numbers of inputs and output of the layer. To know more about Xavier initialization, you can refer to Glorot and Bengio's 2009 paper; details are given in the *See also* section.

There's more...

Anyone who sees the agent learn to play for the first time will be amazed by it--it seems so human-like. The initial moves are always clumsy; slowly, the agent learns which way to go, though it is slow and often misses the ball. However, as the learning continues, the agent becomes an expert.

Yet it is very unlike us; once we learn to play a game, we can easily use that knowledge in any other similar situation. The RL agent will not be able to do so--even a simple thing such as changing the size of environment space will bring it back to zero. Transfer learning, a technique being investigated by researchers, can help the agent use the knowledge it learned in one environment space in another environment space, and perhaps pave the way for true artificial general intelligence one day.

AlphaGo Zero

Recently, DeepMind published an article about AlphaGo Zero, the latest evolution of AlphaGo. According to the results they have published, AlphaGo Zero is even more powerful and the strongest Go player in History. AlphaGo starts tabula rasa, that is, it starts from a blank state, and it uses only the board states and the games it plays against itself to tune the neural network and predict the right moves.

AlphaGo Zero uses a deep neural network, that takes as an input the raw board representations (present and history) and outputs both move probabilities and a value. Thus this neural network combines the role of both policy network and value network. The network is trained from games of self-play, unlike previous AlphaGo versions (they were trained using supervised learning). At each position, a Monte Carlo Tree Search (MCTS) is performed, guided by the neural network. The neural network is trained by a self-play reinforcement learning algorithm that uses MCTS to play each move.

Initially, the neural network has its weights randomly initialized. At each iteration step, many games of self-play are generated. At each time step, an MCTS search is performed for the possible policies using the previous iteration of the neural network., then a move is played by sampling the search probabilities. This is repeated till this particular game terminates. The game state, the policy taken and rewards for each time step of the game are stored. In parallel, the neural network is trained from the data sampled uniformly among all the time steps of the previous iteration(s) of self-play. The weights of the neural network are adjusted so as to minimize the error between the predicted value and the self-play winner, and to maximize the similarity of the neural network move probabilities to the search probabilities.

With only 3 days of training on a single machine with four TPUs, AlphaGo Zero beat AlphaGo by 100-0. AlphaGo Zero is based solely on RL. The detail of its implementation can be read in the paper *Mastering the game of Go without human knowledge* published in Nature, October 2017.

See also

- https://arxiv.org/pdf/1602.01783.pdf
- http://ufal.mff.cuni.cz/~straka/courses/npfl114/2016/sutton-bookdraft2016sep.pdf
- http://karpathy.github.io/2016/05/31/rl/
- Xavier Glorot and Yoshua Bengio, Understanding the difficulty of training deep feedforward neural networks, Proceedings of the Thirteenth International Conference on Artificial Intelligence and Statistics, 2010, http://proceedings.mlr.press/v9/glorot10a/glorot10a.pdf

10
Mobile Computation

In this chapter, we will discuss using deep learning on mobile devices and we will present a number of recipes for the following:

- Installing TensorFlow mobile for macOS and Android
- Playing with TensorFlow and Android examples
- Installing TensorFlow mobile for macOS and iPhone
- Optimizing a TensorFlow graph for mobile devices
- Transforming a TensorFlow graph for mobile devices

Introduction

In this section, we will present a number of use cases for mobile deep learning. This is a very different situation from the desktop or cloud deep learning where GPUs and electricity are commonly available. In fact, on a mobile device, it is very important to preserve the battery and GPUs are frequently not available. However, deep learning can be very useful in a number of situations. Let's review them:

- **Image recognition**: Modern phones have powerful cameras and users are keen to try effects on images and pictures. Frequently, it is also important to understand what is in the pictures, and there are multiple pre-trained models that can be adapted for this, as discussed in the chapters dedicated to CNNs. A good example of a model used for image recognition is given at `https://github.com/TensorFlow/models/tree/master/official/resnet`.

- **Object localization**: Identifying moving objects is a key operation and is required for video and image processing. One can, for instance, imagine that if multiple persons are recognized in an image, then the camera will use multiple focus points. A collection of examples for object localization is given at `https://github.com/TensorFlow/models/tree/master/research/object_detection`.

- **Optical character recognition**: Recognizing handwritten characters is fundamental in for many activities such as text classification and recommendation. Deep learning can provide fundamental help for carrying out these activities. We looked at a few examples of MNIST recognition in the chapters dedicated to CNNs. Information on MNIST can also be found at `https://github.com/TensorFlow/models/tree/master/official/mnist`.

- **Speech recognition**: Voice recognition is a common interface for accessing modern phones. Deep learning is therefore used to recognize voices and spoken commands. The progress made in this area over the last few years has been impressive.

- **Translation**: Dealing with multiple languages is part of the modern multicultural world. Phones are becoming more and more accurate for on-the-fly translations across languages, and deep learning has helped to break barriers, which was impossible to even imagine a few years ago. We looked at some examples of machine translation during the chapter dedicated to RNNs.

- **Gesture recognition**: Phones are starting to use gestures as interfaces for receiving commands. Of course, there are models for this.

- **Compression**: Compression is a key aspect in mobile phones. As you can imagine, it is beneficial to reduce the space before sending an image or a video over the network. Similarly, it might be convenient to compress data before storing locally on the device. In all these situations, deep learning can help. A model using RNNSs for compression is located at `https://github.com/TensorFlow/models/tree/master/research/compression`.

TensorFlow, mobile, and the cloud

As discussed, phones typically do not have GPUs and it is important to save battery. So many expensive computations need to be offloaded to the cloud to alleviate the cost. Of course, it is a matter of compromising different factors including the cost of executing a deep learning model on mobile, the cost of moving data off to the cloud, the cost of the battery for this transfer, and the cost of cloud computing. There is no single solution, and the optimal strategy depends on your particular situation.

Installing TensorFlow mobile for macOS and Android

In this recipe, we will learn how to set up TensorFlow for a mobile environment. My environment is macOS and I develop for Android. However, other configurations will be described during the following recipes.

Getting ready

We will use Android studio, the official **integrated development environment (IDE)** for Google's Android operating system.

How to do it...

We proceed with installing TensorFlow mobile for macOS and Android as follows:

1. Install Android Studio from `https://developer.android.com/studio/install.html`.

2. Create a new project name `AndroidExampleTensorflow` as illustrated in the following screenshot:

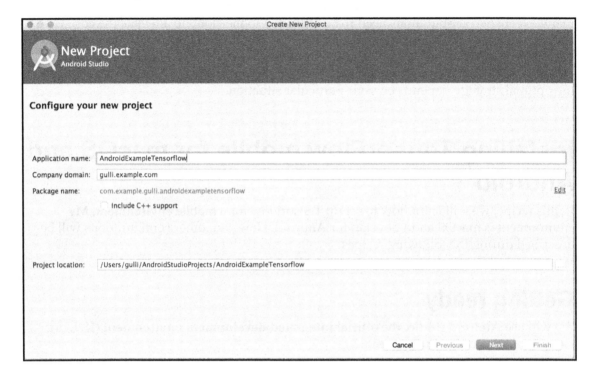

An example of creating TensorFlow mobile application in AndroidStudio, first step **Select Phone and Table** option as explained in the following figure:

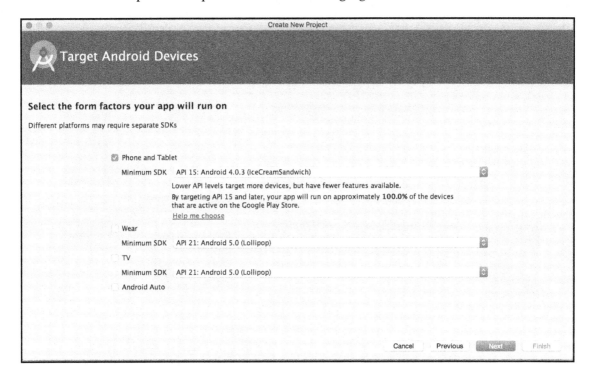

An example of creating TensorFlow mobile application in AndroidStudio, second step And select an **Empty activity** as shown in the following figure:

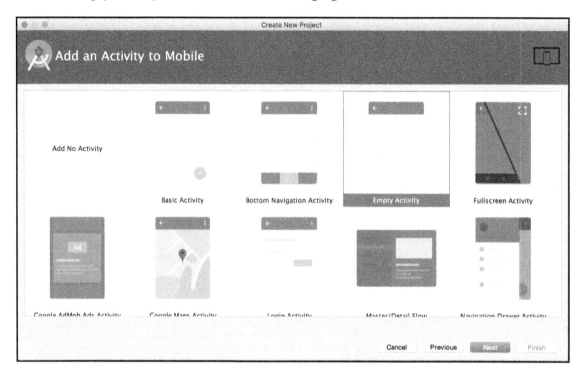

An example of creating TensorFlow mobile application in AndroidStudio, third step Then customize the `MainActivity` as shown in the following figure:

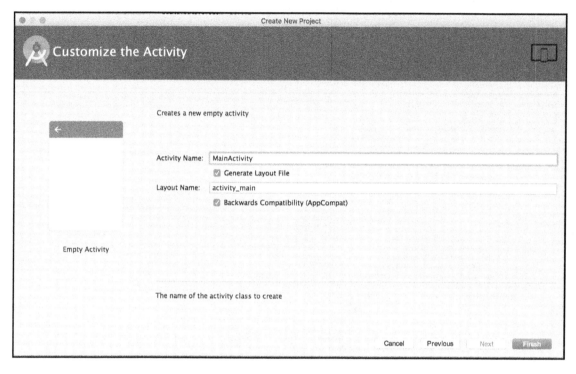

An example of creating TensorFlow mobile application in AndroidStudio, fourth step

3. Insert the following lines in your `build.gradle` app, as illustrated in the following code:

```
// added for automatically connect to TensorFlow via maven
repositories {
jcenter()
maven {
url 'https://google.bintray.com/TensorFlow'
}
}
dependencies {
compile fileTree(dir: 'libs', include: ['*.jar'])
androidTestCompile('com.android.support.test.espresso:espresso-
core:2.2.2', {
exclude group: 'com.android.support', module: 'support-annotations'
})
```

```
compile 'com.android.support:appcompat-v7:26.+'
compile 'com.android.support.constraint:constraint-layout:1.0.2'
// added for automatically compile TensorFlow
compile 'org.TensorFlow:TensorFlow-android:+'
testCompile 'junit:junit:4.12'
}
```

The following screenshot shows the code inserted:

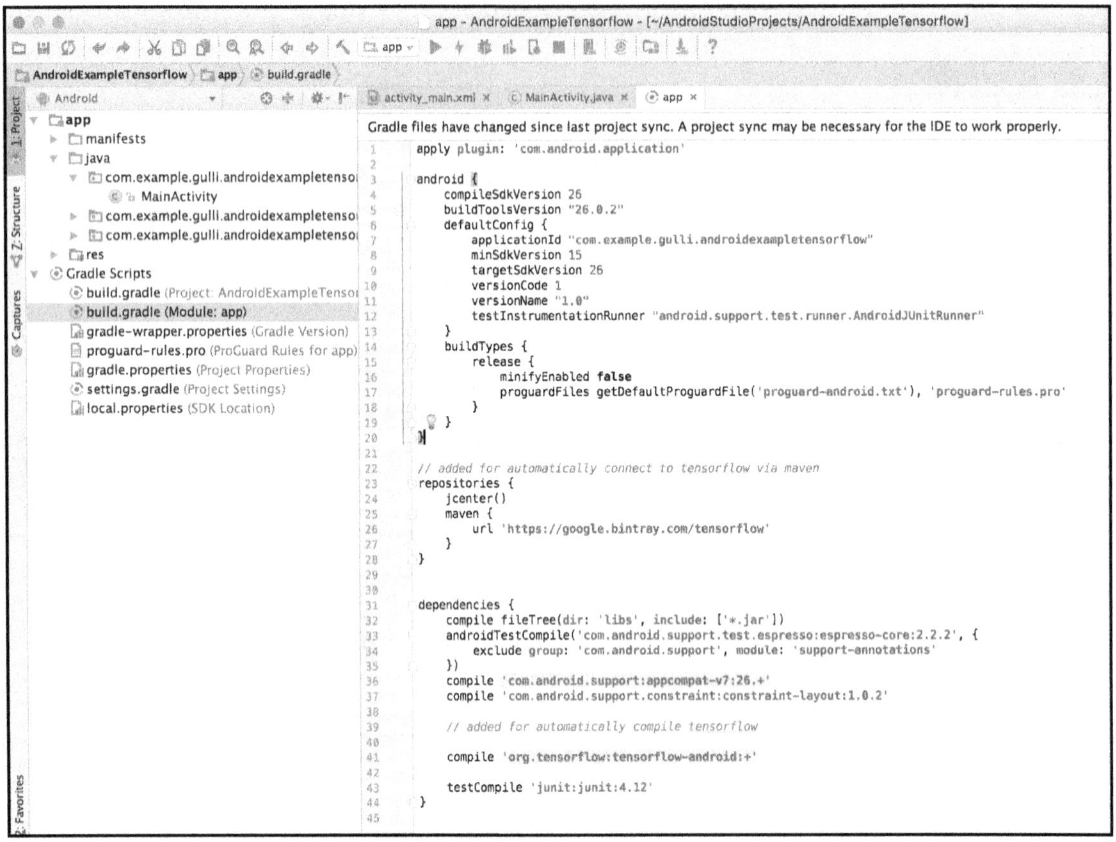

4. Run the project and get the results:

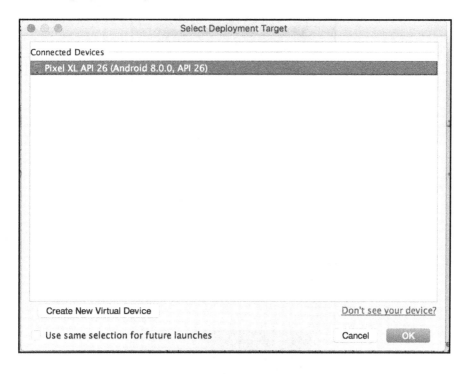

An example of compilation with the AndroidStudio, showing the connected devices.

An example of creating TensorFlow mobile application in AndroidStudio. A simple `Hello World` application

How it works...

Setting up Android TensorFlow with Android Studio is very simple. You just need to add a few configuration lines to your app's `build.gradle` file and Android Studio will do everything on your behalf.

There's more...

If you want to build directly from a TensorFlow source then you need to install Bazel and TensorFlow. Bazel is a fast, scalable, multi-language, and extensible build system. Google uses the build tool Blaze internally and released the open source part of the Blaze tool as Bazel; the name is an anagram of Blaze.

This page will guide you through the process: `https://github.com/TensorFlow/TensorFlow/tree/master/TensorFlow/examples/android/`.

If you are running macOS, the process is very simple:

1. Install Bazel by following the instructions at `https://docs.bazel.build/versions/master/install.html`. For macOS, we are going to use Homebrew:

   ```
   /usr/bin/ruby -e "$(curl -fsSL \
   https://raw.githubusercontent.com/Homebrew/install/master/install)"
   brew install bazel
   bazel version
   brew upgrade bazel
   ```

2. Clone the TensorFlow distribution from GitHub.

   ```
   git clone https://github.com/TensorFlow/TensorFlow.git
   ```

Playing with TensorFlow and Android examples

In this recipe, we will consider the standard Android examples presented in the TensorFlow distribution and install them on our mobile device.

Getting ready

TensorFlow mobile Android apps are available on GitHub at the following address: `https://github.com/TensorFlow/TensorFlow/tree/master/TensorFlow/examples/android`. In October 2017, the page contained the following examples:

- **TF Classify**: Uses the Google Inception model to classify camera frames in real time, displaying the top results in an overlay on the camera image.

- **TF Detect**: Demonstrates an SSD-Mobilenet model trained using the TensorFlow Object Detection API. This was introduced in speed/accuracy trade-offs for modern convolutional object detectors to localize and track objects (from 80 categories) in the camera preview in real time.
- **TF Stylize**: Uses a model based on *A Learned Representation For Artistic Style* to restyle the camera preview image to that of a number of different art styles.
- **TF Speech**: Runs a simple speech recognition model built in the audio training tutorial. Listens for a small set of words, and highlights them in the UI when they are recognized.

How to do it...

We proceed with the recipe as follows:

1. The best way to install the packages is to use the pre-built APK which is created every night. Point your browser to `https://ci.TensorFlow.org/view/Nightly/job/nightly-android/` and download `TensorFlow_demo.apk` as shown in the following screenshot:

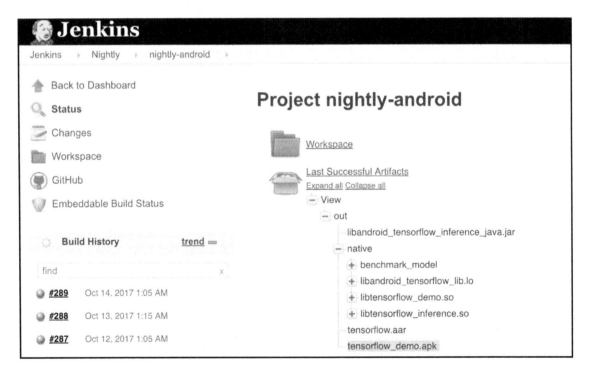

2. Install the applications on your device. In my example, I will use the Pixel XL emulated device available in Android Studio. This is a terminal device emulated directly from inside Android Studio. The command `adb devices` lists all the attached devices. In this case, I have an emulator for the Pixel XL and i can install the `TensorFlow_demo` apk.

```
adb devices
List of devices attached
emulator-5554 device
adb install -r TensorFlow_demo.apk
```

After the installation, the emulator will have a new set of TensorFlow applications available for use as shown in the following figure.

3. Run your favorite application. For instance, the following image is an example of TF Stylize, used for restyling the camera preview image to that of a number of different art styles via Transfer Learning:

The following image is an example of TF Speech (remember to activate the microphone for the emulator):

How it works...

Installing TensorFlow examples for Android is pretty easy if you use the nightly build demo and the `adb` tool for installing the APK on the device.

Installing TensorFlow mobile for macOS and iPhone

In this recipe, we will learn how to set up TensorFlow in a mobile environment. My environment is macOS, and the idea here is to develop for iOS and iPhone.

Getting ready

We will use the Xcode development environment and CocoaPods for pre-installing TensorFlow. I will assume that Xcode is already installed in your environment. If not, please download it from `https://developer.apple.com/xcode/`.

How to do it...

We will proceed with the recipe as follows:

1. Install cocoapods with the following commands

```
sudo gem install cocoapods
pod setup
Setting up CocoaPods master repo
$ /usr/local/git/current/bin/git clone
https://github.com/CocoaPods/Specs.git master --progress
Cloning into 'master'...
remote: Counting objects: 1602077, done.
remote: Compressing objects: 100% (243/243), done.
remote: Total 1602077 (delta 125), reused 172 (delta 74), pack-
reused 1601747
Receiving objects: 100% (1602077/1602077), 432.12 MiB | 1.83 MiB/s,
done.
Resolving deltas: 100% (849517/849517), done.
Checking out files: 100% (188907/188907), done.
```

2. Install TensorFlow distribution with CocoaPods:

```
cd TensorFlow/TensorFlow/examples/ios/benchmark
pod install
Analyzing dependencies
Downloading dependencies
Installing TensorFlow-experimental (1.1.1)
Generating Pods project
Integrating client project
[!] Please close any current Xcode sessions and use
`tf_benchmark_example.xcworkspace` for this project from now on.
Sending stats
Pod installation complete! There is 1 dependency from the Podfile
and 1 total pod installed.
```

3. Download some sample data from Inception v1. Extract the label and graph files into the data folders inside both the `simple` and `camera` folders:

```
mkdir -p ~/graphs
  curl -o ~/graphs/inception5h.zip \
https://storage.googleapis.com/download.TensorFlow.org/models/incep
tion5h.zip \
  && unzip ~/graphs/inception5h.zip -d ~/graphs/inception5h
  cp ~/graphs/inception5h/* TensorFlow/examples/ios/benchmark/data/
  cp ~/graphs/inception5h/* TensorFlow/examples/ios/camera/data/
  cp ~/graphs/inception5h/* TensorFlow/examples/ios/simple/data/
```

4. Download an image used as a test from and copy it into the benchmark directory:

```
https://upload.wikimedia.org/wikipedia/commons/5/55/Grace_Hopper.jpg
```

```
cp grace_hopper.jpg ../../benchmark/data/
```

An image of Grace Hopper

5. Open the sample project used previously. The following command will open Xcode with TensorFlow already available: After that, run compile, as shown in the following code and image:

```
open tf_benchmark_example.xcworkspace
```

6. Look at the results in the iPhone simulator. The image used in step 4 is recognized as being an image of a *military uniform*, according to the Inception v1 categories:

An example of Iphone application for Tensorflow computation

How it works...

Xcode and CocoaPods are used for compiling a TensorFlow application used for classifying images in different Inception categories. The result is visualized using an iPhone simulator.

There's more...

You can use TensorFlow directly from your applications. More information is available here: `https://github.com/TensorFlow/TensorFlow/blob/master/TensorFlow/examples/ios/README.md`.

Optimizing a TensorFlow graph for mobile devices

In this recipe, we will consider the different options to optimize TensorFlow code running on a mobile device. Different options are analyzed, from reducing the size of the model to quantization.

Getting ready

We are going to use Bazel for building the different components of TensorFlow. Therefore, the first step is to make sure that both Bazel and TensorFlow are installed.

How to do it...

We proceed with the optimization as follows:

1. Install Android Studio from `https://developer.android.com/studio/install.html`.

2. Install Bazel by following the instructions at `https://docs.bazel.build/` `versions/master/install.html`. For macOS, we are going to use Homebrew:

```
/usr/bin/ruby -e "$(curl -fsSL \
https://raw.githubusercontent.com/Homebrew/install/master/install)"
brew install bazel
bazel version
brew upgrade bazel
```

3. Clone the TensorFlow distribution from GitHub:

```
git clone https://github.com/TensorFlow/TensorFlow.git
```

4. Build the graph transformer that summarizes the graph itself:

```
cd ~/TensorFlow/
bazel build TensorFlow/tools/graph_transforms:summarize_graph
[2,326 / 2,531] Compiling
TensorFlow/core/kernels/cwise_op_greater.cc
INFO: From Linking
TensorFlow/tools/graph_transforms/summarize_graph:
clang: warning: argument unused during compilation: '-pthread' [-
Wunused-command-line-argument]
Target //TensorFlow/tools/graph_transforms:summarize_graph up-to-
date:
bazel-bin/TensorFlow/tools/graph_transforms/summarize_graph
INFO: Elapsed time: 1521.260s, Critical Path: 103.87s
```

7. Download a TensorFlow graph to be used as an example. In this case, we will use Inception v1 TensorFlow graph:

```
mkdir -p ~/graphs
 curl -o ~/graphs/inception5h.zip \
https://storage.googleapis.com/download.TensorFlow.org/models/incep
tion5h.zip \
 && unzip ~/graphs/inception5h.zip -d ~/graphs/inception5h
```

8. Summarize the Inception graph and notice the number of const parameters: 13.46Million. Each of them is stored with 32-bit floats, and this is quite expensive:

```
bazel-bin/TensorFlow/tools/graph_transforms/summarize_graph --
in_graph=/Users/gulli/graphs/TensorFlow_inception_graph.pb
Found 1 possible inputs: (name=input, type=float(1), shape=[])
No variables spotted.
Found 3 possible outputs: (name=output, op=Identity) (name=output1,
op=Identity) (name=output2, op=Identity)
Found 13462015 (13.46M) const parameters, 0 (0) variable
```

```
parameters, and 0 control_edges
370 nodes assigned to device '/cpu:0'Op types used: 142 Const, 64
BiasAdd, 61 Relu, 59 Conv2D, 13 MaxPool, 9 Concat, 5 Reshape, 5
MatMul, 3 Softmax, 3 Identity, 3 AvgPool, 2 LRN, 1 Placeholder
To use with TensorFlow/tools/benchmark:benchmark_model try these
arguments:
bazel run TensorFlow/tools/benchmark:benchmark_model -- --
graph=/Users/gulli/graphs/TensorFlow_inception_graph.pb --
show_flops --input_layer=input --input_layer_type=float --
input_layer_shape= --output_layer=output,output1,output2
```

9. Compile the tool for quantizing the const operations down to 8 bits:

```
bazel build TensorFlow/tools/graph_transforms:transform_graph
INFO: From Linking
TensorFlow/tools/graph_transforms/transform_graph:
clang: warning: argument unused during compilation: '-pthread' [-
Wunused-command-line-argument]
Target //TensorFlow/tools/graph_transforms:transform_graph up-to-
date:
bazel-bin/TensorFlow/tools/graph_transforms/transform_graph
INFO: Elapsed time: 294.421s, Critical Path: 28.83s
```

10. Run the tool for quantizing the Inception V1 graph:

```
bazel-bin/TensorFlow/tools/graph_transforms/transform_graph --
in_graph=/Users/gulli/graphs/inception5h/TensorFlow_inception_graph
.pb --out_graph=/tmp/TensorFlow_inception_quantized.pb --
inputs='Mul:0' --outputs='softmax:0' --
transforms='quantize_weights'
2017-10-15 18:56:01.192498: I
TensorFlow/tools/graph_transforms/transform_graph.cc:264] Applying
quantize_weights
```

11. Compare the two models:

```
ls -lah
/Users/gulli/graphs/inception5h/TensorFlow_inception_graph.pb
-rw-r----- 1 gulli 5001 51M Nov 19 2015
/Users/gulli/graphs/inception5h/TensorFlow_inception_graph.pb
ls -lah /tmp/TensorFlow_inception_quantized.pb
-rw-r--r-- 1 gulli wheel 13M Oct 15 18:56
/tmp/TensorFlow_inception_quantized.pb
```

How it works...

Quantization helps to reduce the size of a model by downsizing the const operations from 32 bit down to 8 bits. In general, the model will not suffer significant degradation of performance. However, this has to be verified on a case by case basis.

Profiling a TensorFlow graph for mobile devices

In this recipe, we will consider the different options to optimize TensorFlow code for running on a mobile device. Different options are analyzed, from reducing the size of the model to quantization.

Getting ready

We are going to use Bazel for building the different components of TensorFlow. Therefore, the first step is to make sure that both Bazel and TensorFlow are installed.

How to do it...

We proceed with profiling as follows:

1. Install Android Studio from `https://developer.android.com/studio/install.html`.

2. Install Bazel by following the instructions at `https://docs.bazel.build/versions/master/install.html`. For macOS, we are going to use Homebrew:

   ```
   /usr/bin/ruby -e "$(curl -fsSL \
   https://raw.githubusercontent.com/Homebrew/install/master/install)"
   brew install bazel
   bazel version
   brew upgrade bazel
   ```

3. Clone the TensorFlow distribution from GitHub:

   ```
   git clone https://github.com/TensorFlow/TensorFlow.git
   ```

4. Build the graph transformer which profiles the graph itself:

```
cd ~/TensorFlow/
bazel build -c opt TensorFlow/tools/benchmark:benchmark_model
INFO: Found 1 target...
Target //TensorFlow/tools/benchmark:benchmark_model up-to-date:
bazel-bin/TensorFlow/tools/benchmark/benchmark_model
INFO: Elapsed time: 0.493s, Critical Path: 0.01s
```

5. Benchmark the model by running the following command on the desktop:

```
bazel-bin/TensorFlow/tools/benchmark/benchmark_model --
graph=/Users/gulli/graphs/TensorFlow_inception_graph.pb --
show_run_order=false --show_time=false --show_memory=false --
show_summary=true --show_flops=true
Graph: [/Users/gulli/graphs/TensorFlow_inception_graph.pb]
Input layers: [input:0]
Input shapes: [1,224,224,3]
Input types: [float]
Output layers: [output:0]
Num runs: [1000]
Inter-inference delay (seconds): [-1.0]
Inter-benchmark delay (seconds): [-1.0]
Num threads: [-1]
Benchmark name: []
Output prefix: []
Show sizes: [0]
Warmup runs: [2]
Loading TensorFlow.
Got config, 0 devices
Running benchmark for max 2 iterations, max -1 seconds without
detailed stat logging, with -1s sleep between inferences
count=2 first=279182 curr=41827 min=41827 max=279182 avg=160504
std=118677
Running benchmark for max 1000 iterations, max 10 seconds without
detailed stat logging, with -1s sleep between inferences
count=259 first=39945 curr=44189 min=36539 max=51743 avg=38651.1
std=1886
Running benchmark for max 1000 iterations, max 10 seconds with
detailed stat logging, with -1s sleep between inferences
count=241 first=40794 curr=39178 min=37634 max=153345 avg=41644.8
std=8092
Average inference timings in us: Warmup: 160504, no stats: 38651,
with stats: 41644
```

```
Number of nodes executed: 141
=============================== Summary by node type ===============================
         [Node type]       [count]      [avg ms]      [avg %]      [cdf %]     [mem KB]   [times called]
              Conv2D            22        45.729       77.520%      77.520%    10077.888            22
                 LRN             2         4.495        7.620%      85.140%     3211.264             2
             MaxPool             6         3.119        5.287%      90.427%     3562.496             6
             BiasAdd            24         2.269        3.846%      94.274%        0.000            24
                Relu            23         1.071        1.816%      96.089%        0.000            23
              MatMul             2         0.851        1.443%      97.532%        8.128             2
              Concat             3         0.726        1.231%      98.763%     2706.368             3
             AvgPool             1         0.514        0.871%      99.634%       32.512             1
               Const            51         0.162        0.275%      99.908%        0.000            51
             Softmax             1         0.027        0.046%      99.954%        0.000             1
                _Arg             1         0.008        0.014%      99.968%        0.000             1
                NoOp             1         0.008        0.014%      99.981%        0.000             1
             Reshape             2         0.005        0.008%      99.990%        0.000             2
             _Retval             1         0.004        0.007%      99.997%        0.000             1
            Identity             1         0.002        0.003%     100.000%        0.000             1

Timings (microseconds): count=241 first=57594 curr=57181 min=50932 max=265096 avg=59057.9 std=14447
Memory (bytes): count=241 curr=19598656(all same)
141 nodes observed
```

6. Benchmark the model by running the following command on a target android device running a 64-bit ARM processor. Note that the following command pushes the inception graph onto the device and runs a shell, where the benchmark can be executed:

```
bazel build -c opt --config=android_arm64 \
TensorFlow/tools/benchmark:benchmark_model
adb push bazel-bin/TensorFlow/tools/benchmark/benchmark_model \
/data/local/tmp
adb push /tmp/TensorFlow_inception_graph.pb /data/local/tmp/
adb push ~gulli/graphs/inception5h/TensorFlow_inception_graph.pb
/data/local/tmp/
/Users/gulli/graphs/inception5h/TensorFlow_inception_graph.pb: 1
file pushed. 83.2 MB/s (53884595 bytes in 0.618s)
adb shell
generic_x86:/ $
/data/local/tmp/benchmark_model --
graph=/data/local/tmp/TensorFlow_inception_graph.pb --
show_run_order=false --show_time=false --show_memory=false --
show_summary=true
```

How it works...

This model spends a lot of time on Conv2D operations, as expected. Overall this takes about 77.5 percent of the average time on my desktop machine. If you run this on a mobile device, it is critical to take the time to execute each layer in the neural network and make sure they are under control. The other aspect to consider is the memory occupation. In this case, it is ~10 Mb for the desktop execution.

Transforming a TensorFlow graph for mobile devices

In this recipe, we will learn how to transform a TensorFlow graph so that all the training-only nodes are removed. This will reduce the size of the graph and make it more suitable for mobile devices.

> *What is a graph transform tool? According to https://github.com/tensorflow/tensorflow/blob/master/tensorflow/tools/graph_transforms/README.md "When you have finished training a model and want to deploy it in production, you'll often want to modify it to better run in its final environment. For example if you're targeting a phone you might want to shrink the file size by quantizing the weights, or optimize away batch normalization or other training-only features. The Graph Transform framework offers a suite of tools for modifying computational graphs, and a framework to make it easy to write your own modifications".*

Getting ready

We are going to use Bazel for building the different components of TensorFlow. Therefore, the first step is to make sure that both Bazel and TensorFlow are installed.

How to do it...

Here is how we proceed with transforming a TensorFlow:

1. Install Android Studio from `https://developer.android.com/studio/install.html`.

2. Install Bazel by following the instructions at `https://docs.bazel.build/versions/master/install.html`. For macOS, we are going to use Homebrew:

```
/usr/bin/ruby -e "$(curl -fsSL \
https://raw.githubusercontent.com/Homebrew/install/master/install)"
brew install bazel
bazel version
brew upgrade bazel
```

3. Clone the TensorFlow distribution from GitHub:

```
git clone https://github.com/TensorFlow/TensorFlow.git
```

4. Build the graph transformer which summarizes the graph itself:

```
bazel run TensorFlow/tools/graph_transforms:summarize_graph -- --
in_graph=/Users/gulli/graphs/inception5h/TensorFlow_inception_graph
.pb
WARNING: /Users/gulli/TensorFlow/TensorFlow/core/BUILD:1783:1: in
includes attribute of cc_library rule
//TensorFlow/core:framework_headers_lib:
'../../external/nsync/public' resolves to 'external/nsync/public'
not below the relative path of its package 'TensorFlow/core'. This
will be an error in the future. Since this rule was created by the
macro 'cc_header_only_library', the error might have been caused by
the macro implementation in
/Users/gulli/TensorFlow/TensorFlow/TensorFlow.bzl:1054:30.
INFO: Found 1 target...
Target //TensorFlow/tools/graph_transforms:summarize_graph up-to-
date:
bazel-bin/TensorFlow/tools/graph_transforms/summarize_graph
INFO: Elapsed time: 0.395s, Critical Path: 0.01s
INFO: Running command line: bazel-
bin/TensorFlow/tools/graph_transforms/summarize_graph '--
in_graph=/Users/gulli/graphs/inception5h/TensorFlow_inception_graph
.pb'
Found 1 possible inputs: (name=input, type=float(1), shape=[])
No variables spotted.
Found 3 possible outputs: (name=output, op=Identity) (name=output1,
op=Identity) (name=output2, op=Identity)
Found 13462015 (13.46M) const parameters, 0 (0) variable
parameters, and 0 control_edges
370 nodes assigned to device '/cpu:0'Op types used: 142 Const, 64
BiasAdd, 61 Relu, 59 Conv2D, 13 MaxPool, 9 Concat, 5 Reshape, 5
MatMul, 3 Softmax, 3 Identity, 3 AvgPool, 2 LRN, 1 Placeholder
To use with TensorFlow/tools/benchmark:benchmark_model try these
arguments:
bazel run TensorFlow/tools/benchmark:benchmark_model -- --
graph=/Users/gulli/graphs/inception5h/TensorFlow_inception_graph.pb
--show_flops --input_layer=input --input_layer_type=float --
input_layer_shape= --output_layer=output,output1,output2
```

5. Strip all the nodes used for training, which are not needed when the graph is used for inference on mobile devices:

```
bazel run TensorFlow/tools/graph_transforms:transform_graph -- --
in_graph=/Users/gulli/graphs/inception5h/TensorFlow_inception_graph
.pb --out_graph=/tmp/optimized_inception_graph.pb --
transforms="strip_unused_nodes fold_constants(ignore_errors=true)
fold_batch_norms fold_old_batch_norms"
```

```
WARNING: /Users/gulli/TensorFlow/TensorFlow/core/BUILD:1783:1: in
includes attribute of cc_library rule
//TensorFlow/core:framework_headers_lib:
'../../external/nsync/public' resolves to 'external/nsync/public'
not below the relative path of its package 'TensorFlow/core'. This
will be an error in the future. Since this rule was created by the
macro 'cc_header_only_library', the error might have been caused by
the macro implementation in
/Users/gulli/TensorFlow/TensorFlow/TensorFlow.bzl:1054:30.
INFO: Found 1 target...
Target //TensorFlow/tools/graph_transforms:transform_graph up-to-
date:
bazel-bin/TensorFlow/tools/graph_transforms/transform_graph
INFO: Elapsed time: 0.578s, Critical Path: 0.01s
INFO: Running command line: bazel-
bin/TensorFlow/tools/graph_transforms/transform_graph '--
in_graph=/Users/gulli/graphs/inception5h/TensorFlow_inception_graph
.pb' '--out_graph=/tmp/optimized_inception_graph.pb' '--
transforms=strip_unused_nodes fold_constants(ignore_errors=true)
fold_batch_norms fold_old_batch_norms'
2017-10-15 22:26:59.357129: I
TensorFlow/tools/graph_transforms/transform_graph.cc:264] Applying
strip_unused_nodes
2017-10-15 22:26:59.367997: I
TensorFlow/tools/graph_transforms/transform_graph.cc:264] Applying
fold_constants
2017-10-15 22:26:59.387800: I
TensorFlow/core/platform/cpu_feature_guard.cc:137] Your CPU
supports instructions that this TensorFlow binary was not compiled
to use: SSE4.2 AVX AVX2 FMA
2017-10-15 22:26:59.388676: E
TensorFlow/tools/graph_transforms/transform_graph.cc:279]
fold_constants: Ignoring error Must specify at least one target to
fetch or execute.
2017-10-15 22:26:59.388695: I
TensorFlow/tools/graph_transforms/transform_graph.cc:264] Applying
fold_batch_norms
2017-10-15 22:26:59.388721: I
TensorFlow/tools/graph_transforms/transform_graph.cc:264] Applying
fold_old_batch_norms
```

How it works...

In order to create a lighter model that can be loaded on the device, we have deleted all the unneeded nodes with the `strip_unused_nodes` rule which was applied by the graph' transforms tool. This operation removes all operations used for learning and leaves the ones used for inference intact.

11
Generative Models and CapsNet

In this chapter, we will present a number of recipes for:

- Learning to forge MNIST images with Simple GAN
- Learning to forge MNIST images with DCGAN
- Learning to forge Celebrity Faces and other datasets with DCGAN
- Implementing Variational Autoencoders
- Learning to beat the previous MNIST state-of-the-art results with Capsule Networks

Introduction

In this chapter, we will discuss how **Generative Adversarial Networks (GANs)** are used for deep learning in domains where the key method is to train an image generator by simultaneously training a discriminator to challenge the latter for improvement. The same method can be applied to domains different from Images. In addition, we will discuss the Variational Autoencoder.

GANs have been defined as *the most interesting idea in the last 10 years in ML* (https://www. quora.com/What-are-some-recent-and-potentially-upcoming-breakthroughs-in-deep-learning) by Yann LeCun, one of the fathers of Deep Learning. GANs are able to learn how to reproduce synthetic data which looks real. For instance, computers can learn how to paint and create realistic images. The idea was originally proposed by Ian Goodfellow who worked with the University of Montreal, Google Brain, and recently with OpenAI (https://openai.com/).

So what is a GAN?

The key process of GAN can be easily understood by considering it analogous to *art forgery*, which is the process of creating works of art which are falsely credited to other, usually more famous, artists. GANs train two neural networks simultaneously.

The **Generator** *G(Z)* is the one that makes the forgery happen, and the **Discriminator** *D(Y)* is the one that can judge how realistic the reproduction is based on its observations of authentic pieces of art and copies. *D(Y)* takes an input Y (for instance an image) and expresses a vote to judge how real the input is. In general, a value close to zero denotes *real*, while a value close to one denotes *forgery*. G(Z) takes an input from a random noise Z and trains itself to fool D into thinking that whatever G(Z) produces is real. So the goal of training the discriminator *D(Y)* is to maximize *D(Y)* for every image from the true data distribution and to minimize *D(Y)* for every image not from the true data distribution. So G and D play an opposite game: hence the name adversarial training. Note that we train G and D in an alternating manner, where each of their objectives is expressed as a loss function optimized via a gradient descent. The generative model learns how to forge better and better, and the discriminative model learns how to recognize forgery better and better.

The discriminator network (usually a standard convolutional neural network) tries to classify if an input image is real or generated. The important new idea is to backpropagate both the discriminator and the generator to adjust the generator's parameters in such a way that the generator can learn how to fool the discriminator in an increasing number of situations. In the end, the generator will learn how to produce images that are indistinguishable from the real ones:

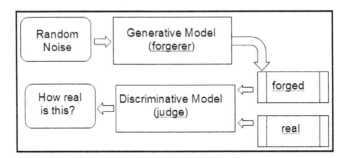

An example of Generator (forger) -Discriminator (judge) model. The Discriminator receives forged and real images

Of course, GANs find the equilibrium in a game with two players. For effective learning, it is necessary that if a player successfully moves downhill in a round of updates, the same update must move the other player downhill too. Think about it! If the forger learns how to fool the judge on every occasion, then the forger himself has nothing more to learn. Sometimes the two players eventually reach an equilibrium, but this is not always guaranteed and the two players can continue playing for a long time. An example of this from both sides is provided in the following figure:

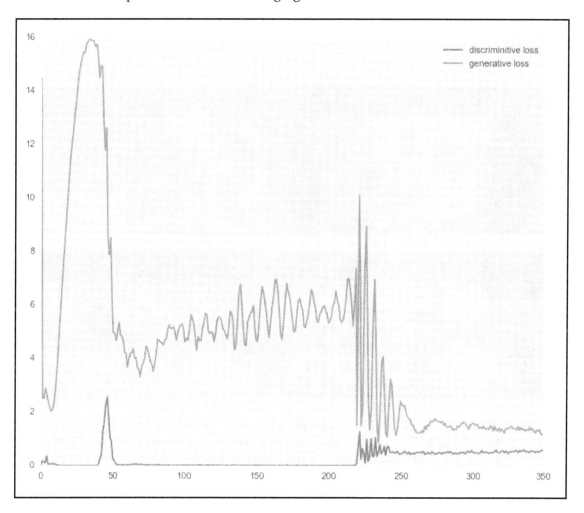

An example of convergence for Generator and Discriminator

Some cool GAN applications

We have established that the generator learns how to forge data. This means that it learns how to create new synthetic data which is created by the network and *looks* real and created by humans. Before going into details about the GAN code, I'd like to share the results of a recent paper (code is available online `https://github.com/hanzhanggit/StackGAN`) in which a GAN was used to synthesize forged images starting with a text description. The results were impressive. The first column is the real image in the test set and all the other columns are the images generated from the same text description in Stage-I and Stage-II of StackGAN. More examples are available on YouTube (`https://www.youtube.com/watch?v=SuRyL5vhCIMfeature=youtu.be`):

Now let us see how a GAN can learn to **forge** the MNIST dataset. In this case, it is a combination of GAN and ConvNets used for the generator and the discriminator networks. In the beginning, the generator creates nothing understandable, but after a few iterations, synthetic forged numbers are progressively clearer and clearer. In the following figure, the panels are ordered by increasing training epochs and you can see the quality improvement among the panels:

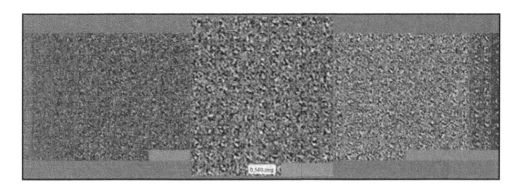

The improved image is as follows:

We can see further improvements in the following image:

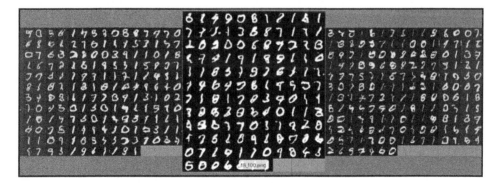

One of the coolest uses of GAN is doing arithmetics on faces in the generator's vector Z. In other words, if we stay in the space of synthetic forged images, it is possible to see things like this: **[smiling woman] - [neutral woman] + [neutral man] = [smiling man]**, or like this: **[man with glasses] - [man without glasses] + [woman without glasses] = [woman with glasses]**. The following figure was taken from: *Unsupervised Representation Learning with Deep Convolutional Generative Adversarial Networks*, Alec Radford, Luke Metz, Soumith Chintala, 2016, `https://arxiv.org/abs/1511.06434`

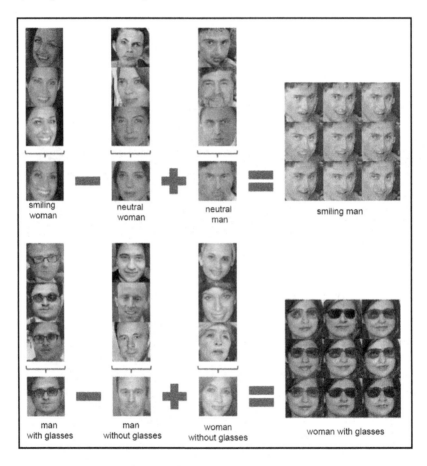

Other cool examples of GANs are provided at `https://github.com/Newmu/dcgan_code`. All images in this paper were generated by a neural network. They are NOT REAL. The full paper is available here: `http://arxiv.org/abs/1511.06434`.

Bedrooms: Generated bedrooms after five epochs of training:

An example of generated bedrooms

Album covers: these images are not real but generated by the GAN. Album covers looks like real:

An example of generated album covers

Learning to forge MNIST images with simple GANs

A good paper to better understand GANs is Generative Adversarial Networks (2014) by Ian J. Goodfellow, Jean Pouget-Abadie, Mehdi Mirza, Bing Xu, David Warde-Farley, Sherjil Ozair, Aaron Courville, Yoshua Bengio. In this recipe, we will learn how to forge MNIST handwritten numbers by using fully-connected layer networks organized in a Generator-Discriminator architecture.

Getting ready

This recipe is based on the code available at `https://github.com/TengdaHan/GAN-TensorFlow`.

How to do it...

We proceed with the recipe as follows:

1. Clone the code from github:

```
git clone https://github.com/TengdaHan/GAN-TensorFlow
```

2. Define a Xavier initializer as described in the paper *Understanding the difficulty of training deep feedforward neural networks (2009) by Xavier Glorot, Yoshua Bengio,* `http://citeseerx.ist.psu.edu/viewdoc/download?doi=10.1.1.207.2059rep=rep1type=pdf` The initializers are proven to allow better convergence for GANs:

```
def xavier_init(size):
    in_dim = size[0]
    xavier_stddev = 1. / tf.sqrt(in_dim / 2.)
    return xavier_stddev
```

3. Define the generator for the input X. First we define a matrix W1 with the dimension [100, K=128], initialized according to a normal distribution. Note that 100 is an arbitrary value for Z, the initial noise used by our generator. Then, we define the bias B1 with the dimension [K=256]. Similarly, we define a matrix W2 with the dimension [K=128, L=784] and a bias B2 with the dimension [L=784]. The two matrices W1 and W2 are initialized by using the `xavier_init` defined in step 1, while B1 and B2 are initialized by using `tf.constant_initializer()`. After that, we compute the multiplication between matrices *X * W1*, sum the bias of B1, and pass it through a RELU activation function for obtaining fc1. This dense layer is then connected with the next dense layer which was created by multiplying the matrices fc1 with W2 and summing the bias of B2. The result is then passed via a sigmoid function. These steps are used to define our two layers' neural network used for the generator:

```
def generator(X):
  with tf.variable_scope('generator'):
    K = 128
    L = 784
    W1 = tf.get_variable('G_W1', [100, K],
      initializer=tf.random_normal_initializer(stddev=xavier_init([100,    K])))
    B1 = tf.get_variable('G_B1', [K],
initializer=tf.constant_initializer())
    W2 = tf.get_variable('G_W2', [K, L],
      initializer=tf.random_normal_initializer(stddev=xavier_init([K,    L])))
    B2 = tf.get_variable('G_B2', [L],
initializer=tf.constant_initializer())
    # summary
    tf.summary.histogram('weight1', W1)
    tf.summary.histogram('weight2', W2)
    tf.summary.histogram('biases1', B1)
    tf.summary.histogram('biases2', B2)
    fc1 = tf.nn.relu((tf.matmul(X, W1) + B1))
    fc2 = tf.matmul(fc1, W2) + B2
    prob = tf.nn.sigmoid(fc2)
    return prob
```

4. Define the discriminator for input X. In principle, this is very similar to the generator. The main difference is that if the parameter reuse is true, then we call `scope.reuse_variables()` to trigger a reuse. Then we define two dense layers. The first layer uses a matrix W1 of dimensions [J=784, K=128] with a bias B1 of dimension [K=128], and it is based on the standard multiplication of X by W1. This result is added to B1 and passed to a RELU activation function for getting the result fc1. The second one uses a matrix W2 of the dimension [K=128, L=1] with a bias B2 of dimension [L=1], and it is based on the standard multiplication of fc1 by W2. This result is added to B2 and passed to a sigmoid function:

```
def discriminator(X, reuse=False):
  with tf.variable_scope('discriminator'):
    if reuse:
      tf.get_variable_scope().reuse_variables()
    J = 784
    K = 128
    L = 1
    W1 = tf.get_variable('D_W1', [J, K],
    initializer=tf.random_normal_initializer(stddev=xavier_init([J,  K])))
    B1 = tf.get_variable('D_B1', [K],
initializer=tf.constant_initializer())
    W2 = tf.get_variable('D_W2', [K, L],
initializer=tf.random_normal_initializer(stddev=xavier_init([K, L])))
    B2 = tf.get_variable('D_B2', [L],
initializer=tf.constant_initializer())
    # summary
    tf.summary.histogram('weight1', W1)
    tf.summary.histogram('weight2', W2)
    tf.summary.histogram('biases1', B1)
    tf.summary.histogram('biases2', B2)
    fc1 = tf.nn.relu((tf.matmul(X, W1) + B1))
    logits = tf.matmul(fc1, W2) + B2
    prob = tf.nn.sigmoid(logits)
    return prob, logits
```

5. Now let's define some useful additional functions. First, we import a bunch of standard modules:

```
import tensorflow as tf
import numpy as np
import matplotlib.pyplot as plt
import matplotlib.gridspec as gridspec
import os
import argparse
```

6. Then we read the data from the MNIST dataset and define an auxiliary function for plotting samples:

```
def read_data():
  from tensorflow.examples.tutorials.mnist import input_data
  mnist = input_data.read_data_sets("../MNIST_data/", one_hot=True)
  return mnist

def plot(samples):
  fig = plt.figure(figsize=(8, 8))
  gs = gridspec.GridSpec(8, 8)
  gs.update(wspace=0.05, hspace=0.05)
  for i, sample in enumerate(samples):
    ax = plt.subplot(gs[i])
    plt.axis('off')
    ax.set_xticklabels([])
    ax.set_yticklabels([])
    ax.set_aspect('equal')
    plt.imshow(sample.reshape(28, 28), cmap='Greys_r')
  return fig
```

7. Now let's define the training function. First, let's read the MNIST data, and then define a matrix X of shape 28 x 28 with one channel for a standard MNIST handwritten character. Then let's define a z noise vector of size 100—a common choice proposed in the seminal GANs paper. The next step is to call the generator on z and assign the result to G. After that, we pass X to the discriminator without reuse. Then we pass the forged/fake G result to the discriminator, reusing the learned weight. One important aspect of this is how we chose the loss function for the discriminator, which is a sum of two cross entropies: one for real characters, where all the real MNIST characters have a label set to one, and one for forged characters, where all the forged characters have a label set to zero. The discriminator and the generator run in an alternate sequence for 100,000 steps. Every 500 steps, a sample is drawn from the learned distribution for printing what that generator has learned so far. This is what defines a new epoch, and the results are shown in the next section. Let's see the code snippet which implements what we just described.

```
def train(logdir, batch_size):
  from model_fc import discriminator, generator
  mnist = read_data()
  with tf.variable_scope('placeholder'):
    # Raw image
    X = tf.placeholder(tf.float32, [None, 784])
    tf.summary.image('raw image', tf.reshape(X, [-1, 28, 28, 1]), 3)
    # Noise
```

```
   z = tf.placeholder(tf.float32, [None, 100]) # noise
   tf.summary.histogram('Noise', z)

 with tf.variable_scope('GAN'):
   G = generator(z)
   D_real, D_real_logits = discriminator(X, reuse=False)
   D_fake, D_fake_logits = discriminator(G, reuse=True)
   tf.summary.image('generated image', tf.reshape(G, [-1, 28, 28, 1]), 3)
 with tf.variable_scope('Prediction'):
   tf.summary.histogram('real', D_real)
   tf.summary.histogram('fake', D_fake)

 with tf.variable_scope('D_loss'):
   d_loss_real = tf.reduce_mean(
   tf.nn.sigmoid_cross_entropy_with_logits(
   logits=D_real_logits, labels=tf.ones_like(D_real_logits)))
   d_loss_fake = tf.reduce_mean(
   tf.nn.sigmoid_cross_entropy_with_logits(
    logits=D_fake_logits, labels=tf.zeros_like(D_fake_logits)))
   d_loss = d_loss_real + d_loss_fake

 tf.summary.scalar('d_loss_real', d_loss_real)
 tf.summary.scalar('d_loss_fake', d_loss_fake)
 tf.summary.scalar('d_loss', d_loss)

 with tf.name_scope('G_loss'):
   g_loss = tf.reduce_mean(tf.nn.sigmoid_cross_entropy_with_logits
   (logits=D_fake_logits, labels=tf.ones_like(D_fake_logits)))
   tf.summary.scalar('g_loss', g_loss)
   tvar = tf.trainable_variables()
   dvar = [var for var in tvar if 'discriminator' in var.name]
   gvar = [var for var in tvar if 'generator' in var.name]

 with tf.name_scope('train'):
   d_train_step = tf.train.AdamOptimizer().minimize(d_loss,
var_list=dvar)
   g_train_step = tf.train.AdamOptimizer().minimize(g_loss,
var_list=gvar)

 sess = tf.Session()
 init = tf.global_variables_initializer()
 sess.run(init)
 merged_summary = tf.summary.merge_all()
 writer = tf.summary.FileWriter('tmp/mnist/'+logdir)
 writer.add_graph(sess.graph)
 num_img = 0
 if not os.path.exists('output/'):
   os.makedirs('output/')
```

```
for i in range(100000):
    batch_X, _ = mnist.train.next_batch(batch_size)
    batch_noise = np.random.uniform(-1., 1., [batch_size, 100])
    if i % 500 == 0:
        samples = sess.run(G, feed_dict={z: np.random.uniform(-1., 1., [64,
100])})
        fig = plot(samples)
        plt.savefig('output/%s.png' % str(num_img).zfill(3),
bbox_inches='tight')
        num_img += 1
        plt.close(fig)

    _, d_loss_print = sess.run([d_train_step, d_loss],
feed_dict={X: batch_X, z: batch_noise})
    _, g_loss_print = sess.run([g_train_step, g_loss],
    feed_dict={z: batch_noise})
    if i % 100 == 0:
        s = sess.run(merged_summary, feed_dict={X: batch_X, z: batch_noise})
        writer.add_summary(s, i)
        print('epoch:%d g_loss:%f d_loss:%f' % (i, g_loss_print, d_loss_print))

    if __name__ == '__main__':
        parser = argparse.ArgumentParser(description='Train vanila GAN using
fully-connected layers networks')
        parser.add_argument('--logdir', type=str, default='1', help='logdir for
Tensorboard, give a string')
        parser.add_argument('--batch_size', type=int, default=64, help='batch
size: give a int')
        args = parser.parse_args()
        train(logdir=args.logdir, batch_size=args.batch_size)
```

How it works...

At each epoch, the generator makes a number of predictions (it creates forged MNIST images) and the discriminator tries to learn how to produce forged images after mixing the prediction with real MNIST images. After 32 epochs, the generator learns to forge this set of handwritten numbers. No one has programmed the machine to write, but it has learned how to write numbers that are indistinguishable from the ones written by humans. Note that training GANs can be very difficult because it is necessary to find the equilibrium between two players. If you are interested in the topic, I'd suggest you have a look at the series of tricks collected by practitioners (https://github.com/soumith/ganhacks).

Let's look at a number of practical examples for different epochs to understand how the machine will learn to improve its writing process:

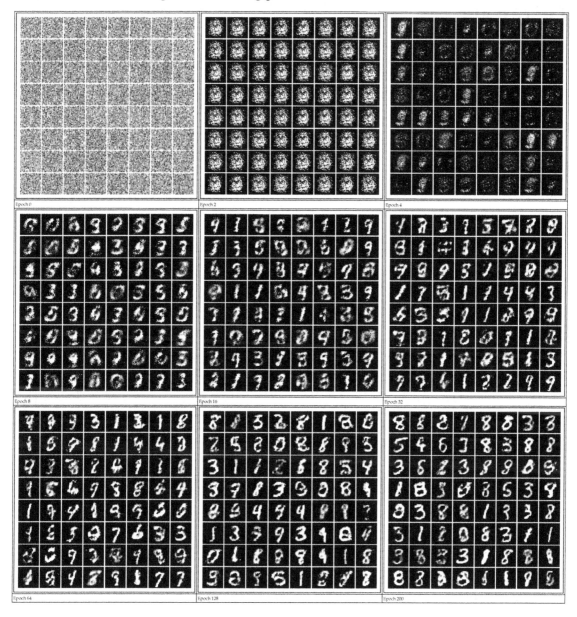

Example of forged MNIST-like characters with a GAN

Learning to forge MNIST images with DCGANs

In this recipe, we will use a simple GAN that uses CNNs for learning how to forge MNIST images and create new ones that are not part of the original dataset. The idea is that CNNs used together with GANs will improve the ability to deal with image datasets. Please note that the previous recipe was using GANs with fully connected networks, while here we focus on CNNs.

Getting ready

This recipe is based on the code available at `https://github.com/TengdaHan/GAN-TensorFlow`.

How to do it...

We proceed with the recipe as follows:

1. Clone the code from github:

```
git clone https://github.com/TengdaHan/GAN-TensorFlow
```

2. Define a Xavier initializer as defined in the paper *Understanding the difficulty of training deep feedforward neural networks (2009) by Xavier Glorot, Yoshua Bengio*. The initializers are proven to allow better convergence for GANs:

```
def xavier_init(size):
    in_dim = size[0]
    xavier_stddev = 1. / tf.sqrt(in_dim / 2.)
    # return tf.random_normal(shape=size, stddev=xavier_stddev)
    return xavier_stddev
```

3. Define a convolutional operation for the given input *x*, weight *w*, bias *b*, and given *stride*. Our code uses the standard `tf.nn.conv2d(...)` module. Note that we use 'SAME' padding, as defined in Chapter 4:

```
def conv(x, w, b, stride, name):
  with tf.variable_scope('conv'):
    tf.summary.histogram('weight', w)
    tf.summary.histogram('biases', b)
    return tf.nn.conv2d(x,
      filter=w,
      strides=[1, stride, stride, 1],
      padding='SAME',
      name=name) + b
```

4. Define a de-convolutional operation for the given input *x*, weight *w*, bias *b*, and given *stride*. Our code uses the standard `tf.nn.conv2d_transpose(...)` module. Again, we use `'SAME'` padding.

```
def deconv(x, w, b, shape, stride, name):
  with tf.variable_scope('deconv'):
    tf.summary.histogram('weight', w)
    tf.summary.histogram('biases', b)
    return tf.nn.conv2d_transpose(x,
      filter=w,
      output_shape=shape,
      strides=[1, stride, stride, 1],
      padding='SAME',
      name=name) + b
```

5. Define a standard `LeakyReLU`, which is a very effective activation function for GANs:

```
def lrelu(x, alpha=0.2):
  with tf.variable_scope('leakyReLU'):
    return tf.maximum(x, alpha * x)
```

6. Define the generator. First, we define a fully connected layer with input size 100 (an arbitrary size for Z, the initial noise used by our generator). The fully connected layer consists of a matrix W1 with the dimension [100, 7*7*256], initialized according to a normal distribution, and a bias B1 with the dimension [7*7*256]. The layer uses ReLu as an activation function. After the fully connected layer, the generator applies two deconvolutional operations, deconv1 and deconv2, both with stride=2. After the first deconv1 operation is done, results are batch normalized. Note that the second deconvolutional operation is preceded by dropout, with a probability of 40percent. The last stage is a sigmoid used as non-linear activation as reported in the below code snippet:

```
def generator(X, batch_size=64):
  with tf.variable_scope('generator'):
    K = 256
    L = 128
    M = 64
    W1 = tf.get_variable('G_W1', [100, 7*7*K],
initializer=tf.random_normal_initializer(stddev=0.1))
    B1 = tf.get_variable('G_B1', [7*7*K],
initializer=tf.constant_initializer())
    W2 = tf.get_variable('G_W2', [4, 4, M, K],
initializer=tf.random_normal_initializer(stddev=0.1))
    B2 = tf.get_variable('G_B2', [M],
initializer=tf.constant_initializer())
    W3 = tf.get_variable('G_W3', [4, 4, 1, M],
initializer=tf.random_normal_initializer(stddev=0.1))
    B3 = tf.get_variable('G_B3', [1],
initializer=tf.constant_initializer())
    X = lrelu(tf.matmul(X, W1) + B1)
    X = tf.reshape(X, [batch_size, 7, 7, K])
    deconv1 = deconv(X, W2, B2, shape=[batch_size, 14, 14, M], stride=2,
name='deconv1')
    bn1 = tf.contrib.layers.batch_norm(deconv1)
    deconv2 = deconv(tf.nn.dropout(lrelu(bn1), 0.4), W3, B3,
shape=[batch_size, 28, 28, 1], stride=2, name='deconv2')
    XX = tf.reshape(deconv2, [-1, 28*28], 'reshape')
    return tf.nn.sigmoid(XX)
```

7. Define the discriminator. As in the previous recipe, if the parameter reuse is true, then we call `scope.reuse_variables()` to trigger a reuse. The discriminator uses two convolutional layers. The first one is followed by batch normalization while the second one is preceded by a dropout with a probability of 40 percent and followed again by a batch normalization step. After that, we have a dense layer with the activation function ReLU followed by another dense layer with the activation function based on the sigmoid:

```
def discriminator(X, reuse=False):
  with tf.variable_scope('discriminator'):
    if reuse:
      tf.get_variable_scope().reuse_variables()
    K = 64
    M = 128
    N = 256
    W1 = tf.get_variable('D_W1', [4, 4, 1, K],
initializer=tf.random_normal_initializer(stddev=0.1))
    B1 = tf.get_variable('D_B1', [K],
initializer=tf.constant_initializer())
    W2 = tf.get_variable('D_W2', [4, 4, K, M],
initializer=tf.random_normal_initializer(stddev=0.1))
    B2 = tf.get_variable('D_B2', [M],
initializer=tf.constant_initializer())
    W3 = tf.get_variable('D_W3', [7*7*M, N],
initializer=tf.random_normal_initializer(stddev=0.1))
    B3 = tf.get_variable('D_B3', [N],
initializer=tf.constant_initializer())
    W4 = tf.get_variable('D_W4', [N, 1],
initializer=tf.random_normal_initializer(stddev=0.1))
    B4 = tf.get_variable('D_B4', [1],
initializer=tf.constant_initializer())
    X = tf.reshape(X, [-1, 28, 28, 1], 'reshape')
    conv1 = conv(X, W1, B1, stride=2, name='conv1')
    bn1 = tf.contrib.layers.batch_norm(conv1)
    conv2 = conv(tf.nn.dropout(lrelu(bn1), 0.4), W2, B2, stride=2,
name='conv2')
    bn2 = tf.contrib.layers.batch_norm(conv2)
    flat = tf.reshape(tf.nn.dropout(lrelu(bn2), 0.4), [-1, 7*7*M],
name='flat')
    dense = lrelu(tf.matmul(flat, W3) + B3)
    logits = tf.matmul(dense, W4) + B4
    prob = tf.nn.sigmoid(logits)
    return prob, logits
```

8. Then we read the data from the MNIST dataset, and define an auxiliary function for plotting samples:

```
import numpy as np
import matplotlib.pyplot as plt
import matplotlib.gridspec as gridspec
import os
import argparse

def read_data():
    from tensorflow.examples.tutorials.mnist import input_data
    mnist = input_data.read_data_sets("../MNIST_data/", one_hot=True)
    return mnist

def plot(samples):
    fig = plt.figure(figsize=(8, 8))
    gs = gridspec.GridSpec(8, 8)
    gs.update(wspace=0.05, hspace=0.05)
    for i, sample in enumerate(samples):
        ax = plt.subplot(gs[i])
        plt.axis('off')
        ax.set_xticklabels([])
        ax.set_yticklabels([])
        ax.set_aspect('equal')
        plt.imshow(sample.reshape(28, 28), cmap='Greys_r')
        return fig
```

9. Now let's define the training function. First, let's read the MNIST data, and then define a matrix X of shape 28 x 28 with one channel for a standard MNIST handwritten character. Then let's define az noise vector of size 100—a common choice proposed in the seminal GANs paper. The next step is to call the generator on z and assign the result to G. After that, we pass X to the discriminator without reuse. Then we pass the forged/fake G result to the discriminator, reusing the learned weight. One important aspect of this is how we chose the loss function for the discriminator, which is a sum of two cross entropies: one for real characters where all the real MNIST characters have a label set to one, and one for forgetting characters where all the forged characters have a label set to zero. The discriminator and the generator run in an alternate sequence for 100,000 steps. Every 500 steps, a sample is drawn from the learned distribution for printing what that generator has learned so far. This is what defines a new epoch, and the results are shown during the next section. The training function code snippet is reported in the following snippet:

```
def train(logdir, batch_size):
    from model_conv import discriminator, generator
```

```
mnist = read_data()
with tf.variable_scope('placeholder'):
  # Raw image
  X = tf.placeholder(tf.float32, [None, 784])
  tf.summary.image('raw image', tf.reshape(X, [-1, 28, 28, 1]), 3)
  # Noise
  z = tf.placeholder(tf.float32, [None, 100]) # noise
  tf.summary.histogram('Noise', z)
with tf.variable_scope('GAN'):
  G = generator(z, batch_size)
  D_real, D_real_logits = discriminator(X, reuse=False)
  D_fake, D_fake_logits = discriminator(G, reuse=True)
  tf.summary.image('generated image', tf.reshape(G, [-1, 28, 28, 1]), 3)

  with tf.variable_scope('Prediction'):
    tf.summary.histogram('real', D_real)
    tf.summary.histogram('fake', D_fake)

  with tf.variable_scope('D_loss'):
    d_loss_real = tf.reduce_mean(
    tf.nn.sigmoid_cross_entropy_with_logits(
logits=D_real_logits, labels=tf.ones_like(D_real_logits)))

    d_loss_fake = tf.reduce_mean(
tf.nn.sigmoid_cross_entropy_with_logits(
logits=D_fake_logits, labels=tf.zeros_like(D_fake_logits)))
    d_loss = d_loss_real + d_loss_fake
    tf.summary.scalar('d_loss_real', d_loss_real)
    tf.summary.scalar('d_loss_fake', d_loss_fake)
    tf.summary.scalar('d_loss', d_loss)

  with tf.name_scope('G_loss'):
    g_loss =   tf.reduce_mean(tf.nn.sigmoid_cross_entropy_with_logits
(logits=D_fake_logits, labels=tf.ones_like(D_fake_logits)))
    tf.summary.scalar('g_loss', g_loss)
    tvar = tf.trainable_variables()
    dvar = [var for var in tvar if 'discriminator' in var.name]
    gvar = [var for var in tvar if 'generator' in var.name]

  with tf.name_scope('train'):
    d_train_step = tf.train.AdamOptimizer().minimize(d_loss, var_list=dvar)
    g_train_step = tf.train.AdamOptimizer().minimize(g_loss, var_list=gvar)

  sess = tf.Session()
  init = tf.global_variables_initializer()
  sess.run(init)
  merged_summary = tf.summary.merge_all()
  writer = tf.summary.FileWriter('tmp/'+'gan_conv_'+logdir)
```

```
    writer.add_graph(sess.graph)
    num_img = 0

    if not os.path.exists('output/'):
        os.makedirs('output/')
    for i in range(100000):
        batch_X, _ = mnist.train.next_batch(batch_size)
        batch_noise = np.random.uniform(-1., 1., [batch_size, 100])
        if i % 500 == 0:
            samples = sess.run(G, feed_dict={z: np.random.uniform(-1., 1., [64,
100])})
            fig = plot(samples)
            plt.savefig('output/%s.png' % str(num_img).zfill(3),
bbox_inches='tight')
            num_img += 1
            plt.close(fig)

        _, d_loss_print = sess.run([d_train_step, d_loss],
feed_dict={X: batch_X, z: batch_noise})
        _, g_loss_print = sess.run([g_train_step, g_loss],
feed_dict={z: batch_noise})

    if i % 100 == 0:
        s = sess.run(merged_summary, feed_dict={X: batch_X, z: batch_noise})
        writer.add_summary(s, i)
        print('epoch:%d g_loss:%f d_loss:%f' % (i, g_loss_print, d_loss_print))

    if __name__ == '__main__':
        parser = argparse.ArgumentParser(description='Train vanila GAN using
convolutional networks')
        parser.add_argument('--logdir', type=str, default='1', help='logdir for
Tensorboard, give a string')
        parser.add_argument('--batch_size', type=int, default=64, help='batch
size: give a int')
        args = parser.parse_args()
        train(logdir=args.logdir, batch_size=args.batch_size)
```

How it works...

Using CNN together with GANs results in a faster capacity to learn. Let's look at a number of practical examples of different epochs to understand how the machine will learn to improve its writing process. For instance, compare the results achieved after four iterations in the following recipe with the results achieved after four iterations in the previous recipe. Do you see the difference? I wish that I could learn this art myself!

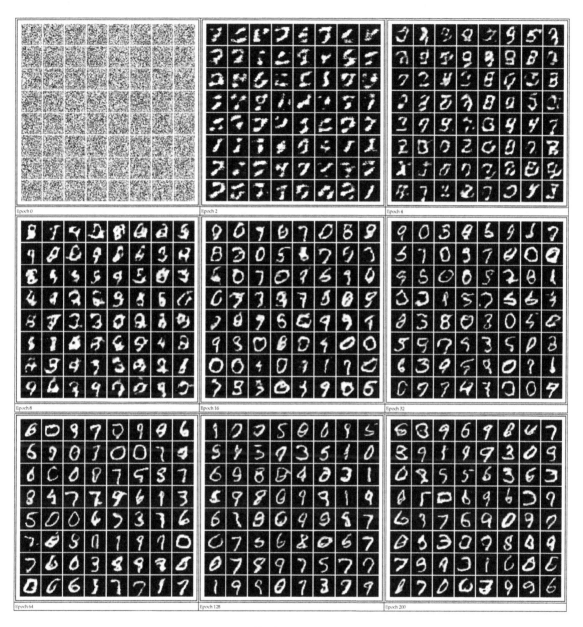

Example of forged MNIST-like with DCGAN

Learning to forge Celebrity Faces and other datasets with DCGAN

The same ideas used for forging MNIST images can be applied to other image domains. In this recipe, you will learn how to use the package located at `https://github.com/carpedm20/DCGAN-tensorflow` to train a DCGAN model on different datasets. The work is based on the paper *Unsupervised Representation Learning with Deep Convolutional Generative Adversarial Networks, Alec Radford, Luke Metz, Soumith Chintal, 2015.* Quoting the abstract:

In recent years, supervised learning with convolutional networks (CNNs) has seen huge adoption in computer vision applications. Comparatively, unsupervised learning with CNNs has received less attention. In this work we hope to help bridge the gap between the success of CNNs for supervised learning and unsupervised learning. We introduce a class of CNNs called deep convolutional generative adversarial networks (DCGANs), that have certain architectural constraints, and demonstrate that they are a strong candidate for unsupervised learning. Training on various image datasets, we show convincing evidence that our deep convolutional adversarial pair learns a hierarchy of representations from object parts to scenes in both the generator and discriminator. Additionally, we use the learned features for novel tasks - demonstrating their applicability as general image representations.

Note that the generator has the architecture represented in the following diagram:

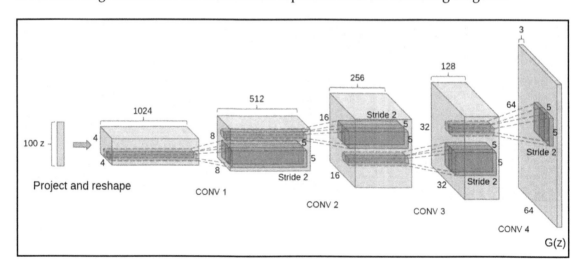

Note that in the package there are changes with respect to the original paper to avoid the fast convergence of D (discriminator) network, G (generator) network is updated twice for each D network update.

Getting ready

This recipe is based on the code available at `https://github.com/carpedm20/DCGAN-tensorflow`.

How to do it...

We proceed with the recipe as follows:

1. Clone the code from Github:

```
git clone https://github.com/carpedm20/DCGAN-tensorflow
```

2. Download the dataset with the following:

```
python download.py mnist celebA
```

3. To train a model with the downloaded dataset, use the following:

```
python main.py --dataset celebA --input_height=108 --train --crop
```

4. To test it with an existing model, use the following:

```
python main.py --dataset celebA --input_height=108 --crop
```

5. Alternatively, you can use your own dataset by doing the following:

```
$ mkdir data/DATASET_NAME
 ... add images to data/DATASET_NAME ...
 $ python main.py --dataset DATASET_NAME --train
 $ python main.py --dataset DATASET_NAME
 $ # example
 $ python main.py --dataset=eyes --input_fname_pattern="*_cropped.png" --
train
```

How it works...

The generator learns how to produce forged images of celebrities and the discriminator learns how to distinguish the forged images from the real ones. Each epoch in the two networks competes to improve and reduce losses. The first five epochs are reported in the following table:

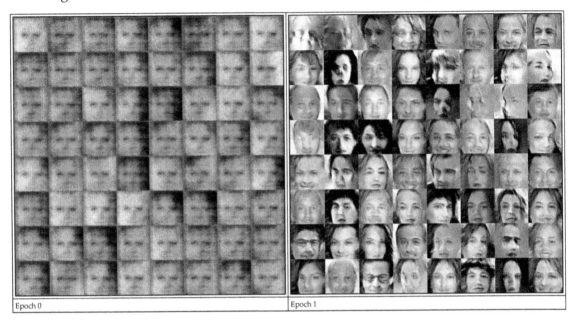

Epoch 0   Epoch 1

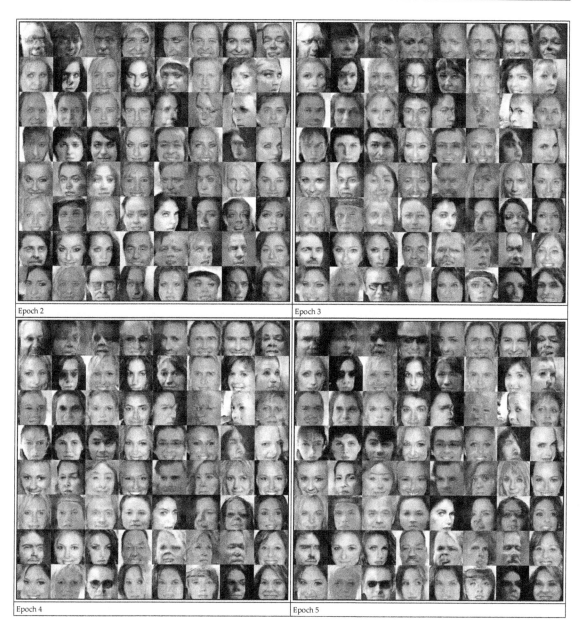

Epoch 2

Epoch 3

Epoch 4

Epoch 5

Example of forged celebrities with a DCGAN

There's more...

Content-aware fill is a tool used by photographers to fill in unwanted or missing parts of images. The paper `Semantic Image Inpainting with Perceptual and Contextual Losses`, by Raymond A. Yeh, Chen Chen, Teck Yian Lim, Alexander G. Schwing, Mark Hasegawa-Johnson, Minh N., 2016 uses a DCGAN for image completion, and it learns how to fill in parts of images.

Implementing Variational Autoencoders

Variational Autoencoders (**VAE**) are a mix of the best of both worlds of the neural networks and the Bayesian inference. They are the coolest neural networks and have emerged as one of the popular approaches to unsupervised learning. They are Autoencoders with a twist. Along with the conventional Encoder and the Decoder network of the Autoencoders (see Chapter 8, *Autoencoders*), they have additional stochastic layers.

The stochastic layer, after the Encoder network, samples the data using a Gaussian distribution, and the one after the Decoder network samples the data using Bernoulli's distribution.

Like GANs, Variational Autoencoders can be used to generate images and figures based on the distribution they have been trained on. VAEs allow one to set complex priors in the latent and thus learn powerful latent representations.

The following diagram describes a VAE. The Encoder network $q_\Phi(z|x)$ approximates the true but intractable posterior distribution $p(z|x)$, where x is the input to the VAE and z is the latent representation. The decoder network $p_\theta(x|z)$ takes the d-dimensional latent variables (also called latent space) as its input and generate new images following the same distribution as $P(x)$. The latent representation z is sampled from $z|x \sim N(\mu_{z|x}, \Sigma z|x$, and the output of the decoder network samples $x|z$ from $x|z \sim N(\mu_{x|z}, \Sigma x|z$:

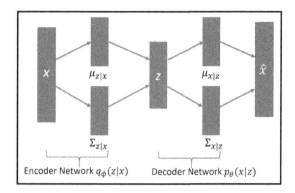

Example of Encoder-Decoder for Autoencoders.

Getting ready...

Now that we have the basic architecture of VAEs, the question arises how can they be trained, since the maximum likelihood of the training data and posterior density are intractable? The network is trained by maximizing the lower bound of the log data likelihood. Thus, the loss term consists of two components: generation loss, which is obtained from the decoder network through sampling, and the KL divergence term, also called the latent loss.

Generation loss ensures that the image generated by the decoder and the image used to train the network is the same, and latent loss ensures that the posterior distribution $q_\phi(z|x)$ is close to the prior $p_\theta(z)$. Since the encoder uses Gaussian distribution for sampling, the latent loss measures how closely the latent variables match a unit Gaussian.

Once the VAE is trained, we can use only the decoder network to generate new images.

How to do it...

The code here is based on the paper Autoencoding Variational Bayes by Kingma and Welling (`https://arxiv.org/pdf/1312.6114.pdf`), and is adapted from GitHub: `https://jmetzen.github.io/2015-11-27/vae.html`.

1. The first step is as always importing the necessary modules. For this recipe we will require Numpy, Matplolib, and TensorFlow:

```
import numpy as np
import tensorflow as tf
import matplotlib.pyplot as plt
%matplotlib inline
```

2. Next, we define the VariationalAutoencoder class. The `class __init__` `method` defines the hyperparameters such as the learning rate, batch size, the placeholders for the input, and the weight and bias variables for the encoder and decoder network. It also builds the computational graph according to the network architecture of the VAE. We initialize the weights using Xavier initialization in this recipe. Instead of defining our own method for Xavier initialization, we use the `tf.contrib.layers.xavier_initializer()` TensorFlow to do the task. Lastly, we define the loss (generation and latent) and optimizer ops:

```
class VariationalAutoencoder(object):
  def __init__(self, network_architecture,    transfer_fct=tf.nn.softplus,
learning_rate=0.001, batch_size=100):
      self.network_architecture = network_architecture
      self.transfer_fct = transfer_fct
      self.learning_rate = learning_rate
      self.batch_size = batch_size
      # Place holder for the input
      self.x = tf.placeholder(tf.float32, [None,
network_architecture["n_input"]])
      # Define weights and biases
      network_weights =
self._initialize_weights(**self.network_architecture)
      # Create autoencoder network
      # Use Encoder Network to determine mean and
      # (log) variance of Gaussian distribution in latent
      # space
      self.z_mean, self.z_log_sigma_sq = \
      self._encoder_network(network_weights["weights_encoder"],
    network_weights["biases_encoder"])
      # Draw one sample z from Gaussian distribution
      n_z = self.network_architecture["n_z"]
      eps = tf.random_normal((self.batch_size, n_z), 0, 1,
dtype=tf.float32)
      # z = mu + sigma*epsilon
      self.z =
tf.add(self.z_mean,tf.multiply(tf.sqrt(tf.exp(self.z_log_sigma_sq)), eps))
      # Use Decoder network to determine mean of
```

```
    # Bernoulli distribution of reconstructed input
    self.x_reconstr_mean = \
    self._decoder_network(network_weights["weights_decoder"],
  network_weights["biases_decoder"])
    # Define loss function based variational upper-bound and
    # corresponding optimizer
    # define generation loss
    generation_loss = \
  -tf.reduce_sum(self.x * tf.log(1e-10 + self.x_reconstr_mean)
+ (1-self.x) * tf.log(1e-10 + 1 - self.x_reconstr_mean), 1)
    latent_loss = -0.5 * tf.reduce_sum(1 + self.z_log_sigma_sq
- tf.square(self.z_mean)- tf.exp(self.z_log_sigma_sq), 1)
    self.cost = tf.reduce_mean(generation_loss + latent_loss)      #
average over batch
    # Define the optimizer
    self.optimizer = \
tf.train.AdamOptimizer(learning_rate=self.learning_rate).minimize(self.cost
)
    # Initializing the tensor flow variables
    init = tf.global_variables_initializer()
  # Launch the session
    self.sess = tf.InteractiveSession()
    self.sess.run(init)
def _initialize_weights(self, n_hidden_recog_1, n_hidden_recog_2,
n_hidden_gener_1, n_hidden_gener_2,
n_input, n_z):
  initializer = tf.contrib.layers.xavier_initializer()
  all_weights = dict()
  all_weights['weights_encoder'] = {
  'h1': tf.Variable(initializer(shape=(n_input, n_hidden_recog_1))),
  'h2': tf.Variable(initializer(shape=(n_hidden_recog_1,
n_hidden_recog_2))),
  'out_mean': tf.Variable(initializer(shape=(n_hidden_recog_2, n_z))),
  'out_log_sigma': tf.Variable(initializer(shape=(n_hidden_recog_2,
n_z)))}
  all_weights['biases_encoder'] = {
  'b1': tf.Variable(tf.zeros([n_hidden_recog_1], dtype=tf.float32)),
  'b2': tf.Variable(tf.zeros([n_hidden_recog_2], dtype=tf.float32)),
  'out_mean': tf.Variable(tf.zeros([n_z], dtype=tf.float32)),
  'out_log_sigma': tf.Variable(tf.zeros([n_z], dtype=tf.float32))}

  all_weights['weights_decoder'] = {
  'h1': tf.Variable(initializer(shape=(n_z, n_hidden_gener_1))),
  'h2': tf.Variable(initializer(shape=(n_hidden_gener_1,
n_hidden_gener_2))),
  'out_mean': tf.Variable(initializer(shape=(n_hidden_gener_2, n_input))),
  'out_log_sigma': tf.Variable(initializer(shape=(n_hidden_gener_2,
n_input)))}
```

```
      all_weights['biases_decoder'] = {
      'b1': tf.Variable(tf.zeros([n_hidden_gener_1],      dtype=tf.float32)),
      'b2': tf.Variable(tf.zeros([n_hidden_gener_2],
dtype=tf.float32)),'out_mean': tf.Variable(tf.zeros([n_input],
dtype=tf.float32)),
      'out_log_sigma': tf.Variable(tf.zeros([n_input], dtype=tf.float32))}
      return all_weights
```

3. We build the encoder network and the decoder network. The first layer of the Encoder network is taking the input and generating a reduced latent representation of the input. The second layer maps the input to a Gaussian distribution. The network learns these transformations:

```
def _encoder_network(self, weights, biases):
  # Generate probabilistic encoder (recognition network), which
  # maps inputs onto a normal distribution in latent space.
  # The transformation is parametrized and can be learned.
  layer_1 = self.transfer_fct(tf.add(tf.matmul(self.x,      weights['h1']),
biases['b1']))
  layer_2 = self.transfer_fct(tf.add(tf.matmul(layer_1,   weights['h2']),
biases['b2']))
  z_mean = tf.add(tf.matmul(layer_2, weights['out_mean']),
biases['out_mean'])
  z_log_sigma_sq = \
tf.add(tf.matmul(layer_2, weights['out_log_sigma']),
biases['out_log_sigma'])
  return (z_mean, z_log_sigma_sq)

def _decoder_network(self, weights, biases):
  # Generate probabilistic decoder (decoder network), which
  # maps points in latent space onto a Bernoulli distribution in data
space.
  # The transformation is parametrized and can be learned.
  layer_1 = self.transfer_fct(tf.add(tf.matmul(self.z, weights['h1']),
biases['b1']))
  layer_2 = self.transfer_fct(tf.add(tf.matmul(layer_1, weights['h2']),
biases['b2']))
  x_reconstr_mean = \
tf.nn.sigmoid(tf.add(tf.matmul(layer_2, weights['out_mean']),
  biases['out_mean']))
  return x_reconstr_mean
```

4. The class `VariationalAutoencoder` also contains some helper functions to generate and reconstruct data, and to fit the VAE:

```
def fit(self, X):
    opt, cost = self.sess.run((self.optimizer, self.cost),
    feed_dict={self.x: X})
    return cost

def generate(self, z_mu=None):
""" Generate data by sampling from latent space.
If z_mu is not None, data for this point in latent space is
generated. Otherwise, z_mu is drawn from prior in latent
space.
"""
    if z_mu is None:
        z_mu = np.random.normal(size=self.network_architecture["n_z"])
# Note: This maps to mean of distribution, we could alternatively
# sample from Gaussian distribution
    return self.sess.run(self.x_reconstr_mean,
        feed_dict={self.z: z_mu})

def reconstruct(self, X):
""" Use VAE to reconstruct given data. """
    return self.sess.run(self.x_reconstr_mean,
        feed_dict={self.x: X})
```

5. Once the VAE class is done, we define a function train, which uses the VAE class object and trains it for a given data.

```
def train(network_architecture, learning_rate=0.001,
batch_size=100, training_epochs=10, display_step=5):
    vae = VariationalAutoencoder(network_architecture,
    learning_rate=learning_rate,
    batch_size=batch_size)
    # Training cycle
    for epoch in range(training_epochs):
        avg_cost = 0.
        total_batch = int(n_samples / batch_size)
        # Loop over all batches
        for i in range(total_batch):
            batch_xs, _ = mnist.train.next_batch(batch_size)
            # Fit training using batch data
            cost = vae.fit(batch_xs)
            # Compute average loss
            avg_cost += cost / n_samples * batch_size
            # Display logs per epoch step
        if epoch % display_step == 0:
```

```
      print("Epoch:", '%04d' % (epoch+1),
          "cost=", "{:.9f}".format(avg_cost))
   return vae
```

6. Let us now use the VAE class and train function. We use the VAE for our favorite MNIST dataset:

```
# Load MNIST data in a format suited for tensorflow.
# The script input_data is available under this URL:
#https://raw.githubusercontent.com/tensorflow/tensorflow/master/tensorflow/
examples/tutorials/mnist/input_data.py

from tensorflow.examples.tutorials.mnist import input_data
mnist = input_data.read_data_sets('MNIST_data', one_hot=True)
n_samples = mnist.train.num_examples
```

7. We define the network-architecture and perform training of VAE on MNIST dataset. In this case, we keep the latent dimensions 2 for simplicity.

```
network_architecture = \
dict(n_hidden_recog_1=500, # 1st layer encoder neurons
n_hidden_recog_2=500, # 2nd layer encoder neurons
n_hidden_gener_1=500, # 1st layer decoder neurons
n_hidden_gener_2=500, # 2nd layer decoder neurons
n_input=784, # MNIST data input (img shape: 28*28)
n_z=2) # dimensionality of latent space
vae = train(network_architecture, training_epochs=75)
```

8. Let us now see if the VAE really reconstructs the input or not. The output shows that digits are indeed reconstructed, and since we have used a 2D latent space, there is a significant blurring of the images:

```
x_sample = mnist.test.next_batch(100)[0]
x_reconstruct = vae.reconstruct(x_sample)
plt.figure(figsize=(8, 12))
for i in range(5):
  plt.subplot(5, 2, 2*i + 1)
  plt.imshow(x_sample[i].reshape(28, 28),   vmin=0, vmax=1, cmap="gray")
  plt.title("Test input")
  plt.colorbar()
  plt.subplot(5, 2, 2*i + 2)
  plt.imshow(x_reconstruct[i].reshape(28, 28), vmin=0, vmax=1, cmap="gray")
  plt.title("Reconstruction")
  plt.colorbar()
  plt.tight_layout()
```

Following is the output of the preceding code:

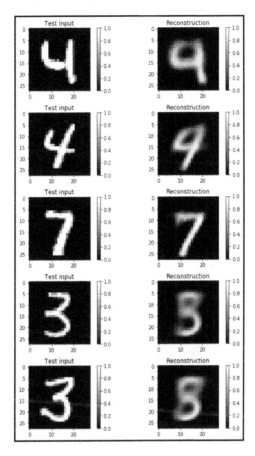

An example of MNIST reconstructed characters

9. The following are the samples of handwritten digits generated using the trained VAE:

```
nx = ny = 20
x_values = np.linspace(-3, 3, nx)
y_values = np.linspace(-3, 3, ny)
canvas = np.empty((28*ny, 28*nx))
for i, yi in enumerate(x_values):
  for j, xi in enumerate(y_values):
    z_mu = np.array([[xi, yi]]*vae.batch_size)
    x_mean = vae.generate(z_mu)
    canvas[(nx-i-1)*28:(nx-i)*28, j*28:(j+1)*28] = x_mean[0].reshape(28,
28)
plt.figure(figsize=(8, 10))
Xi, Yi = np.meshgrid(x_values, y_values)
plt.imshow(canvas, origin="upper", cmap="gray")
plt.tight_layout()
```

Following is the range of MNIST like characters generated by autoencoders:

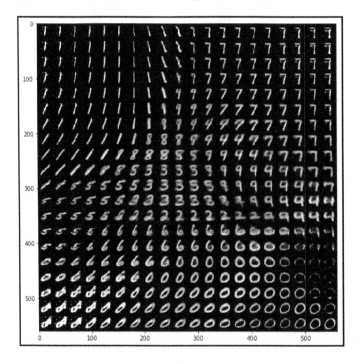

A range of MNIST like characters generated by autoencoders

How it works...

VAE learns to reconstruct and at the same time generate new images. The generated images are dependent upon the latent space. The images generated have the same distribution as the dataset they are trained on.

We can also see the data in the latent space by defining a transform function within the VariationalAutoencoder class:

```
def transform(self, X):
    """Transform data by mapping it into the latent space."""
    # Note: This maps to mean of distribution, we could alternatively
sample from Gaussian distribution
    return self.sess.run(self.z_mean,   feed_dict={self.x: X})
```

The latent representation of the MNIST dataset using the transform function is as follows:

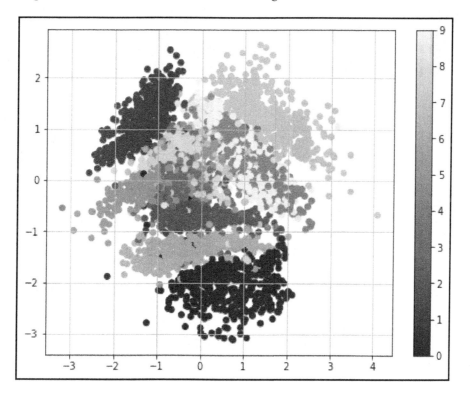

There's More...

The generated images of the VAE depend on the latent space dimensions. The blurring reduces the dimension of the latent space is increased. The reconstructed images for 5-d, 10-d, and 20-d latent dimensions respectively, are as follows:

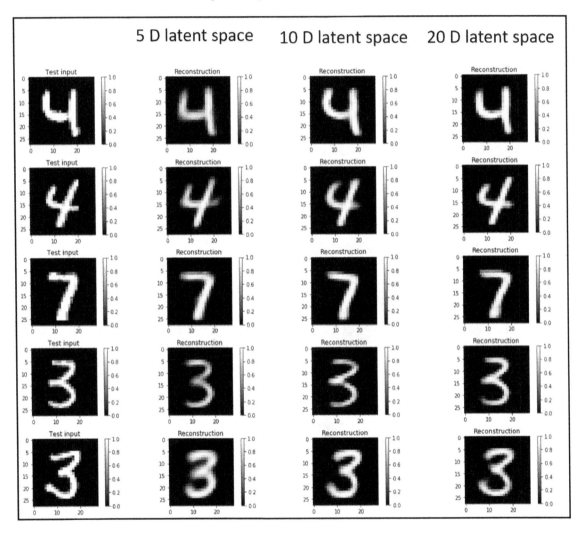

See also...

- The paper by Kingma and Welling is the seminal paper in this field. They go through the complete building thought process along with its elegant maths. For anyone interested in VAEs, this is a must read: `https://arxiv.org/pdf/1312.6114.pdf` .

- Another interesting read is the paper by Carl Doersch, A Tutorial on Variational Encoders: `https://arxiv.org/pdf/1606.05908.pdf`.

- The Github link contains another implementation of VAEs, along with the reproduction of the images from the Kingma and Welling paper: `https://github.com/hwalsuklee/tensorflow-mnist-VAE`.

Learning to beat the previous MNIST state-of-the-art results with Capsule Networks

Capsule Networks (or CapsNets) is a very recent and innovative type of deep learning network. This technique was introduced at the end of October 2017 in a seminal paper titled Dynamic Routing Between Capsules by Sara Sabour, Nicholas Frost and Geoffrey Hinton (`https://arxiv.org/abs/1710.09829`). Hinton is one of the fathers of Deep Learning and, therefore, the whole Deep Learning community is excited to see the progress made with capsules. Indeed, CapsNets are already beating the best CNN at MNIST classification which is... well, impressive!

So what is the problem with CNNs? In CNNs each layer *understands* an image at a progressive level of granularity. As we discussed in multiple recipes, the first layer will most likely recognize straight lines or simple curves and edges, while subsequent layers will start to understand more complex shapes such as rectangles and complex forms such as human faces.

Now, one critical operation used for CNNs is pooling. Pooling aims to create the positional invariance and it is generally used after each CNN layer to make any problem computationally tractable. However, pooling introduces a significant problem because it forces us to lose all the positional data. This is not good. Think about a face: it consists in two eyes, a mouth, and a nose, and what is important is that there is a spatial relationship between these parts (the mouth is below the nose, which is typically below the eyes). Indeed, Hinton said:

> *The pooling operation used in convolutional neural networks is a big mistake and the fact that it works so well is a disaster.*

Technically, we do not need positional invariance; instead, we need equivariance. Equivariance is a fancy term for indicating that we want to understand the rotation or proportion change in an image, and we want to adapt the network accordingly. In this way, the spatial positioning of the different components in an image is not lost.

So what is new with Capsule Networks? According to the authors, our brain has modules called **capsules**, and each capsule specializes in handling particular types of information. In particular, there are capsules that work well for understanding the concept of position, the concept of size, the concept of orientation, the concept of deformation, the textures, and so on and so forth. In addition to that, the authors suggest that our brain has particularly efficient mechanisms for dynamically routing each piece of information to the capsule, which is considered best suited for handling a particular type of information.

So, the main difference between CNN and CapsNets is that with a CNN you keep adding layers for creating a deep network, while with CapsNet you nest a neural layer inside another. A capsule is a group of neurons and introduces more structure in the net; it produces a vector to signal the existence of an entity in the image. In particular, Hinton uses the length of the activity vector to represent the probability that the entity exists, and its orientation to represent the instantiation parameters. When multiple predictions agree, a higher-level capsule becomes active. For each possible parent, the capsule produces an additional prediction vector.

Now a second innovation comes in place: we will use dynamic routing across capsules and will no longer use the raw idea of pooling. A lower-level capsule prefers to send its output to the higher-level capsule, and the activity vectors have a big scalar product, with the prediction coming from the lower-level capsule. The parent with the largest scalar prediction vector product increases the capsule bond. All the other parents decrease their bond.

In other words, the idea is that if a higher-level capsule agrees with a lower level one, then it will ask to send more information of that type. If there is no agreement, it will ask to send less of them. This dynamic routing using the agreement method is superior to the current mechanisms such as max-pooling and, according to Hinton, routing is ultimately a way to parse the image. Indeed, Max-pooling is ignoring anything but the largest value, while dynamic routing selectively propagates information according to the agreement between lower layers and upper layers.

A third difference is that a new nonlinear activation function has been introduced. Instead of adding a squashing function to each layer as in CNN, CapsNet adds a squashing function to a nested set of layers. The nonlinear activation function is represented in the following figure and it is called the squashing function (equation 1):

$$\mathbf{v}_j = \frac{||\mathbf{s}_j||^2}{1 + ||\mathbf{s}_j||^2} \frac{\mathbf{s}_j}{||\mathbf{s}_j||} \tag{1}$$

where $\mathbf{v}_j$ is the vector output of capsule j and $\mathbf{s}_j$ is its total input.

Squashing function as seen in Hinton's seminal paper

Moreover, Hinton and others show that a discriminatively trained, multi-layer capsule system achieves state-of-the-art performance on MNIST and is considerably better than a convolutional network at recognizing highly overlapping digits.

The paper *Dynamic Routing Between Capsules* shows us simple CapsNet architecture:

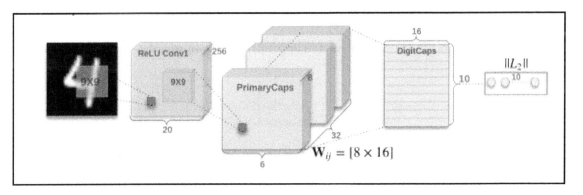

A simple CapsNet architecture

The architecture is shallow, with only two convolutional layers and one fully connected layer. Conv1 has 256, 9×9 convolution kernels with a stride of 1, and ReLU activation. The role of this layer is to convert pixel intensities to the activities of local feature detectors that are then used as input to the primary capsules. PrimaryCapsules is a convolutional capsule layer with 32 channels; each primary capsule contains eight convolutional units with a 9×9 kernel and a stride of 2. In total, PrimaryCapsules has [32, 6, 6] capsule outputs (each output is an 8D vector) and each capsule in the [6, 6] grid is sharing its weight with each other. The final layer (DigitCaps) has one 16D capsule per digit class and each one of these capsules receives input from all the other capsules in the layer below. Routing happens only between two consecutive capsule layers (such as PrimaryCapsules and DigitCaps).

Getting ready

This recipe is based on the code available at `https://github.com/debarko/CapsNet-Tensorflow`, which in its turn is based on the code located at `https://github.com/naturomics/CapsNet-Tensorflow.git`.

How to do it...

Here is how is how we proceed with the recipe:

1. Clone the code from github under an Apache Licence:

```
git clone https://github.com/naturomics/CapsNet-Tensorflow.git
 $ cd CapsNet-Tensorflow
```

2. Download MNIST and create the appropriate structure:

```
mkdir -p data/mnist
wget -c -P data/mnist \\
http://yann.lecun.com/exdb/mnist/{train-images-idx3-ubyte.gz,train-labels-i
dx1-ubyte.gz,t10k-images-idx3-ubyte.gz,t10k-labels-idx1-ubyte.gz}
gunzip data/mnist/*.gz
```

3. Start the training process:

```
python main.py
```

4. Let's see the code used for defining a capsule. Each capsule takes a 4D tensor as input and returns a 4D tensor. It is possible to define a capsule as either a fully connected network (the DigiCaps) or a convolutional one (the Primary Capsules). Note that Primary is a collection of ConvNets and after them the nonlinear squashing function is applied. Primary capsules will communicate with DigiCaps via dynamic routing:

```python
# capsLayer.py
#
import numpy as np
import tensorflow as tf
from config import cfg
epsilon = 1e-9
class CapsLayer(object):
''' Capsule layer.
Args:
input: A 4-D tensor.
num_outputs: the number of capsule in this layer.
vec_len: integer, the length of the output vector of a capsule.
layer_type: string, one of 'FC' or "CONV", the type of this layer,
fully connected or convolution, for the future expansion capability
with_routing: boolean, this capsule is routing with the
lower-level layer capsule.
Returns:
A 4-D tensor.
'''
def __init__(self, num_outputs, vec_len, with_routing=True,
layer_type='FC'):
  self.num_outputs = num_outputs
  self.vec_len = vec_len
  self.with_routing = with_routing
  self.layer_type = layer_type

def __call__(self, input, kernel_size=None, stride=None):
'''
The parameters 'kernel_size' and 'stride' will be used while 'layer_type'
equal 'CONV'
'''
  if self.layer_type == 'CONV':
    self.kernel_size = kernel_size
    self.stride = stride

    if not self.with_routing:
    # the PrimaryCaps layer, a convolutional layer
    # input: [batch_size, 20, 20, 256]
      assert input.get_shape() ==  [cfg.batch_size, 20, 20, 256]
```

```
        capsules = []
        for i in range(self.vec_len):
          # each capsule i: [batch_size, 6, 6, 32]
          with tf.variable_scope('ConvUnit_' + str(i)):
            caps_i = tf.contrib.layers.conv2d(input,        self.num_outputs,
self.kernel_size, self.stride,
padding="VALID")
            caps_i = tf.reshape(caps_i, shape=(cfg.batch_size, -1, 1, 1))
            capsules.append(caps_i)
        assert capsules[0].get_shape() == [cfg.batch_size, 1152, 1, 1]
# [batch_size, 1152, 8, 1]
        capsules = tf.concat(capsules, axis=2)
        capsules = squash(capsules)
        assert capsules.get_shape() == [cfg.batch_size, 1152, 8, 1]
        return(capsules)

    if self.layer_type == 'FC':
      if self.with_routing:
        # the DigitCaps layer, a fully connected layer
        # Reshape the input into [batch_size, 1152, 1, 8, 1]
        self.input = tf.reshape(input, shape=(cfg.batch_size, -1, 1,
input.shape[-2].value, 1))
      with tf.variable_scope('routing'):
        # b_IJ: [1, num_caps_l, num_caps_l_plus_1, 1, 1]
        b_IJ = tf.constant(np.zeros([1, input.shape[1].value,
self.num_outputs, 1, 1], dtype=np.float32))
        capsules = routing(self.input, b_IJ)
        capsules = tf.squeeze(capsules, axis=1)
      return(capsules)
```

5. The routing algorithm is described in the paper *Dynamic Routing Between Capsules* and the relevant section of the paper has been explained, together with the definition of Equation 2 and Equation 3. The goal of the routing algorithm is to pass information from lower layer capsules into higher-level ones and *understand* where there is agreement. The agreement is computed by simply using a scalar product between the current output v_j of each capsule j in the layer above, and the prediction $\hat{u}_{j|i}$ made by the capsule i:

For all but the first layer of capsules, the total input to a capsule s_j is a weighted sum over all "prediction vectors" $\hat{u}_{j|i}$ from the capsules in the layer below and is produced by multiplying the output u_i of a capsule in the layer below by a weight matrix W_{ij}

$$s_j = \sum_i c_{ij} \hat{u}_{j|i}, \qquad \hat{u}_{j|i} = W_{ij} u_i \qquad (2)$$

where the c_{ij} are coupling coefficients that are determined by the iterative dynamic routing process.

The coupling coefficients between capsule i and all the capsules in the layer above sum to 1 and are determined by a "routing softmax" whose initial logits b_{ij} are the log prior probabilities that capsule i

---

should be coupled to capsule j.

$$c_{ij} = \frac{\exp(b_{ij})}{\sum_k \exp(b_{ik})} \qquad (3)$$

The log priors can be learned discriminatively at the same time as all the other weights. They depend on the location and type of the two capsules but not on the current input image[2]. The initial coupling coefficients are then iteratively refined by measuring the agreement between the current output v_j of each capsule, j, in the layer above and the prediction $\hat{u}_{j|i}$ made by capsule i.

The agreement is simply the scalar product $a_{ij} = \mathbf{v}_j.\hat{\mathbf{u}}_{j|i}$. This agreement is treated as if it were a log likelihood and is added to the initial logit, b_{ij} before computing the new values for all the coupling coefficients linking capsule i to higher level capsules.

In convolutional capsule layers each unit in a capsule is a convolutional unit. Therefore, each capsule will output a grid of vectors rather than a single vector output.

Procedure 1 Routing algorithm.

1: **procedure** ROUTING($\hat{\mathbf{u}}_{j|i}, r, l$)
2:      for all capsule i in layer l and capsule j in layer $(l+1)$: $b_{ij} \leftarrow 0$.
3:      **for** r iterations **do**
4:          for all capsule i in layer l: $\mathbf{c}_i \leftarrow \texttt{softmax}(\mathbf{b}_i)$ ▷ `softmax` computes Eq. 3
5:          for all capsule j in layer $(l+1)$: $\mathbf{s}_j \leftarrow \sum_i c_{ij}\hat{\mathbf{u}}_{j|i}$
6:          for all capsule j in layer $(l+1)$: $\mathbf{v}_j \leftarrow \texttt{squash}(\mathbf{s}_j)$ ▷ `squash` computes Eq. 1
7:          for all capsule i in layer l and capsule j in layer $(l+1)$: $b_{ij} \leftarrow b_{ij} + \hat{\mathbf{u}}_{j|i}.\mathbf{v}_j$
        return $\mathbf{v}_j$

The following method implements the steps described in Procedure 1 in the preceding images. Note that the input is a 4D tensor from 1,152 capsules in the layer l. The output is a Tensor of shape `[batch_size, 1, length(v_j)=16, 1]` representing the vector output `v_j` of capsule j in the layer l+1:

```
def routing(input, b_IJ):
''' The routing algorithm.
Args:
input: A Tensor with [batch_size, num_caps_l=1152, 1, length(u_i)=8, 1]
shape, num_caps_l meaning the number of capsule in the layer l.
Returns:
A Tensor of shape [batch_size, num_caps_l_plus_1, length(v_j)=16, 1]
representing the vector output `v_j` in the layer l+1
Notes:
u_i represents the vector output of capsule i in the layer l, and
v_j the vector output of capsule j in the layer l+1.
'''
    # W: [num_caps_j, num_caps_i, len_u_i, len_v_j]
    W = tf.get_variable('Weight', shape=(1, 1152, 10, 8, 16),
dtype=tf.float32,
    initializer=tf.random_normal_initializer(stddev=cfg.stddev))
    # Eq.2, calc u_hat
    # do tiling for input and W before matmul
    # input => [batch_size, 1152, 10, 8, 1]
    # W => [batch_size, 1152, 10, 8, 16]
    input = tf.tile(input, [1, 1, 10, 1, 1])
    W = tf.tile(W, [cfg.batch_size, 1, 1, 1, 1])
```

```
assert input.get_shape() == [cfg.batch_size, 1152, 10, 8, 1]
# in last 2 dims:
# [8, 16].T x [8, 1] => [16, 1] => [batch_size, 1152, 10, 16, 1]
u_hat = tf.matmul(W, input, transpose_a=True)
assert u_hat.get_shape() == [cfg.batch_size, 1152, 10, 16, 1]
# line 3,for r iterations do
for r_iter in range(cfg.iter_routing):
  with tf.variable_scope('iter_' + str(r_iter)):
    # line 4:
    # => [1, 1152, 10, 1, 1]
    c_IJ = tf.nn.softmax(b_IJ, dim=2)
    c_IJ = tf.tile(c_IJ, [cfg.batch_size, 1, 1, 1, 1])
    assert c_IJ.get_shape() == [cfg.batch_size, 1152, 10, 1, 1]
    # line 5:
    # weighting u_hat with c_IJ, element-wise in the last two dims
    # => [batch_size, 1152, 10, 16, 1]
    s_J = tf.multiply(c_IJ, u_hat)
    # then sum in the second dim, resulting in [batch_size, 1, 10, 16, 1]
    s_J = tf.reduce_sum(s_J, axis=1, keep_dims=True)
    assert s_J.get_shape() == [cfg.batch_size, 1, 10, 16, 16]
    # line 6:
    # squash using Eq.1,
    v_J = squash(s_J)
    assert v_J.get_shape() == [cfg.batch_size, 1, 10, 16, 1]
    # line 7:
    # reshape & tile v_j from [batch_size ,1, 10, 16, 1] to [batch_size,
10, 1152, 16, 1]
    # then matmul in the last tow dim: [16, 1].T x [16, 1] => [1, 1],
reduce mean in the
    # batch_size dim, resulting in [1, 1152, 10, 1, 1]
    v_J_tiled = tf.tile(v_J, [1, 1152, 1, 1, 1])
    u_produce_v = tf.matmul(u_hat, v_J_tiled, transpose_a=True)
    assert u_produce_v.get_shape() == [cfg.batch_size, 1152, 10, 1, 1]
    b_IJ += tf.reduce_sum(u_produce_v, axis=0, keep_dims=True)
  return(v_J)
```

6. Now let us review the nonlinear activation squashing function. The input is a 4D vector with the shape `[batch_size, num_caps, vec_len, 1]` and the output is a 4-D tensor with the same shape as a vector but squashed in the third and fourth dimensions. Given a vector input, the goal is to compute the value represented in the Equation 1 which is shown as follows:

$$\mathbf{v}_j = \frac{\|\mathbf{s}_j\|^2}{1 + \|\mathbf{s}_j\|^2} \frac{\mathbf{s}_j}{\|\mathbf{s}_j\|} \tag{1}$$

where $\mathbf{v}_j$ is the vector output of capsule j and $\mathbf{s}_j$ is its total input.

```
def squash(vector):
'''Squashing function corresponding to Eq. 1
Args:
vector: A 5-D tensor with shape [batch_size, 1, num_caps, vec_len, 1],
Returns:
A 5-D tensor with the same shape as vector but squashed in 4rd and 5th
dimensions.
'''
  vec_squared_norm = tf.reduce_sum(tf.square(vector), -2, keep_dims=True)
  scalar_factor = vec_squared_norm / (1 + vec_squared_norm) /
tf.sqrt(vec_squared_norm + epsilon)
  vec_squashed = scalar_factor * vector # element-wise
return(vec_squashed)
```

7. During the previous steps, we have defined what a capsule is, the dynamic routing algorithm among capsules, and the nonlinear squashing function. Now we can define the proper CapsNet. A loss function is built for training and the Adam Optimizer is chosen. The method `build_arch(...)` defines the CapsNet represented in the following figure:

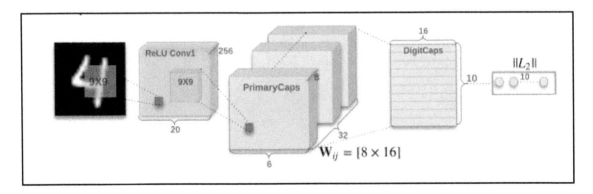

Note that the paper describes a technique of reconstruction as a regularization method. From the paper:

> *We use an additional reconstruction loss to encourage the digit capsules to encode the instantiation parameters of the input digit. During training, we mask out all but the activity vector of the correct digit capsule.*

Then we use this activity vector to reconstruct.

The output of the digit capsule is fed into a decoder consisting of three fully connected layers that model the pixel intensities as described in Fig. 2. We minimize the sum of squared differences between the output of the logistic units and the pixel intensities. We scale down this reconstruction loss by 0.0005 so that it does not dominate the margin loss during training. The method `build_arch(..)` implemented as follows is also used for creating the Decoder:

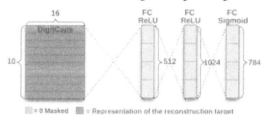

Figure 2: Decoder structure to reconstruct a digit from the DigitCaps layer representation. The euclidean distance between the image and the output of the Sigmoid layer is minimized during training. We use the true label as reconstruction target during training.

```
#capsNet.py
#
import tensorflow as tf
from config import cfg
from utils import get_batch_data
from capsLayer import CapsLayer
epsilon = 1e-9

class CapsNet(object):
  def __init__(self, is_training=True):
    self.graph = tf.Graph()
    with self.graph.as_default():
      if is_training:
        self.X, self.labels = get_batch_data()
        self.Y = tf.one_hot(self.labels, depth=10, axis=1,
```

```
dtype=tf.float32)
        self.build_arch()
        self.loss()
        self._summary()

        # t_vars = tf.trainable_variables()
        self.global_step = tf.Variable(0, name='global_step',
trainable=False)
        self.optimizer = tf.train.AdamOptimizer()
        self.train_op =    self.optimizer.minimize(self.total_loss,
global_step=self.global_step) # var_list=t_vars)

    elif cfg.mask_with_y:
      self.X = tf.placeholder(tf.float32,
        shape=(cfg.batch_size, 28, 28, 1))
      self.Y = tf.placeholder(tf.float32, shape=(cfg.batch_size, 10, 1))
      self.build_arch()
    else:
      self.X = tf.placeholder(tf.float32,
      shape=(cfg.batch_size, 28, 28, 1))
      self.build_arch()
    tf.logging.info('Setting up the main structure')

def build_arch(self):
  with tf.variable_scope('Conv1_layer'):
    # Conv1, [batch_size, 20, 20, 256]
    conv1 = tf.contrib.layers.conv2d(self.X, num_outputs=256,
      kernel_size=9, stride=1,
      padding='VALID')
    assert conv1.get_shape() == [cfg.batch_size, 20, 20, 256]# Primary
Capsules layer, return [batch_size, 1152, 8, 1]

  with tf.variable_scope('PrimaryCaps_layer'):
    primaryCaps = CapsLayer(num_outputs=32, vec_len=8,
with_routing=False, layer_type='CONV')
    caps1 = primaryCaps(conv1, kernel_size=9, stride=2)
    assert caps1.get_shape() == [cfg.batch_size, 1152, 8, 1]

  # DigitCaps layer, return [batch_size, 10, 16, 1]
  with tf.variable_scope('DigitCaps_layer'):
    digitCaps = CapsLayer(num_outputs=10, vec_len=16,   with_routing=True,
layer_type='FC')
    self.caps2 = digitCaps(caps1)

  # Decoder structure in Fig. 2
  # 1. Do masking, how:
  with tf.variable_scope('Masking'):
    # a). calc ||v_c||, then do softmax(||v_c||)
```

```
    # [batch_size, 10, 16, 1] => [batch_size, 10, 1, 1]
    self.v_length = tf.sqrt(tf.reduce_sum(tf.square(self.caps2),
axis=2, keep_dims=True) + epsilon)
    self.softmax_v = tf.nn.softmax(self.v_length, dim=1)
    assert self.softmax_v.get_shape() == [cfg.batch_size, 10, 1, 1]
    # b). pick out the index of max softmax val of the 10 caps
    # [batch_size, 10, 1, 1] => [batch_size] (index)
    self.argmax_idx = tf.to_int32(tf.argmax(self.softmax_v, axis=1))
    assert self.argmax_idx.get_shape() == [cfg.batch_size, 1, 1]
    self.argmax_idx = tf.reshape(self.argmax_idx, shape=(cfg.batch_size, ))

    # Method 1.
    if not cfg.mask_with_y:
      # c). indexing
      # It's not easy to understand the indexing process with  argmax_idx
      # as we are 3-dim animal
      masked_v = []
      for batch_size in range(cfg.batch_size):
        v = self.caps2[batch_size][self.argmax_idx[batch_size], :]
        masked_v.append(tf.reshape(v, shape=(1, 1, 16, 1)))
        self.masked_v = tf.concat(masked_v, axis=0)
        assert self.masked_v.get_shape() == [cfg.batch_size, 1, 16, 1]

    # Method 2. masking with true label, default mode
    else:
      self.masked_v = tf.matmul(tf.squeeze(self.caps2), tf.reshape(self.Y,
(-1, 10, 1)), transpose_a=True)
      self.v_length = tf.sqrt(tf.reduce_sum(tf.square(self.caps2), axis=2,
keep_dims=True) + epsilon)

  # 2. Reconstruct the MNIST images with 3 FC layers
  # [batch_size, 1, 16, 1] => [batch_size, 16] => [batch_size, 512]
  with tf.variable_scope('Decoder'):
    vector_j = tf.reshape(self.masked_v, shape=(cfg.batch_size, -1))
    fc1 = tf.contrib.layers.fully_connected(vector_j, num_outputs=512)
    assert fc1.get_shape() == [cfg.batch_size, 512]
    fc2 = tf.contrib.layers.fully_connected(fc1, num_outputs=1024)
    assert fc2.get_shape() == [cfg.batch_size, 1024]
    self.decoded = tf.contrib.layers.fully_connected(fc2, num_outputs=784,
activation_fn=tf.sigmoid)
```

8. Another important part defined in the paper is the margin loss function. This is explained in the snippet quote from the paper below (Equation 4) and implemented in the loss(..) method which consists of three losses, the margin loss, the reconstruction loss and the total loss:

> We are using the length of the instantiation vector to represent the probability that a capsule's entity exists, so we would like the top-level capsule for digit class k to have a long instantiation vector if and only if that digit is present in the image. To allow for multiple digits, we use a separate margin loss, L_k for each digit capsule, k:
>
> $$L_c = T_c \max(0, m^+ - \|\mathbf{v}_c\|)^2 + \lambda (1 - T_c) \max(0, \|\mathbf{v}_c\| - m^-)^2 \qquad (4)$$
>
> where $T_c = 1$ iff a digit of class c is present[3] and $m^+ = 0.9$ and $m^- = 0.1$. The λ down-weighting of the loss for absent digit classes stops the initial learning from shrinking the lengths of the activity vectors of all the digit capsules. We suggest $\lambda = 0.5$. The total loss is simply the sum of the losses of all digit capsules.

```
def loss(self):
    # 1. The margin loss
    # [batch_size, 10, 1, 1]
    # max_l = max(0, m_plus-||v_c||)^2
    max_l = tf.square(tf.maximum(0., cfg.m_plus - self.v_length))
    # max_r = max(0, ||v_c||-m_minus)^2
    max_r = tf.square(tf.maximum(0., self.v_length - cfg.m_minus))
    assert max_l.get_shape() == [cfg.batch_size, 10, 1, 1]
    # reshape: [batch_size, 10, 1, 1] => [batch_size, 10]
    max_l = tf.reshape(max_l, shape=(cfg.batch_size, -1))
    max_r = tf.reshape(max_r, shape=(cfg.batch_size, -1))
    # calc T_c: [batch_size, 10]
    T_c = self.Y
    # [batch_size, 10], element-wise multiply
    L_c = T_c * max_l + cfg.lambda_val * (1 - T_c) * max_r

    self.margin_loss = tf.reduce_mean(tf.reduce_sum(L_c, axis=1))
    # 2. The reconstruction loss
    orgin = tf.reshape(self.X, shape=(cfg.batch_size, -1))
    squared = tf.square(self.decoded - orgin)
    self.reconstruction_err = tf.reduce_mean(squared)

    # 3. Total loss
    # The paper uses sum of squared error as reconstruction   error, but we
    # have used reduce_mean in `# 2 The reconstruction loss` to calculate
    # mean squared error. In order to keep in line with the paper,the
    # regularization scale should be 0.0005*784=0.392
    self.total_loss = self.margin_loss + cfg.regularization_scale *
self.reconstruction_err
```

9. In addition, it might be convenient to define a _summary(...) method to report the losses and the accuracy:

```
#Summary
def _summary(self):
  train_summary = []
  train_summary.append(tf.summary.scalar('train/margin_loss',
self.margin_loss))train_summary.append(tf.summary.scalar('train/reconstruct
ion_loss', self.reconstruction_err))
  train_summary.append(tf.summary.scalar('train/total_loss',
self.total_loss))
  recon_img = tf.reshape(self.decoded, shape=(cfg.batch_size, 28, 28, 1))
  train_summary.append(tf.summary.image('reconstruction_img', recon_img))
  correct_prediction = tf.equal(tf.to_int32(self.labels), self.argmax_idx)
  self.batch_accuracy = tf.reduce_sum(tf.cast(correct_prediction,
tf.float32))
  self.test_acc = tf.placeholder_with_default(tf.constant(0.), shape=[])
  test_summary = []
  test_summary.append(tf.summary.scalar('test/accuracy', self.test_acc))
  self.train_summary = tf.summary.merge(train_summary)
  self.test_summary = tf.summary.merge(test_summary)
```

How it works...

CapsNets are very different from state-of-the-art deep learning networks. Instead of adding more layers and making the network deeper, CapsNets use a shallow network where capsule layers are nested inside other layers. Each capsule specializes in detecting a specific entity in an image, and a dynamic routing mechanism is used to send the detected entity to parents layers. With CNNs you have to consider thousands of images from many different perspectives in order to recognize an object from different angles. Hinton believes the redundancies in the layers will allow capsule networks to identify objects from multiple angles and in different scenarios with less data that is typically used by CNNs.

Let's examine the network as shown by tensorboad:

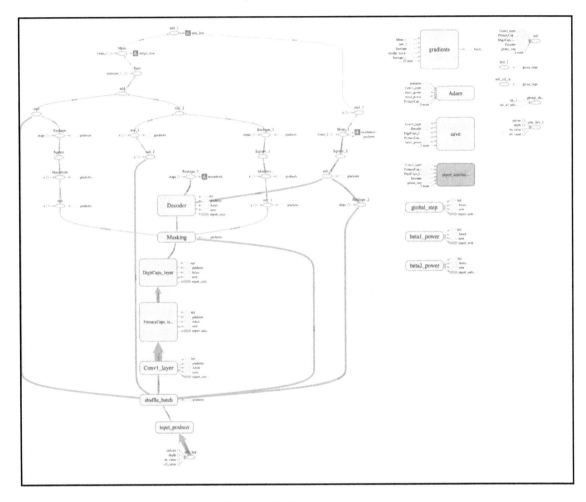

An example of CapsNet as defined in the code and shown by tensorboard

The results are impressive as shown in the following diagram taken from the seminal paper. CapsNet has a low test error (0.25 percent) on a three-layer network previously only achieved in deeper networks. The baseline is a standard CNN with three convolutional layers of 256,256—128 channels. Each has 5 x 5 kernels and a stride of 1. The last convolutional layers are followed by two fully connected layers of size 328,192. The last fully connected layer is connected with dropout to a 10 class softmax layer with cross-entropy losses:

Figure 3: Sample MNIST test reconstructions of a CapsNet with 3 routing iterations. (l, p, r) represents the label, the prediction and the reconstruction target respectively. The two rightmost columns show two reconstructions of a failure example and it explains how the model confuses a 5 and a 3 in this image. The other columns are from correct classifications and shows that model picks on the details while smoothing the noise.

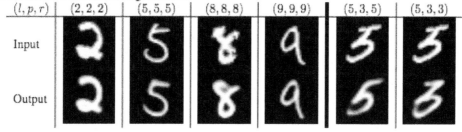

Table 1: CapsNet classification test accuracy. The MNIST average and standard deviation results are reported from 3 trials.

Method	Routing	Reconstruction	MNIST (%)	MultiMNIST (%)
Baseline	-	-	0.39	8
CapsNet	1	no	$0.34_{\pm 0.032}$	-
CapsNet	1	yes	$0.29_{\pm 0.011}$	7
CapsNet	3	no	$0.35_{\pm 0.036}$	-
CapsNet	3	yes	$\mathbf{0.25}_{\pm 0.005}$	5

Let's examine the reduction of margin loss, reconstruction loss, and total loss:

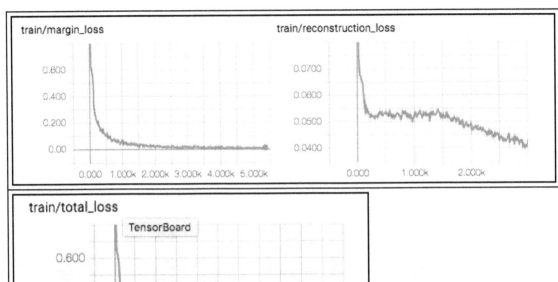

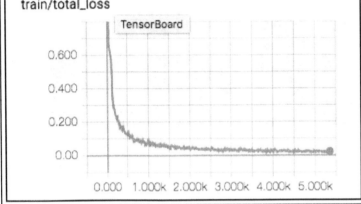

Let's also examine the increase in accuracy; after 500 iterations it achieves 92 percent and 98.46 percent in 3,500 iterations:

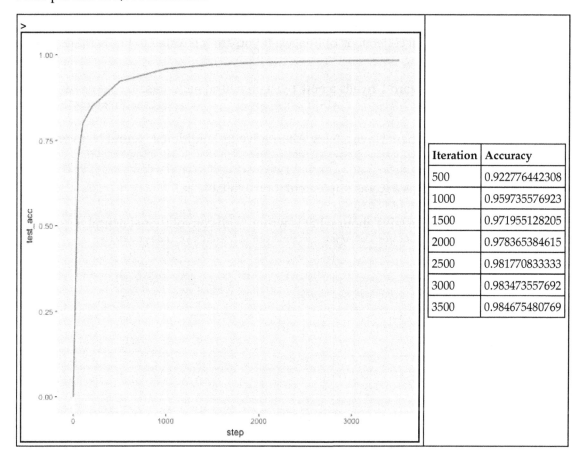

Iteration	Accuracy
500	0.922776442308
1000	0.959735576923
1500	0.971955128205
2000	0.978365384615
2500	0.981770833333
3000	0.983473557692
3500	0.984675480769

Examples of increase in accuracy for CapsNet

There's more...

CapsNets work very well on MNIST but there is a lot of research work to be done in terms of understanding if the same impressive results can be achieved on other datasets such as CIFAR, or on more general collections of images. If you are interested to know more please have a look at the following:

- Google's AI Wizard Unveils a new twist on neural networks: `https://www.wired.com/story/googles-ai-wizard-unveils-a-new-twist-on-neural-networks/`
- Google Researchers Have a New Alternative to Traditional Neural Networks: `https://www.technologyreview.com/the-download/609297/google-researchers-have-a-new-alternative-to-traditional-neural-networks/`
- Keras-CapsNet is a Keras implementation available at `https://github.com/XifengGuo/CapsNet-Keras`
- Geoffrey Hinton talks about what is wrong with convolutional neural nets: `https://www.youtube.com/watch?v=rTawFwUvnLEfeature=youtu.be`

12
Distributed TensorFlow and Cloud Deep Learning

In this chapter, we will discuss using distributed TensorFlow and Cloud deep learning. We will present a number of recipes for:

- Working with TensorFlow and GPUs
- Playing with Distributed TensorFlow: multiple GPUs and one CPU
- Playing with Distributed TensorFlow: multiple servers
- Training a Distributed TensorFlow MNIST classifier
- Working with TensorFlow Serving and Docker
- Running Distributed TensorFlow on Google Cloud (GCP) with Compute Engine
- Running Distributed TensorFlow on Google CloudML
- Running Distributed TensorFlow on Microsoft Azure
- Running Distributed TensorFlow on Amazon AWS

Introduction

Each TensorFlow computation is described in terms of a graph. This allows a natural degree of flexibility in the structure and the placement of operations that can be split across distributed nodes of computation. The graph can be split into multiple subgraphs that are assigned to different nodes in a cluster of servers.

I strongly suggest the reader have a look to the paper Large Scale Distributed Deep Networks Jeffrey Dean, Greg S. Corrado, Rajat Monga, Kai Chen, Matthieu Devin, Quoc V. Le, Mark Z. Mao, Marc'Aurelio Ranzato, Andrew Senior, Paul Tucker, Ke Yang, and Andrew Y. Ng. NIPS, 2012, `https://research.google.com/archive/large_deep_networks_nips2012.html`

One key result of the paper is to prove that it is possible to run distributed **stochastic gradient descent (SDG)** where multiple nodes are working in parallel on data-shards and update independently and asynchronously the gradient by sending updates to a parameter server. Quoting the abstract of the paper:

> *Our experiments reveal several surprising results about large-scale nonconvex optimization. Firstly, asynchronous SGD, rarely applied to nonconvex problems, works very well for training deep networks, particularly when combined with Adagrad adaptive learning rates.*

This is well explained by the following picture taken from the paper itself:

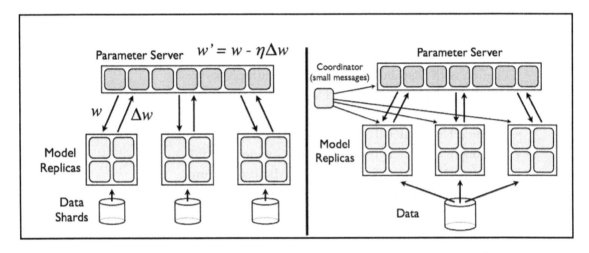

An example of distributed gradient descent with a parameter server as taken from `https://research.google.com/archive/large_deep_networks_nips2012.html`

Another document you should read is the white paper *TensorFlow: Large-Scale Machine Learning on Heterogeneous Distributed Systems* Martín Abadi, and others November, 2015, `http://download.tensorflow.org/paper/whitepaper2015.pdf`

Considering some examples contained in it we can see a fragment of TensorFlow code shown on the left in the picture below which is then represented as a graph on the right:

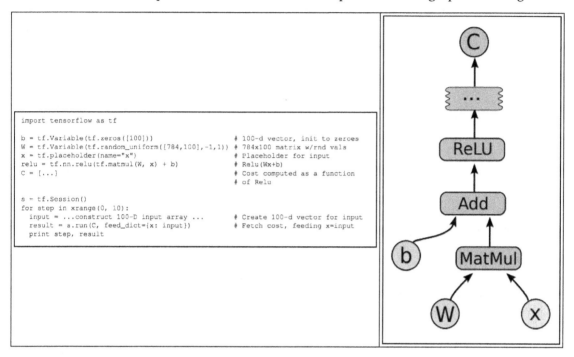

```
import tensorflow as tf

b = tf.Variable(tf.zeros([100]))              # 100-d vector, init to zeroes
W = tf.Variable(tf.random_uniform([784,100],-1,1))  # 784x100 matrix w/rnd vals
x = tf.placeholder(name="x")                  # Placeholder for input
relu = tf.nn.relu(tf.matmul(W, x) + b)        # Relu(Wx+b)
C = [...]                                      # Cost computed as a function
                                              # of Relu

s = tf.Session()
for step in xrange(0, 10):
    input = ...construct 100-D input array ...  # Create 100-d vector for input
    result = s.run(C, feed_dict={x: input})    # Fetch cost, feeding x=input
    print step, result
```

An example of TensorFlow graph as taken from http://download.tensorflow.org/paper/whitepaper2015.pdf

A graph can be partitioned across multiple nodes by having local computations and by transparently adding to the graph remote communication nodes when needed. This is well explained in the following figure which is still taken from the paper mentioned earlier:

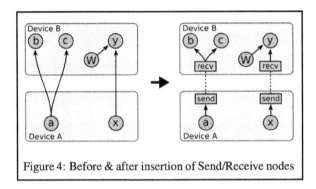

Figure 4: Before & after insertion of Send/Receive nodes

An example of distributed TensorFlow graph computation as taken from http://download.tensorflow.org/paper/whitepaper2015.pdf

Gradient descent and all the major optimizer algorithms can be computed in either a centralized way (left side of the figure below) or in a distributed way (right side). The latter involves a master process which talks with multiple workers provisioning both GPUs and CPUs:

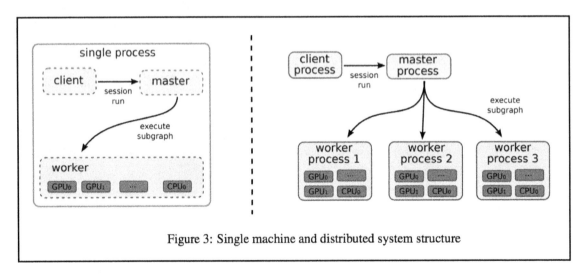

Figure 3: Single machine and distributed system structure

An example of single machine and distributed system structure as taken from An example of distributed TensorFlow graph computation as taken from http://download.tensorflow.org/paper/whitepaper2015.pdf

Distributed computations can be either synchronous (all the workers are updating at the same time the gradient on sharded data) or asynchronous (the update did not happen at the same time). The latter typically allows higher scalability with larger graph computations still working pretty well in terms of convergence to an optimal solution. Again the pictures are taken from the TensorFlow white paper and I strongly encourage the interested reader to have a look to this paper if you want to know more:

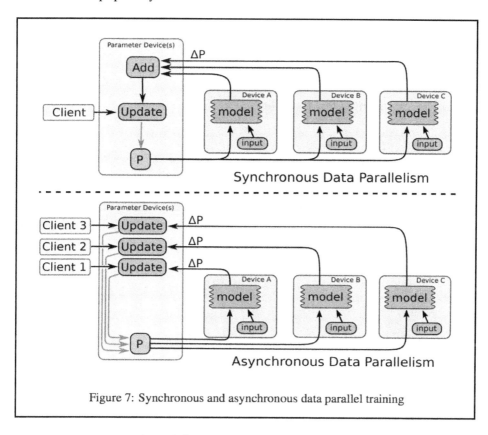

Figure 7: Synchronous and asynchronous data parallel training

An example of synchronous and asynchronous data parallel training

Working with TensorFlow and GPUs

In this recipe we will learn how to use TensorFlow with GPUs: the operation performed is a simple matrix multiplication either on CPU or on GPU.

Getting ready

The first step is to install a version of TensorFlow that supports GPUs. The official TensorFlow Installation Instruction is your starting point https://www.tensorflow.org/. Remember that you need to have an environment supporting GPUs either via CUDA or CuDNN.

How to do it...

We proceed with the recipe as follows:

1. Start by importing a few modules

```
import sys
import numpy as np
import tensorflow as tf
from datetime import datetime
```

2. Get from command line the type of processing unit that you desire to use (either "gpu" or "cpu")

```
device_name = sys.argv[1] # Choose device from cmd line. Options: gpu or cpu
shape = (int(sys.argv[2]), int(sys.argv[2]))
if device_name == "gpu":
  device_name = "/gpu:0"
else:
  device_name = "/cpu:0"
```

3. Execute the matrix multiplication either on GPU or on CPU. The key instruction is with tf.device(device_name). It creates a new context manager, telling TensorFlow to perform those actions on either the GPU or the CPU

```
with tf.device(device_name):
  random_matrix = tf.random_uniform(shape=shape, minval=0, maxval=1)
  dot_operation = tf.matmul(random_matrix, tf.transpose(random_matrix))
  sum_operation = tf.reduce_sum(dot_operation)

startTime = datetime.now()
with tf.Session(config=tf.ConfigProto(log_device_placement=True)) as session:
  result = session.run(sum_operation)
  print(result)
```

4. Print some debug timing just to verify what is the difference between CPU and GPU

```
print("Shape:", shape, "Device:", device_name)
print("Time taken:", datetime.now() - startTime)
```

How it works...

This recipe explains how to assign TensorFlow computations either to CPUs or to GPUs. The code is pretty simple and it will be used as a basis for the next recipe.

Playing with Distributed TensorFlow: multiple GPUs and one CPU

We will show an example of data parallelism where data is split across multiple GPUs

Getting ready

This recipe is inspired by a good blog posting written by Neil Tenenholtz and available online: https://clindatsci.com/blog/2017/5/31/distributed-tensorflow

How to do it...

We proceed with the recipe as follows:

1. Consider this piece of code which runs a matrix multiplication on a single GPU.

```
# single GPU (baseline)
import tensorflow as tf
# place the initial data on the cpu
with tf.device('/cpu:0'):
  input_data = tf.Variable([[1., 2., 3.],
    [4., 5., 6.],
    [7., 8., 9.],
    [10., 11., 12.]])
b = tf.Variable([[1.], [1.], [2.]])

# compute the result on the 0th gpu
with tf.device('/gpu:0'):
  output = tf.matmul(input_data, b)
```

```
# create a session and run
with tf.Session() as sess:
  sess.run(tf.global_variables_initializer())
  print sess.run(output)
```

2. Partition the code with in graph replication as in the following snippet between 2 different GPUs. Note that the CPU is acting as the master node distributing the graph and collecting the final results.

```
# in-graph replication
import tensorflow as tf
num_gpus = 2
# place the initial data on the cpu
with tf.device('/cpu:0'):
  input_data = tf.Variable([[1., 2., 3.],
    [4., 5., 6.],
    [7., 8., 9.],
    [10., 11., 12.]])
  b = tf.Variable([[1.], [1.], [2.]])

# split the data into chunks for each gpu
inputs = tf.split(input_data, num_gpus)
outputs = []

# loop over available gpus and pass input data
for i in range(num_gpus):
  with tf.device('/gpu:'+str(i)):
    outputs.append(tf.matmul(inputs[i], b))

# merge the results of the devices
with tf.device('/cpu:0'):
  output = tf.concat(outputs, axis=0)

# create a session and run
with tf.Session() as sess:
  sess.run(tf.global_variables_initializer())
  print sess.run(output)
```

How it works...

This is a very simple recipe where the graph is split in two parts by the CPU acting as master and distributed to two GPUs acting as distributed workers. The result of the computation is collected back to the CPU.

Playing with Distributed TensorFlow: multiple servers

In this recipe, we will learn how to distribute a TensorFlow computation across multiple servers. The key assumption is that the code is the same for both the workers and the parameter servers. Therefore the role of each computation node is passed a command line argument.

Getting ready

Again, this recipe is inspired by a good blog posting written by Neil Tenenholtz and available online: `https://clindatsci.com/blog/2017/5/31/distributed-tensorflow`

How to do it...

We proceed with the recipe as follows:

1. Consider this piece of code where we specify the cluster architecture with one master running on 192.168.1.1:1111 and two workers running on 192.168.1.2:1111 and 192.168.1.3:1111 respectively.

```
import sys
import tensorflow as tf

# specify the cluster's architecture
cluster = tf.train.ClusterSpec({'ps': ['192.168.1.1:1111'],
    'worker': ['192.168.1.2:1111',
    '192.168.1.3:1111']
})
```

2. Note that the code is replicated on multiple machines and therefore it is important to know what is the role of the current execution node. This information we get from the command line. A machine can be either a worker or a parameter server (ps).

```
# parse command-line to specify machine
job_type = sys.argv[1] # job type: "worker" or "ps"
task_idx = sys.argv[2] # index job in the worker or ps list
# as defined in the ClusterSpec
```

3. Run the training server where given a cluster, we bless each computational with a role (either worker or ps), and an id.

```
# create TensorFlow Server. This is how the machines communicate.
server = tf.train.Server(cluster, job_name=job_type, task_index=task_idx)
```

4. The computation is different according to the role of the specific computation node:

   - If the role is a parameter server, then the condition is to join the server. Note that in this case there is no code to execute because the workers will continuously push updates and the only thing that the Parameter Server has to do is waiting.
   - Otherwise the worker code is executed on a specific device within the cluster. This part of code is similar to the one executed on a single machine where we first build the model and then we train it locally. Note that all the distribution of the work and the collection of the updated results is done transparently by Tensoflow. Note that TensorFlow provides a convenient `tf.train.replica_device_setter` that automatically assigns operations to devices.

```
# parameter server is updated by remote clients.
# will not proceed beyond this if statement.
if job_type == 'ps':
  server.join()
else:
  # workers only
  with tf.device(tf.train.replica_device_setter(
    worker_device='/job:worker/task:'+task_idx,
    cluster=cluster)):
# build your model here as if you only were using a single machine

with tf.Session(server.target):
  # train your model here
```

How it works...

In this recipe, we have seen how to create a cluster with multiple computation nodes. A node can be either playing the role of a Parameter server or playing the role of a worker.

In both cases the code executed is the same but the execution of the code is different according to parameters collected from the command line. The parameter server only needs to wait until the workers send updates. Note that `tf.train.replica_device_setter(..)` takes the role of automatically assigning operations to available devices, while `tf.train.ClusterSpec(..)` is used for cluster setup.

There is more...

An example of distributed training for MNIST is available online on `https://github.com/ischlag/distributed-tensorflow-example/blob/master/example.py`

In addition, note that You can decide to have more than one parameter server for efficiency reasons. Using parameters the server can provide better network utilization, and it allows to scale models to more parallel machines. It is possible to allocate more than one parameter server. The interested reader can have a look to `https://www.tensorflow.org/deploy/distributed`

Training a Distributed TensorFlow MNIST classifier

This recipe is used to train a full MNIST classifier in a distributed way. This recipe is inspired by the blog post in `http://ischlag.github.io/2016/06/12/async-distributed-tensorflow/` and the code running on TensorFlow 1.2 is available here `https://github.com/ischlag/distributed-tensorflow-example`

Getting ready

This recipe is based on the previous one. So it might be convenient to read them in order.

How to do it...

We proceed with the recipe as follows:

1. Import a few standard modules and define the TensorFlow cluster where the computation is run. Then start a server for a specific task

```
import tensorflow as tf
import sys
import time
# cluster specification
parameter_servers = ["pc-01:2222"]
workers = [ "pc-02:2222",
"pc-03:2222",
"pc-04:2222"]
cluster = tf.train.ClusterSpec({"ps":parameter_servers, "worker":workers})
# input flags
tf.app.flags.DEFINE_string("job_name", "", "Either 'ps' or 'worker'")
tf.app.flags.DEFINE_integer("task_index", 0, "Index of task within the
job")FLAGS = tf.app.flags.FLAGS
# start a server for a specific task
server = tf.train.Server(
  cluster,
  job_name=FLAGS.job_name,
  task_index=FLAGS.task_index)
```

2. Read MNIST data and define the hyperparameters used for training

```
# config
batch_size = 100
learning_rate = 0.0005
training_epochs = 20
logs_path = "/tmp/mnist/1"
# load mnist data set
from tensorflow.examples.tutorials.mnist import input_data
mnist = input_data.read_data_sets('MNIST_data', one_hot=True)
```

3. Check if your role is Parameter Server or Worker. If worker then define a simple dense neural network, define an optimizer, and the metric used for evaluating the classifier (for example accuracy).

```
if FLAGS.job_name == "ps":
  server.join()
elif FLAGS.job_name == "worker":
# Between-graph replication
with tf.device(tf.train.replica_device_setter(
```

```
    worker_device="/job:worker/task:%d" % FLAGS.task_index,
    cluster=cluster)):
# count the number of updates
    global_step = tf.get_variable( 'global_step', [], initializer =
tf.constant_initializer(0),
trainable = False)

    # input images
    with tf.name_scope('input'):
        # None -> batch size can be any size, 784 -> flattened mnist image
        x = tf.placeholder(tf.float32, shape=[None, 784], name="x-input")
        # target 10 output classes
        y_ = tf.placeholder(tf.float32, shape=[None, 10], name="y-input")

    # model parameters will change during training so we use tf.Variable
    tf.set_random_seed(1)
    with tf.name_scope("weights"):
        W1 = tf.Variable(tf.random_normal([784, 100]))
        W2 = tf.Variable(tf.random_normal([100, 10]))

    # bias
    with tf.name_scope("biases"):
        b1 = tf.Variable(tf.zeros([100]))
        b2 = tf.Variable(tf.zeros([10]))

    # implement model
    with tf.name_scope("softmax"):
        # y is our prediction
        z2 = tf.add(tf.matmul(x,W1),b1)
        a2 = tf.nn.sigmoid(z2)
        z3 = tf.add(tf.matmul(a2,W2),b2)
        y = tf.nn.softmax(z3)

    # specify cost function
    with tf.name_scope('cross_entropy'):
        # this is our cost
        cross_entropy = tf.reduce_mean(
-tf.reduce_sum(y_ * tf.log(y), reduction_indices=[1]))

    # specify optimizer
    with tf.name_scope('train'):
        # optimizer is an "operation" which we can execute in a session
        grad_op = tf.train.GradientDescentOptimizer(learning_rate)
        train_op = grad_op.minimize(cross_entropy, global_step=global_step)

    with tf.name_scope('Accuracy'):
        # accuracy
        correct_prediction = tf.equal(tf.argmax(y,1), tf.argmax(y_,1))
```

```
accuracy = tf.reduce_mean(tf.cast(correct_prediction, tf.float32))

# create a summary for our cost and accuracy
tf.summary.scalar("cost", cross_entropy)
tf.summary.scalar("accuracy", accuracy)
# merge all summaries into a single "operation" which we can execute in a
session
summary_op = tf.summary.merge_all()
init_op = tf.global_variables_initializer()
print("Variables initialized ...")
```

4. Start a supervisor which acts as a Chief machine for the distributed setting. The chief is the worker machine which manages all the rest of the cluster. The session is maintained by the chief and the key instruction is sv = tf.train.Supervisor(is_chief=(FLAGS.task_index == 0)). Also, with prepare_or_wait_for_session(server.target) the supervisor will wait for the model to be ready for use. Note that each worker will take care of different batched models and the final model is then available for the chief.

```
sv = tf.train.Supervisor(is_chief=(FLAGS.task_index == 0),
begin_time = time.time()
frequency = 100
with sv.prepare_or_wait_for_session(server.target) as sess:
  # create log writer object (this will log on every machine)
  writer = tf.summary.FileWriter(logs_path, graph=tf.get_default_graph())
  # perform training cycles
  start_time = time.time()
  for epoch in range(training_epochs):
    # number of batches in one epoch
    batch_count = int(mnist.train.num_examples/batch_size)
    count = 0
    for i in range(batch_count):
      batch_x, batch_y = mnist.train.next_batch(batch_size)
      # perform the operations we defined earlier on batch
      _, cost, summary, step = sess.run(
      [train_op, cross_entropy, summary_op, global_step],
      feed_dict={x: batch_x, y_: batch_y})
      writer.add_summary(summary, step)
      count += 1
      if count % frequency == 0 or i+1 == batch_count:
        elapsed_time = time.time() - start_time
        start_time = time.time()
        print("Step: %d," % (step+1),
          " Epoch: %2d," % (epoch+1), " Batch: %3d of %3d," % (i+1,
batch_count),
          " Cost: %.4f," % cost,
```

```
        "AvgTime:%3.2fms" % float(elapsed_time*1000/frequency))
        count = 0
    print("Test-Accuracy: %2.2f" % sess.run(accuracy, feed_dict={x:
mnist.test.images, y_: mnist.test.labels}))
    print("Total Time: %3.2fs" % float(time.time() - begin_time))
    print("Final Cost: %.4f" % cost)
  sv.stop()
  print("done")
```

How it works...

This recipe describes an example of distributed MNIST classifier. In this example, TensorFlow allows us to define a cluster of three machines. One acts as parameter server and two more machines are used as workers working on separate batches of the training data.

Working with TensorFlow Serving and Docker

In this recipe we will show how to run a Docker container for TensorFlow Serving, a set of components to export a trained TensorFlow model and use the standard `tensorflow_model_server` to serve it. The TensorFlow Serving server discovers new exported models and runs a gRPC service for serving them.

Getting ready

We will use Docker and will assume that you are familiar with the system. If not, please make sure that you have a look to `https://www.docker.com/` and install it. What we are going to do is to build a version of TF Serving.

How to do it...

Here is how we proceed with the recipe:

1. Download Dockerfile.devel from `https://github.com/tensorflow/serving/blob/master/tensorflow_serving/tools/docker/Dockerfile.devel`

2. Build a container by running

```
docker build --pull -t $USER/tensorflow-serving-devel -f Dockerfile.devel
```

3. Run the container

```
docker run -it $USER/tensorflow-serving-devel
```

4. Clone the TensorFlow Serving, configure and test the server

```
git clone --recurse-submodules https://github.com/tensorflow/serving
cd serving/tensorflow
./configure
cd ..
bazel test tensorflow_serving/...
```

5. Now let's see an example of saving a model so that the Server can save it. This step is inspired by an example used for building a MNIST trainer and serving the model (see `https://github.com/tensorflow/serving/blob/master/tensorflow_serving/example/mnist_saved_model.py`). The first step is to import the builder as saved_model_builder. Then the bulk of the work is done by the `SavedModelBuilder()` which saves a *snapshot* of the trained model to reliable storage. Note that here `export_path` is /tmp/mnist_model/

```
from tensorflow.python.saved_model import builder as saved_model_builder
...
export_path_base = sys.argv[-1]
export_path = os.path.join(
  compat.as_bytes(export_path_base),
  compat.as_bytes(str(FLAGS.model_version)))
print 'Exporting trained model to', export_path
builder = saved_model_builder.SavedModelBuilder(export_path)
builder.add_meta_graph_and_variables(
  sess, [tag_constants.SERVING],
  signature_def_map={
    'predict_images':
    prediction_signature,
    signature_constants.DEFAULT_SERVING_SIGNATURE_DEF_KEY:
    classification_signature,
```

```
    },
    legacy_init_op=legacy_init_op)
builder.save()
```

6. The model can then be served with a simple command

```
tensorflow_model_server --port=9000 --model_name=mnist --
model_base_path=/tmp/mnist_model/
```

How it works...

In February 2016 Google released TensorFlow Serving (`https://www.tensorflow.org/serving/`), a high-performance serving system for machine learned models, designed for production environments. In August 2017, there are over 800 projects within Google using TensorFlow Serving in production.

There is more...

TensoFlow Serving is a very versatile piece of software and in this recipe, we have just scratched the surface of the potential uses. If you have interest in knowing more about advanced functionalities. such as running in large batches, or loading models dynamically, you should have a look to `https://github.com/tensorflow/serving/blob/master/tensorflow_serving/g3doc/serving_advanced.md`

Running Distributed TensorFlow on Google Cloud (GCP) with Compute Engine

In this recipe, we are going to learn how to use Google Tensorflow on Google Cloud (GCP). The example we are going to review is the classical MNIST.

Getting ready

It would be good to have a look to how GCP works in `https://cloud.google.com/`. Note that GCP offers $300 free credit to get started with any GCP product. In addition, there are free usage limits on some products for eligible customers, during and after the free trial. (Offer is subject to change, see `https://cloud.google.com/free/`).

How to do it...

Here is how we proceed with the recipe:

1. Create a new Google Cloud project from the Web console `https://pantheon.google.com/cloud-resource-manager`

The following screen is displayed when you click on **create project**:

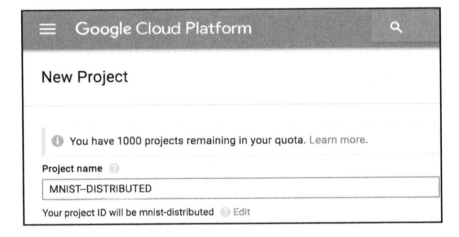

2. Enable billing for this project by selecting the related voice on the left bar of the console. Then enable the **Compute Engine** and **Cloud Machine Learning APIs** for the project:

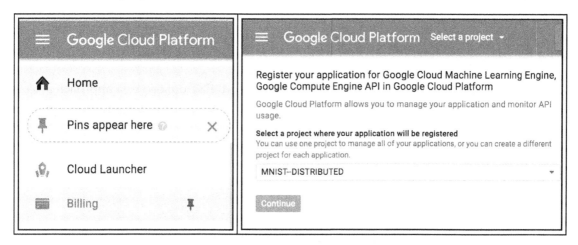

3. Login to the web cloudshell `https://pantheon.google.com/cloudshell/editor`?

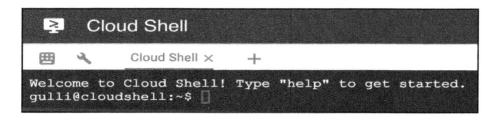

4. From the console run the following commands for configuring the zone where the computation will be executed, for downloading the sample code and for creating the VMs used for running the code. Finally connect to the machine:

```
gcloud config set compute/zone us-east1-c
gcloud config set project [YOUR_PROJECT_ID]
git clone https://github.com/GoogleCloudPlatform/cloudml-dist-mnist-example
cd cloudml-dist-mnist-example
gcloud compute instances create template-instance \
 --image-project ubuntu-os-cloud \
 --image-family ubuntu-1604-lts \
 --boot-disk-size 10GB \
 --machine-type n1-standard-1
gcloud compute ssh template-instance
```

5. Now, after logging into the machine we need to setup the environment by installing PIP and TensorFlow with these commands.

```
sudo apt-get update
sudo apt-get -y upgrade \
 && sudo apt-get install -y python-pip python-dev
sudo pip install tensorflow
sudo pip install --upgrade tensorflow
```

6. We will have multiple workers operating on MNIST data so best approach is to create a storage bucket shared among all the workers and copy the MNIST data in this bucket

```
BUCKET="mnist-$RANDOM-$RANDOM"
gsutil mb -c regional -l us-east1 gs://${BUCKET}
sudo ./scripts/create_records.py
gsutil cp /tmp/data/train.tfrecords gs://${BUCKET}/data/
gsutil cp /tmp/data/test.tfrecords gs://${BUCKET}/data/
```

7. We are now going to create multiple workers (worker-0, worker-1) which are clones of the initial template-instance machine. We don't want the machines to delete the disks when they are turned off so that's why we have the first command.

```
gcloud compute instances set-disk-auto-delete template-instance \
 --disk template-instance --no-auto-delete
gcloud compute instances delete template-instance
gcloud compute images create template-image \
 --source-disk template-instance
gcloud compute instances create \
 master-0 worker-0 worker-1 ps-0 \
 --image template-image \
 --machine-type n1-standard-4 \
 --scopes=default,storage-rw
```

8. The final step is to run the computation for distributed training.

```
./scripts/start-training.sh gs://${BUCKET}
```

How it works...

The demo script moves the code to each VM and starts the distributed computation. The two workers are running in parallel on the same MNIST data shared on a common storage bucket. When the computation is concluded the script will print the location of the trained model.

There is more...

If we don't want to manage TensorFlow than we can decide to use the managed version run by Google on your behalf. This is the CloudML service described during the next recipe. In addition if you decide t use GPUs with CloudML then this URL is a good starting point `https://cloud.google.com/ml-engine/docs/using-gpus`

Running Distributed TensorFlow on Google CloudML

CloudML is a managed version of Tensorflow run by Google. Instead of running TF by yourself you can simply use CloudML and forget all the issues related to infrastructure and scalability.

Getting ready

Here we assume that you have already created a Cloud Platform Project, enabling billing for your project, and enable the Google Compute Engine and the Cloud Machine Learning APIs. These steps are similar to the ones described in the previous recipes. This recipe is inspired by the MNIST training code available in `https://cloud.google.com/ml-engine/docs/distributed-tensorflow-mnist-cloud-datalab`.

How to do it...

We proceed with running distributed TensorFlow on Google CloudML:

1. The first step is simply to download the example code

git clone `https://github.com/GoogleCloudPlatform/cloudml-dist-mnist-example`
cd cloudml-dist-mnist-example

2. Then we download the data and save in a GCP storage bucket

```
PROJECT_ID=$(gcloud config list project --format "value(core.project)")
BUCKET="${PROJECT_ID}-ml"
gsutil mb -c regional -l us-central1 gs://${BUCKET}
./scripts/create_records.py
gsutil cp /tmp/data/train.tfrecords gs://${BUCKET}/data/
gsutil cp /tmp/data/test.tfrecords gs://${BUCKET}/data/
```

3. Submitting a training job is a very easy: we can simply invoke the training step with CloudML engine. In this example, the trainer code runs for 1000 iterations in the region us-central1. The input data is taken from a storage bucket and the output bucket will be submitted to a different storage bucket.

```
JOB_NAME="job_$(date +%Y%m%d_%H%M%S)"
gcloud ml-engine jobs submit training ${JOB_NAME} \
 --package-path trainer \
 --module-name trainer.task \
 --staging-bucket gs://${BUCKET} \
 --job-dir gs://${BUCKET}/${JOB_NAME} \
 --runtime-version 1.2 \
 --region us-central1 \
 --config config/config.yaml \
 -- \
 --data_dir gs://${BUCKET}/data \
 --output_dir gs://${BUCKET}/${JOB_NAME} \
 --train_steps 10000
```

4. If you want You can control the training process by accessing the CloudML console in `https://pantheon.google.com/mlengine/`
5. Once the training is concluded, it is possible to serve the model directly from CloudML

```
MODEL_NAME=MNIST
gcloud ml-engine models create --regions us-central1 ${MODEL_NAME}
VERSION_NAME=v1
```

```
ORIGIN=$(gsutil ls gs://${BUCKET}/${JOB_NAME}/export/Servo | tail -1)
gcloud ml-engine versions create \
 --origin ${ORIGIN} \
 --model ${MODEL_NAME} \
${VERSION_NAME}
gcloud ml-engine versions set-default --model ${MODEL_NAME} ${VERSION_NAME}
```

6. Once the model is served online it is possible to access the server and make a prediction. The request.json is created by using the script `make_request.py` which reads data from MNIST, performs a one hot encoding and then write the features with a well-formatted json schema.

```
gcloud ml-engine predict --model ${MODEL_NAME} --json-instances
request.json
```

How it works...

CloudML is a convenient solution for using a managed version of TensorFlow run by Google. Instead of directly taking care of the infrastructure and operations, it is possible to focus directly on developing machine learning models.

There is more...

One very cool feature of CloudML is the capacity of auto-tuning the hyperparameters contained in your model by running multiple trials in parallel. This provides you optimized values for hyperparameters, which maximizes your model's predictive accuracy. If you are interested in knowing more, then it might be beneficial to have a look at `https://cloud.google.com/ml-engine/docs/hyperparameter-tuning-overview`

Running Distributed TensorFlow on Microsoft Azure

Microsoft Azure offers a service called Batch AI that allows us to run our machine learning models on clusters of Azure virtual machines.

Getting ready

As the first step we need to have an Azure account: if you do not already have one, you can create one for free here: `https://azure.microsoft.com/en-us/services/batch-ai/`. The Azure offers $200 credit for 30 days to new users. This recipe will follow the example provided by Microsoft Azure to run MNIST on two GPUs using TensorFlow distributed, the relevant codes are available on Github: `https://github.com/Azure/batch-shipyard/tree/master/recipes/TensorFlow-Distributed`

How to do it...

We proceed with the recipe as follows:

1. The first step would be to install Azure CLI. The details for installing Azure CLI on different OS platforms can be obtained from here `https://docs.microsoft.com/en-us/cli/azure/install-azure-cli?view=azure-cli-latest`.

2. Before creating a cluster you would require to login in Azure, using command `az login`. It will generate a code and provide you with a website address, where you will be asked to verify your credentials, once all the steps on the website are over, you will be asked to close, and your az credentials will be verified.

3. Configure the default location, create and configure a resource group.

```
az group create --name myResourceGroup --location eastus
az configure --defaults group=myResourceGroup
az configure --defaults location=eastus
```

4. Next, we will require creating a storage using <az storage account create> command, and set the environmental variables depending upon your OS, details about environment variables and their values are given at `https://docs.microsoft.com/en-us/azure/batch-ai/quickstart-cli`

5. Download and extract the preprocessed MNIST database

```
wget
"https://batchaisamples.blob.core.windows.net/samples/mnist_dataset_origina
l.zip?st=2017-09-29T18%3A29%3A00Z&se=2099-12-31T08%3A00%3A00Z&sp=rl&sv=2016
-05-31&sr=b&sig=Qc1RA3zsXIP4oeioXutkL1PXIrHJO0pHJlppS2rID3I%3D" -O
mnist_dataset_original.zip
unzip mnist_dataset_original.zip
```

6. Download the `mnist_replica`

```
wget
"https://raw.githubusercontent.com/Azure/BatchAI/master/recipes/TensorFlow/
TensorFlow-GPU-
Distributed/mnist_replica.py?token=AcZzrcpJGDHCUzsCyjlWiKVNfBuDdkqwks5Z4dPr
wA%3D%3D" -O mnist_replica.py
```

7. Next create an Azure File Share, where you upload the downloaded MNIST dataset and `mnist_replica.py` files.

```
az storage share create --name batchaisample
az storage directory create --share-name batchaisample --name mnist_dataset
az storage file upload --share-name batchaisample --source t10k-images-
idx3-ubyte.gz --path mnist_dataset
az storage file upload --share-name batchaisample --source t10k-labels-
idx1-ubyte.gz --path mnist_dataset
az storage file upload --share-name batchaisample --source train-images-
idx3-ubyte.gz --path mnist_dataset
az storage file upload --share-name batchaisample --source train-labels-
idx1-ubyte.gz --path mnist_dataset
az storage directory create --share-name batchaisample --name
tensorflow_samples
az storage file upload --share-name batchaisample --source mnist_replica.py
--path tensorflow_samples
```

8. Now we create a cluster, for this recipe, the cluster consists of two GPU nodes of standard_NC6 size, with standard Ubuntu LTS or Ubuntu DVSM. The cluster can be created using Azure CLI command:

For Linux:

```
az batchai cluster create -n nc6 -i UbuntuDSVM -s Standard_NC6 --min 2 --
max 2 --afs-name batchaisample --afs-mount-path external -u $USER -k
~/.ssh/id_rsa.pub
```

For Windows:

```
az batchai cluster create -n nc6 -i UbuntuDSVM -s Standard_NC6 --min 2 --
max 2 --afs-name batchaisample --afs-mount-path external -u <user_name> -p
<password>
```

9. The next step is creating job creation parameters in job.json file:

```
{
  "properties": {
    "nodeCount": 2,
    "tensorFlowSettings": {
      "parameterServerCount": 1,
      "workerCount": 2,
      "pythonScriptFilePath": "$AZ_BATCHAI_INPUT_SCRIPT/mnist_replica.py",
      "masterCommandLineArgs": "--job_name=worker --num_gpus=1 --
ps_hosts=$AZ_BATCHAI_PS_HOSTS --worker_hosts=$AZ_BATCHAI_WORKER_HOSTS --
task_index=$AZ_BATCHAI_TASK_INDEX --data_dir=$AZ_BATCHAI_INPUT_DATASET --
output_dir=$AZ_BATCHAI_OUTPUT_MODEL",
      "workerCommandLineArgs": "--job_name=worker --num_gpus=1 --
ps_hosts=$AZ_BATCHAI_PS_HOSTS --worker_hosts=$AZ_BATCHAI_WORKER_HOSTS --
task_index=$AZ_BATCHAI_TASK_INDEX --data_dir=$AZ_BATCHAI_INPUT_DATASET --
output_dir=$AZ_BATCHAI_OUTPUT_MODEL",
      "parameterServerCommandLineArgs": "--job_name=ps --num_gpus=0 --
ps_hosts=$AZ_BATCHAI_PS_HOSTS --worker_hosts=$AZ_BATCHAI_WORKER_HOSTS --
task_index=$AZ_BATCHAI_TASK_INDEX --data_dir=$AZ_BATCHAI_INPUT_DATASET --
output_dir=$AZ_BATCHAI_OUTPUT_MODEL"
},
    "stdOutErrPathPrefix": "$AZ_BATCHAI_MOUNT_ROOT/external",
    "inputDirectories": [{
    "id": "DATASET",
    "path": "$AZ_BATCHAI_MOUNT_ROOT/external/mnist_dataset"
    }, {
    "id": "SCRIPT",
    "path": "$AZ_BATCHAI_MOUNT_ROOT/external/tensorflow_samples"
    }],
    "outputDirectories": [{
      "id": "MODEL",
      "pathPrefix": "$AZ_BATCHAI_MOUNT_ROOT/external",
    "pathSuffix": "Models"
    }],
    "containerSettings": {
      "imageSourceRegistry": {
      "image": "tensorflow/tensorflow:1.1.0-gpu"
    }
  }
}
}
```

}

10. Finally, create the Batch AI job using the command:

```
az batchai job create -n distibuted_tensorflow --cluster-name nc6 -c
job.json
```

How it works...

Batch AI manages the resources by itself, you just need to specify the job, the location of inputs and where to store the outputs. If during the execution of the job you want to see the results, you can use the command:

```
az batchai job stream-file --job-name myjob --output-directory-id stdouterr
--name stderr.txt
```

Once the job is over, you delete both the job and the cluster using `az batchai job delete` and `az batchai cluster delete` commands.

There's more...

Above we learned how to use Microsoft Azure Batch AI for Distributed TensorFlow using Azure Command Line tool. We can do the same using Jupyter Notebook too. This will involve setting the Azure Active Directory, and making a new App registration. The details can be had at this link: `https://docs.microsoft.com/en-us/azure/azure-resource-manager/resource-group-create-service-principal-portal`.

Azure BatchAI works with other AI deep learning libraries too, we suggest that you should go through the BatchAI Github for more details: `https://github.com/Azure/BatchAI`.

Running Distributed TensorFlow on Amazon AWS

Amazon AWS offers P2.x machine featuring NVIDIA K8 GPU. To be able to use, again the first step involves creating an Amazon AWS account. If you do not have one already, you can create it using the link: `https://portal.aws.amazon.com/billing/signup?nc2=h_ct redirect_url=https%3A%2F%2Faws.amazon.com%2Fregistration-confirmation#/start` . Once you login into your account, your dashboard looks like this:

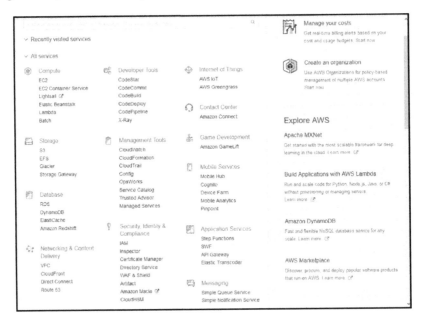

You can see that Amazon AWS provides a host of services, but here we are concerned with using Amazon AWS for Deep learning.

The GPUs are available only in P2 instance creation, and are not available by default, to get this service one has to raise a ticket for increasing resources via AWS support, the support is available in the top right corner, once you go to support, you will see a button **Create case**, choose the button and make following selections:

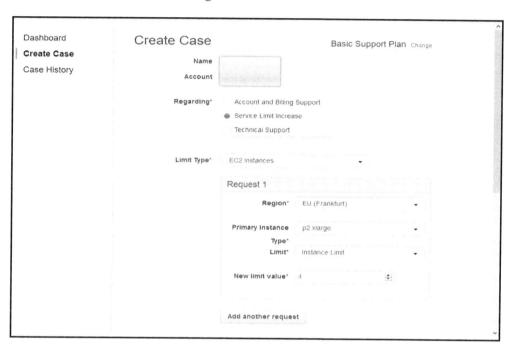

You can choose any region offering **p2.xlarge** instance. The new limit value decides the maximum number of the instances you can use, choose the number carefully because the service is not free and costs roughly $1 per hour. It takes about 24 hours for AWS to respond to the request.

Getting ready

Now that you have the AWS account and p2.xlarge instances available to you, you are ready to create your own instance from EC2 dashboard. The first step is selecting the machine image, as of now, Amazon offers special machine images preloaded with Deep learning libraries you can select the Ubuntu or Linux version. Next, choose the GPU to compute instance type.

You can review and launch the instance with default parameters, or you can configure the settings, choose the storage and configure the security group. Configuring the security group is important, by default SSH security group is set, but if you want to use Jupyter Notebook, you need to add a custom security group for port 8888, you have the option to choose the source from which you will log in to the instance, there are three possibilities Custom, Anywhere or My IP:

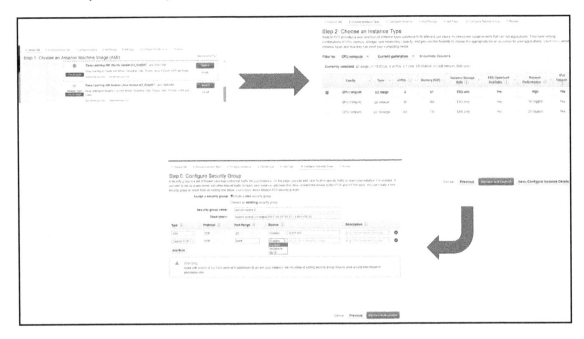

Finally, when you launch the instance, you will be asked to create a key pair, which allows you to login to the particular instance, you will need to create one key-pair and download the respective .pem file, this you will use for logging later.

How to do it...

1. The first step will be connecting to the instance, you can do it either through ssh using the command line, or via browser. We use CLI.

2. To connect first change the mode of `.pem` file.

```
chmod 400 <security-keypair-filename>.pem
```

3. Next use the the command below to SSH the instance. The exact address will be available on the dashboard, when you select connect:

```
ssh -i " <security-keypair-filename>.pem" ubuntu@ec2-
XXXXXXXXXXXXX.compute-1.amazonaws.com
```

4. The machine instance that we have chosen already contains all the deep learning libraries including TensorFlow and so we don't need to install anything:

```
 ⊖ ⊖ ⊜  ubuntu@ip-172-31-19-254: ~/src

* Documentation:   https://help.ubuntu.com
* Management:      https://landscape.canonical.com
* Support:         https://ubuntu.com/advantage

  Get cloud support with Ubuntu Advantage Cloud Guest:
    http://www.ubuntu.com/business/services/cloud

4 packages can be updated.
0 updates are security updates.


*** System restart required ***

The programs included with the Ubuntu system are free software;
the exact distribution terms for each program are described in the
individual files in /usr/share/doc/*/copyright.

Ubuntu comes with ABSOLUTELY NO WARRANTY, to the extent permitted by
applicable law.

ubuntu@ip-172-31-19-254:~$ ls
src
ubuntu@ip-172-31-19-254:~$ cd src
ubuntu@ip-172-31-19-254:~/src$ ls
anaconda2  caffe2          caffe_cpu       keras               OpenBLAS             tensorflow_anaconda3  theano
anaconda3  caffe2_anaconda2 caffe_python3   logs                pytorch              tensorflow_cpu        torch
bin        caffe_anaconda2  cntk            mxnet               README.md            tensorflow_python2
caffe      caffe_anaconda3  demos           Nvidia_Cloud_EULA.pdf  tensorflow_anaconda2  tensorflow_python3
ubuntu@ip-172-31-19-254:~/src$ █
```

5. Each folder contains a readme file which describes how to use the corresponding library:

```
ubuntu@ip-172-31-19-254: ~/src/tensorflow_anaconda3
emo.apk), [native libs](http://ci.tensorflow.org/view/Nightly/job/nightly-android/lastSuccessfulBuild/artifact/out/native/)
([build history](https://ci.tensorflow.org/view/Nightly/job/nightly-android/))

#### *Try your first TensorFlow program*
```shell
$ python
```
```python
>>> import tensorflow as tf
>>> hello = tf.constant('Hello, TensorFlow!')
>>> sess = tf.Session()
>>> sess.run(hello)
'Hello, TensorFlow!'
>>> a = tf.constant(10)
>>> b = tf.constant(32)
>>> sess.run(a+b)
42
>>>
```

For more information

* [TensorFlow website](https://www.tensorflow.org)
* [TensorFlow whitepaper](http://download.tensorflow.org/paper/whitepaper2015.pdf)
* [TensorFlow Model Zoo](https://github.com/tensorflow/models)
* [TensorFlow MOOC on Udacity](https://www.udacity.com/course/deep-learning--ud730)

The TensorFlow community has created amazing things with TensorFlow, please see the [resources section of tensorflow.org](http
s://www.tensorflow.org/about/#community) for an incomplete list.
ubuntu@ip-172-31-19-254:~/src/tensorflow_anaconda3$
```

How it works...

You can run the codes that you have learned on the instance we have created. Once the work is over do not forget to exit, and from dashboard stop the instance. More details about pricing and usage is available here: `https://aws.amazon.com/documentation/ec2/`

There is more...

A large number of docker images and machine images with preconfigured libraries and APIs are available at AWS marketplace. To launch the jupyter notebook , at command line use `<jupyter notebook --ip=0.0.0.0 --no-browser>`. This will result in an output as shown in the following:

Copy/paste this URL into your browser when you connect for the first time to login with a token:
http://0.0.0.0:8888/?token=3156e...

You copy and paste the URL on your browser and you are ready to go.

In addition, the whole process can be simplified by looking at AWS CloudFormation. It creates and configures Amazon Web Services resources with a template. In doing so, it simplifies the process of setting up a distributed deep learning cluster. The interested reader can have a look to `https://aws.amazon.com/blogs/compute/distributed-deep-learning-made-easy/`

A

Learning to Learn with AutoML (Meta-Learning)

The success of deep learning has immensely facilitated the work of feature engineering. Indeed, traditional machine learning depended very much on the selection of the right set of features, and very frequently, this step was more important that the selection of a particular learning algorithm. Deep learning has changed this scenario; creating a right model is still very important but nowadays networks are less sensitive to the selection of a particular set of feature and are much more able to auto-select the features that really matter.

Instead, the introduction of deep learning has increased the focus on the selection of the right neural network architecture. This means that progressively the interest of researchers is shifting from feature engineering to network engineering. **AutoML (Meta Learning)** is an emerging research topic which aims at auto-selecting the most efficient neural network for a given learning task. In other words, AutoML represents a set of methodologies *for learning how to learn efficiently*. Consider for instance the tasks of Machine Translation, or Image Recognition, or Game playing. Typically, the models are manually designed by a team of engineers, data scientist, and domain experts. If you consider that a typical 10-layer network can have ~10^{10} candidate network, you understand how expensive, error prone, and ultimately sub-optimal the process can be.

Meta-learning with recurrent networks and with reinforcement learning

The key idea to tackle this problem is to have a controller network which proposes a *child* model architecture with probability p, given a particular network given in input. The child is trained and evaluated for the particular task to be solved (say for instance that the child gets accuracy R). This evaluation R is passed back to the controller which, in turn, uses R to improve the next candidate architecture. Given this framework, it is possible to model the feedback from the candidate child to the controller as the task of computing the gradient of p and then scale this gradient by R. The controller can be implemented as a Recurrent Neural Network (see the following figure). In doing so, the controller will tend to privilege iteration after iterations candidate areas of architecture that achieve better R and will tend to assign a lower probability to candidate areas that do not score so well.

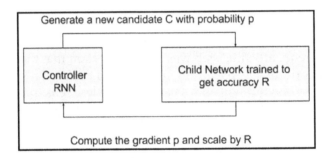

For instance, a controller recurrent neural network can sample a convolutional network. The controller can predict many hyper-parameters such as filter height, filter width, stride height, stride width, and the number of filters for one layer and then can repeat. Every prediction can be carried out by a softmax classifier and then fed into the next RNN time step as input. This is well expressed by the following images taken from *Neural Architecture Search with Reinforcement Learning*, Barret Zoph, Quoc V. Le, https://arxiv.org/abs/1611.01578:

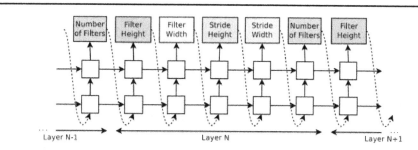

Figure 2: How our controller recurrent neural network samples a simple convolutional network. It predicts filter height, filter width, stride height, stride width, and number of filters for one layer and repeats. Every prediction is carried out by a softmax classifier and then fed into the next time step as input.

Predicting hyperparameters is not enough as it would be optimal to define a set of actions to create new layers in the network. This is particularly difficult because the reward function describing the new layers is most likely not differentiable and therefore it would not be possible to optimize it with standard techniques such as SGD. The solution comes from reinforcement learning and it consists of adopting a policy gradient network similar to the one described in our Chapter 9, *Reinforcement Learning*.

Besides that, parallelism can be used for optimizing the parameters of the controller RNN. Quoc Le & Barret Zoph proposed to adopt a parameter-server scheme where we have a parameter server of S shards, that store the shared parameters for K controller replicas. Each controller replica samples m different child architectures that are trained in parallel as illustrated in the following images, taken from *Neural Architecture Search with Reinforcement Learning*, Barret Zoph, Quoc V. Le, https://arxiv.org/abs/1611.01578:

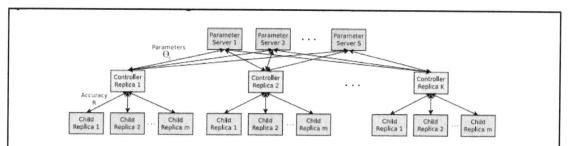

Figure 3: Distributed training for Neural Architecture Search. We use a set of *S* parameter servers to store and send parameters to *K* controller replicas. Each controller replica then samples *m* architectures and run the multiple child models in parallel. The accuracy of each child model is recorded to compute the gradients with respect to θ_c, which are then sent back to the parameter servers.

Quoc and Barret applied AutoML techniques for Neural Architecture Search to the Penn Treebank dataset (https://en.wikipedia.org/wiki/Treebank), a well-known benchmark for language modeling. Their results improve the manually designed networks currently considered the state-of-the-art. In particular, they achieve a test set perplexity of 62.4 on the Penn Treebank, which is 3.6 perplexity better than the previous state-of-the-art model. Similarly, on the CIFAR-10 dataset (https://www.cs.toronto.edu/~kriz/cifar.html), starting from scratch, the method can design a novel network architecture that rivals the best human-invented architecture in terms of test set accuracy. The proposed CIFAR-10 model achieves a test error rate of 3.65, which is 0.09 percent better and 1.05x faster than the previous state-of-the-art model that used a similar architectural scheme.

Meta-learning blocks

In *Learning Transferable Architectures for Scalable Image Recognition*, Barret Zoph, Vijay Vasudevan, Jonathon Shlens, Quoc V. Le, 2017 https://arxiv.org/abs/1707.07012. propose to learn an architectural building block on a small dataset that can be transferred to a large dataset. The authors propose to search for the best convolutional layer (or cell) on the CIFAR-10 dataset and then apply this learned cell to the ImageNet dataset by stacking together more copies of this cell, each with their own parameters. Precisely, all convolutional networks are made of convolutional layers (or cells) with identical structures but different weights. Searching for the best convolutional architectures is therefore reduced to searching for the best cell structures, which is faster more likely to generalize to other problems. Although the cell is not learned directly on ImageNet, an architecture constructed from the best learned cell achieves, among the published work, state-of-the-art accuracy of 82.7 percent top-1 and 96.2 percent top-5 on ImageNet. The model is 1.2 percent better in top-1 accuracy than the best human-invented architectures while having 9 billion fewer FLOPS—a reduction of 28% from the previous state of the art model. What is also important to notice is that the model learned with RNN+RL (Recurrent Neural Networks + Reinforcement Learning) is beating the baseline represented by Random Search (RL) as shown in the figure taken from the paper. In the mean performance of the top-5 and top-25 models identified in RL versus RS, RL is always winning:

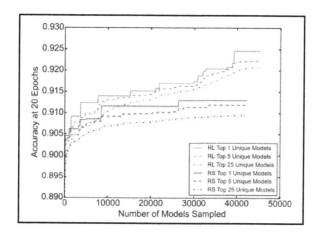

Meta-learning novel tasks

Meta-learning systems can be trained to achieve a large number of tasks and are then tested for their ability to learn new tasks. A famous example of this kind of meta-learning is the so-called Transfer Learning discussed in the Chapter on Advanced CNNs, where networks can successfully learn new image-based tasks from relatively small datasets. However, there is no analogous pre-training scheme for non-vision domains such as speech, language, and text.

Model-Agnostic Meta-Learning for Fast Adaptation of Deep Networks, Chelsea Finn, Pieter Abbeel, Sergey Levine, 2017, `https://arxiv.org/abs/1703.03400` proposes a model-agnostic approach names MAML, compatible with any model trained with gradient descent and applicable to a variety of different learning problems, including classification, regression, and reinforcement learning. The goal of meta-learning is to train a model on a variety of learning tasks, such that it can solve new learning tasks using only a small number of training samples. The meta-learner aims at finding an initialization that rapidly adapts to various problems quickly (in a small number of steps) and efficiently (using only a few examples). A model represented by a parametrized function f_θ with parameters θ. When adapting to a new task T_i, the model's parameters θ become θ_i'. In MAML, the updated parameter vector θ_i' is computed using one or more gradient descent updates on task T_i.

For example, when using one gradient update, $\theta_i^- = \theta - \alpha\nabla_\theta L_{Ti}(f_\theta)$ where L_{Ti} is the loss function for the task T and α is a meta-learning parameter. The MAML algorithm is reported in this figure:

Algorithm 1 Model-Agnostic Meta-Learning

Require: $p(\mathcal{T})$: distribution over tasks

Require: α, β: step size hyperparameters

  1: randomly initialize θ

  2: **while** not done **do**

  3:     Sample batch of tasks $\mathcal{T}_i \sim p(\mathcal{T})$

  4:     **for all** $\mathcal{T}_i$ **do**

  5:         Evaluate $\nabla_\theta \mathcal{L}_{\mathcal{T}_i}(f_\theta)$ with respect to K examples

  6:         Compute adapted parameters with gradient descent: $\theta'_i = \theta - \alpha\nabla_\theta \mathcal{L}_{\mathcal{T}_i}(f_\theta)$

  7:     **end for**

  8:     Update $\theta \leftarrow \theta - \beta\nabla_\theta \sum_{\mathcal{T}_i \sim p(\mathcal{T})} \mathcal{L}_{\mathcal{T}_i}(f_{\theta'_i})$

  9: **end while**

MAML was able to substantially outperform a number of existing approaches on popular few-shot image classification benchmark. Few shot image is a quite challenging problem aiming at learning new concepts from one or a few instances of that concept. As an example, *Human-level concept learning through probabilistic program induction*, Brenden M. Lake, Ruslan Salakhutdinov, Joshua B. Tenenbaum, 2015, `https://www.cs.cmu.edu/ ~rsalakhu/papers/LakeEtA12015Science.pdf`, suggested that humans can learn to identify novel two-wheel vehicles from a single picture such as the one contained in a red box as follows:

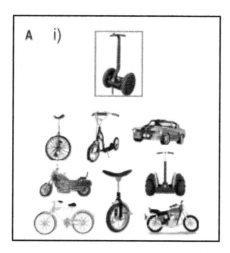

At the end of 2017, the topic of AutoML (or meta-learning) is an active research topic that aims at auto-selecting the most efficient neural network for a given learning task. The goal is to learn how to efficiently and automatically design networks that, in turn, can learn specific tasks or can adapt to new tasks. The main problem is that designing a network cannot simply be described with a differentiable loss function and therefore traditional optimization techniques cannot simply be adopted for meta-learning. Therefore a few solutions have been proposed including the idea of having a controller recurrent network (RNN) and a reward policy based on reinforcement learning and the idea of having a model-agnostic meta-Learning. Both the approaches are very promising but there is certainly still a lot of room for research.

So, if you are interested in a hot topic, this *Learning to learn for deep learning* is certainly a space to consider as your next job.

- Google proposed the adoption of RNNs for the controller in *Using Machine Learning to Explore Neural Network Architecture*; Quoc Le & Barret Zoph, 2017, `https://research.googleblog.com/2017/05/using-machine-learning-to-explore.html`.
- *Neural Architecture Search with Reinforcement Learning*, Barret Zoph, Quoc V. Le, `https://arxiv.org/abs/1611.01578`, is a seminal paper proving more details about Google's approach. However, RNNs are not the only option.
- *Large-Scale Evolution of Image Classifiers*, Esteban Real, Sherry Moore, Andrew Selle, Saurabh Saxena, Yutaka Leon Suematsu, Jie Tan, Quoc Le, Alex Kurakin, 2017, `https://arxiv.org/abs/1703.01041`, proposed to use evolutionary computing where genetic intuitive mutation operations are explored to generate new candidate networks.

- *Learning Transferable Architectures for Scalable Image Recognition*, Barret Zoph, Vijay Vasudevan, Jonathon Shlens, Quoc V. Le, `https://arxiv.org/abs/1707.07012`, proposed the idea of cells learnt on CIFAR and used for improving ImageNet classification.
- *Building A.I. That Can Build A.I.: Google and others, fighting for a small pool of researchers, are looking for automated ways to deal with a shortage of artificial intelligence experts.*, The New York Times, `https://www.nytimes.com/2017/11/05/technology/machine-learning-artificial-intelligence-ai.html`.
- *Model-Agnostic Meta-Learning for Fast Adaptation of Deep Networks*, Chelsea Finn, Pieter Abbeel, Sergey Levine, 2017, `https://arxiv.org/abs/1703.03400`.
- *Learning to Learn by Gradient Descent by Gradient Descent*, Marcin Andrychowicz, Misha Denil, Sergio Gomez, Matthew W. Hoffman, David Pfau, Tom Schaul, Brendan Shillingford, Nando de Freitas, `https://arxiv.org/abs/1606.04474`, shows how the design of an optimization algorithm can be cast as a learning problem, allowing the algorithm to learn to exploit structure in the problems of interest in an automatic way. The LSMT learned algorithms outperform hand-designed competitors on the tasks for which they are trained, and also generalize well to new tasks with similar structure. The code for this algorithm is available on GitHub at `https://github.com/deepmind/learning-to-learn`.

Siamese Network

Siamese Networks are a special type of neural networks introduced by Yann LeCun and his colleagues in NIPS 1994 (`http://www.worldscientific.com/doi/pdf/10.1142/S0218001493000339`). The basic idea behind them is that like the 'Siamese Twins', the network consists of two different Neural Networks, both sharing the same architecture and weights.

Here, you can see the Siamese architecture:

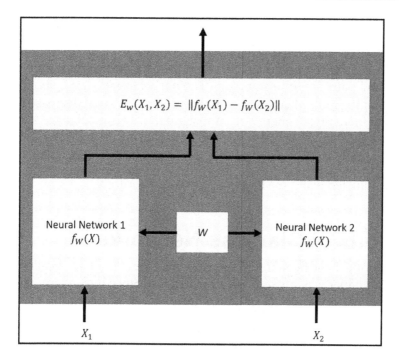

During the training phase the pair-network is presented with a training pair (X_1, X_2), where the two inputs are different yet similar, for example, X_1 = *He is smart*, and X_2 = *He is a wise man*. The two neural networks will produce two different results; the combined network can be thought of as a scalar **energy function** measuring the similarity between the training pair (X_1, X_2), defined as:

$$E_W(X_1, X_2) = \left\| f_W(X_1) - f_W(X_2) \right\|$$

The goal of the Siamese network is that the energy between the training-pair (X_1, X_2) should be less than energy between any other imposter pair (X_1, X_2').

This is achieved by using a **contrastive loss function** for training.

During the training phase the network is given as input a training pair, and a label associated with it, telling it is a genuine pair or an impostor pair: $(X_1, X_2, Y)^i$ is the ith training sample. The contrastive Loss function is calculated:

$$L(W) = \sum_{i=1}^{P} L(W, (X_1, X_2, Y)^i)$$

where, $L(W, (X_1, X_2, Y)^i) = (1 - Y) L_G(E_w(X_1, X_2)^i + YL_I(E_w(X_1, X_2)^i)$ with L_G being the partial loss for a genuine pair, and L_I the partial loss for an impostor pair and P the number of training samples. The label Y has a value 0 when the pairs are genuine and has value 1 when the presented pairs are imposter pairs. The partial loss L_G and L_I should be designed in such a manner that the minimization of contrastive loss $L(W)$ will decrease the energy of genuine pairs and increase the energy of imposter pairs. This is achieved by choosing the partial loss L_G as monotonically increasing and partial loss L_I as monotonically decreasing f. One possible choice is using cosine similarity for calculating the partial loss.

The weights are adjusted using the backpropagation algorithm.

Applications of Siamese Networks

The Siamese networks have been in recent years used for a lot of applications. Their first used in the LeCun paper was for signature verification. Since then a large number of applications have emerged, we will present some of the recent ones:

- Joint Learning of Speaker and Phonetic Similarities with Siamese Networks (https://pdfs.semanticscholar.org/4ffe/ 3394628a8a0ffd4cba1a77ea85e197bd4c22.pdf): They trained a multi-output Siamese network, with one output for phonetic similarity and other for the speaker similarity. They extended the work to include Triamese Network.
- Fully-Convolutional Siamese Network for Object Tracking (https://link. springer.com/chapter/10.1007/978-3-319-48881-3_56): They used convolutional Siamese network trained on ILSVRC15 dataset for object detection in Video.
- Together We stand: Siamese Networks for Similar Question Retrieval (http:// www.aclweb.org/anthology/P16-1036): The paper used Siamese Network to find the semantic similarity between the current and archived questions. They also used convolutional Siamese Networks.

Besides these, Siamese networks have also been explored for face verification/recognition (https://github.com/harveyslash/Facial-Similarity-with-Siamese-Networks-in- Pytorch). They have been used for Question-Answering (https://arxiv.org/pdf/1512. 05193v2.pdf).

A working example - MNIST

The working example is based on the Github page: `https://github.com/ywpkwon/siamese_tf_mnist`. This code here uses Siamese Networks to embed hand-written MNIST digits into 2D space, digits belonging to same class are embedded together. The code consists of three major files:

● `run.py`: It contains the basic wrapper to perform training. It uses the Gradient Descent algorithm to minimize the contrastive loss.

● `inference.py`: This contains the Siamese Class which defines a 3-layered fully connected network. The similarity between the output of two networks in the code is Euclidean. The partial generative loss and the partial imposter Loss are used to then to calculate the Contrastive loss.

● `visualize.py`: This is again just a wrapper to visualize the results.

After first 100,000 training steps, the results are:

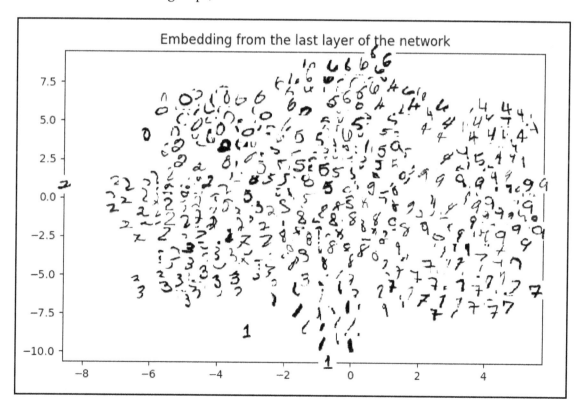

You can see that same (labeled) digits embedded together in the 2D space.

There is another interesting example at `https://github.com/dhwajraj/deep-siamese-text-similarity`.

Here, using Tensorflow, deep Siamese LSTM networks are trained to capture phrase/sentence similarity using character embeddings.

TensorFlow Processing Units

Google services such as Google Search (RankBrain), Street View, Google Photos, and Google Translate have one thing in common: they all use Google's Tensor Processing Unit, or **TPU**, for their computations.

You might be thinking what is a TPU and what is so great about these services? All these services use state-of-the-art machine learning algorithms in the background, and these algorithms involve large computations. TPUs help to accelerate the neural network computations involved. Even AlphaGo, the deep learning program that defeated Lee Sedol in the game of Go, was powered by TPUs. So let us see what exactly a TPU is.

A TPU is a custom application-specific integrated circuit (**ASIC**) built by Google specifically for machine learning and is tailored for Tensorflow. It is built on a 28-nm process, it runs at 700 MHz, and consumes 40 W of energy when running. It is packaged as an external accelerator card that can fit into the existing SATA hard disk slots. A TPU is connected to the host CPUs via a PCIe Gen 3×16 bus, which provides an effective bandwidth of 12.5 GB/s.

The first generation of TPUs is, as of now, targeting inference, that is, use of an already trained model. The training of DNNs, which usually takes more time, was still done on CPUs and GPUs. The second-generation TPUs announced in a May 2017 blog post (`https://www.blog.google/topics/google-cloud/google-cloud-offer-tpus-machine-learning/`) can both train and infer machine learning models.

Components of TPUs

In all the deep learning models covered in this book, irrespective of the learning paradigm, three basic calculations were necessary: multiplication, addition, and application of an activation function.

The first two components are part of matrix multiplication: the weight matrix W needs to be multiplied to input matrix X, generally expressed as $W^T X$; matrix multiplication is computationally expensive on a CPU, and though a GPU parallelizes the operation, still there is scope for improvement.

The TPU has a 65,536 8-bit integer matrix multiplier unit (**MXU**) that gives a peak throughput of 92 TOPS. The major difference between GPU and TPU multiplication is that GPUs contain floating point multipliers, while TPUs contain 8-bit integer multipliers. TPUs also contain a Unified Buffer (**UB**), 24 MB of SRAM that works as registers, and an Activation Unit (**AU**), which contains hardwired activation functions.

The MXU is implemented using systolic array architecture. It contains an array of Arithmetic Logic Units (ALUs) connected to a small number of nearest neighbors in a mesh-like topology. Each data value is read only once but used many times for different operations as it flows through the ALU array, without storing it back to a register. The ALUs in TPUs perform only multiplications and additions in a fixed pattern. The MXU is optimized for matrix multiplication and is not suited for general-purpose computations.

Each TPU also has an off-chip 8-GiB DRAM pool, called weight memory. It has a four-stage pipeline and executes CISC instructions. TPUs, as of now, consist of six neural networks: two MLPs, two CNNs, and two LSTMs.

The TPU is programmed with the help of high-level instructions; some of the instructions used to program TPUs are the following:

- `Read_Weights`: Read weights from memory
- `Read_Host_Memory`: Read data from memory
- `MatrixMultiply/Convolve`: Multiply or convolve with the data and accumulate the results
- `Activate`: Apply the activation functions
- `Write_Host_Memory`: Write the results to the memory

Google has created an API stack to facilitate TPU programming; it translates the API calls from Tensorflow graphs into TPU instructions.

Advantages of TPUs

The first and foremost advantage that TPUs offer over GPUs and CPUs is performance. Google compared the TPU performance to a server-class Intel Haswell CPU and a NVIDIA K80 GPU running the benchmark code representative of 95% of the inference workload; it found that the TPU is 15-30 times faster than both NVIDIA's GPU and Intel's CPU.

The second important parameter is the power consumption. It is important to reduce power consumption since it has a twofold energy benefit: not only does it reduce the amount of power consumed, it also saves power by reducing the cooling cost to dissipate the heat generated while processing. The TPU/CPU per watt performance shows a 30-80 times improvement over other CPU and GPU configurations.

Another advantage of TPUs is their minimal and deterministic design since they have to execute only one task at a time.

> As compared to CPUs and GPUs, the single-threaded TPU has none of the sophisticated microarchitectural features that consume transistors and energy to improve the average case but not the 99th-percentile case: no caches, branch prediction, out-of-order execution, multiprocessing, speculative prefetching, address coalescing, multithreading, context switching, and so forth. Minimalism is a virtue of domain-specific processors.

Accessing TPUs

Google has decided not to sell TPUs directly to others; instead, the TPUs will be made available via the Google cloud platform: Cloud TPU Alpha (`https://cloud.google.com/tpu/`). Cloud TPU Alpha will offer up to 180 teraflops of computing performance and 64 GB of ultra-high bandwidth memory. Users will be able to connect to these Cloud TPUs from custom virtual machines.

Google has also decided to make a cluster of 1,000 cloud TPUs available free of charge to machine learning researchers around the world, with the aim of accelerating the pace of open machine learning research. Access to it will be given to selected individuals for limited amounts of computing time; individuals can sign up using this link: `https://services.google.com/fb/forms/tpusignup/`. According to the Google Blog:

> *"Since the main goal of the TensorFlow Research Cloud is to benefit the open machine learning research community as a whole, successful applicants will be expected to do the following:*
> *Share their TFRC-supported research with the world through peer-reviewed publications, open-source code, blog posts, or other open media*
> *Share concrete, constructive feedback with Google to help us improve the TFRC program and the underlying Cloud TPU platform over time.*
> *Imagine a future in which ML acceleration is abundant and develop new kinds of machine learning models in anticipation of that future"*

Resources on TPUs

- Norman P. Jouppi and others, *In-datacenter performance analysis of a tensor processing unit*, arXiv preprint arXiv:1704.04760 (2017). In this paper, the authors compare the TPU with a server-class Intel Haswell CPU and an NVIDIA k80 GPU. The paper benchmarks TPUs performance as compared to CPUs and K80 GPU.
- This Google Blog explains the TPU and its working in simple terms at: `https://cloud.google.com/blog/big-data/2017/05/an-in-depth-look-at-googles-first-tensor-processing-unit-tpu`

Index

A

accelerated linear algebra (XLA)
  reference 35, 38
  used, for enhancing computational performance
    35, 37
activation functions
  hyperbolic tangent activation function 90
  Linear activation function 91
  Rectified linear units (ReLU) 91
  reference 94
  Sigmoidal activation function 89
  Softmax activation function 92
  threshold activation function: 88
  using 87
activity of the neuron 87
Amazon AWS
  Distributed TensorFlow, running 482, 487
  reference 486
Anaconda
  reference 12
Android Studio
  installation link 369
Android
  examples 377, 381
  reference 377
  TensorFlow mobile, installing 369
AoT (Ahead of Time) 35
AoT Compilation 37
application-specific integrated circuit (ASIC) 501
Artificial Neural Networks (ANNs) 42
Atari game
  playing, with deep Q network (DQN) 346, 348,
    355
autoassociators 291
autoencoders
  about 291
  Overcomplete 293
  Undercomplete 293
AutoML (Meta Learning)
  about 489
  blocks 492
  novel tasks 493
  with recurrent networks 490
  with reinforcement learning 490
Azure BatchAI
  reference 481
Azure CLI
  reference 478

B

backpropagation (BPN) algorithm
  about 87
  gradients, calculating 97, 102
  reference 102
  starting with 99
backward pass 97, 273
batch gradient descent 57
Bayesian optimization 114
Bazel
  about 377
  installation link 387
  reference 377
Boston house prices
  predicting 106, 111
Boston housing price dataset
  reference 61

C

Capsule Networks (CapsNets)
  about 435
  features 436
  issue 435

used, for beating state-of-the-art results 436,
454
capsules 436
celebrity faces
    forging, with DCGAN 420
Central Processing Unit (CPU)
    versus Graphical Processing Unit (GPU) 12
CIFAR-10 classification
    ConvNet, creating 133
Cloud TPU Alpha
    reference 503
CNN
    about 117
    average pooling 121
    in TensorFlow 119
    local receptive fields 118
    mathematical example 118
    max-pooling operator 120
    pooling layers 120
    shared weights and bias 118
    summarizing 122
components, deep learning
    CIFAR10 44
    dataset 43
    ImageNET 44
    MNIST 43
    WORDNET 44
    YouTube-8M 44
compression
    about 368
    reference 368
computational graph 20
connectionist models 83
constants
    about 23
    working with 23, 27, 29
Contrastive Divergence (CD) 272
ConvNet
    creating, for CIFAR-10 classification 129, 132
    creating, for handwritten MNIST numbers
        classification 122, 127, 129
    creating, for Sentiment Analysis 158
    used, for generating music 193
convolution 118
Convolutional Autoencoders (CAE)

about 314
working 319
Convolutional Neural Networks (CNN) 117, 314,
346
CPU/GPU devices
    invoking 38
CSV files
    reading from 61

D

data flow graph
    using 32
data preprocessing 61
data
    feeding 44
    filename queue 45
    reading 44
    reading, from files 45
    training/Learning 47
DBN
    used, for emotion detection 280, 284, 288
DCGAN
    MNIST images, forging with 412, 418
    used, for forging celebrity faces 420
decoder 46
Deep Belief Networks (DBN) 280
deep learning
    TensorFlow 41
Deep neural networks (DNNs) 10, 83
deep Q network (DQN)
    laying Atari game 348, 355, 357
    used, for playing Atari game 346
deep-siamese-text-similarity example
    reference 500
DeepDream network
    creating 150, 153
    reference 155
denoising autoencoder
    about 309
    working 309
dependent variable 51
Diabolo networks 291
Distributed TensorFlow MNIST classifier
    reference 465
    training 465, 469

Distributed TensorFlow
  multiple GPUs and one CPU 461
  multiple servers 463, 465
  reference 465
  running, on Amazon AWS 482, 487
  running, on Google Cloud (GCP) with Compute
    Engine 471, 475
  running, on Google CloudML 475
  running, on Microsoft Azure 477, 481
DNN-based problems
  Python packages 47
Docker
  reference 469
Dockerfile.devel
  download link 470

E

eigen decomposition or singular value
    decomposition (SVD) 252
elbow method 261
embeddings 256
Estimators
  reference 47
execution of graph 20
Exploration-Exploitation trade-off 341

F

feedforward networks 85
filter 118
forward pass 97, 273
fully connected layers 85

G

Gated Recurrent Units (GRUs) 215
Generative Adversarial Networks (GANs)
  about 43, 398
  applications 400
  MNIST images, forging with 405, 410
  reference 403
gesture recognition 368
Google Cloud (GCP)
  Distributed TensorFlow, running with Compute
    Engine 471, 475
  reference 471

Google CloudML
  Distributed TensorFlow, running 475
  feature 477
  reference 475, 476
Google research blog
  reference 11
GPUs
  working with 459
gradient descent algorithms 85
gradient descent optimizer
  reference links 60
  using, in TensorFlow 58
greedy wise training 285

H

handwritten MNIST numbers
  classification, by creating ConvNet 122, 127,
    129
hidden layer 272
hyperbolic tangent activation function 90, 93
Hyperopt
  reference 114
hyperparameters
  optimization, reference 114
  tuning 112, 114

I

image classification
  Inception, using 168
  ResNet, using 168
  VGGNet, using 168
  Xception, using 168
image recognition
  about 367
  reference 367
ImageNet for the Large Scale Visual Recognition
    Challenge (ILSVRC) 150
ImageNET
  reference 44
images
  questions, answering 195, 199, 203
Inception
  image classification 171
  used, for image classification 168

InceptionV3 Net
  used, for transfer learning 184, 188
independent variable 51
integrated development environment (IDE) 369
iPhone
  TensorFlow mobile, installing 381, 386

J

JIT (Just In Time) 35
JIT Compilation 37

K

k-means clustering
  about 258
  reference 264
  working 258, 263
Keras
  reference 116
  using 114
Kohonen networks 264
Kullback-Leiber (KL) 301

L

L1 regularization 53
L2 Regularization 54
learning with a critic 328
Linear activation function 91, 93
Linear regression
  about 52
  reference 52
Logistic regression
  about 52
  performing, on MNIST dataset 75, 80
  reference 53
Long Short Term Memory (LSTM) 214
loss functions
  selecting 54, 56

M

macOS
  TensorFlow mobile, installing 369, 381
matrix manipulation
  performing, TensorFlow used 30, 32
McCulloch Pitts (MCP)

  reference 84
mean square error (MSE) 103, 292
Microsoft Azure
  Distributed TensorFlow, running 477, 481
MLP
  used, for function approximation 106, 111
  using, in MNIST classifier 102
MNIST classifier
  MLP, using 102
MNIST dataset
  Logistic regression, performing 75, 78
  reference 43, 75, 98
MNIST images
  forging, with DCGANs 412, 418
  forging, with simple GANs 405, 410
MNIST
  reference 499
mobile devices
  TensorFlow graph, optimizing 386, 389
  TensorFlow graph, profiling 389, 391
  TensorFlow graph, transforming 392, 395
model
  defining 46
  evaluating 47
MovieLens
  reference 278
multi-layered perceptron 85
multiple linear regression
  performing, on Boston house price estimation 70,
  74

N

natural language processing (NLP) 157, 209
neural network agent
  building, for playing Pac-Man 333, 337
NSynth
  used, for generating music 189

O

object localization
  about 368
  reference 368
OpenAl Gym
  about 329, 333

reference 329, 333
  using 330, 332
optical character recognition 368

P

padding 119
Peephole LSTM 215
Perceptron 84
placeholders
  about 24
  working with 23, 27
policy gradients
  AlphaGo Zero 364
  used, to play Pong game 357, 361, 363
Pong game
  playing, policy gradients used 357, 363, 364
pre-built Deep Learning models
  recycling, for extracting features 183
preloaded data 46
pretrained VGG16 net
  used, for transfer learning 145, 149
principal component analysis (PCA)
  about 252
  using 252, 256
principal components 252
Python packages
  for DNN-based problems 47
  H5fs 48
  Keras 49
  Matplolib 48
  Numpy 48
  OS 48
  Pandas 48
  PythonMagick 48
  seaborn 48
  TFlearn 49
PythonMagick
  reference 48

Q

Q learning
  used, for balancing Cart-Pole wiki 337, 340,
    344, 346
  web links 346

R

random tensors 25
RBM
  reference 280
reader 45
recommender system
  RBM, using 278, 280
Rectified linear units (ReLU) 91
Recurrent Neural Networks (RNNs) 10, 209, 212
regression
  about 51
  L2 Regularization 54
  Linear regression 52
  Logistic regression 53
  regularization 53
regularization 53
reinforcement learning (RL) 251, 327, 329
ReLU activation function 94
ResNet
  used, for image classification 168, 170
Restricted Boltzmann Machine (RBM)
  about 272
  using 274, 277
RFHO
  reference 114

S

self-organized maps (SOM)
  about 264
  using 265, 269, 271
Sentiment Analysis
  ConvNet, creating 158, 161
seq2seq RNN
  about 221
  used, for neural machine translation 218
shallow neural networks 272
Siamese Network
  about 496
  applications 498
  MNIST, working example 499
  reference 496
Sigmoid activation function 89, 93
simple linear regression
  performing, on Boston house price estimation 64,

65, 68
single layer perceptron
  about 94
  using 95
Softmax activation function 92, 94
sparse autoencoder
  about 301
  working 302, 307
speech recognition 368
Stacked Autoencoder (Deep Autoencoders)
  about 320, 322
  working 325, 326
Stacked RBMs 280
sum of squared error (SSE) distance 263
supervised learning 251

T

temporal credit assignment problem 329
tensor processing units (TPUs) 11
TensorFlow 1.x
  migrating, to TensorFlow 0.x 34
TensorFlow computation 455
TensorFlow graph
  optimizing, for mobile devices 386, 389
  profiling, for mobile devices 389, 391
  transforming, for mobile devices 392, 395
TensorFlow mobile
  installing, for Android 369
  installing, for iPhone 381, 386
  installing, for macOS 369, 381
TensorFlow Processing Units (TPU) components
  matrix multiplier unit (MXU) 502
  Unified Buffer (UB) 502
  Activation Unit (AU) 502
  SRAM 502
TensorFlow Processing Units (TPU)
  about 501
  accessing 503
  advantages 503
  components 501
  reference 501
  resources, URL 504
TensorFlow Serving
  and Docker, working with 469, 471
TensorFlow

advanced functionalities 471
and cloud 369
data types, reference 29
examples 377, 381
features 43
for deep learning 41
gradient descent optimizer, using 57
Hello world program 17, 19
installation, weblinks 49
installing 12, 16
matrix manipulations, performing 30, 32
program structure 20, 21
reference 10, 36, 386
working with 459
Text-to-Speech (TTS) systems 189
TF Classify 377
TF Detect 378
TF Speech 378
TF Stylize 378
tf_upgrade.py file
  limitations 35
Threshold activation function 88, 93
transfer learning
  InceptionV3 Net, using 184, 188
  pretrained VGG16 net, using 145, 149
  reference 150
translation 368
transposed convolution layers 315

U

unsupervised learning 252

V

vanilla autoencoder
  about 294
  using 295, 299
variables
  about 24
  saving 28
  working with 23
Variational Autoencoders (VAE)
  implementing 424, 426, 433
variations, gradient descent
  mini-batch gradient descent 57

Stochastic gradient descent 57
  vanilla gradient descent 57
vectors
  sequence, operating on 217
VGG pre-built network
  inspecting 163, 166, 168
VGG16
  used, for image classification 169
VGG19
  used, for image classification 169
  used, for style transfer for image repainting 133, 136, 143, 144
VGGNet
  used, for image classification 168
videos
  classifying, with pre-trained nets 206

W

WaveNet
  used, for generating music 189, 194

web cloudshell
  URL 473
weights 83
Winner take all units (WTU) 264
WORDNET
  reference 44

X

Xception
  image classification 172
  used, for image classification 168
Xcode
  reference 382

Y

YouTube-8M
  reference 44

Z

zeroth layer 85

Lightning Source UK Ltd.
Milton Keynes UK
UKOW05f1803161217
314598UK00004B/106/P